For my parents,
For Eva & Ward, my children.

Linda Vinck

Basic Rhythms of Being

a life in patterns

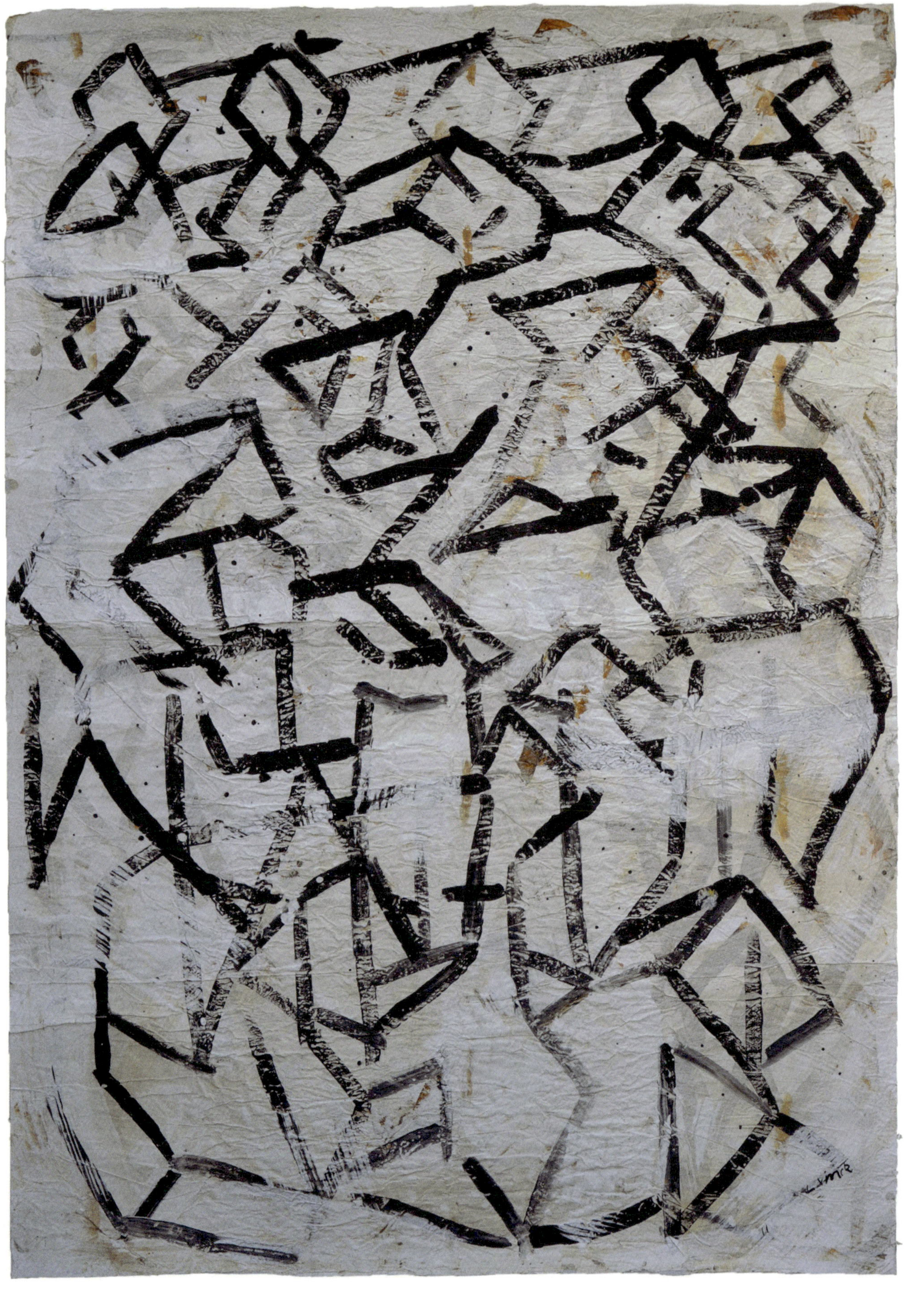

Triangular

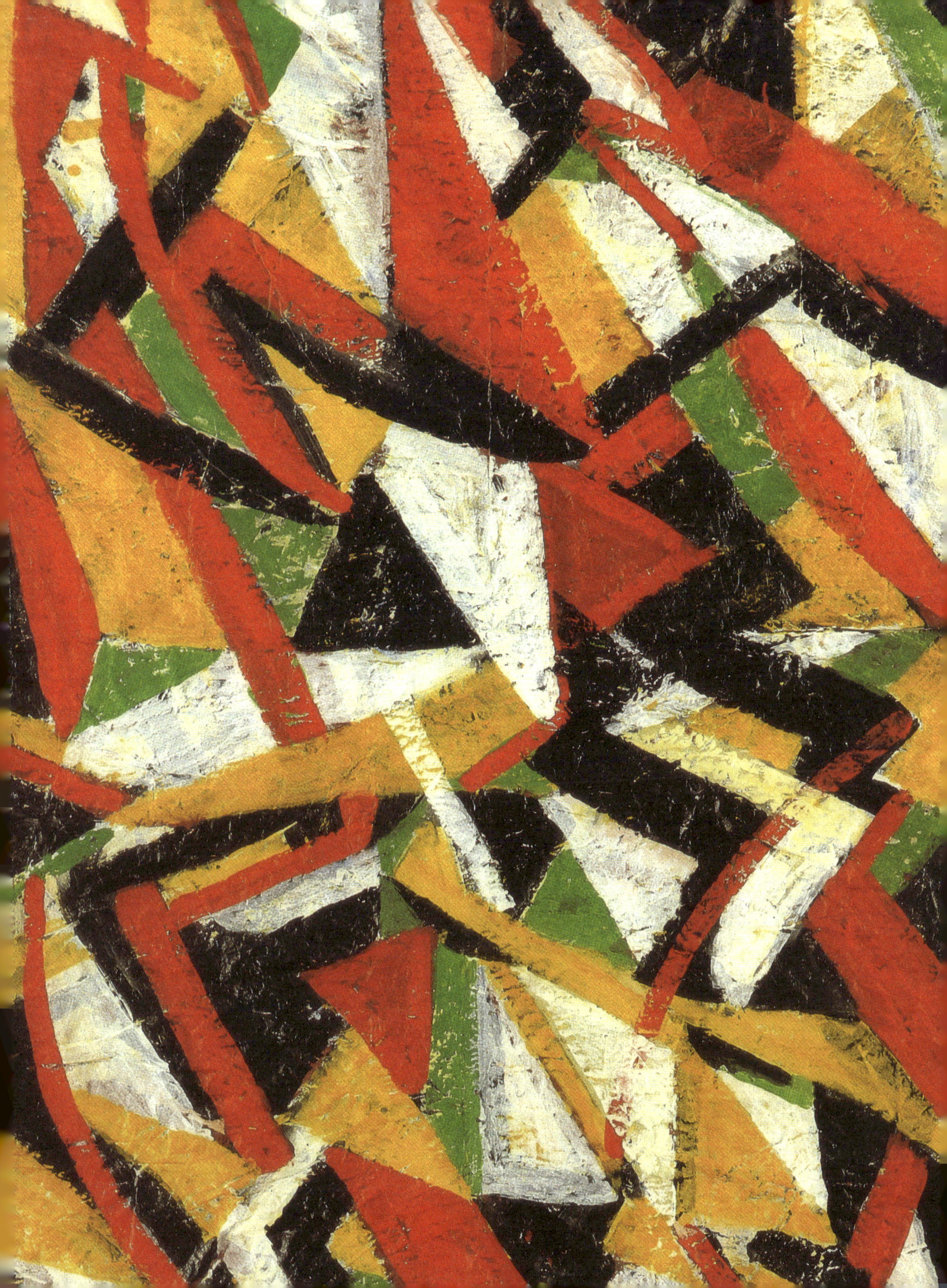

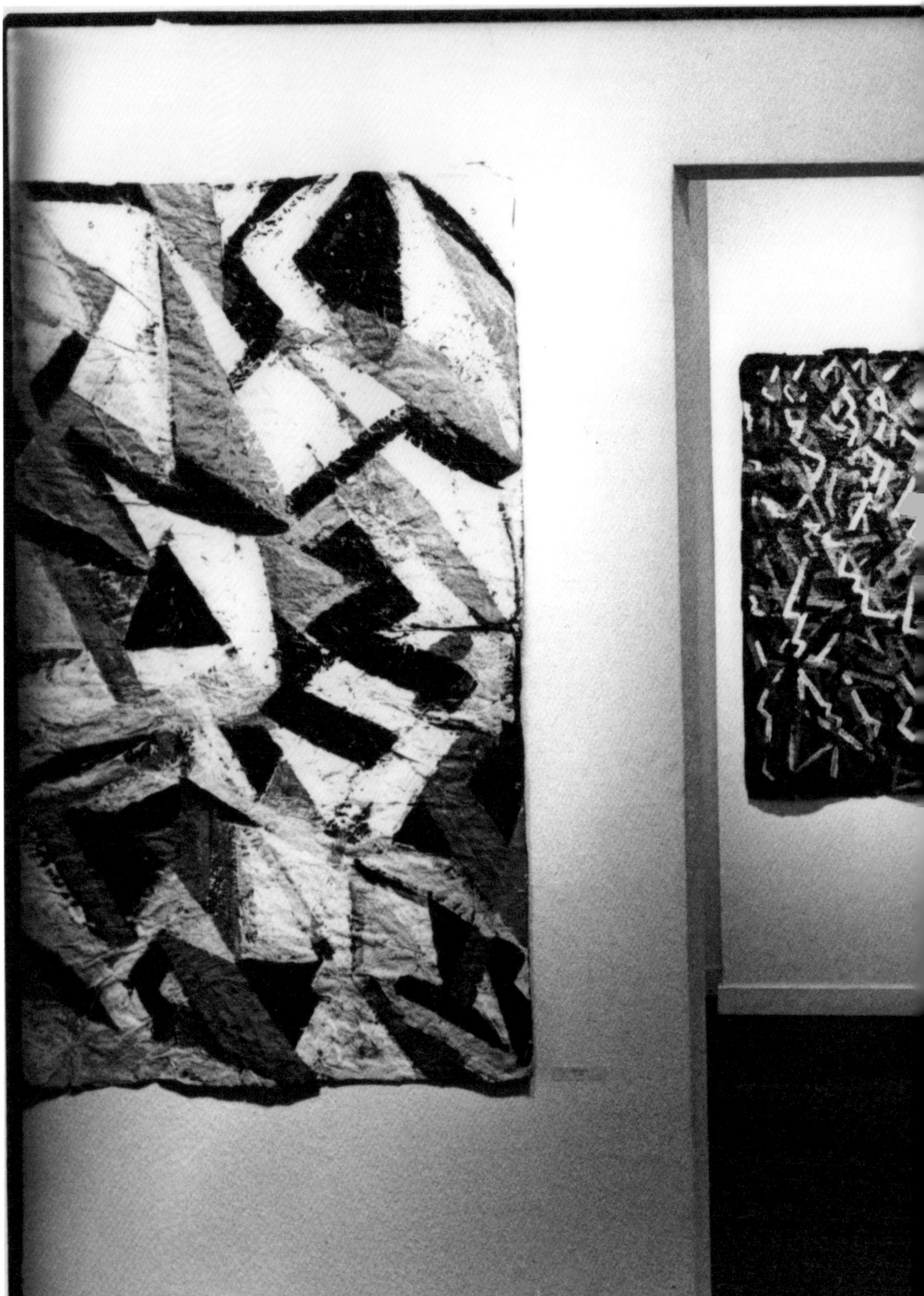

6 Galerie Francis van Hoof, Antwerp, 1989

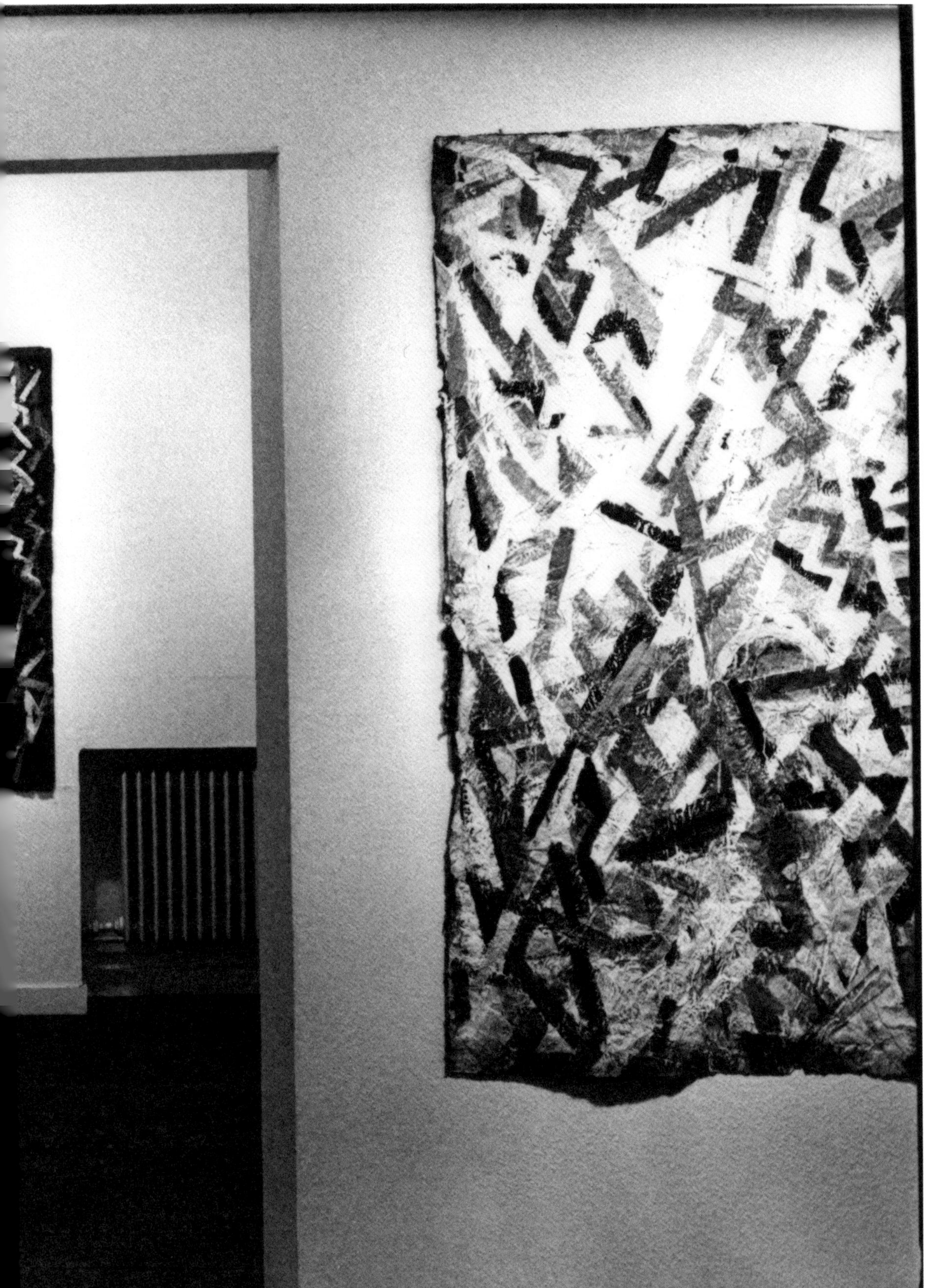

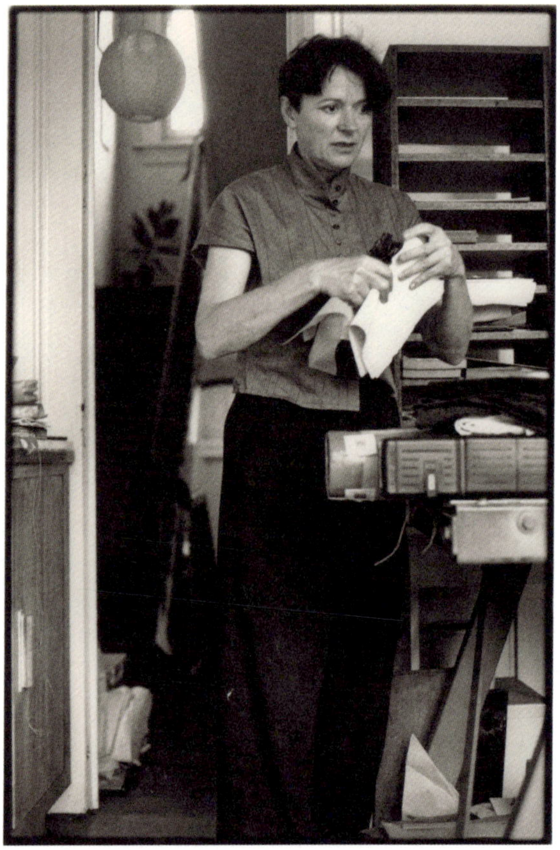

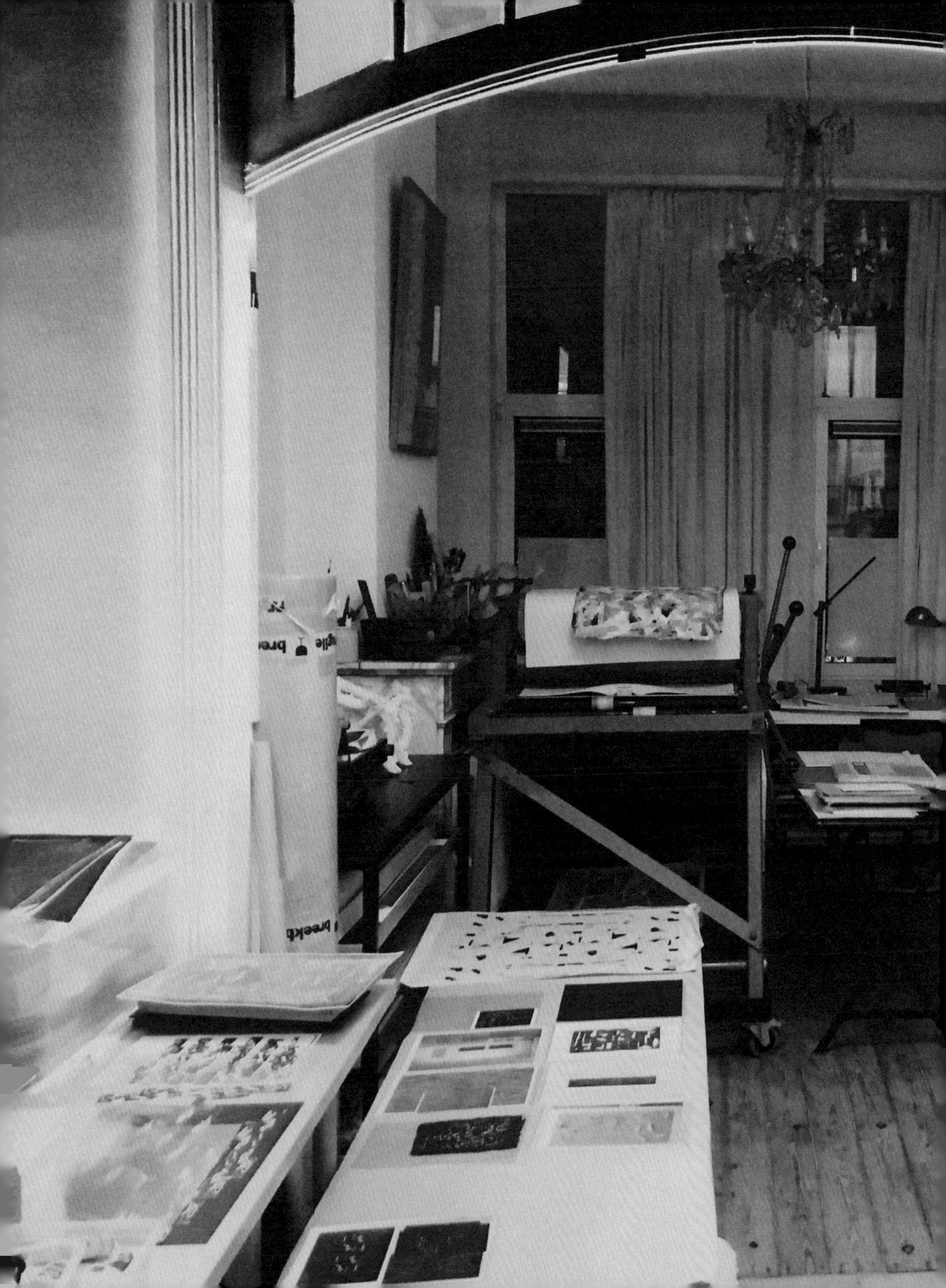

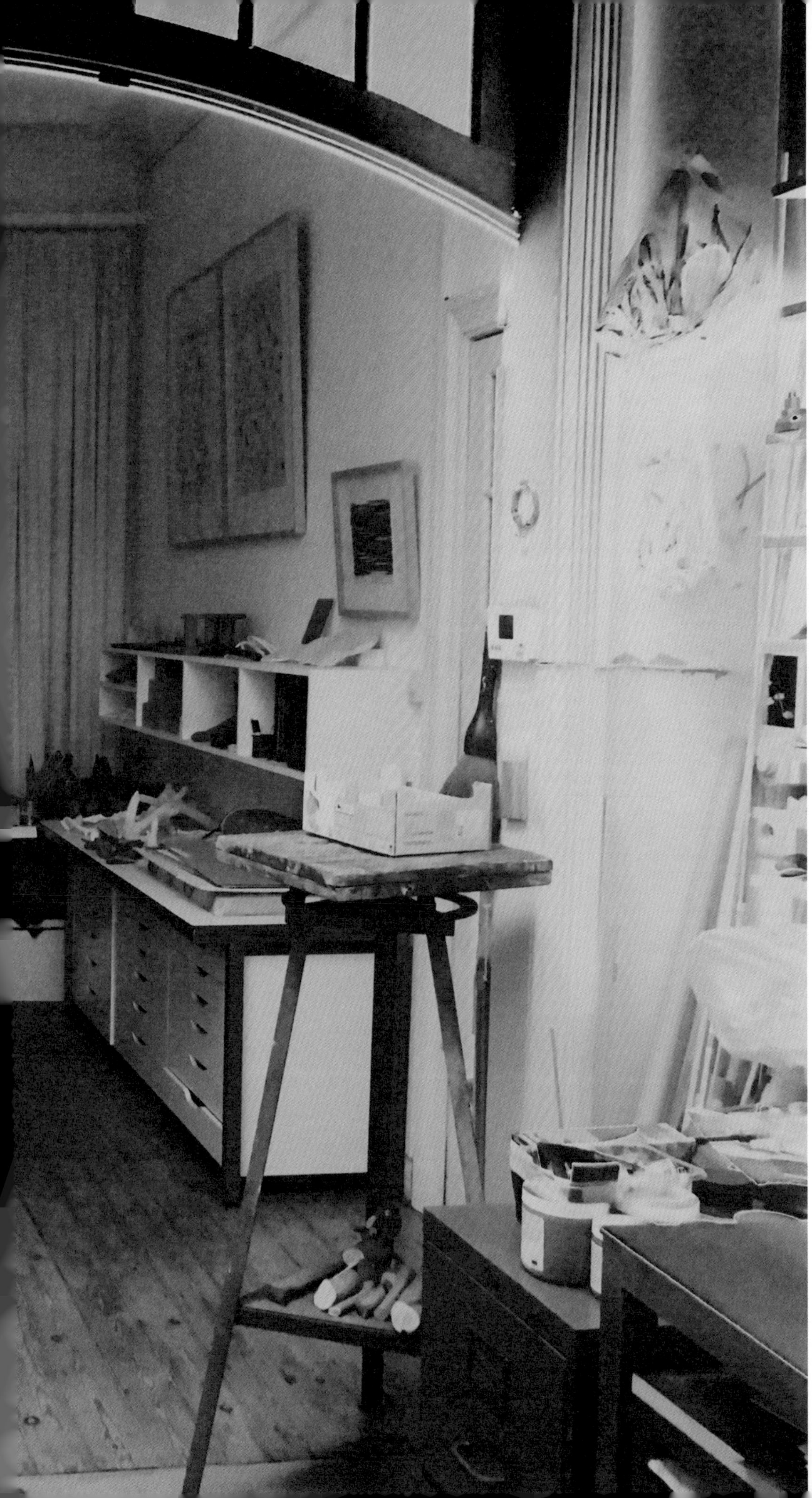

When one beats a drum at regular intervals, the rhythm emerges in the form of time divided into equal parts. The rhythmic intensity will depend on the force with which the parchment of the drum is struck... Shorter intervals imply greater force. The variations will also depend on the combination of beats and intervals. The succession of beats and pauses gives a certain intentionality, something like a direction. The rhythm provokes an expectation, and awakens a yearning. If it is interrupted, we experience a shock.

Something is broken. And if it continues, we expect something to which we cannot put a name. The rhythm is felt as a journey towards something, although it is not known what this something can be. Every rhythm is not merely an empty measure, but a direction; a meaning. The rhythm is not a measurement; it is primal time.

The measurement is not time itself, but a way of calculating it. Each rhythm is an attitude, a vision, and a reflection of the world, which is both different and special. The rhythm that Dante perceives and that moves the stars and souls is called *Love*; Lao Tseu and Chuan Tse hear another rhythm consisting of relative contradictions; Heraclitus felt it as war. It is impossible to reduce all these rhythms to one unit without at the same time the individual content of each of them evaporating.

The rhythm is not a philosophy, but an image of the world. In other words, where the philosophies are based.

Octavio Paz, from 'The Bow and the Lyre' (El arco y la lira), Meulenhoff Amsterdam, 1984

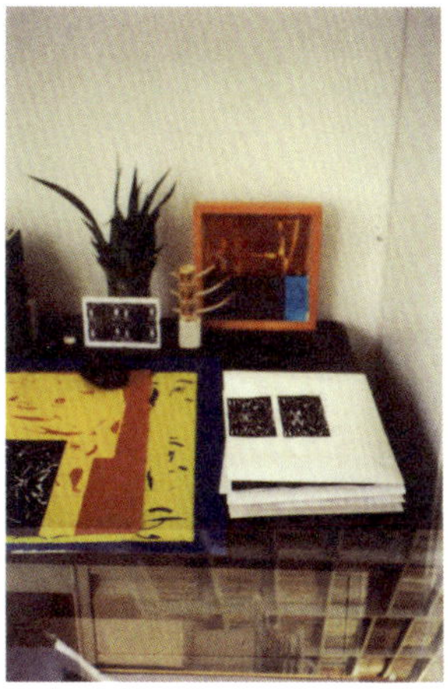

I. Vibration, Sequencing, Energy

Trilling, Sequentie, Energie

Automatic drawings,
***seismographic* notations,**
composing & assemblages

**If you want to find the secrets of the universe,
think in terms of energy, frequency and vibration.**

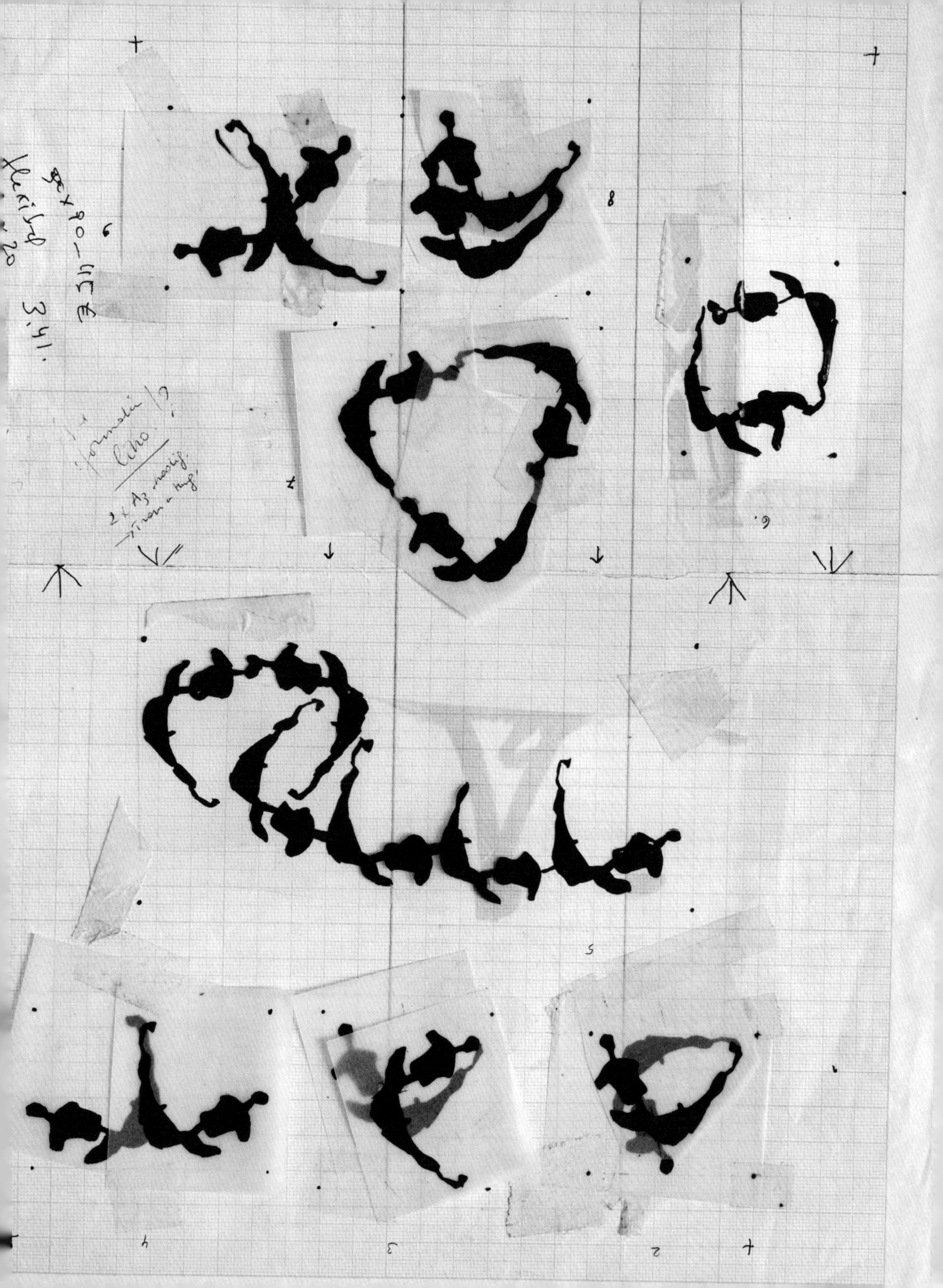

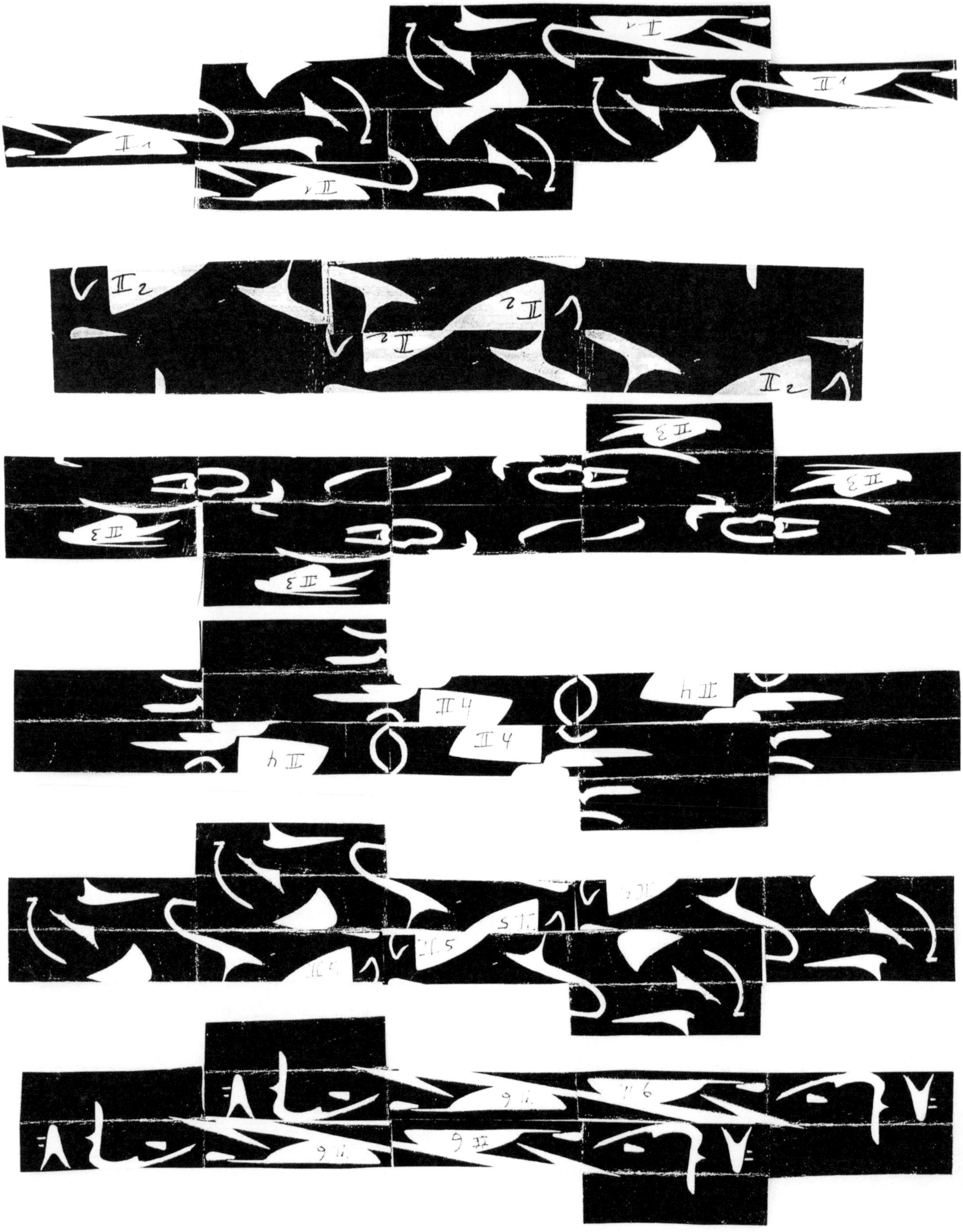

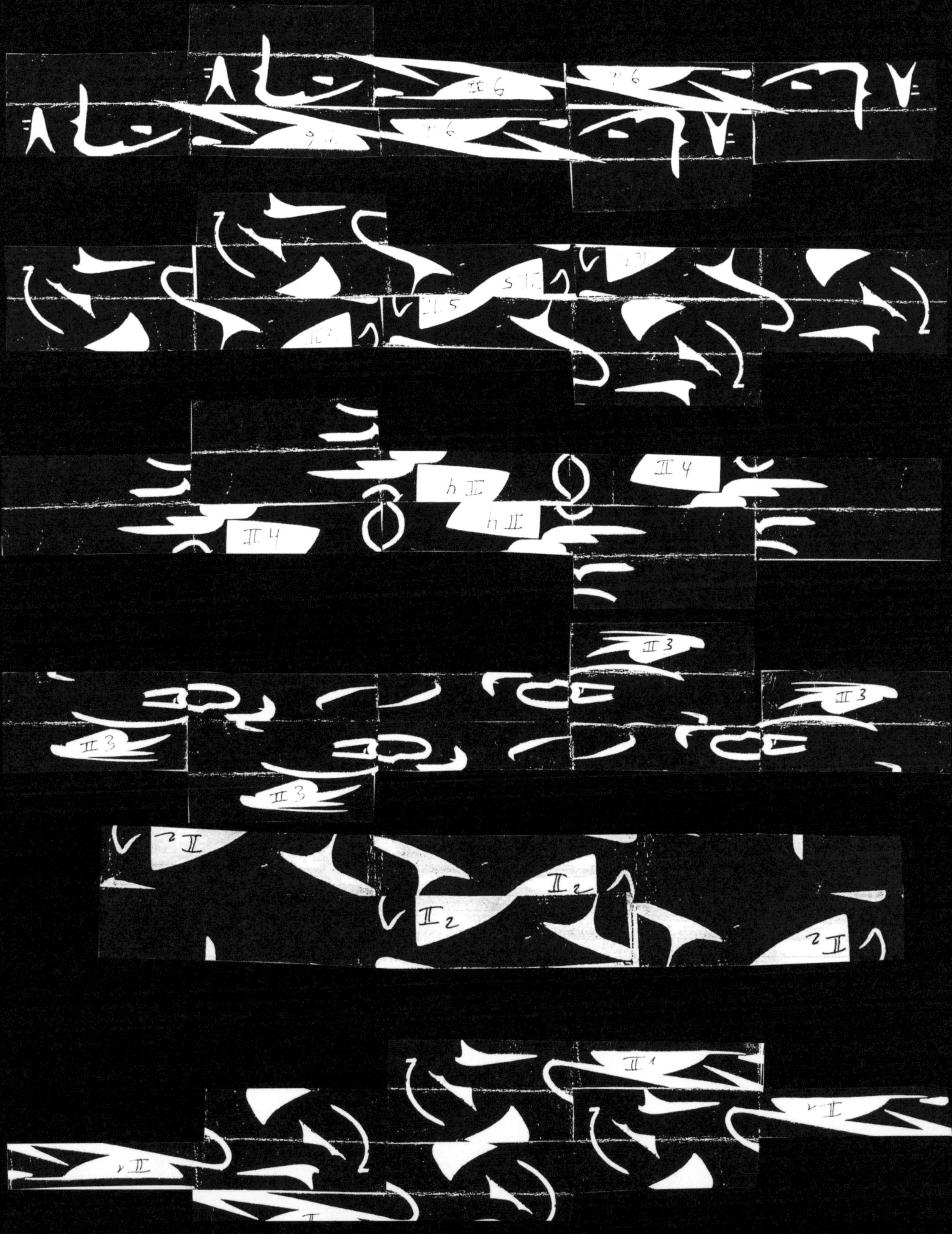

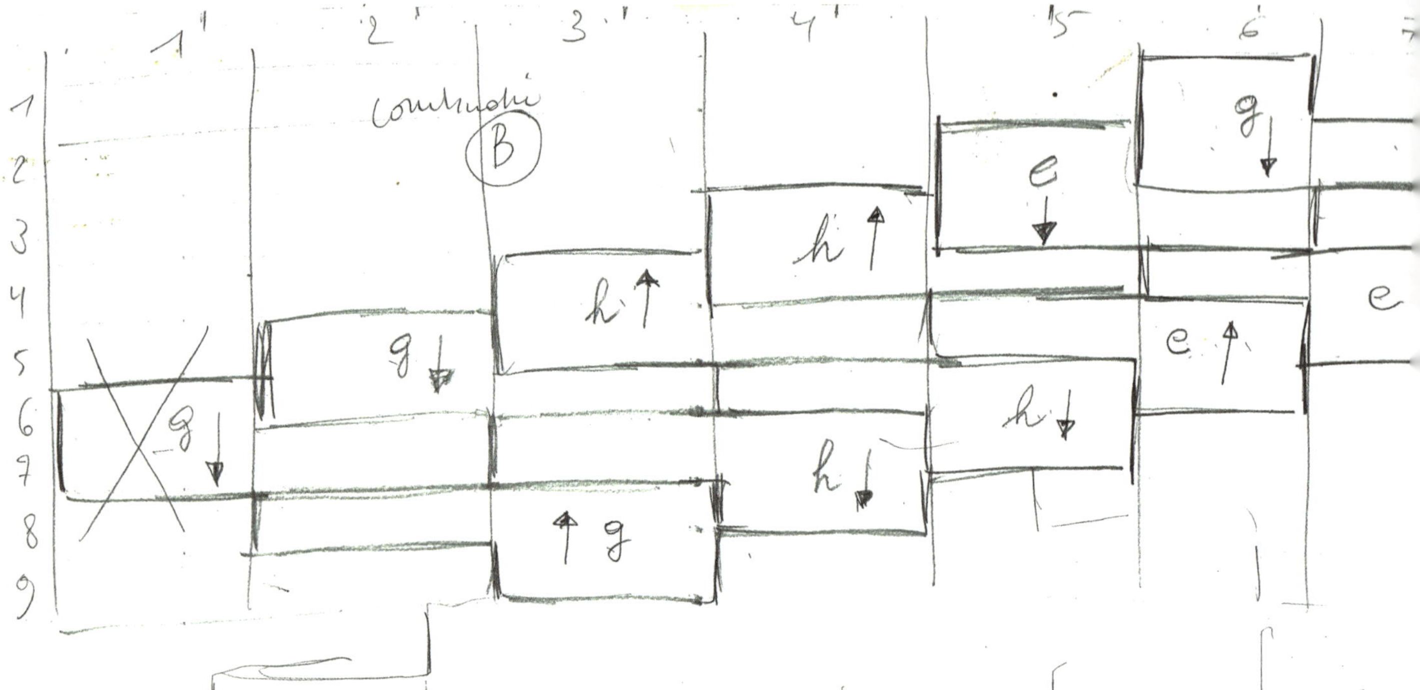

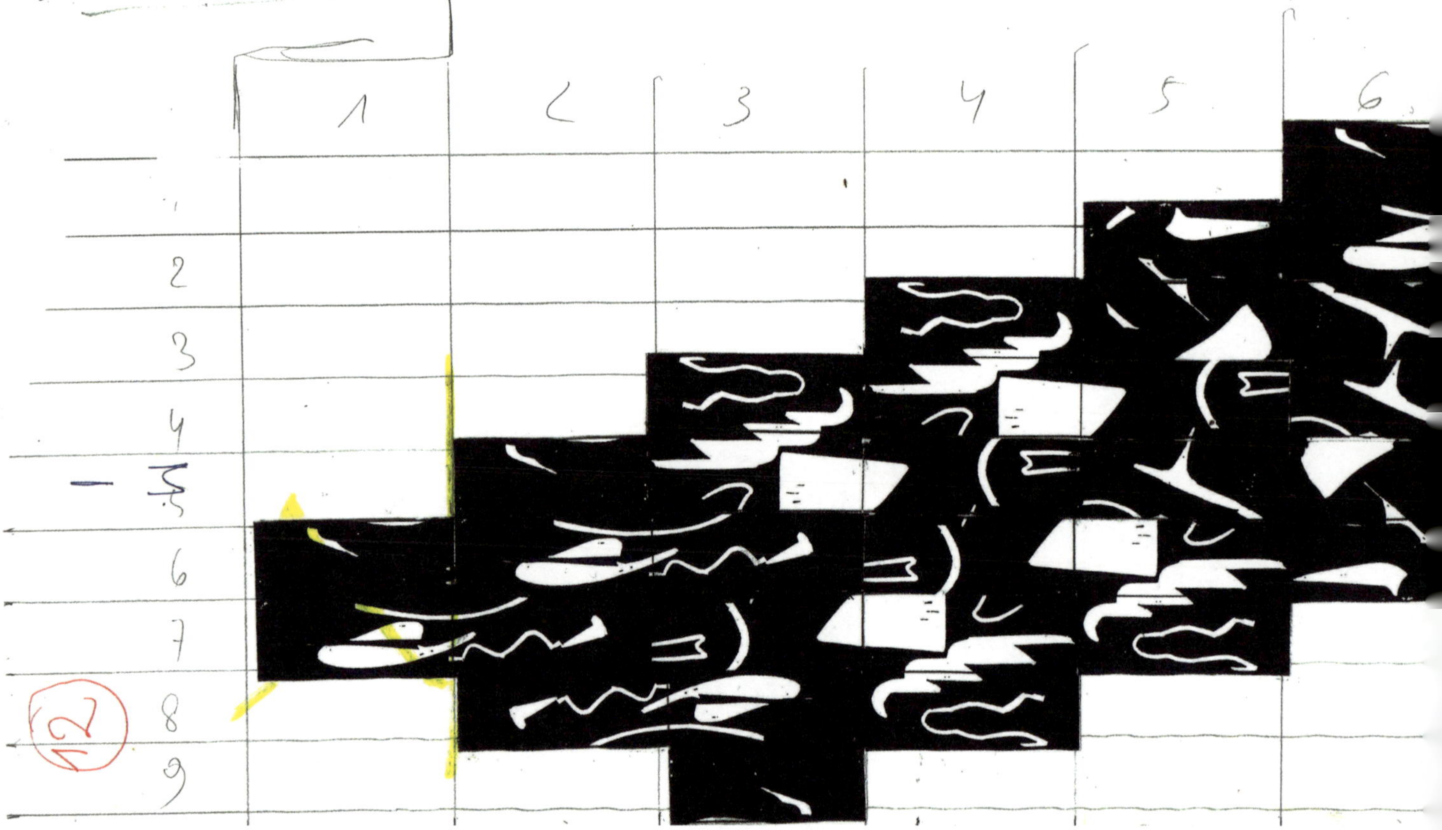

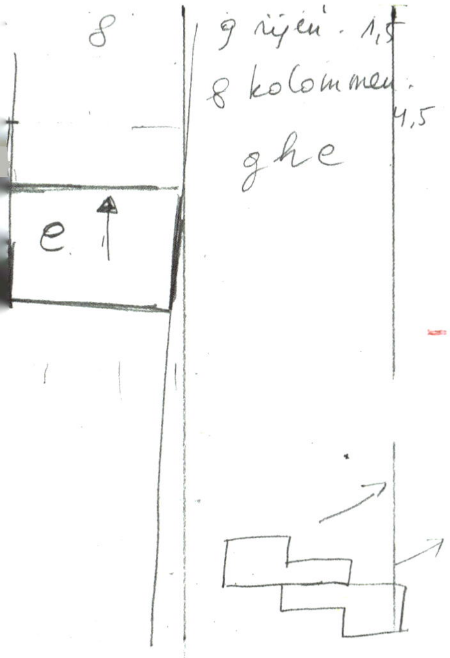
8
9 rijen · 1,5
8 kolommen · 1,5
ghe
e

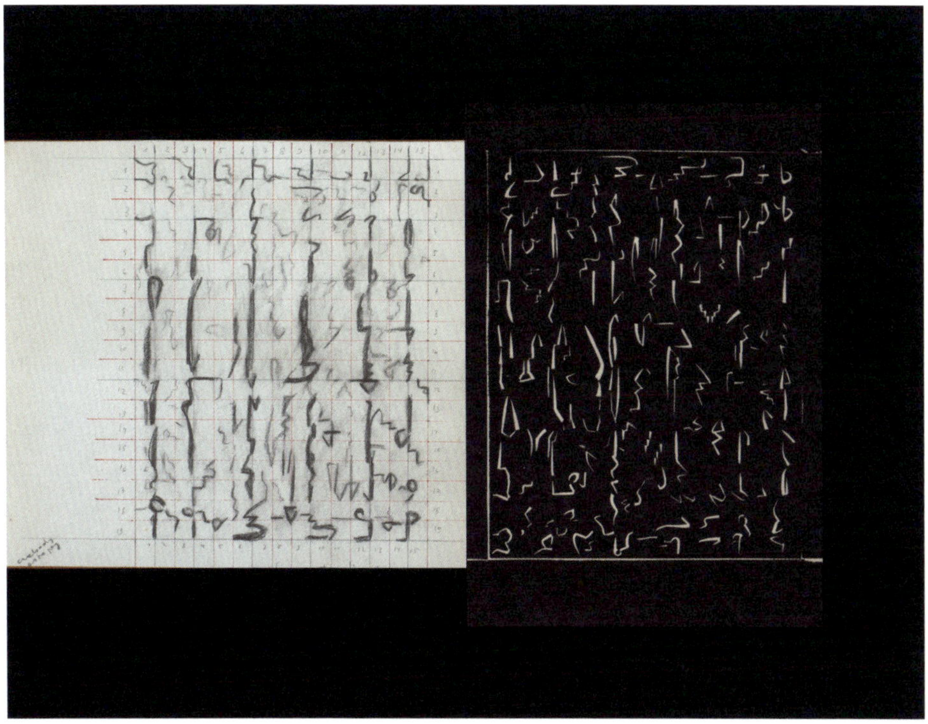

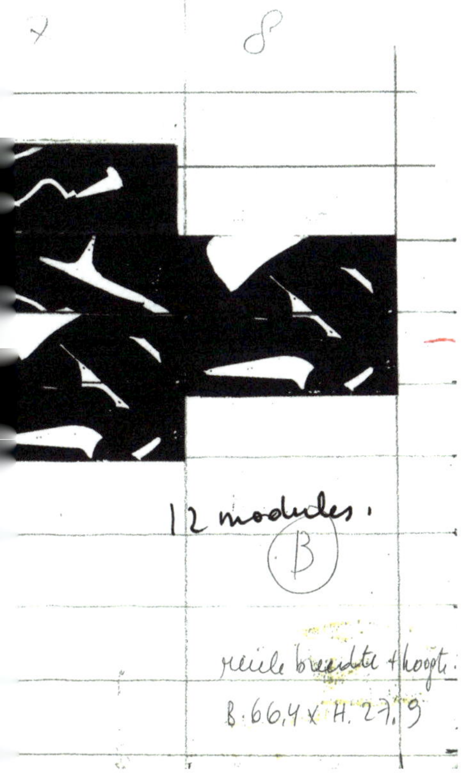
8
12 modules.
B
reële breedte + hoogte.
B. 66,4 x H. 27,9

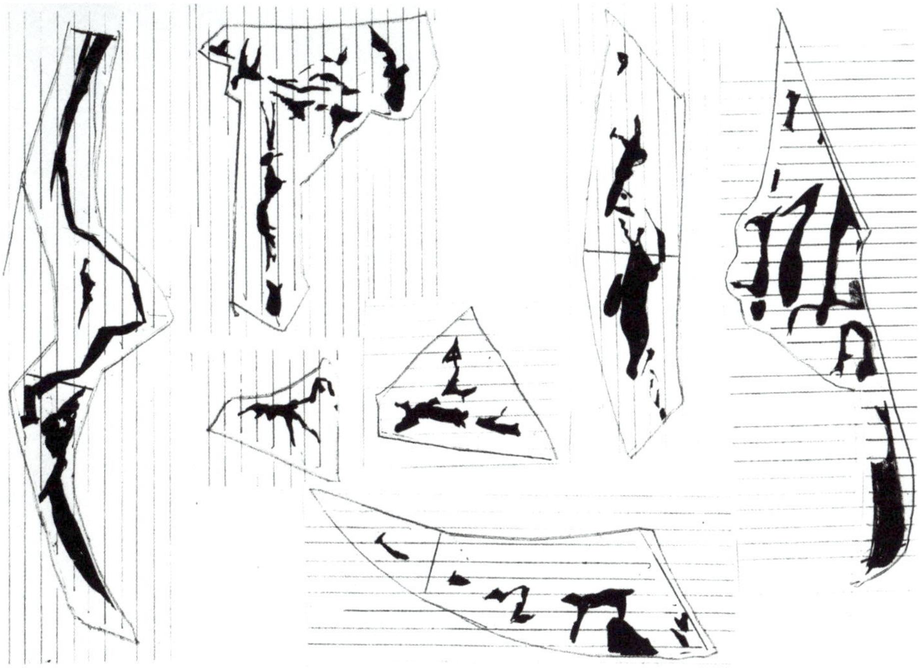

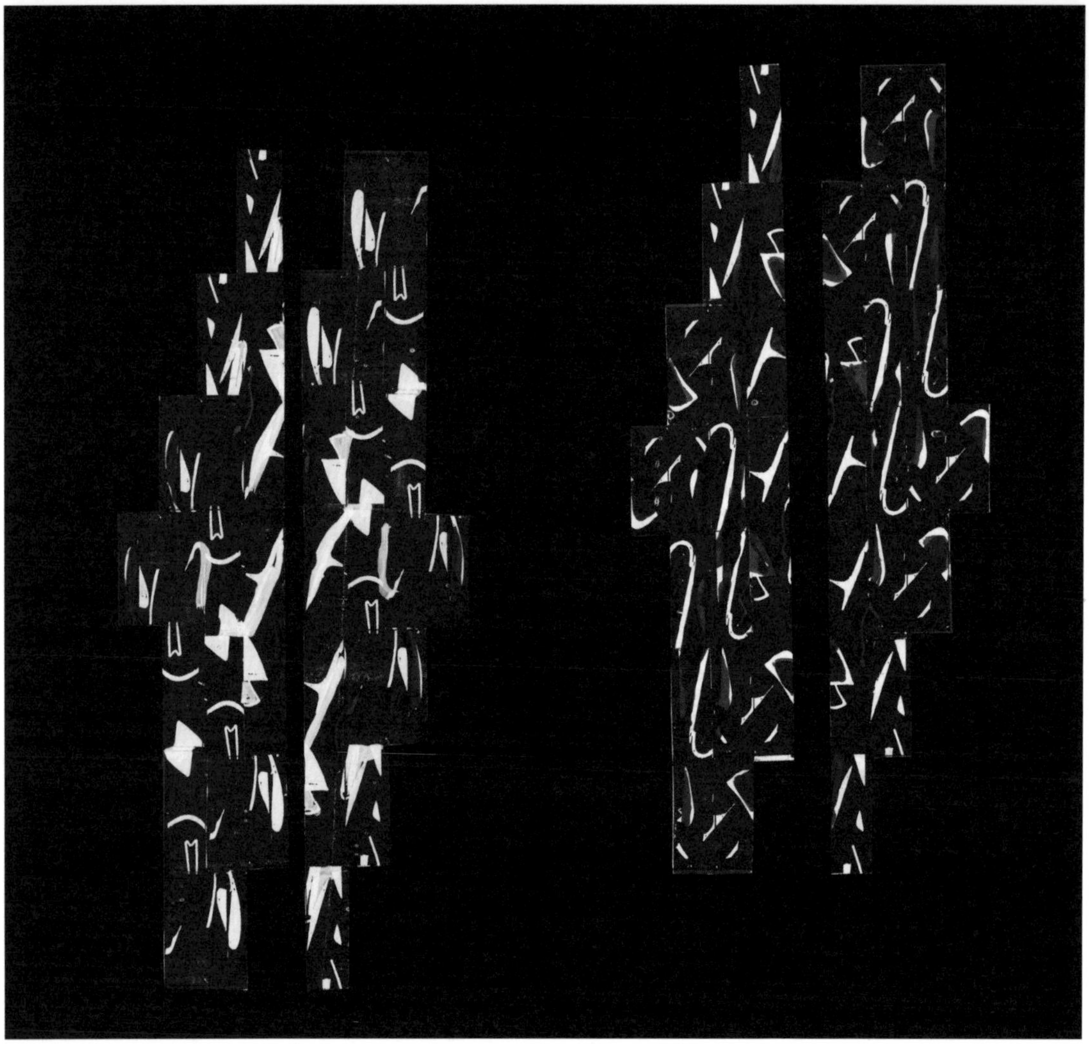

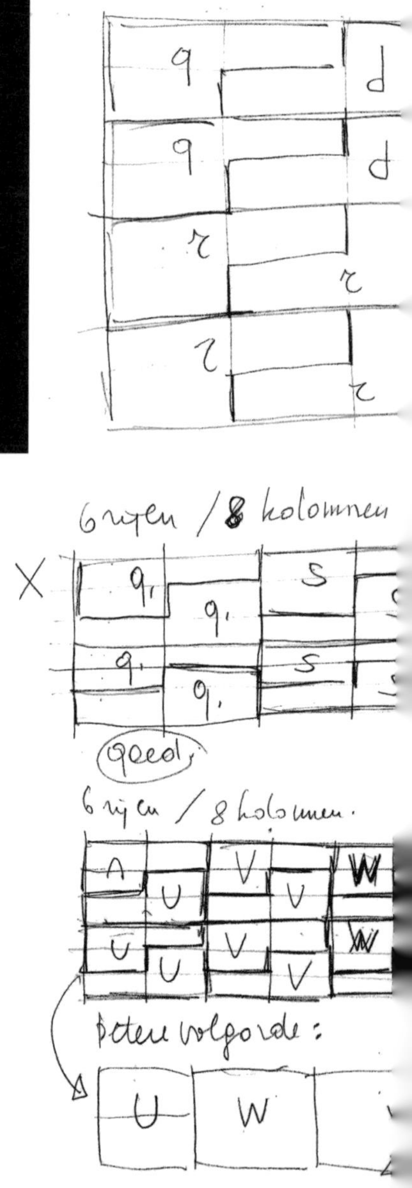

6 rijen / 8 kolommen
goed
6 rijen / 8 kolommen.
betere volgorde:

18 rijen. 9 kolommen.

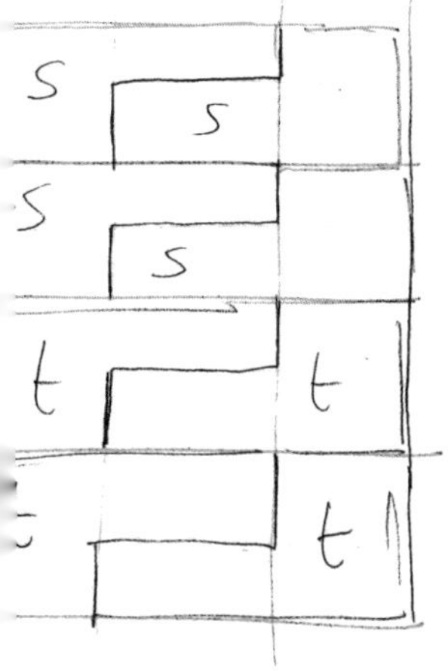

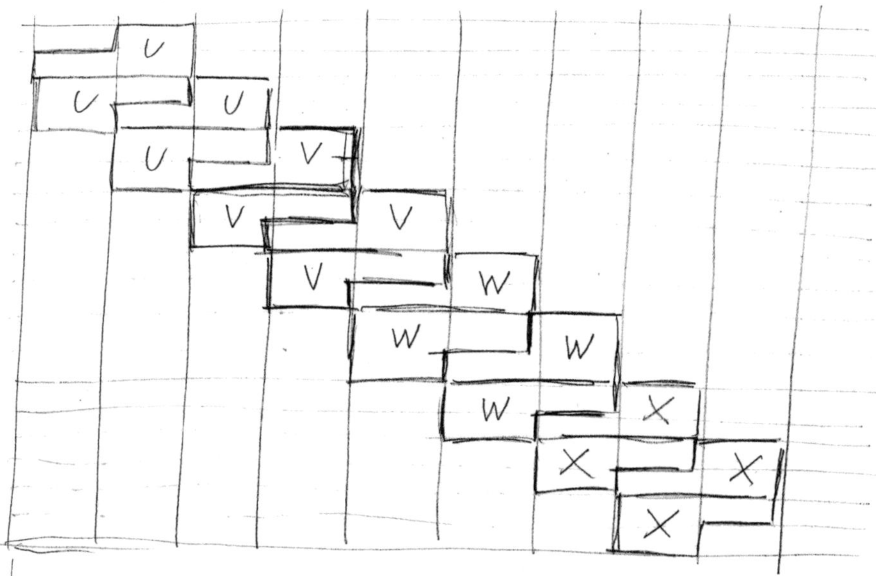

5).

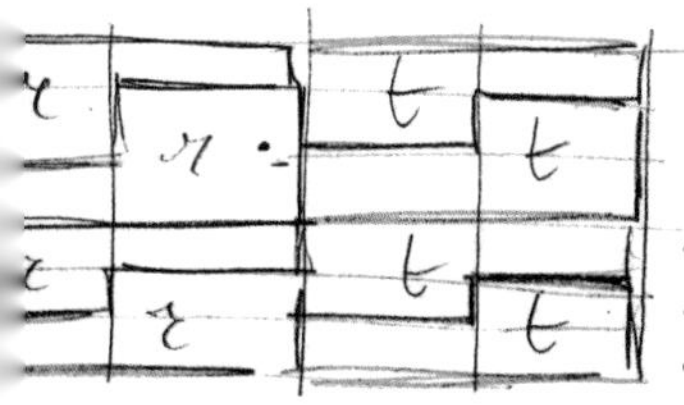

8 rijen - 9 kolommen.

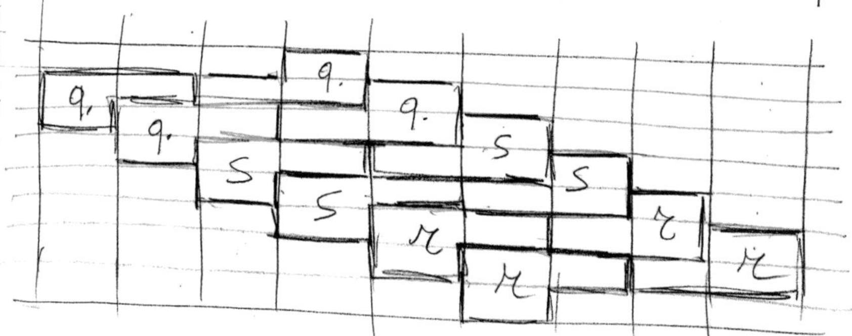

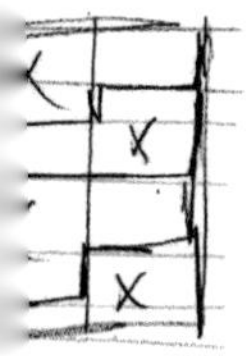

4 rijen / 12 kolommen

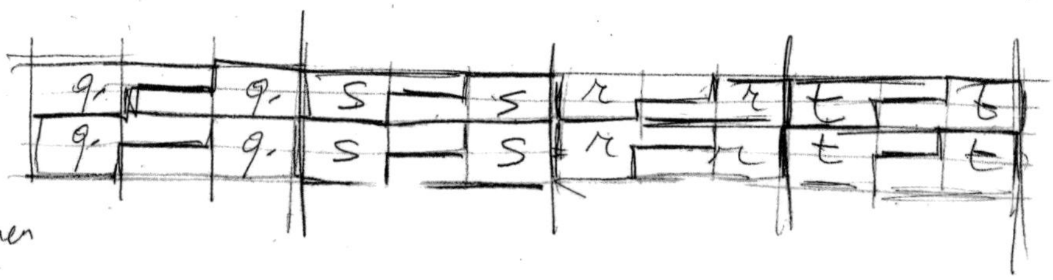

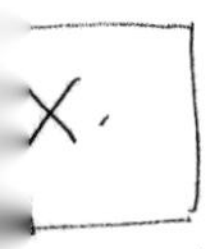

z. goed deze 2 samen

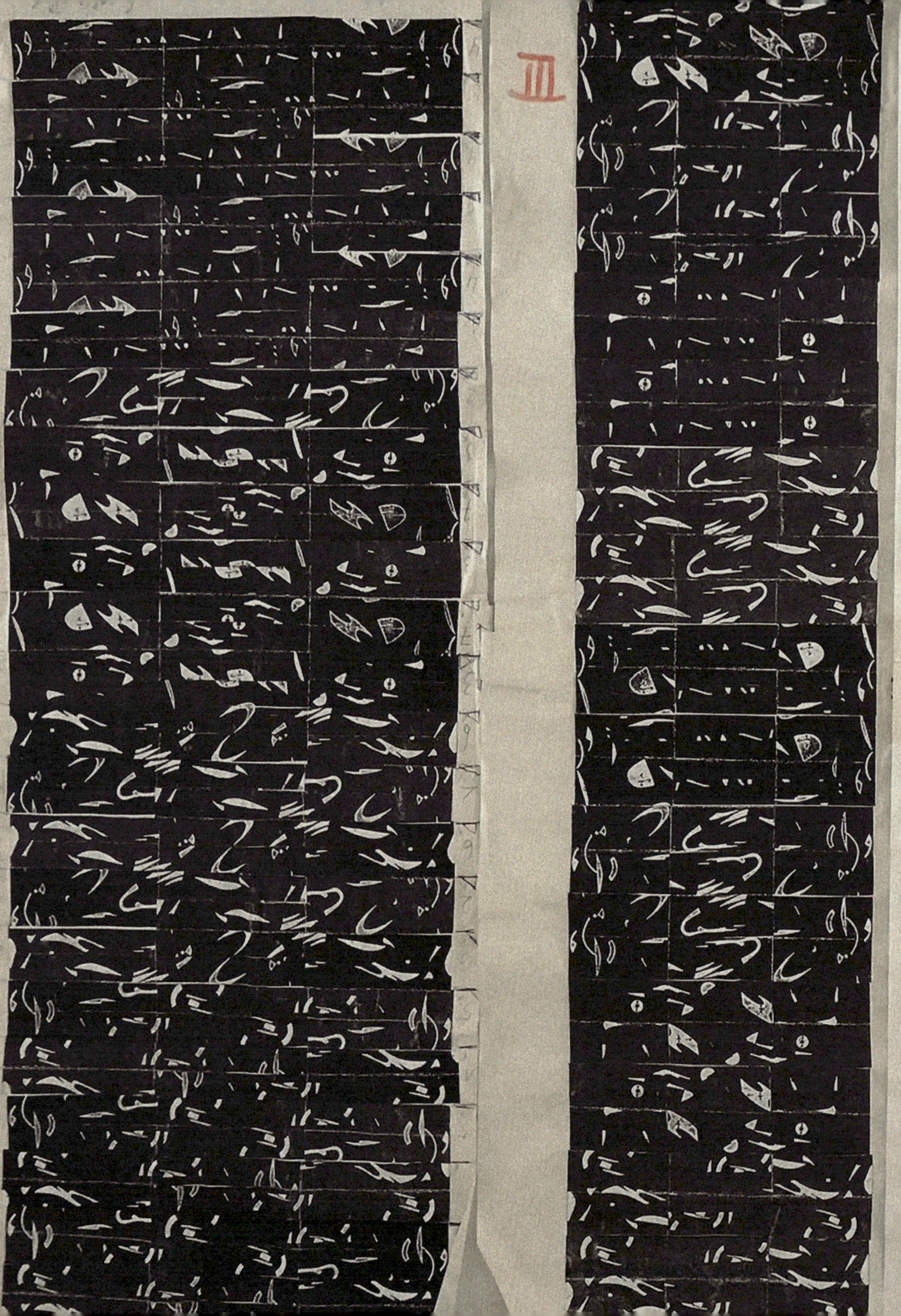

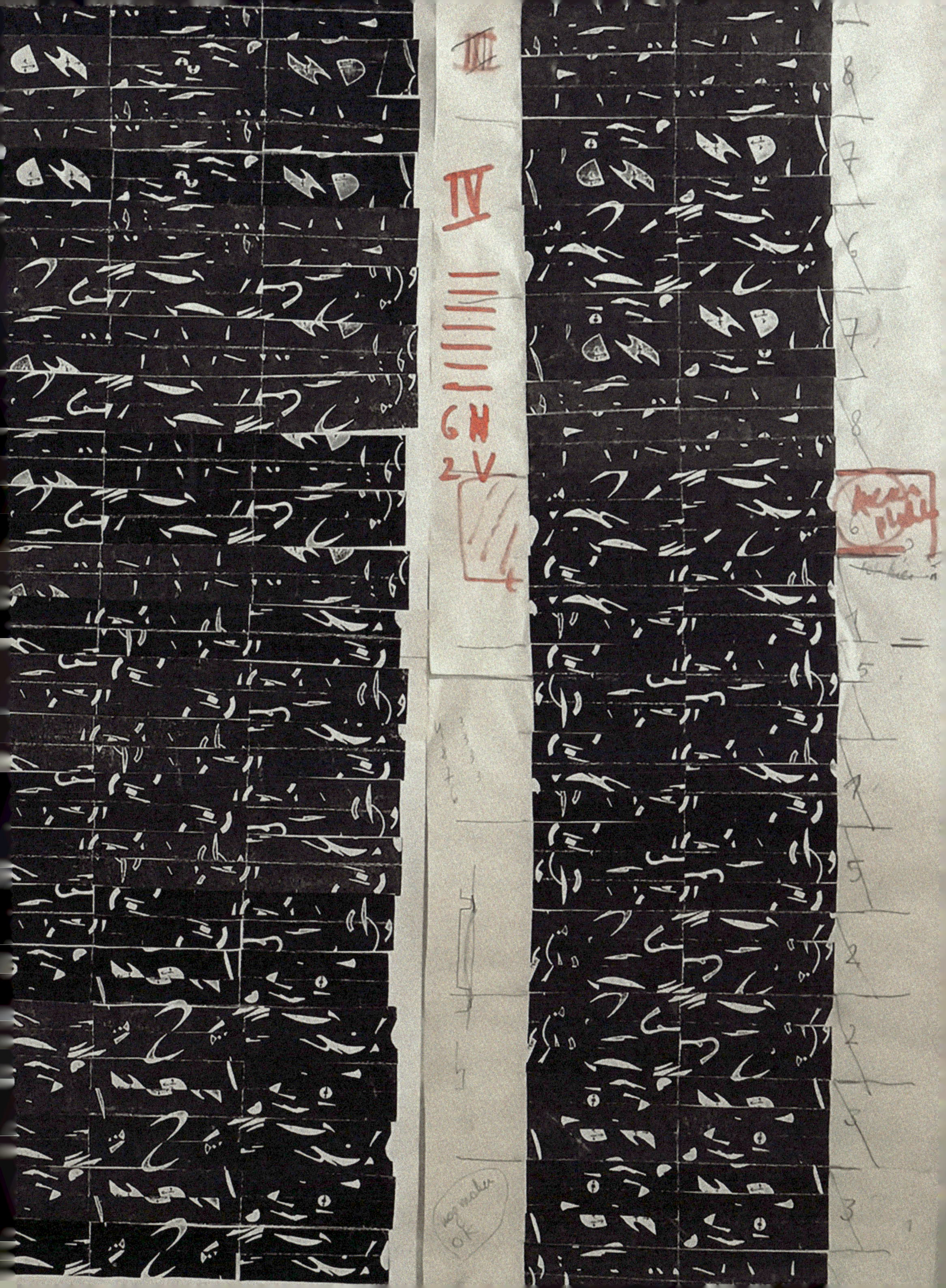
IV
6 H
2 V

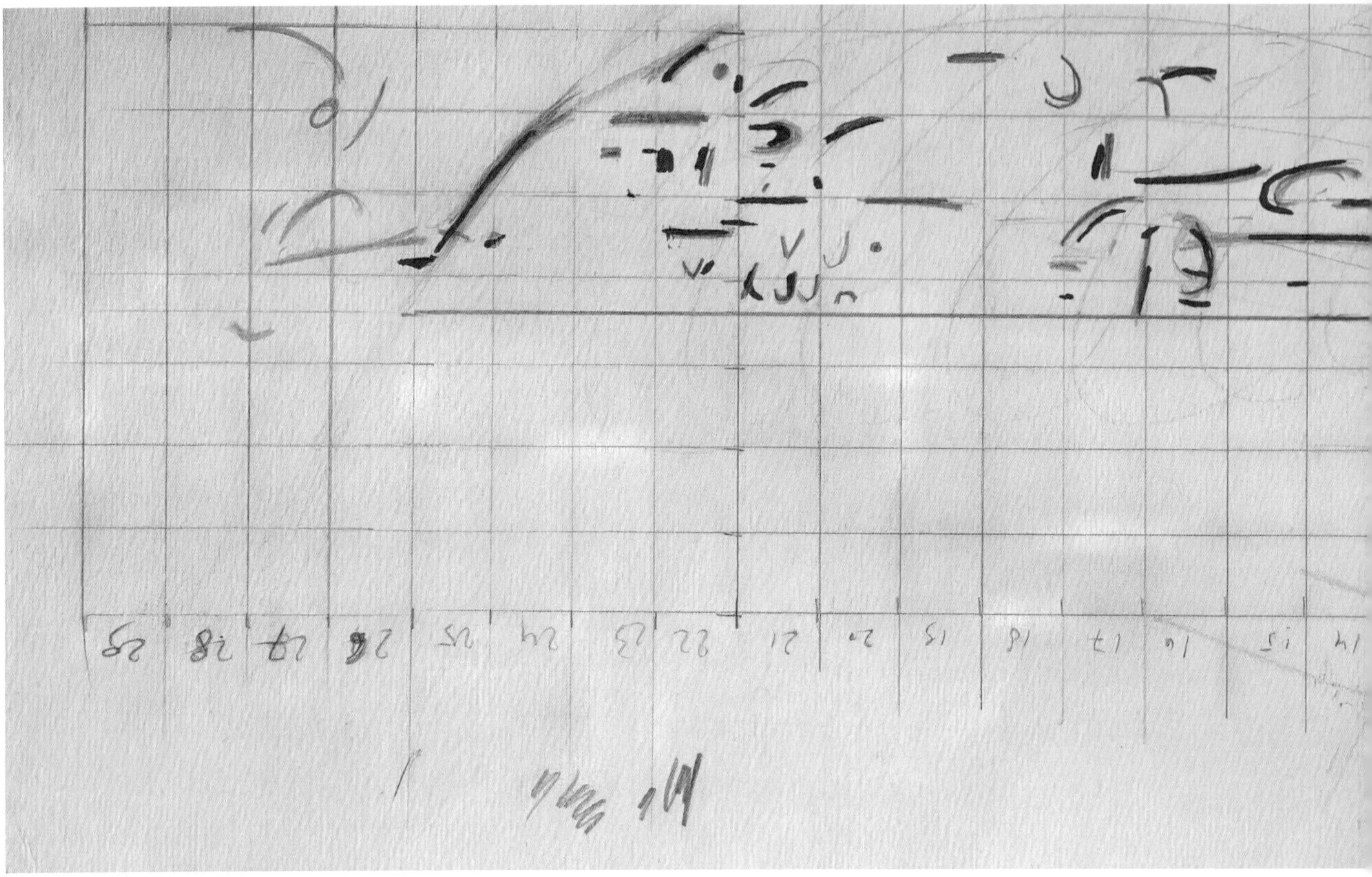

Linda Vinck uses a small number of motifs and modules formed by signs, as she likes to call these elements of her practice, to create her paintings. She arranges these motifs and modules according to a certain rhythm and sequence leading to an enumerative and repetitive organizational system and to arrive at a determined motif. Paths and invisible directions seem to appear in the predefined space of canvas and paper. She borrows these from her signs, notes, and graphemes, to achieve her score – if we think in terms of musical resemblance – and tablet (if we retain the analogy with oriental scribes or calligraphers).

João Vário, from 'Linda Vinck: A special case of enumeration in painting', Antwerp, July 1994

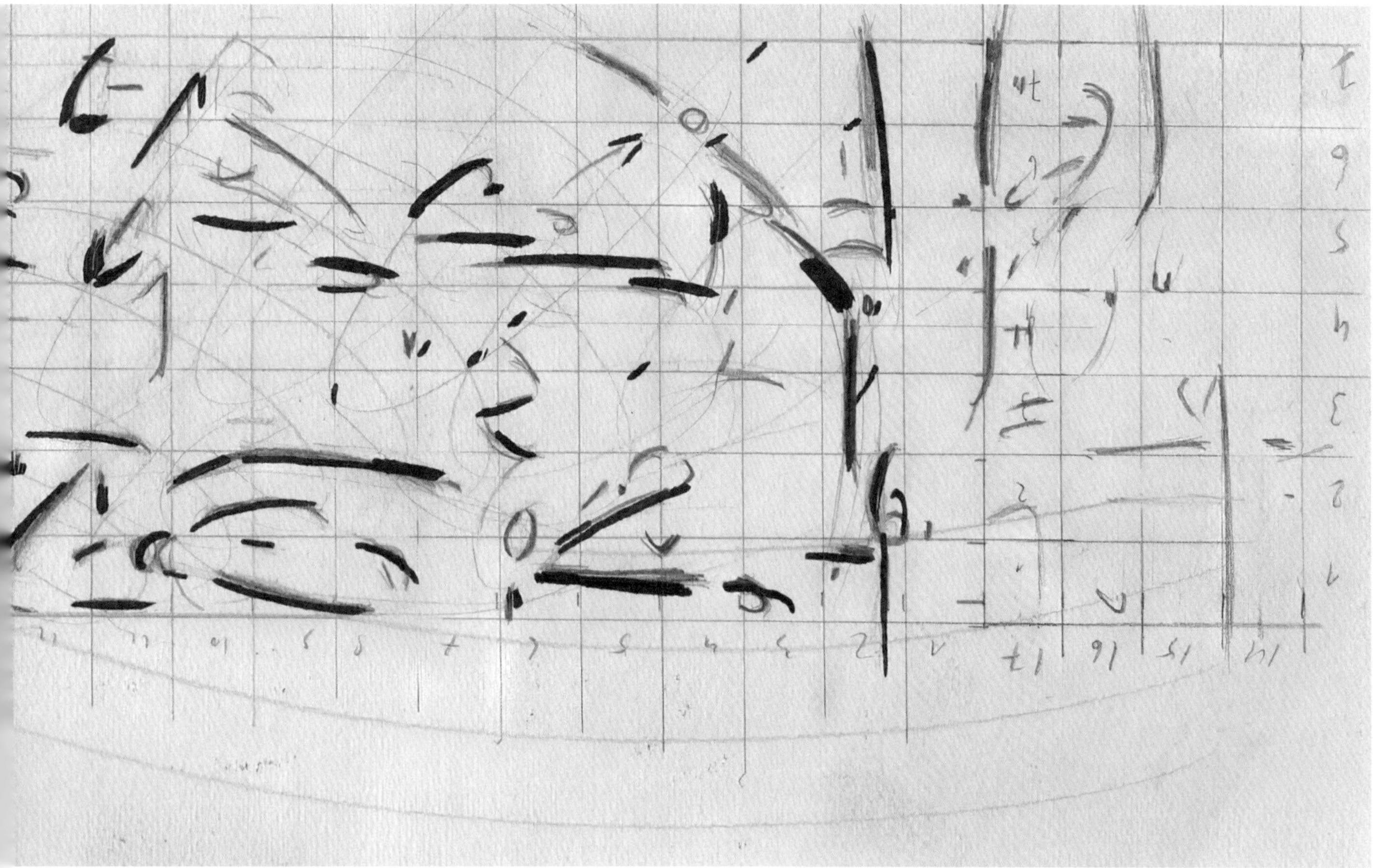

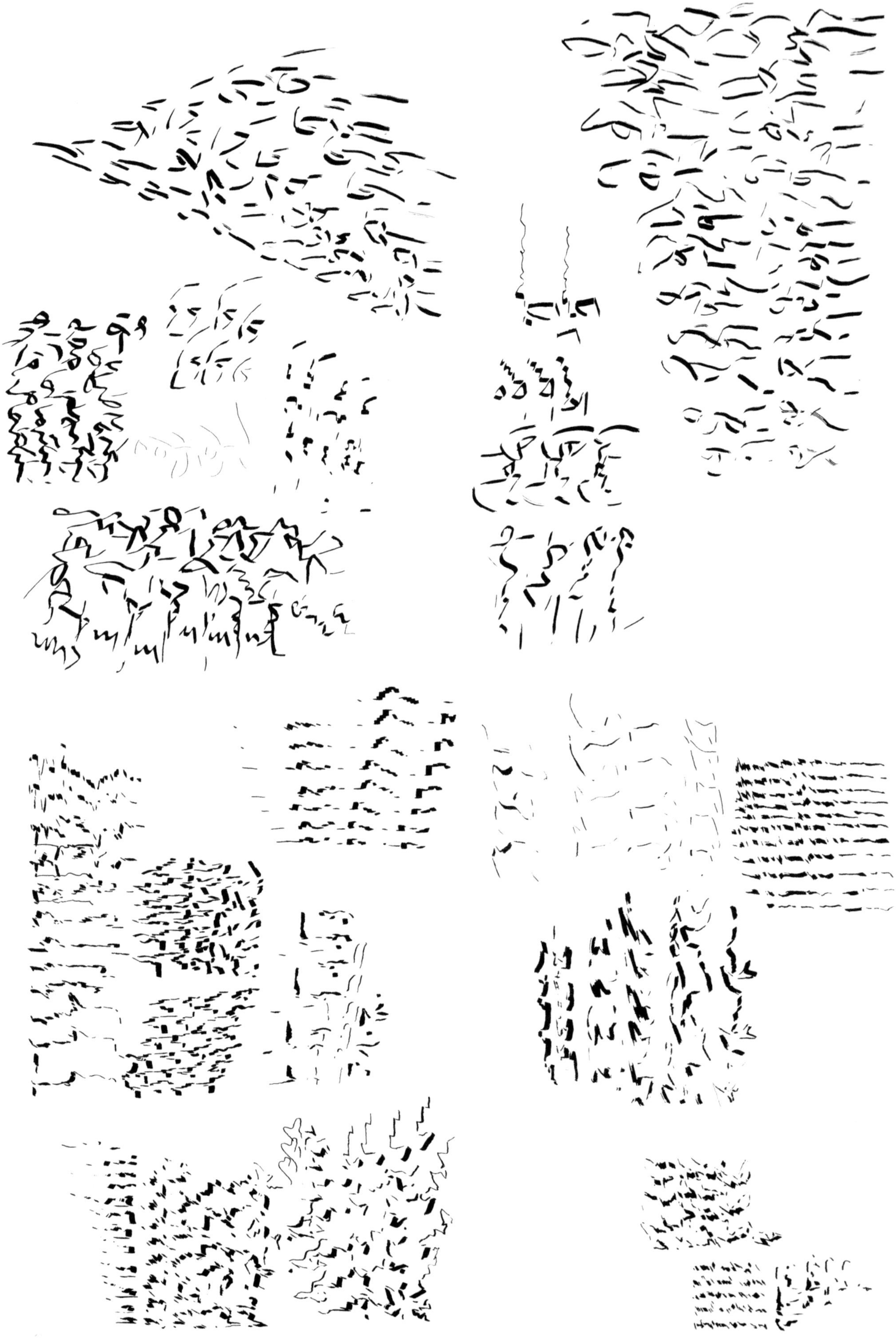

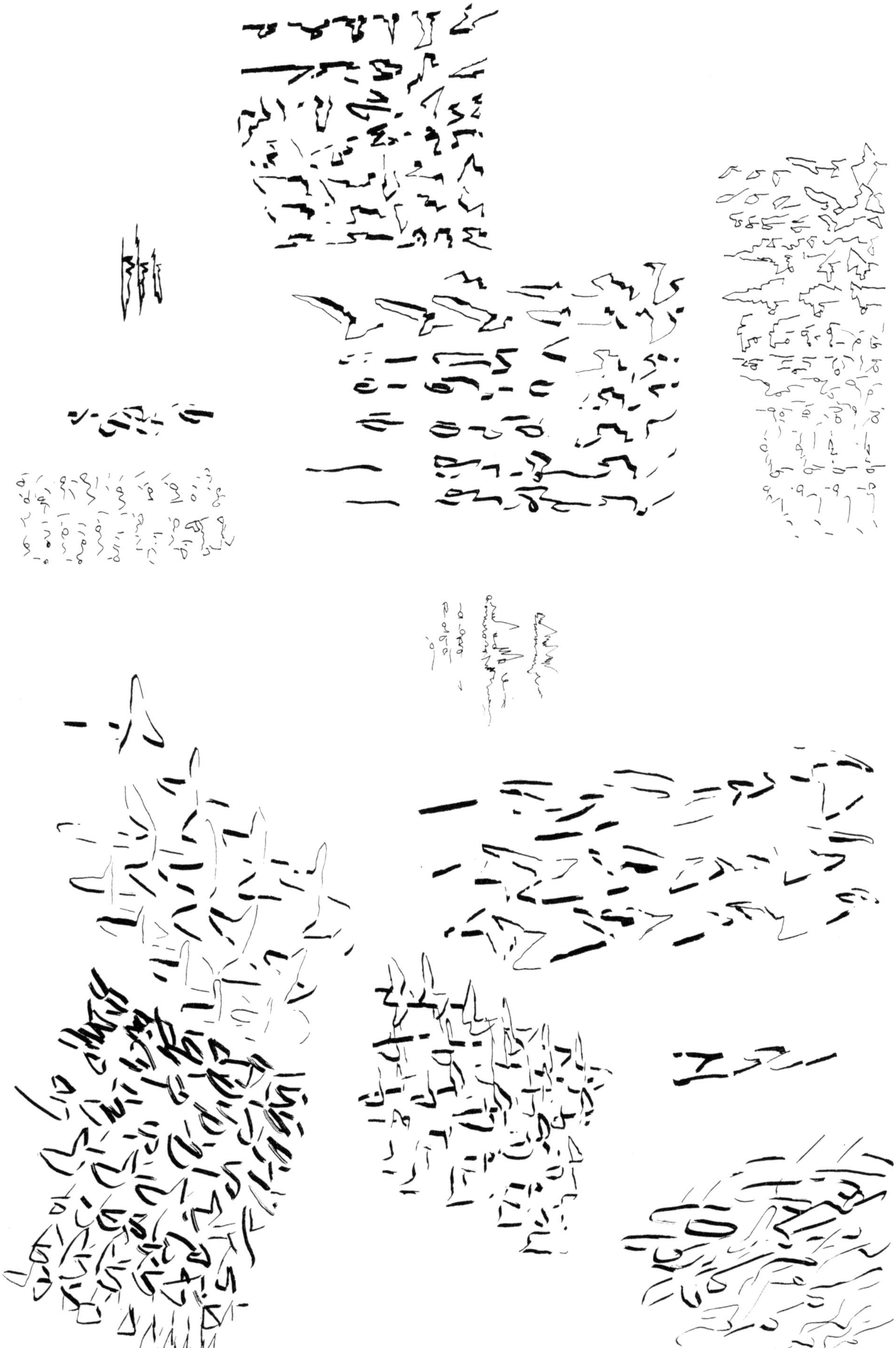

Een lijn wordt licht op dit podium
Van papier, in dit forum van stigma's
Die brandstichtende vogels zijn

Nic van Bruggen, 'BIJ EEN LINOSNEDE, *voor Linda Vinck*', 1986

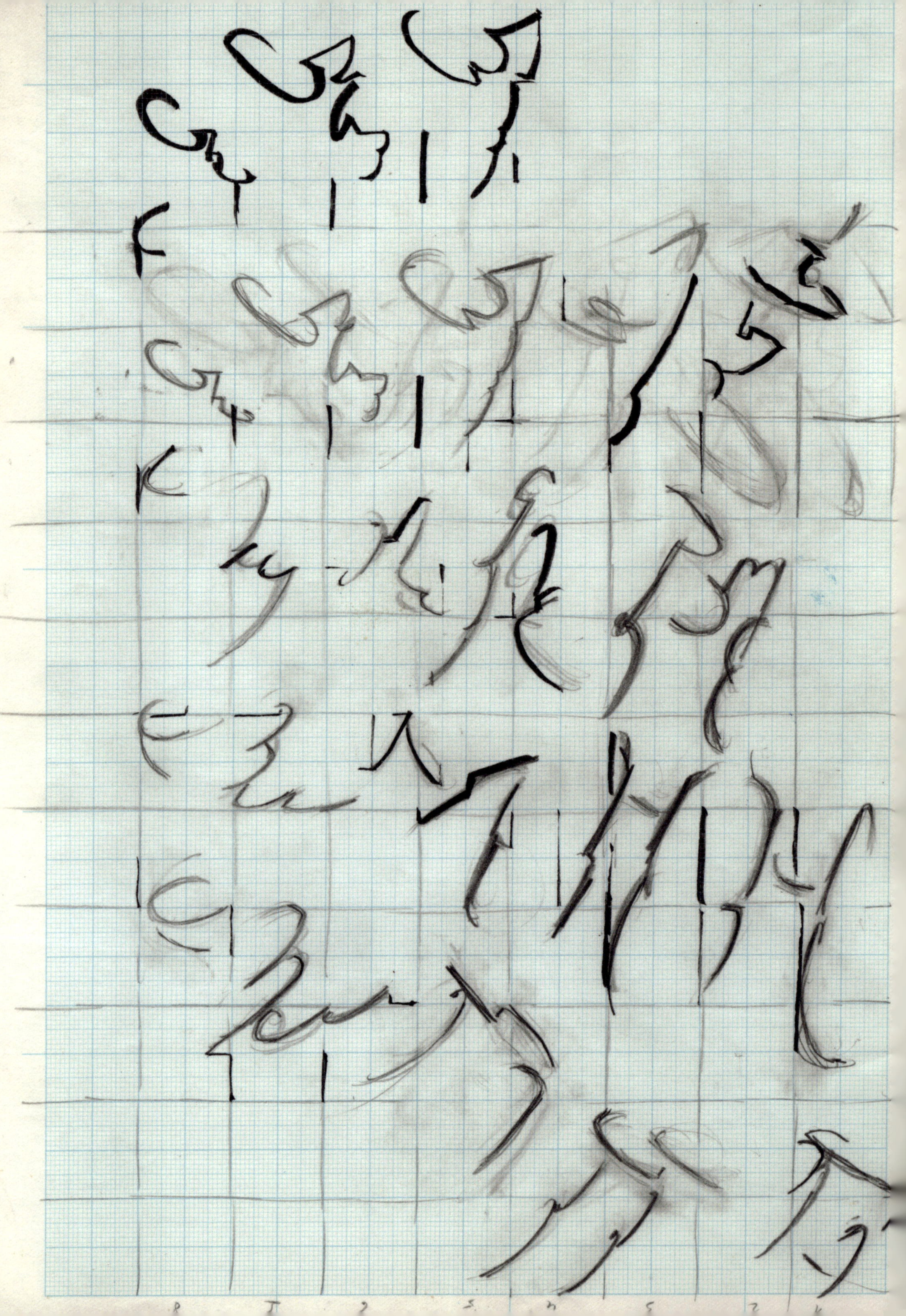

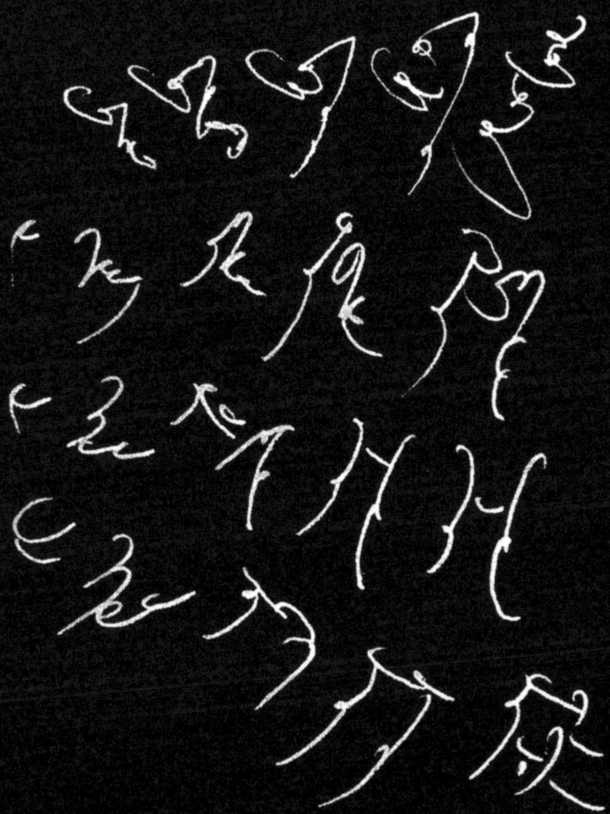

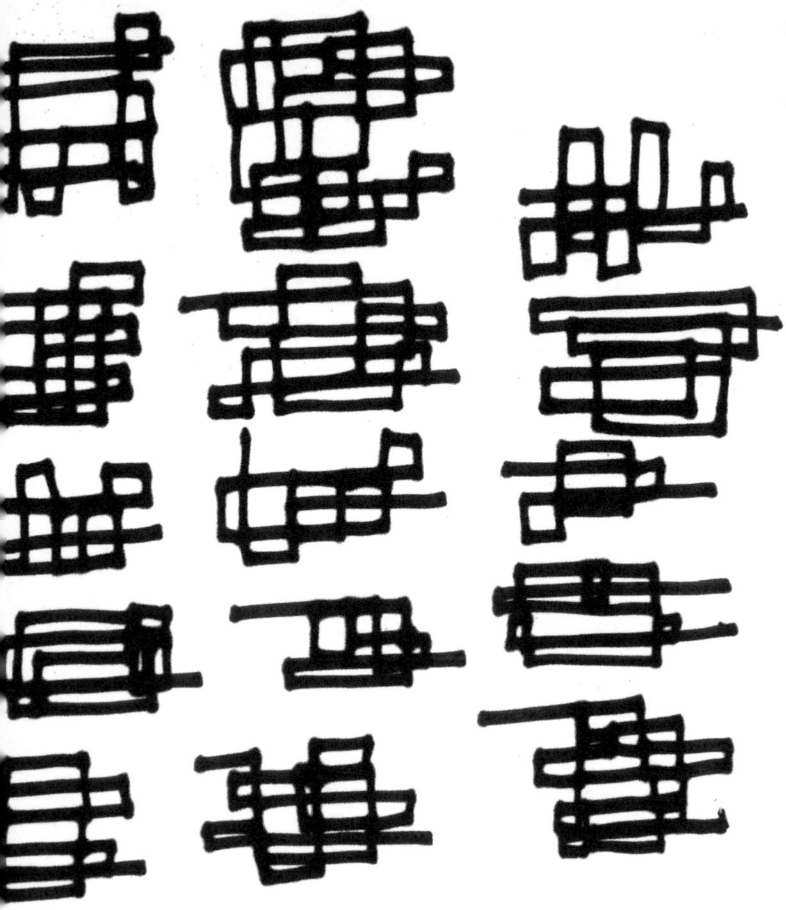

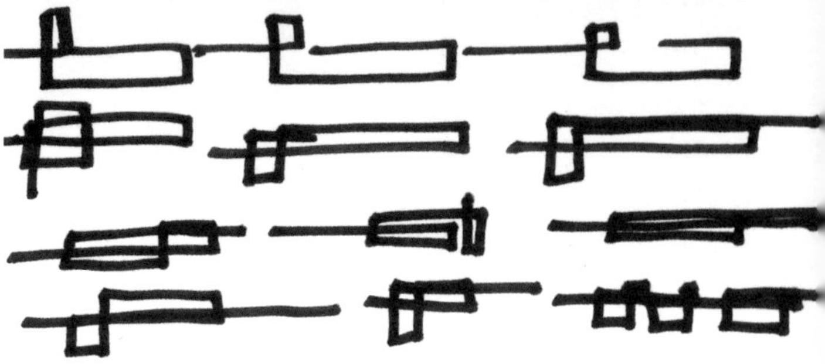

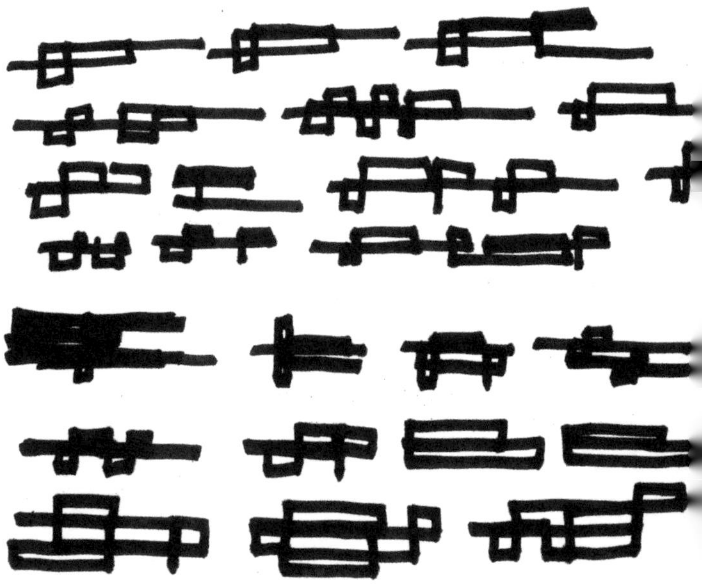

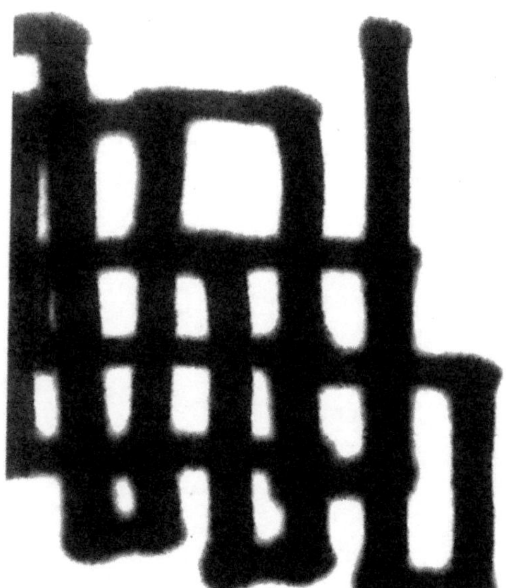

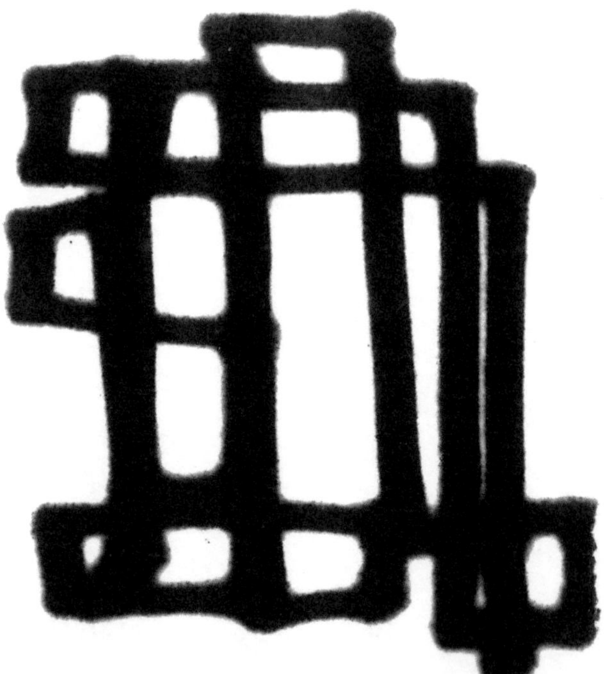

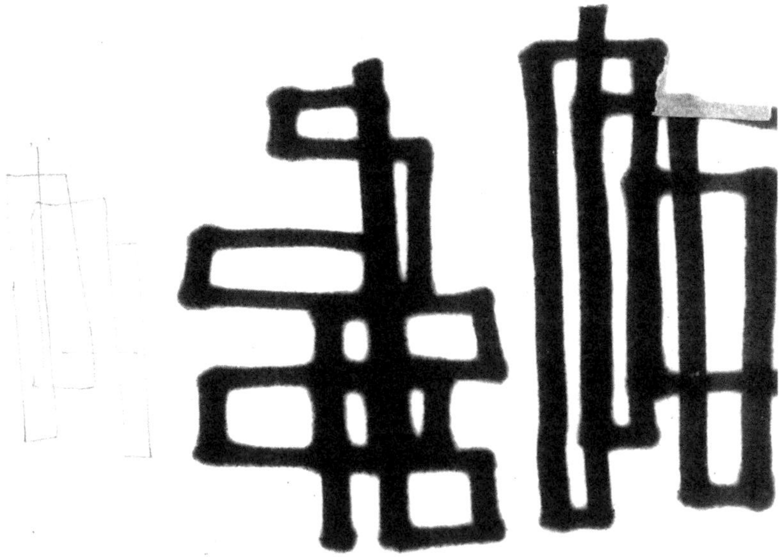

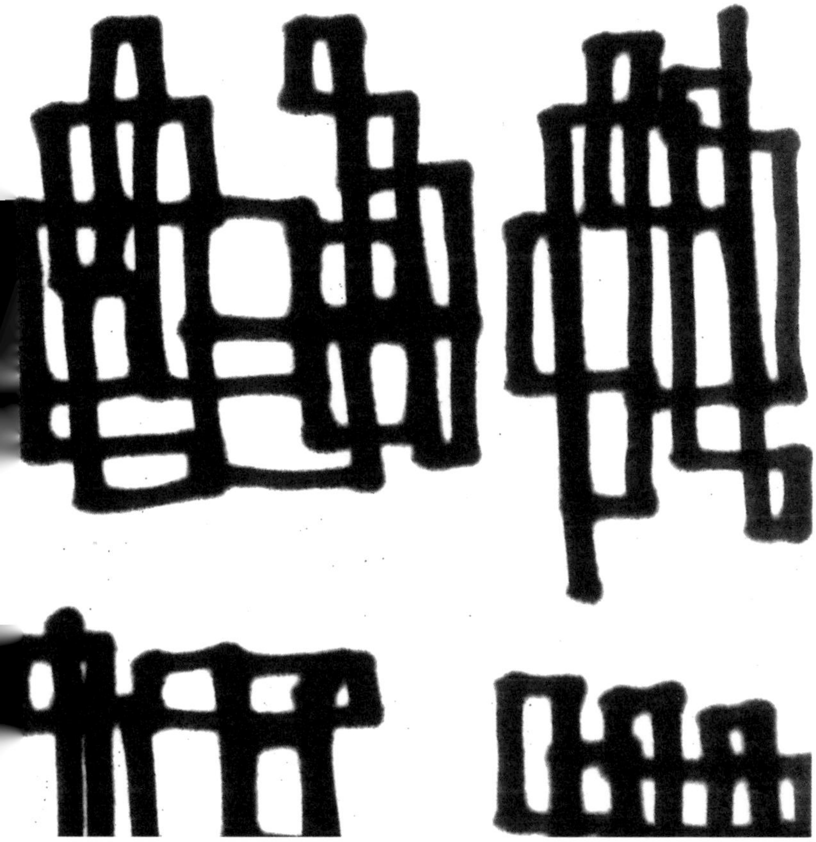

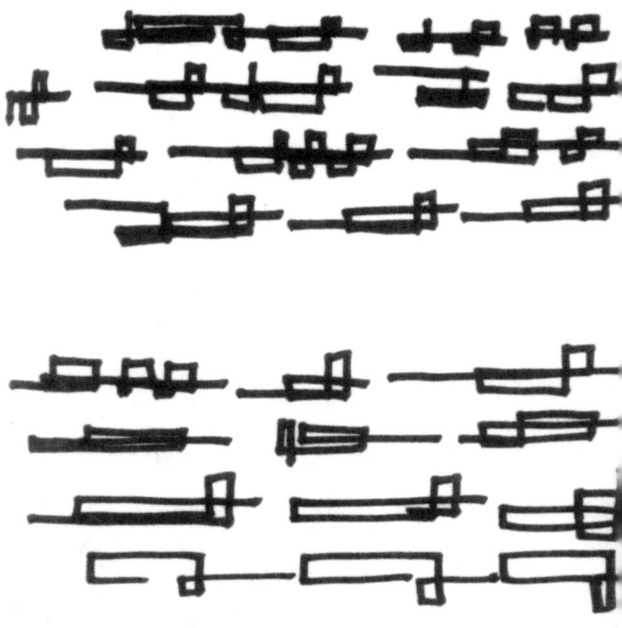

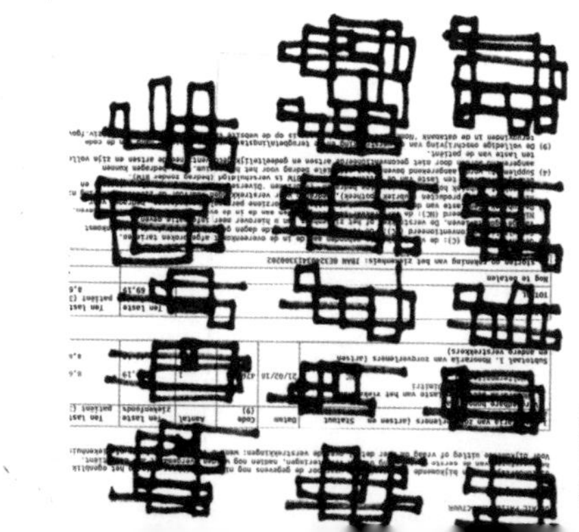

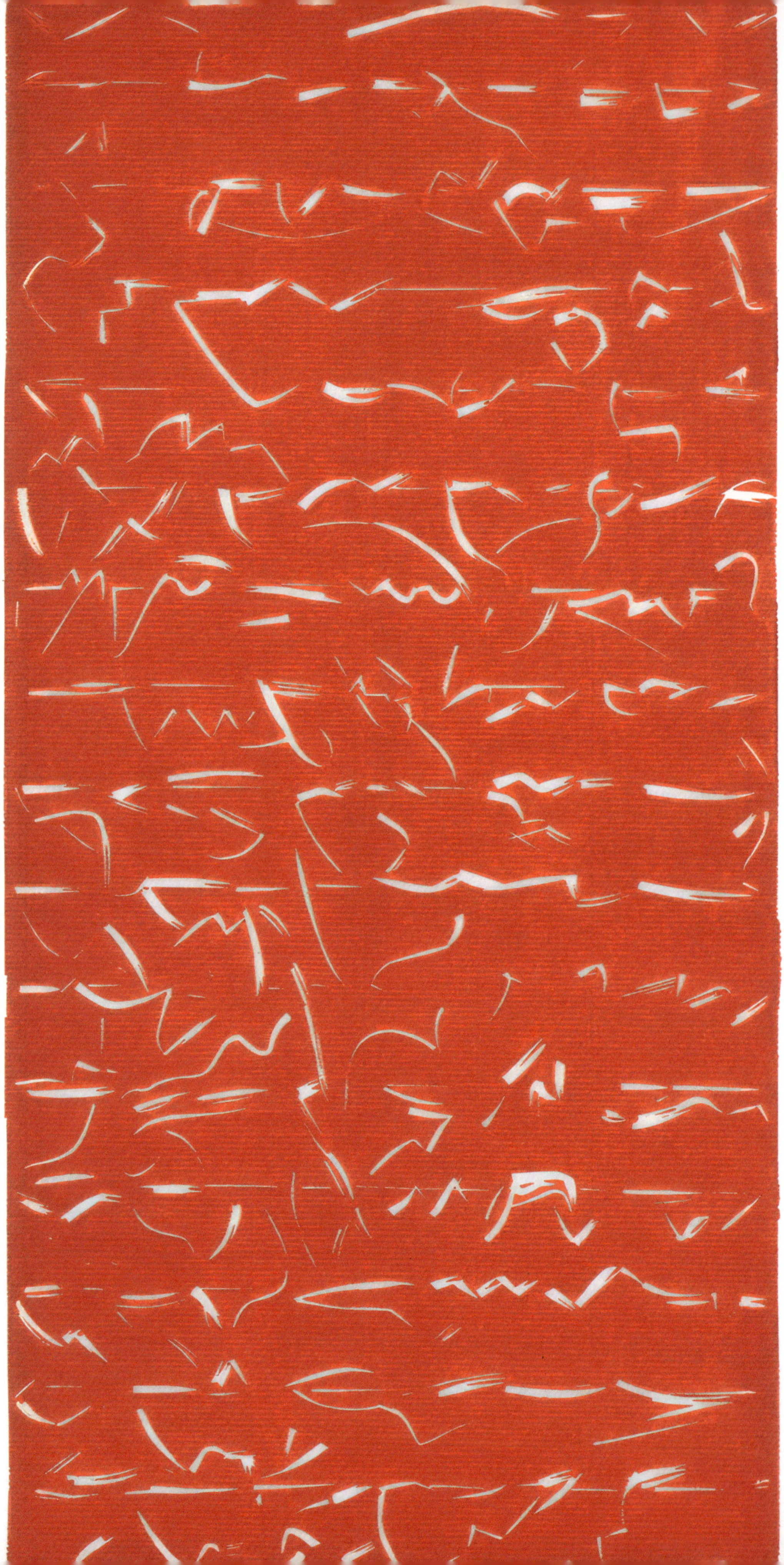

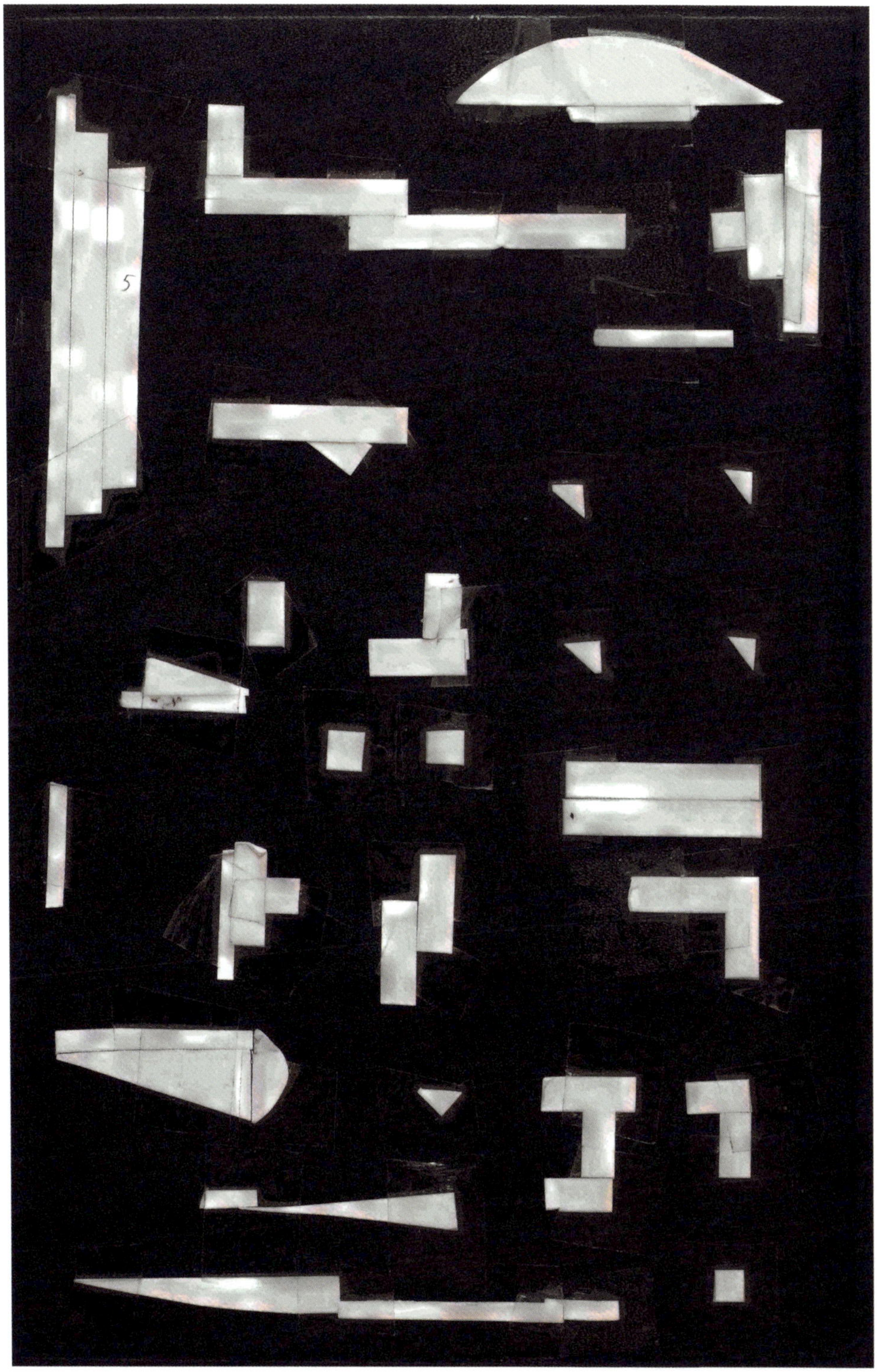

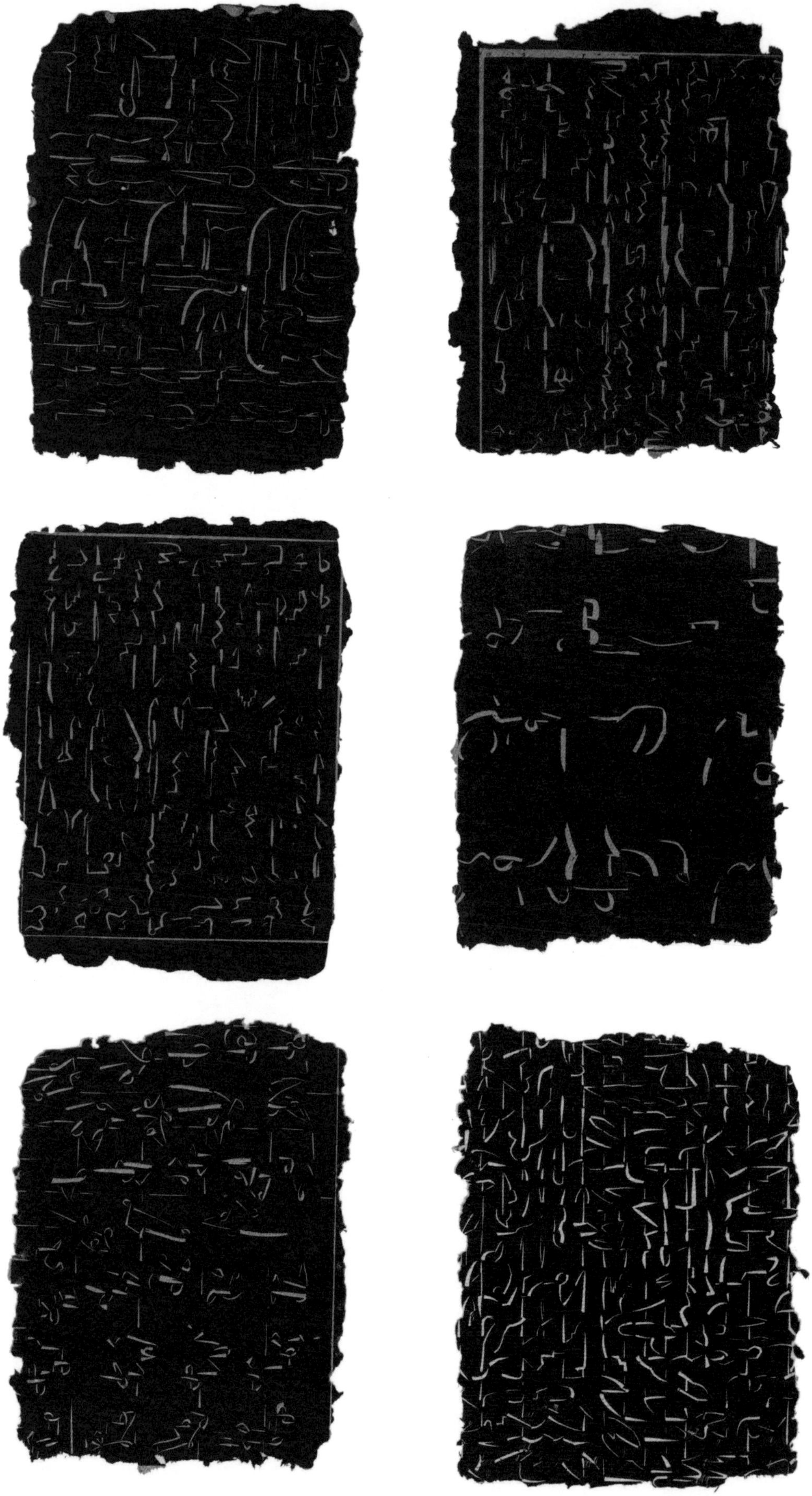

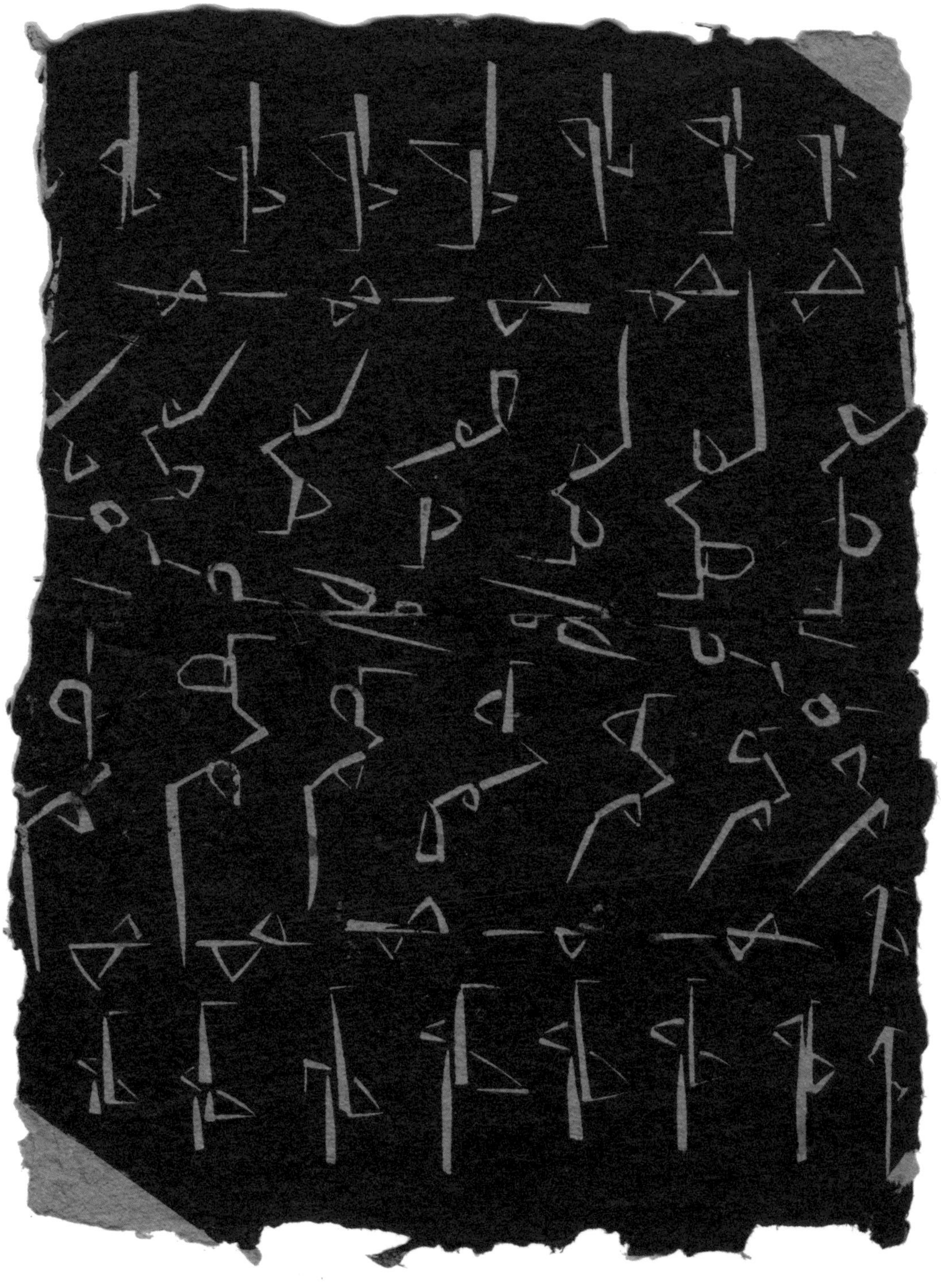

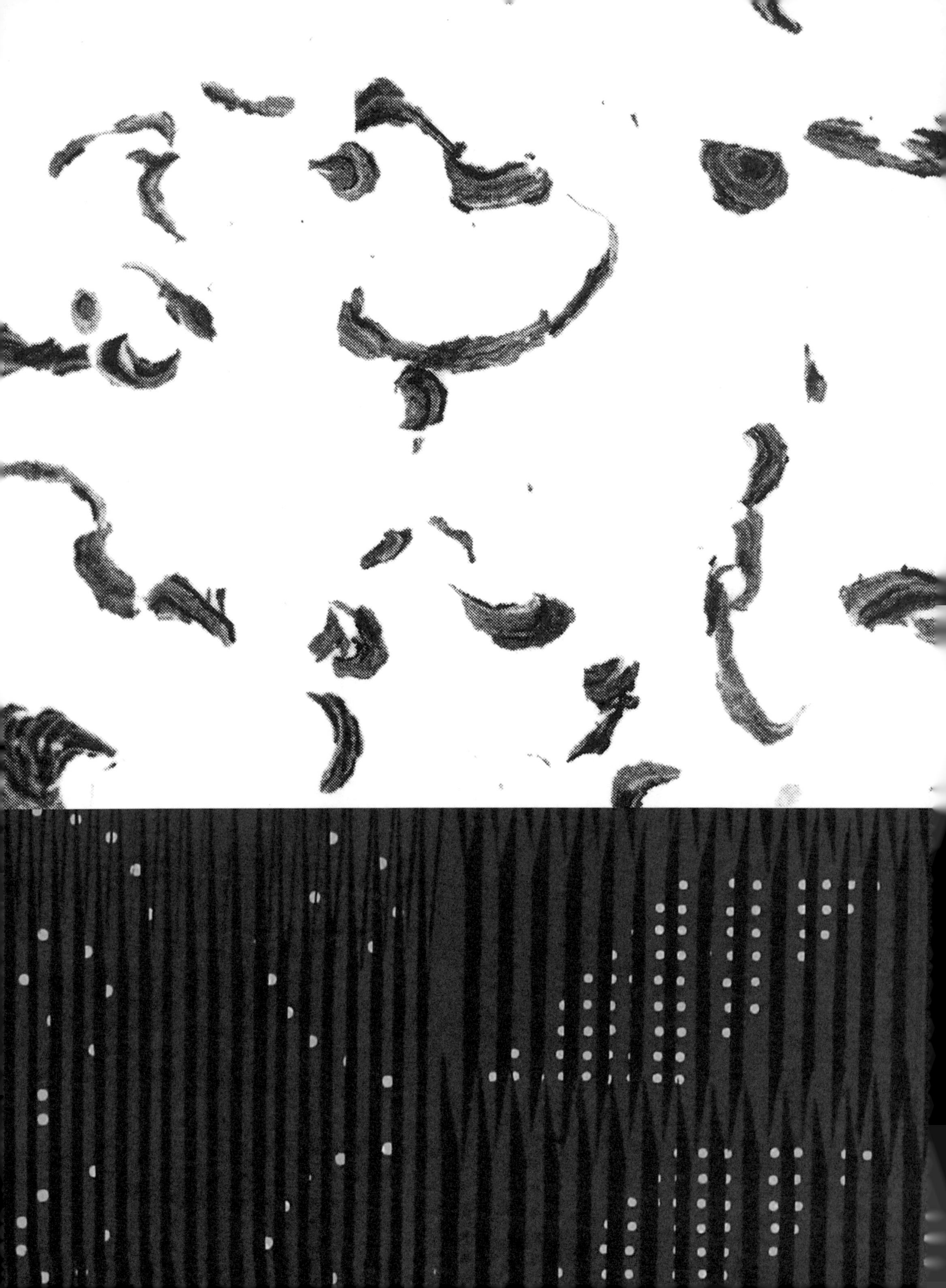

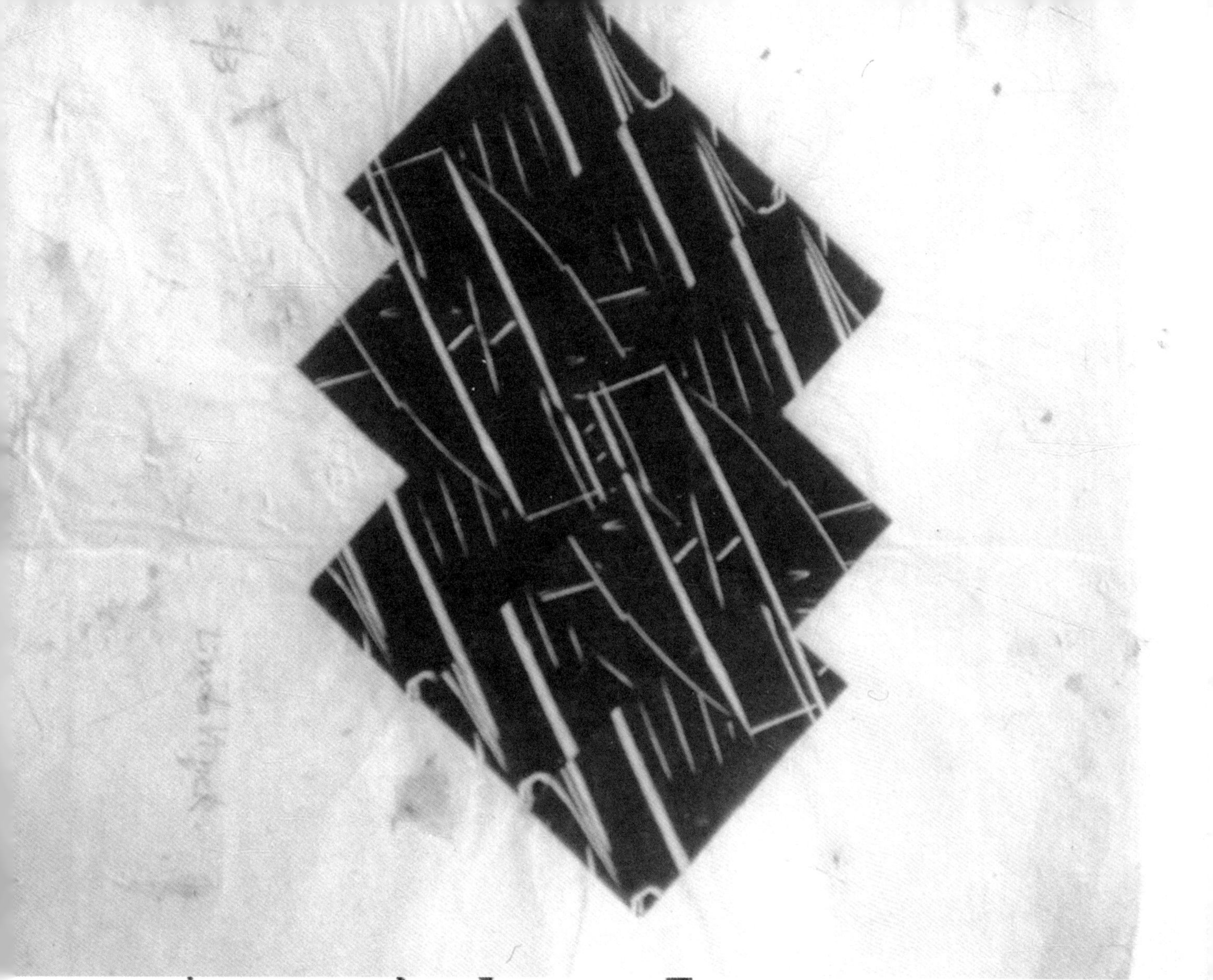

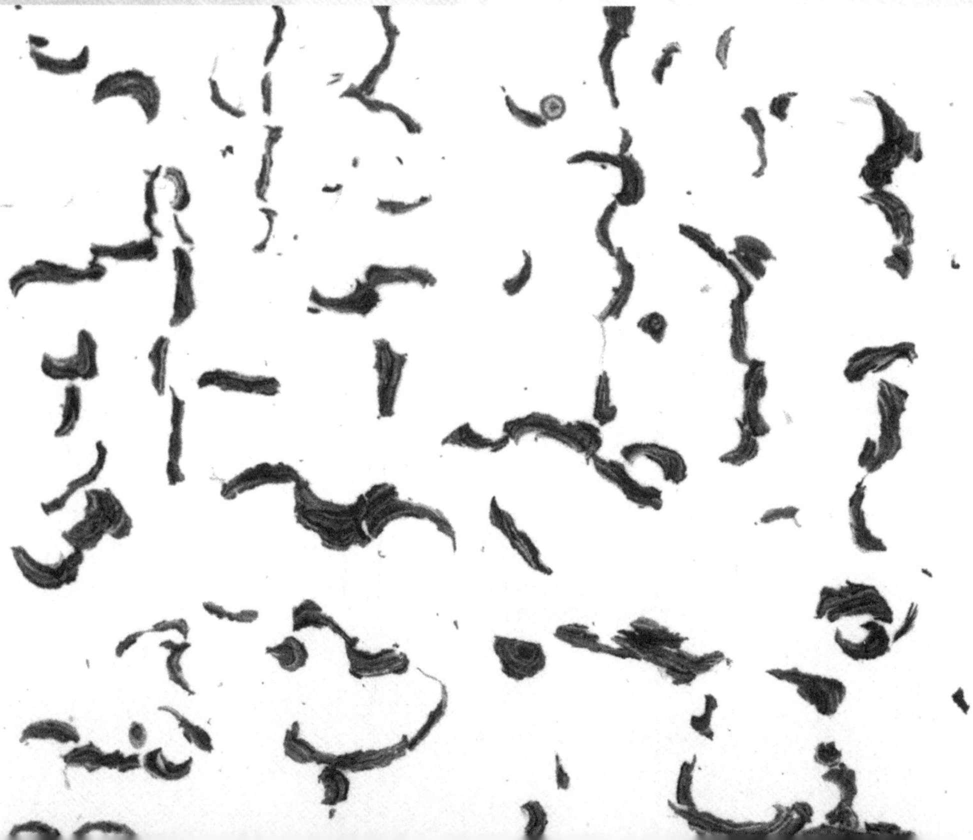

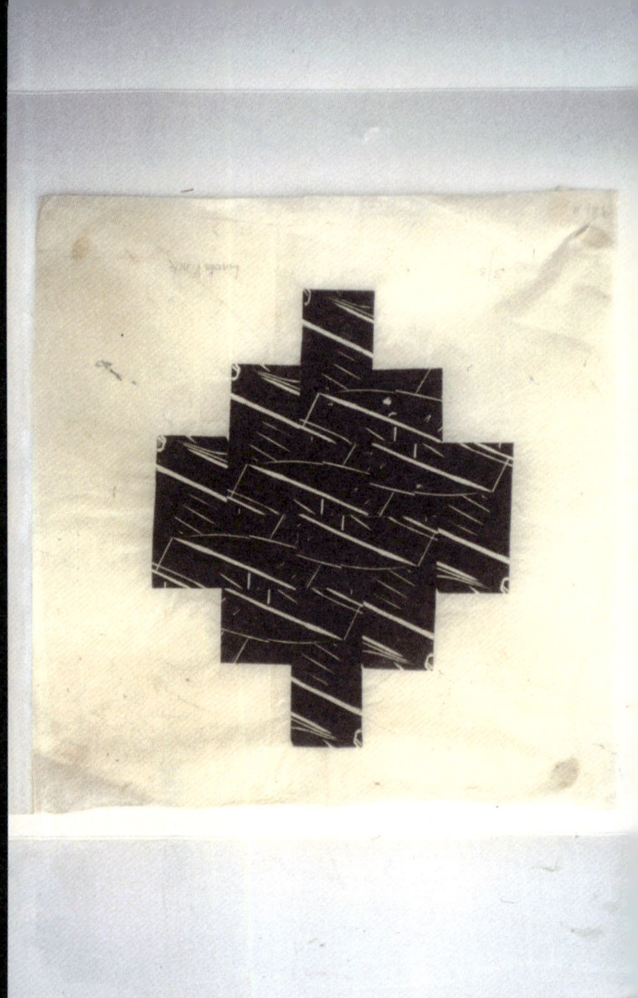

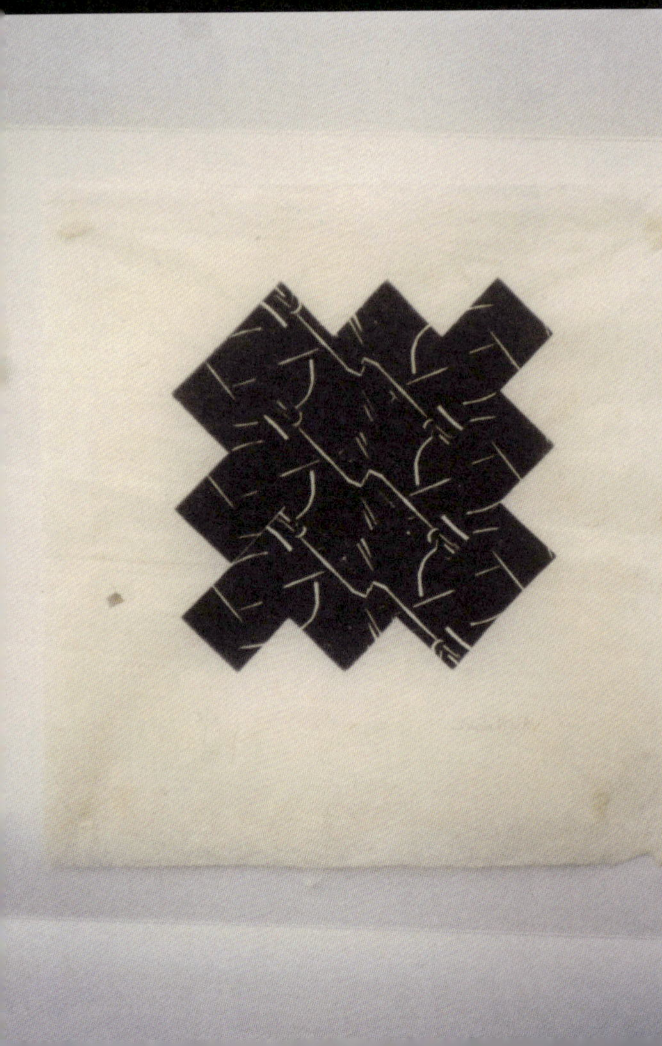

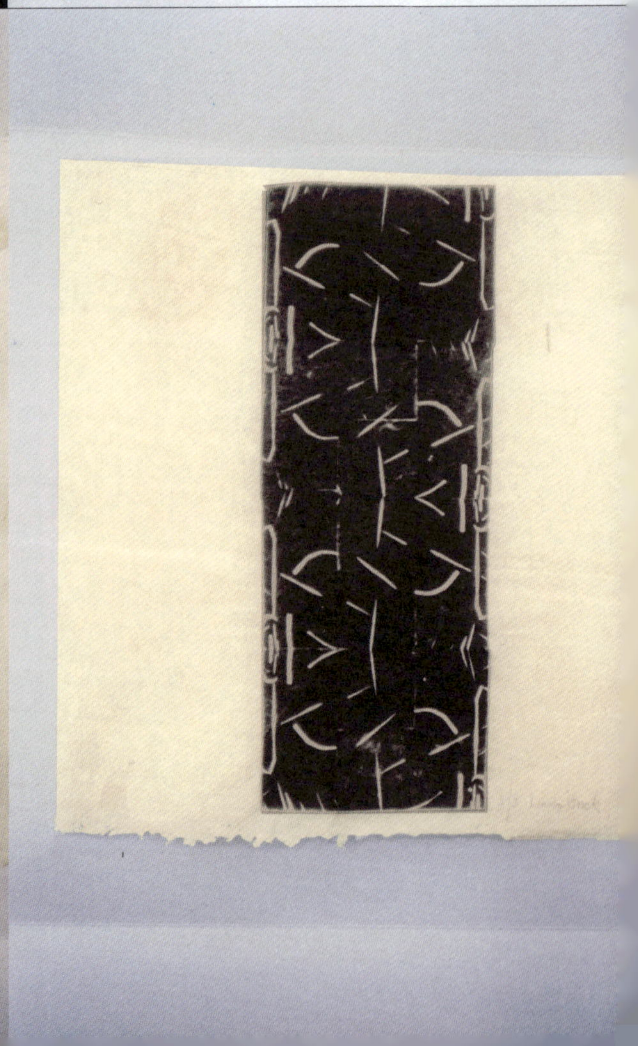

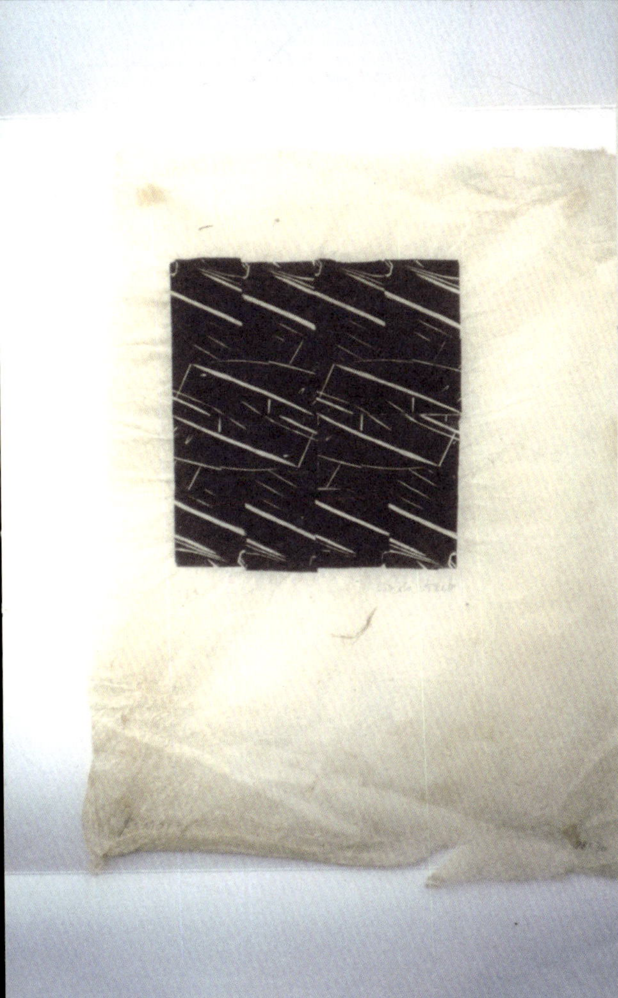

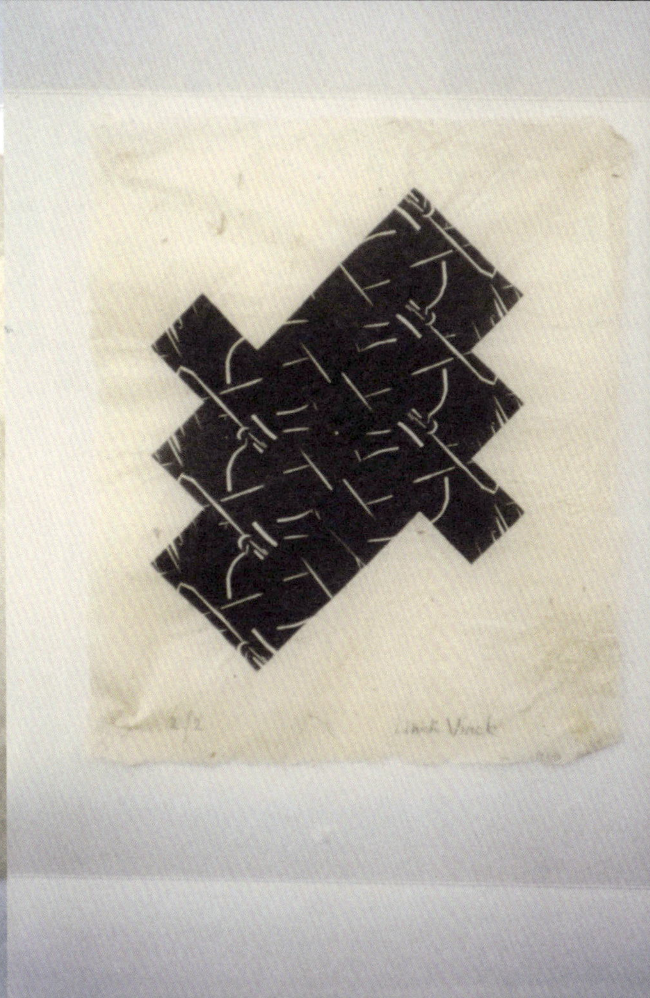

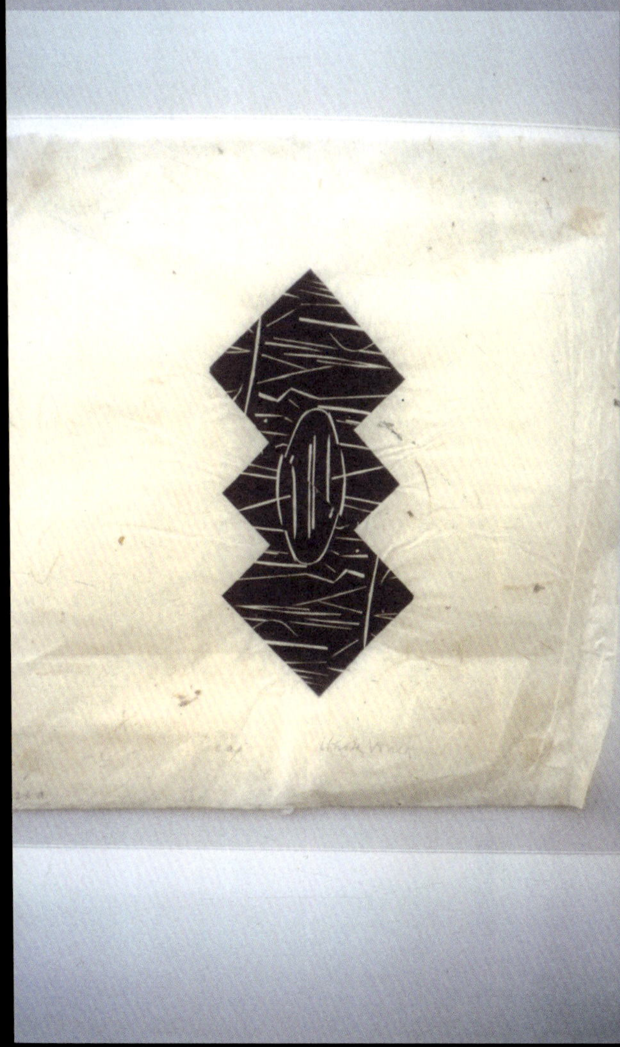

Little Nepal series

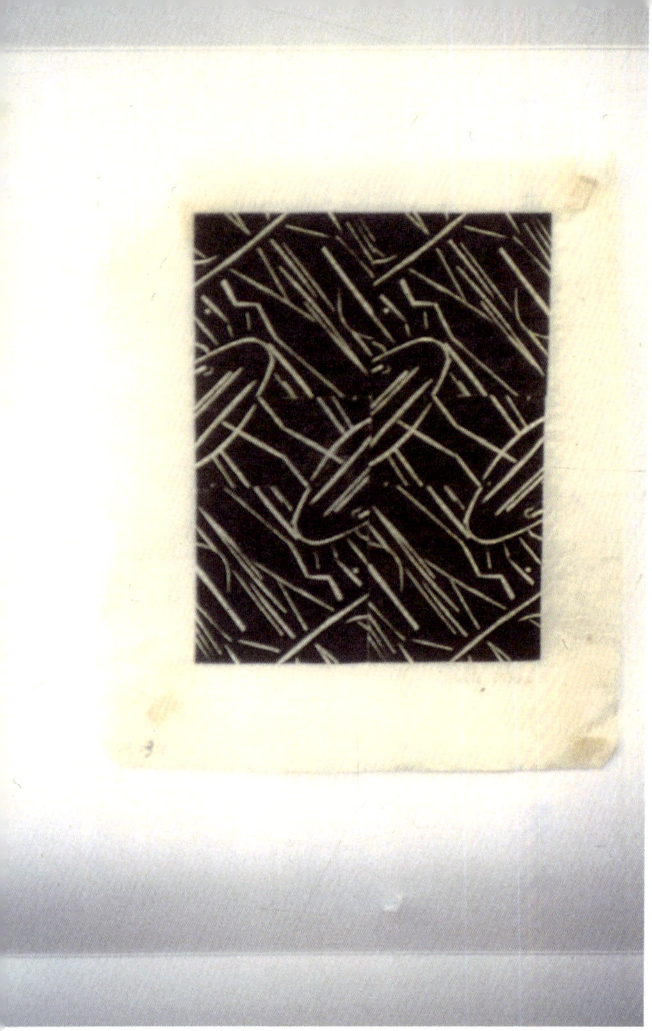

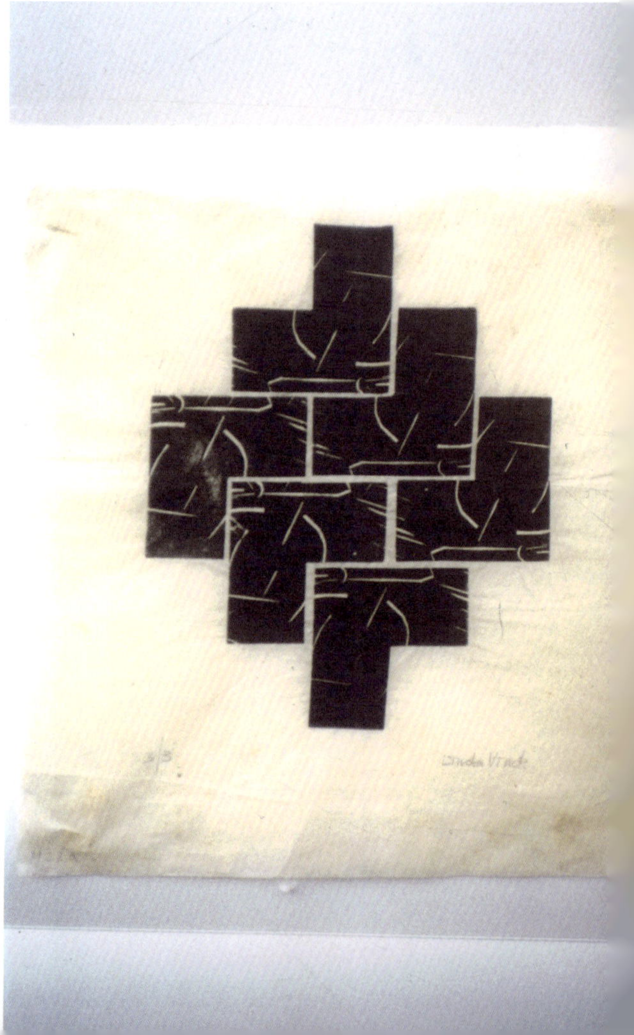

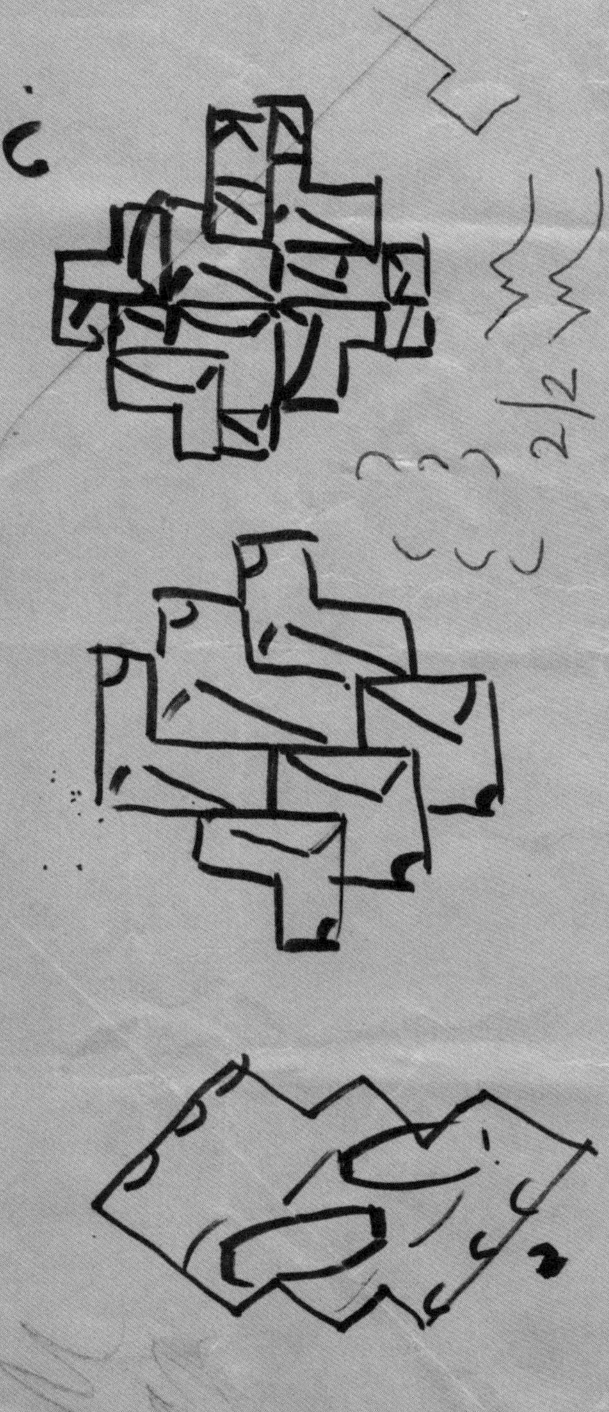

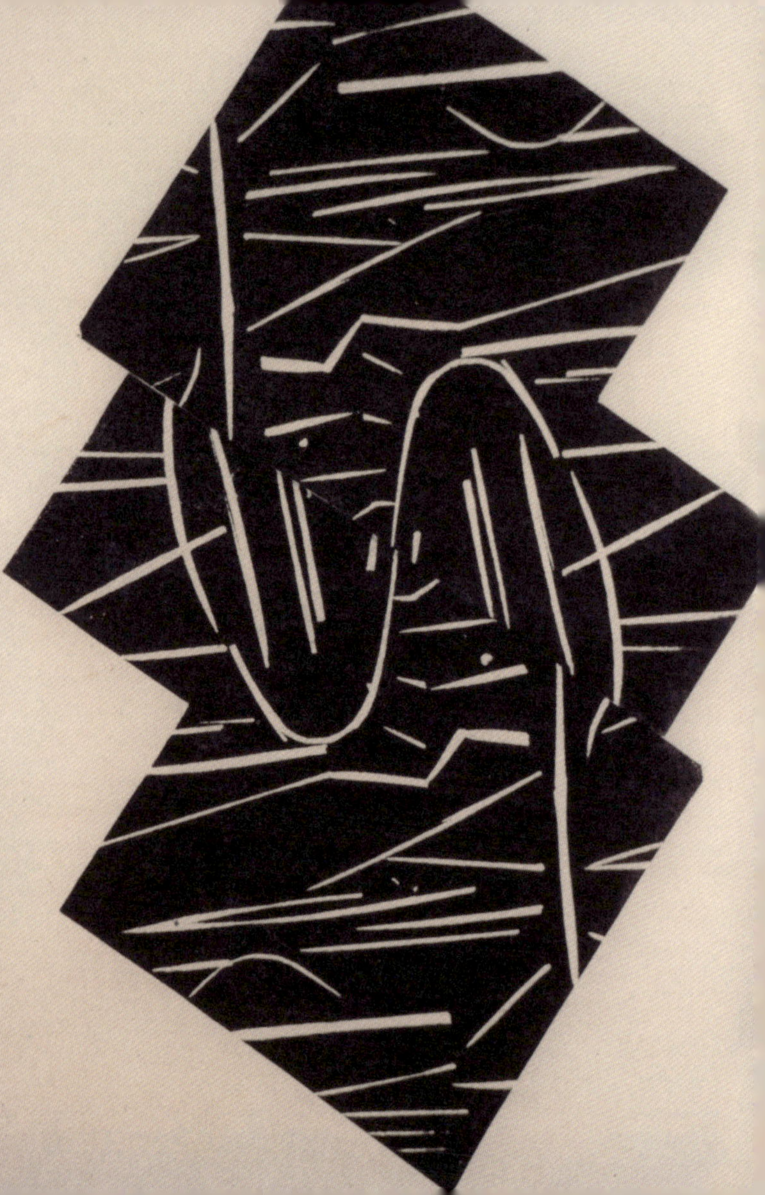

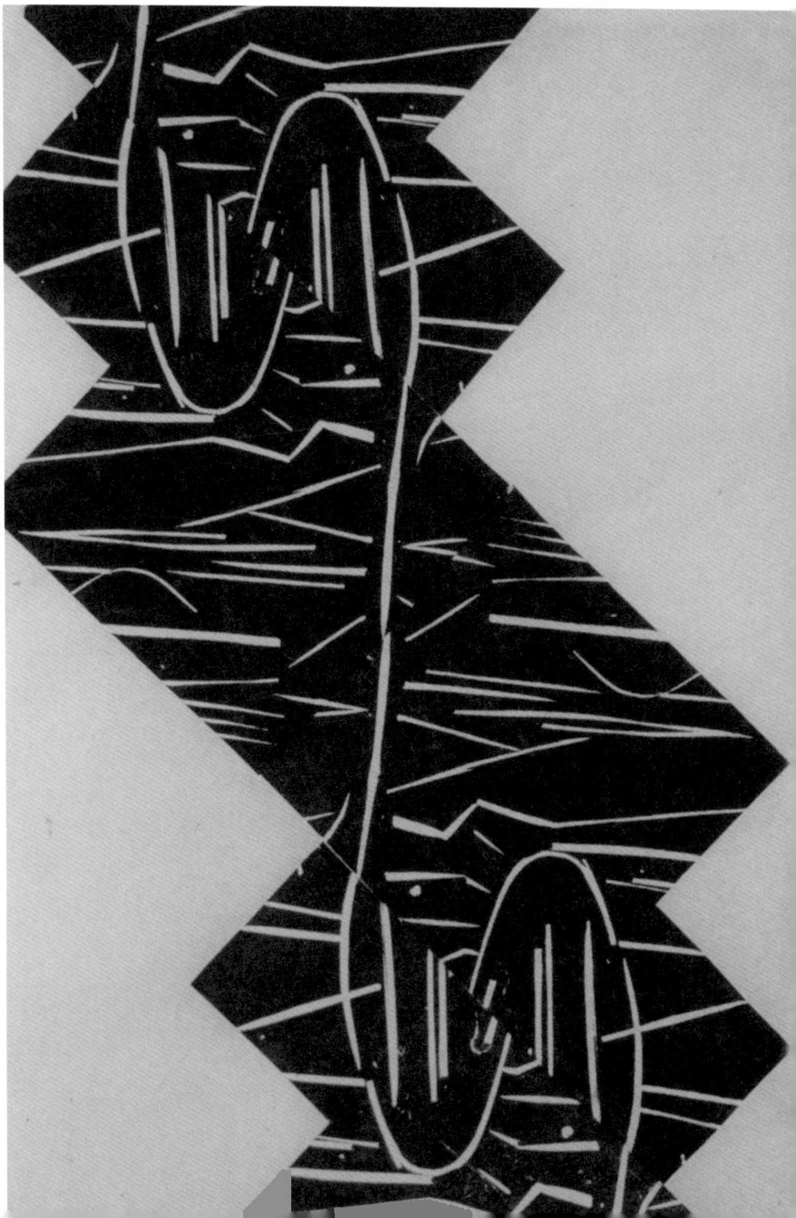

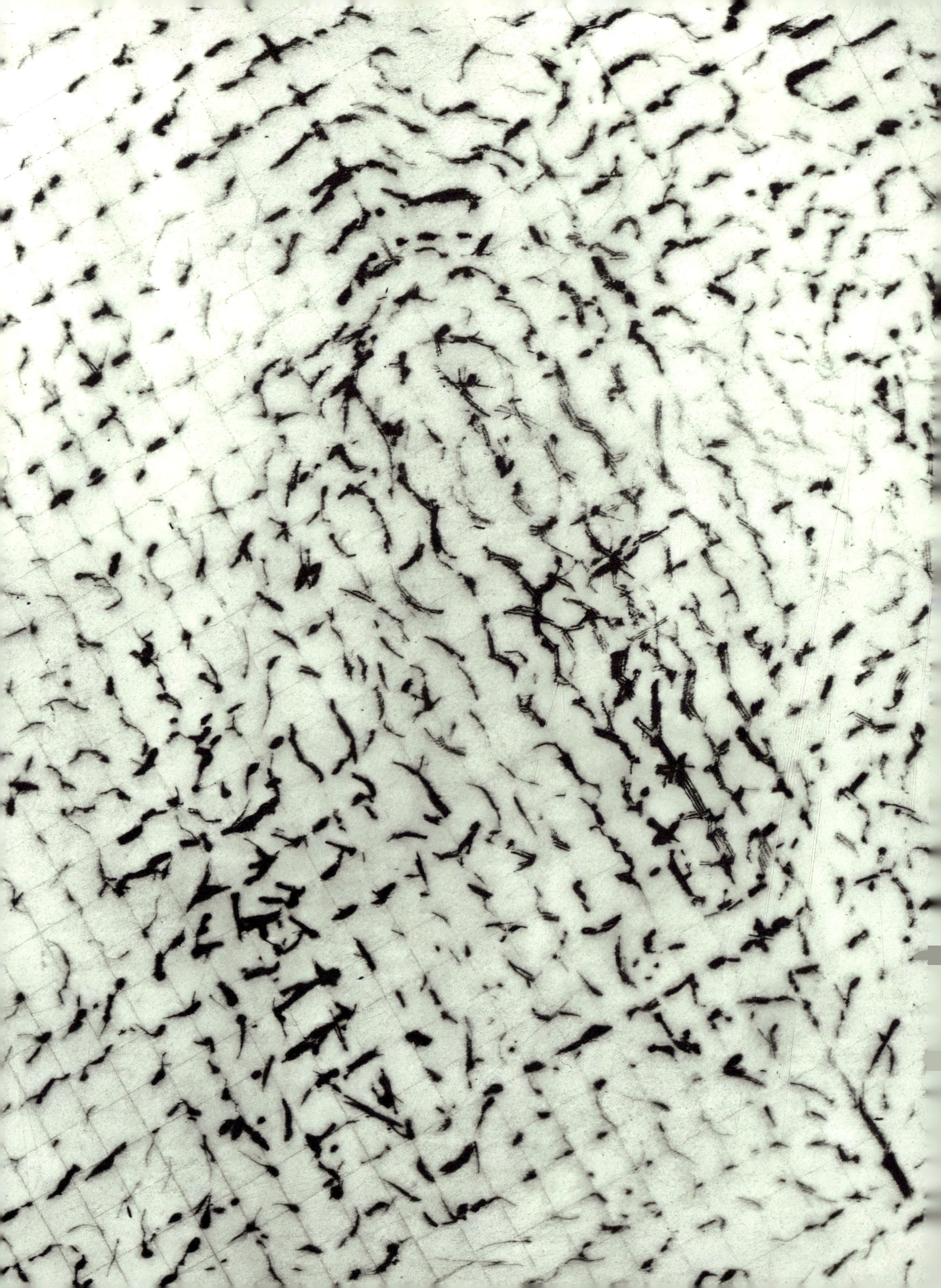

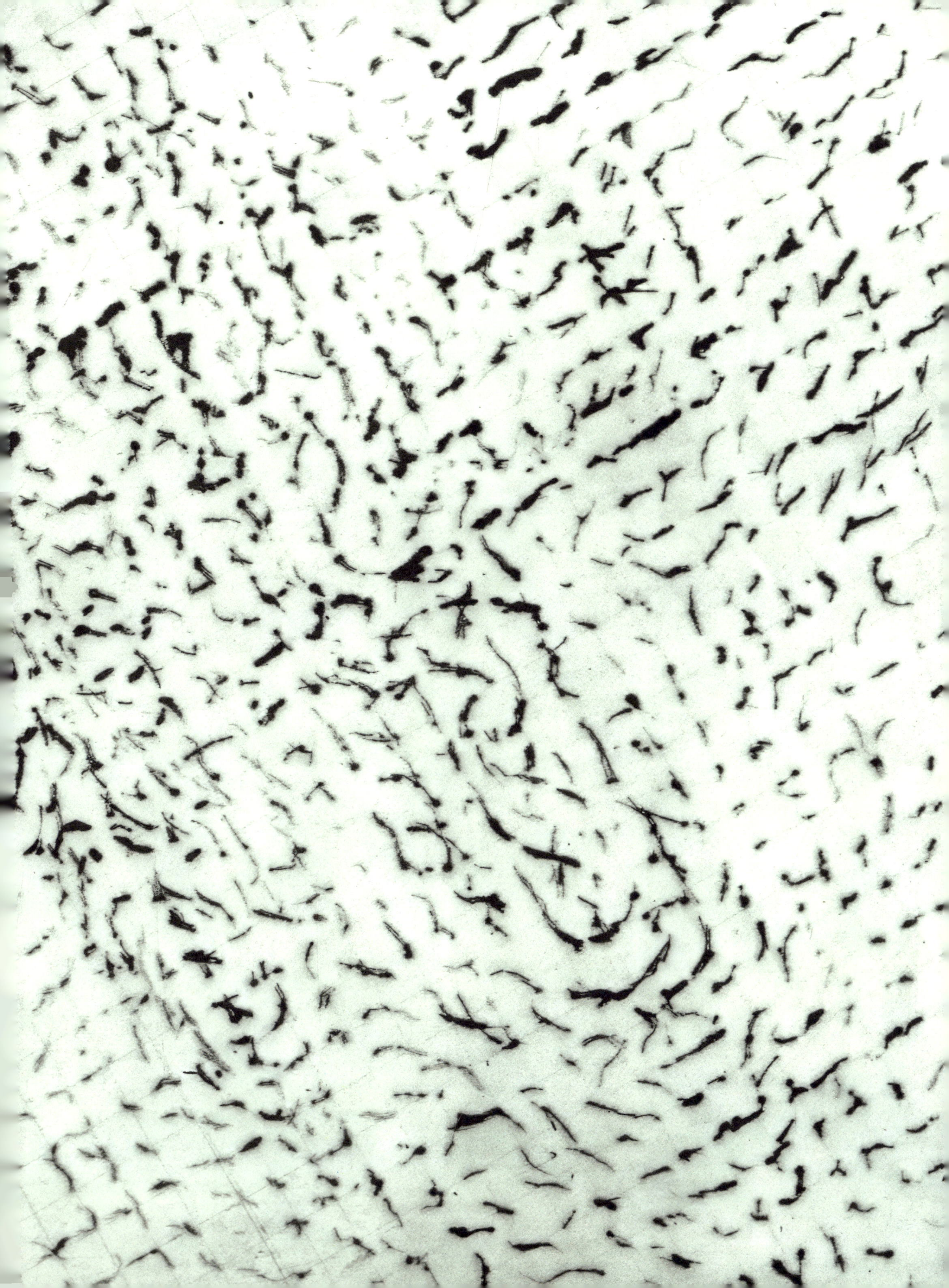

In de scherpte van mijn oog tekent
Een mes de volheid van leegte, het
onzichtbaar herkennen van de hartslag

Nic van Bruggen, 'BIJ EEN LINOSNEDE, *voor Linda Vinck*', 1986

II. Ongoing Stream

Doorlopende stroom

When patterns get along

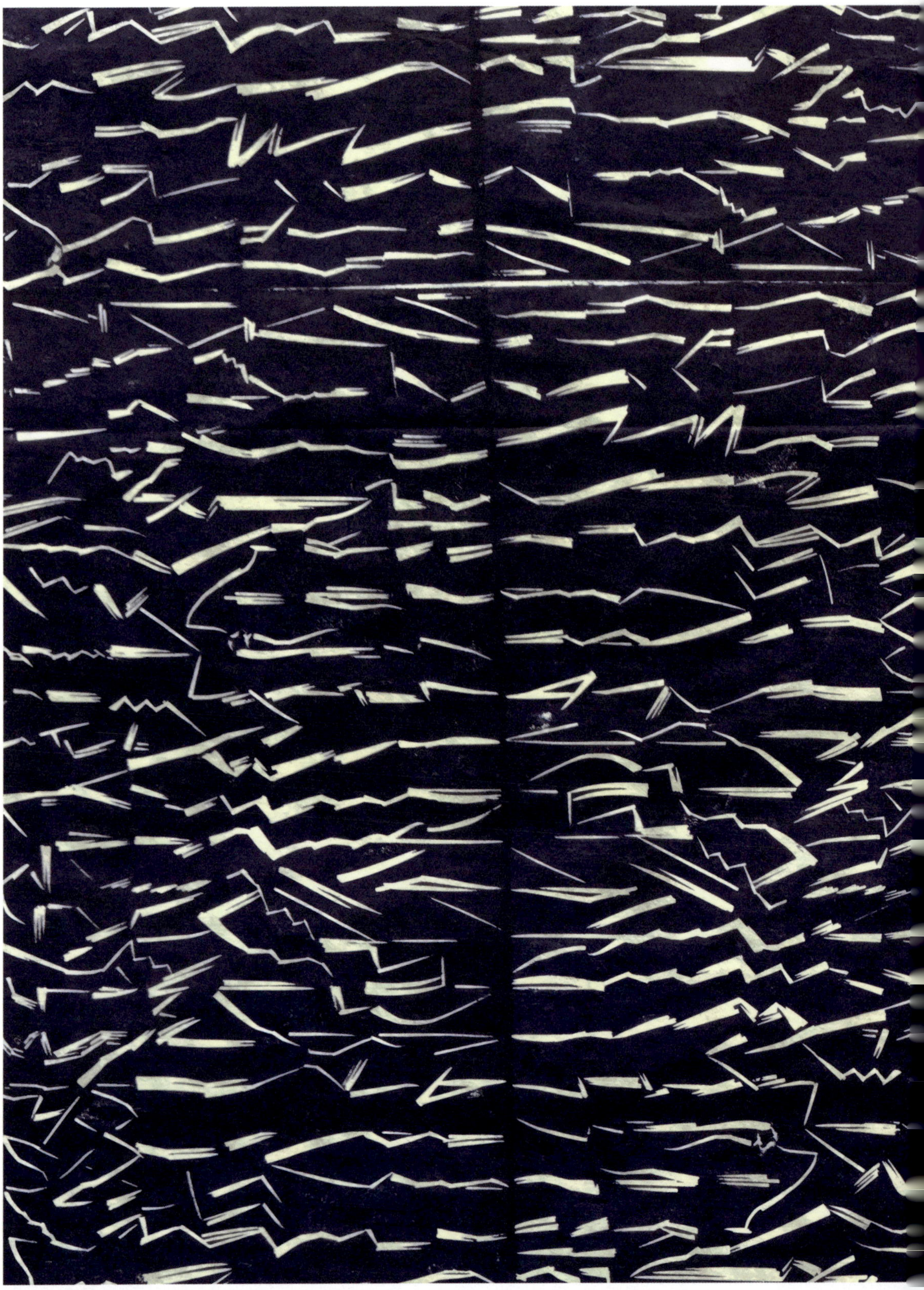

 Contemplation (detail) – Meditation on Peace 2

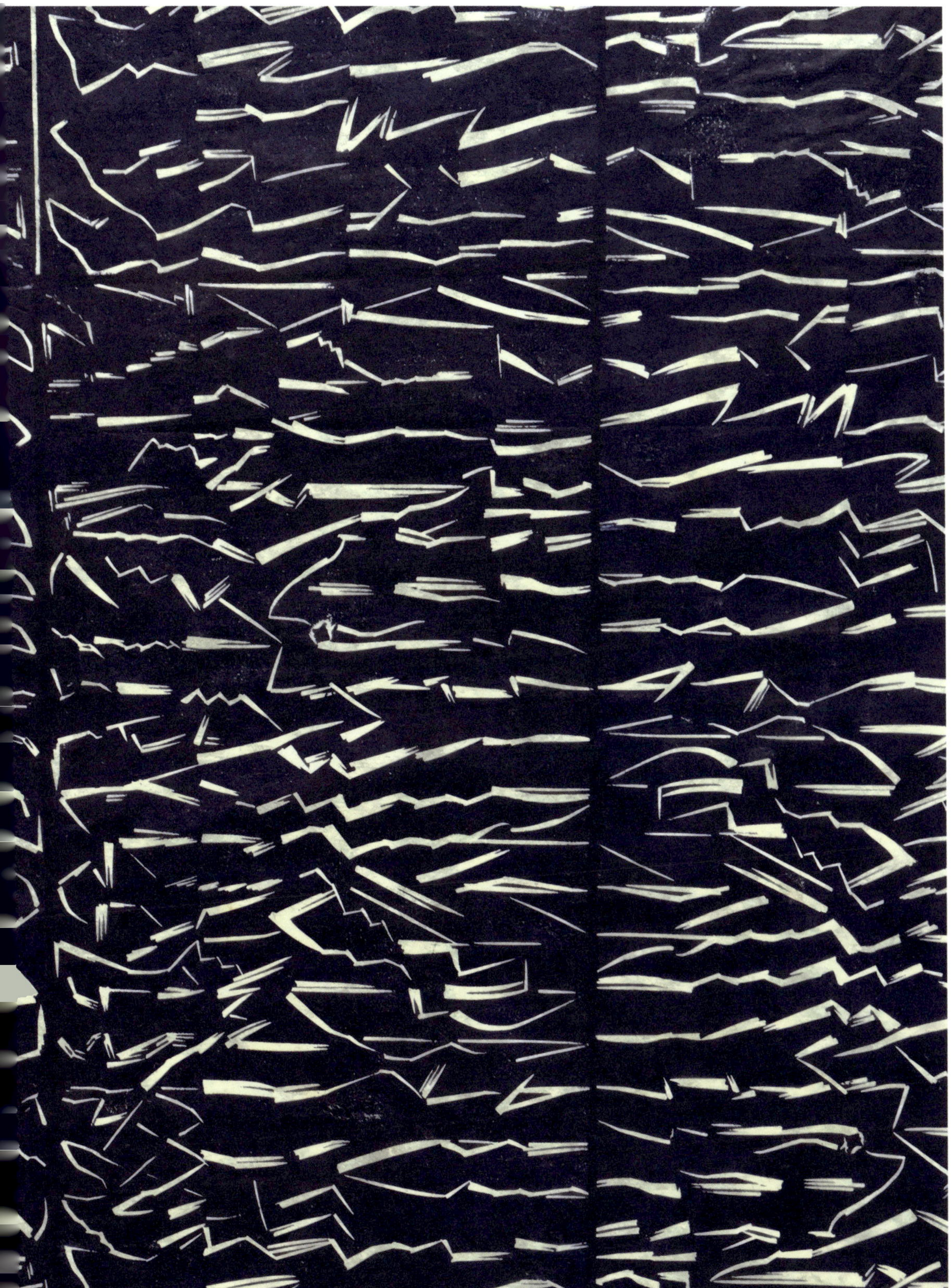

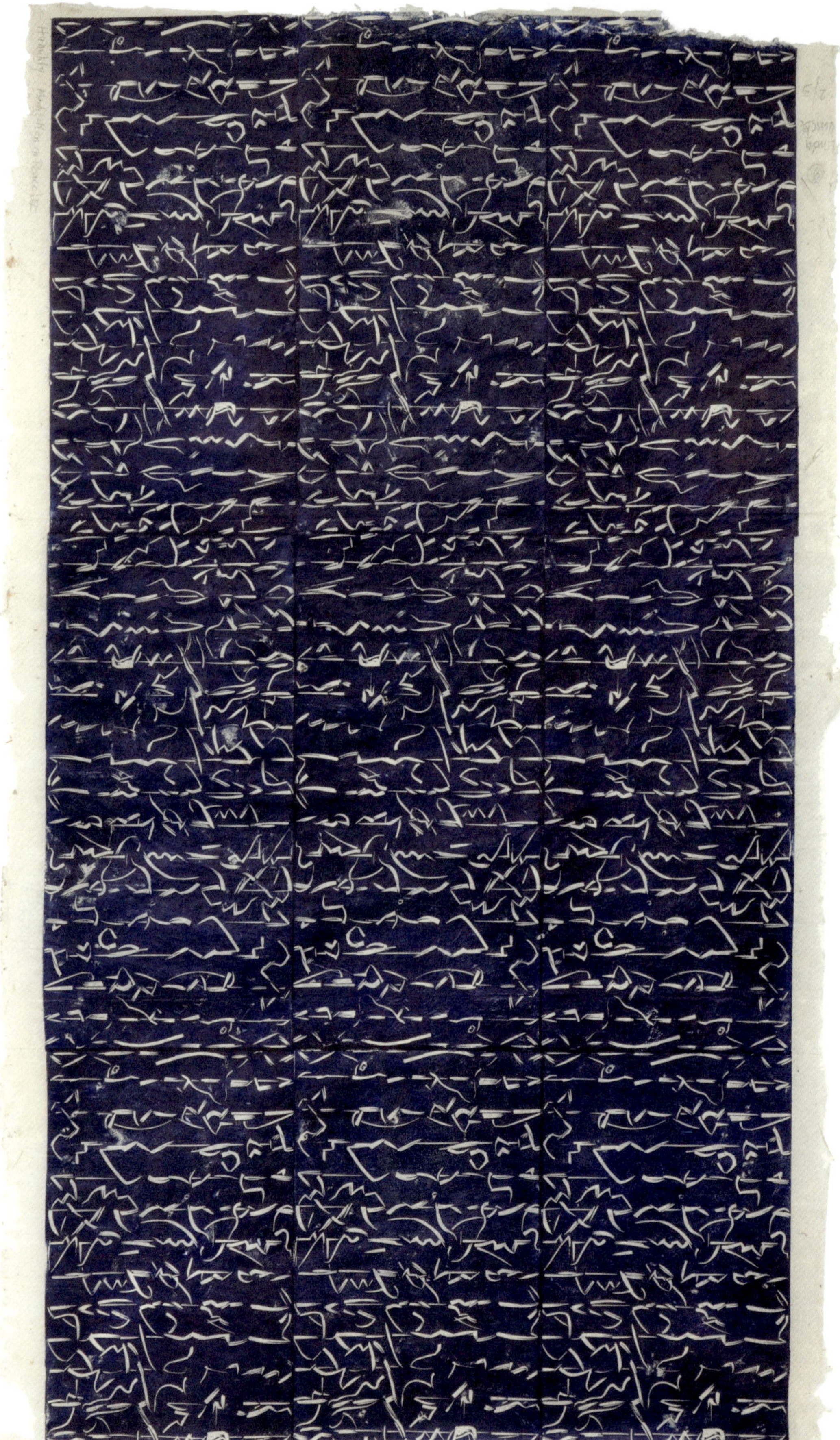

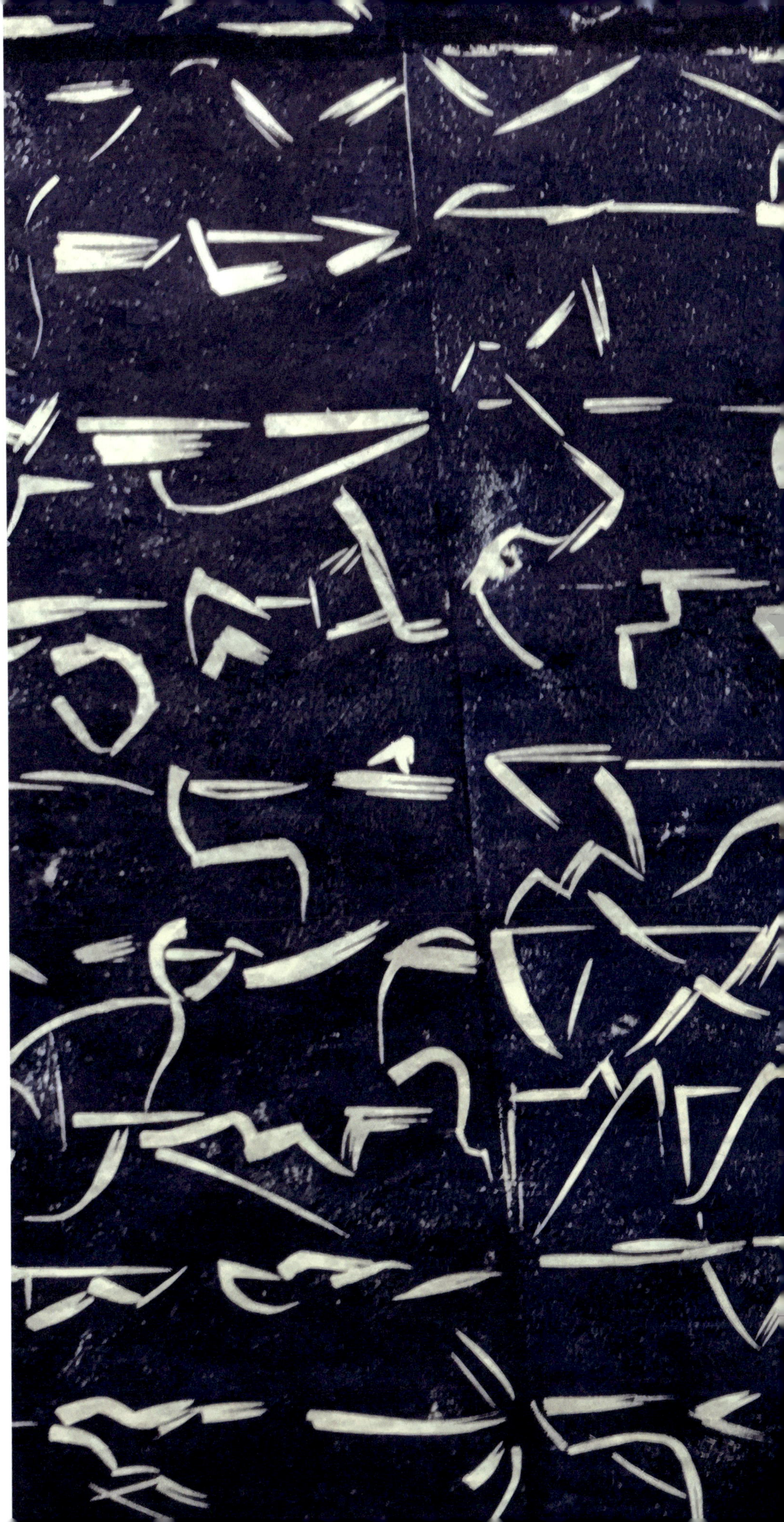

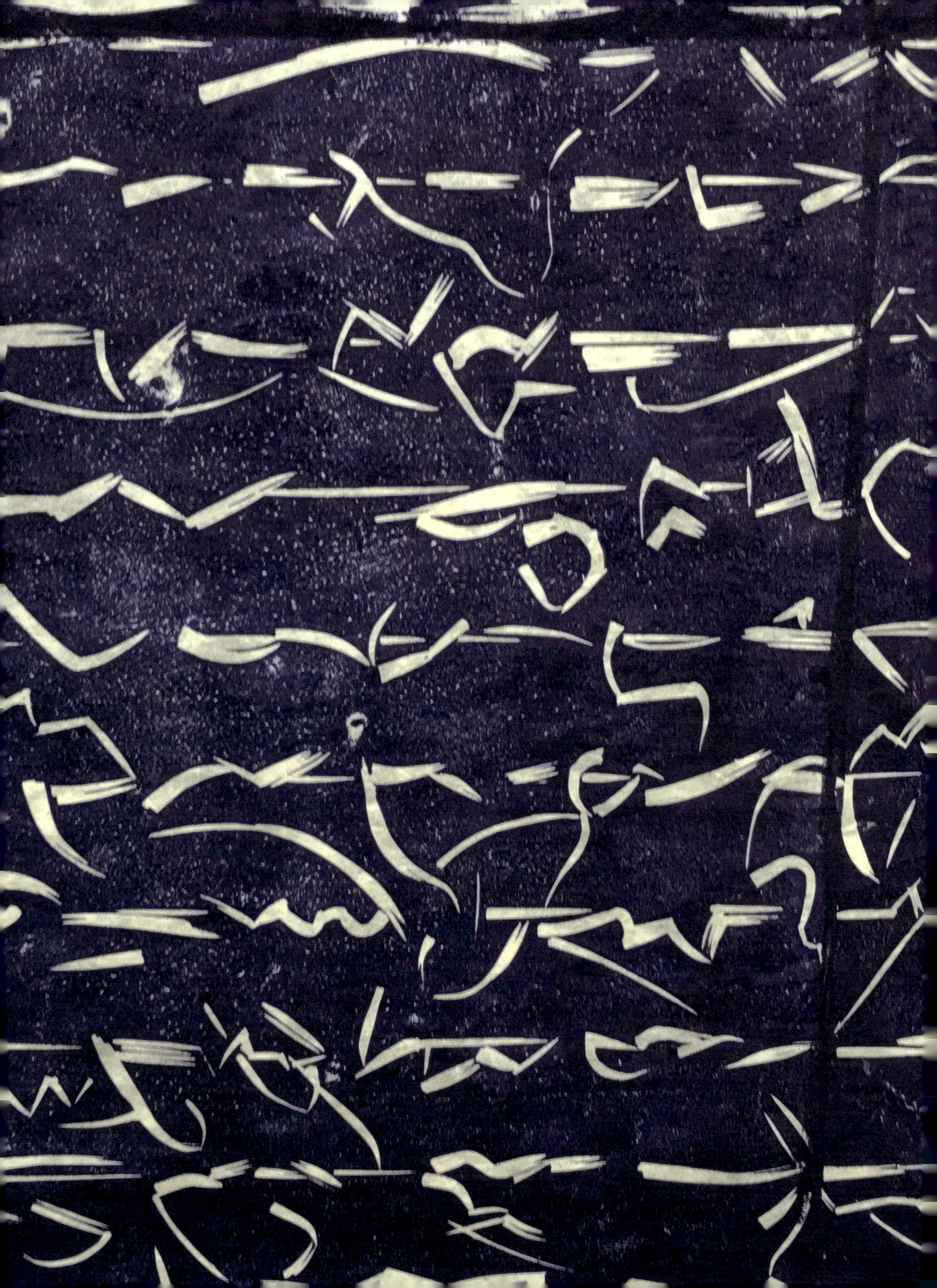

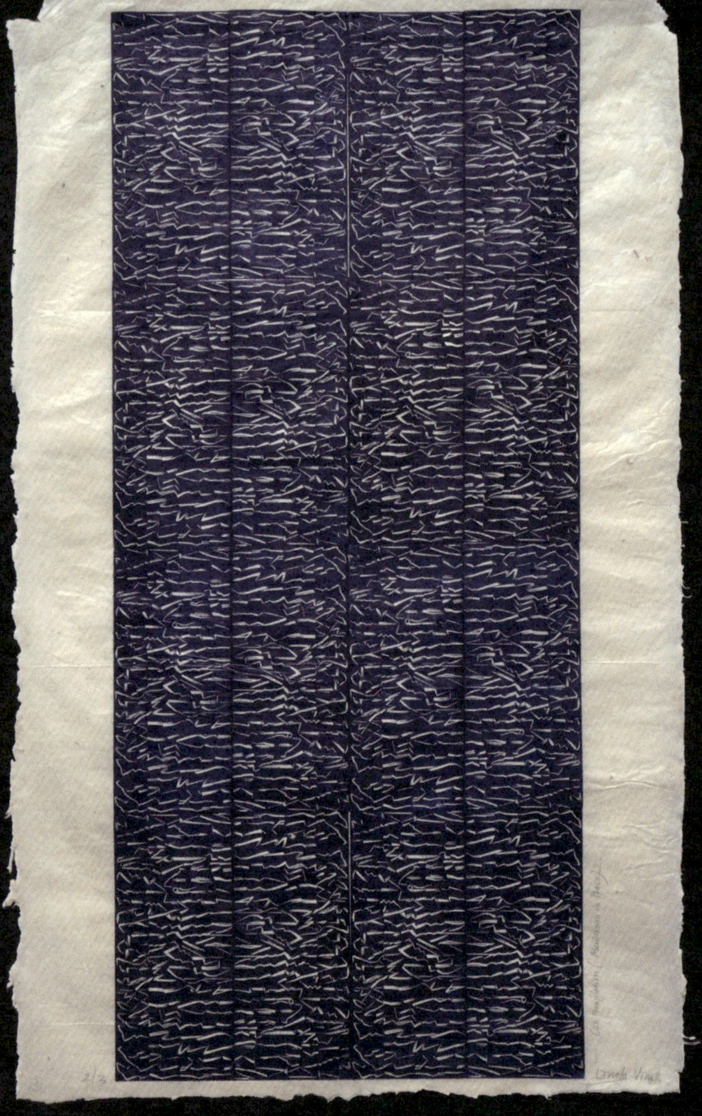

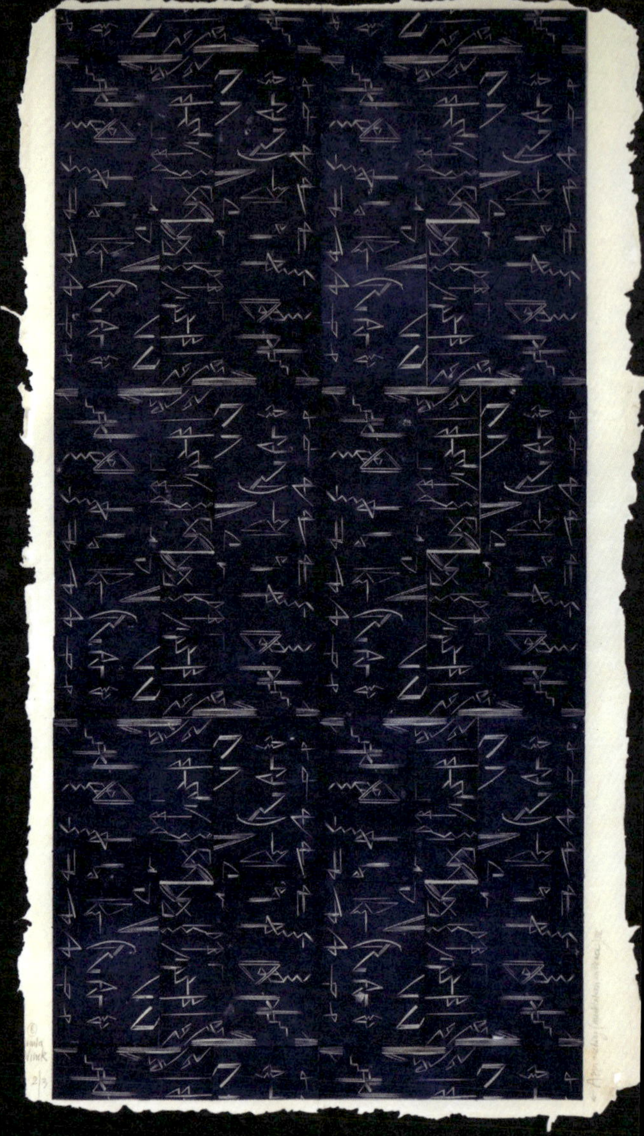

 from left to right: Contemplation, Approaching, Run — Meditation on Peace 2, 3 & 1

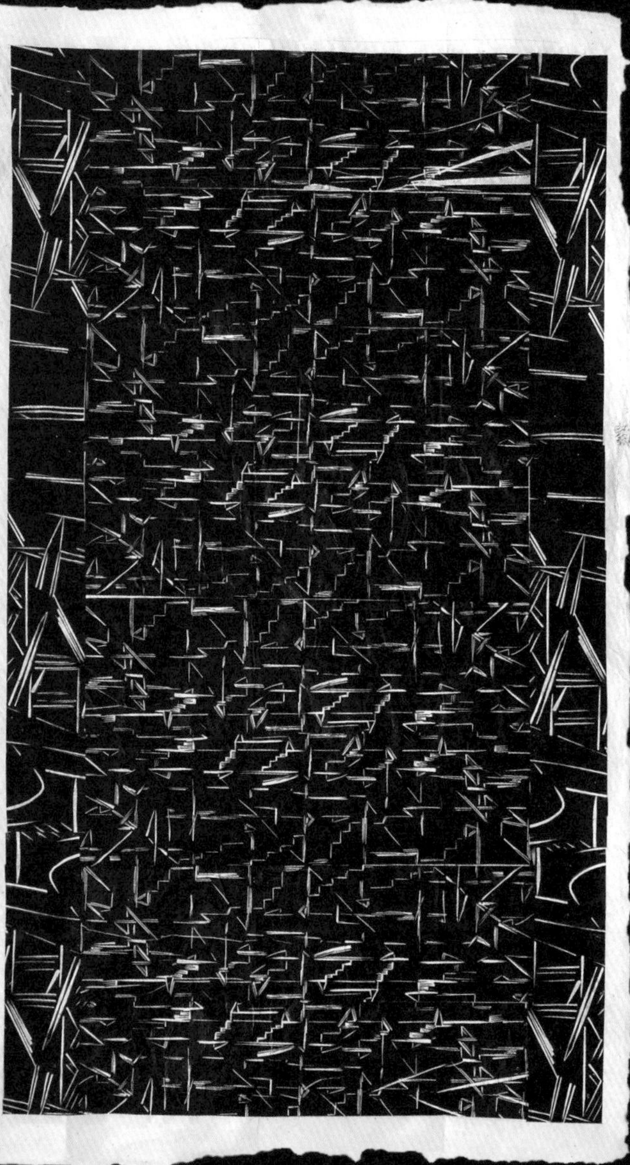

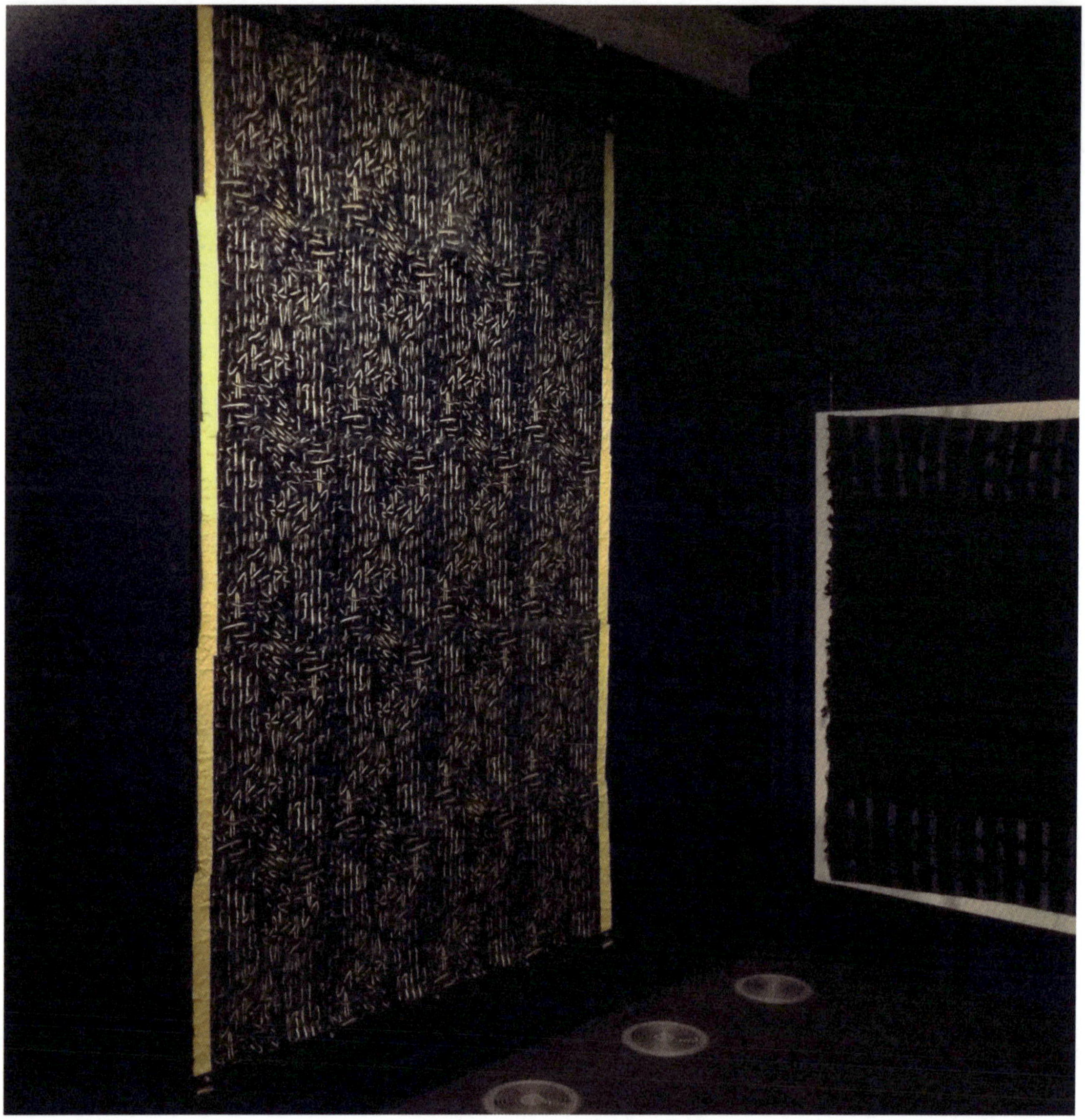

 Patterns of Paradise 2, exhibition 'Bodies of Lace', Museum Texture, Kortrijk, 2016

The work of Linda Vinck is suffused with a unique energy aroused by the primary colours: red, yellow, and blue on the black background of an allusive board. She has constructed a calligraphic scaffolding of undecipherable meaning and a black-stained support.

Her work conveys the impulse of an electronic circuit field in which a type of physical process is unleashed that indicates the unstoppable course of a source of energy, and the composition gives the impression of wanting to break out from the vertical bounds of the support.

Despite the monotonous and repetitive sensation of the sequences, the work oozes plastic beauty and creative harmony, qualities to which a certain narrative intention must be added. An intention that becomes more meaningful in the light of the titles of the pieces *Patterns of Paradise 1* and *2* from 1992, and the later *Kemper meets Chladni* from 1997, where the artist sharply defines the space of the composition. She uses two wooden planks for the piece, one for the background staining and another for the making of the colours.

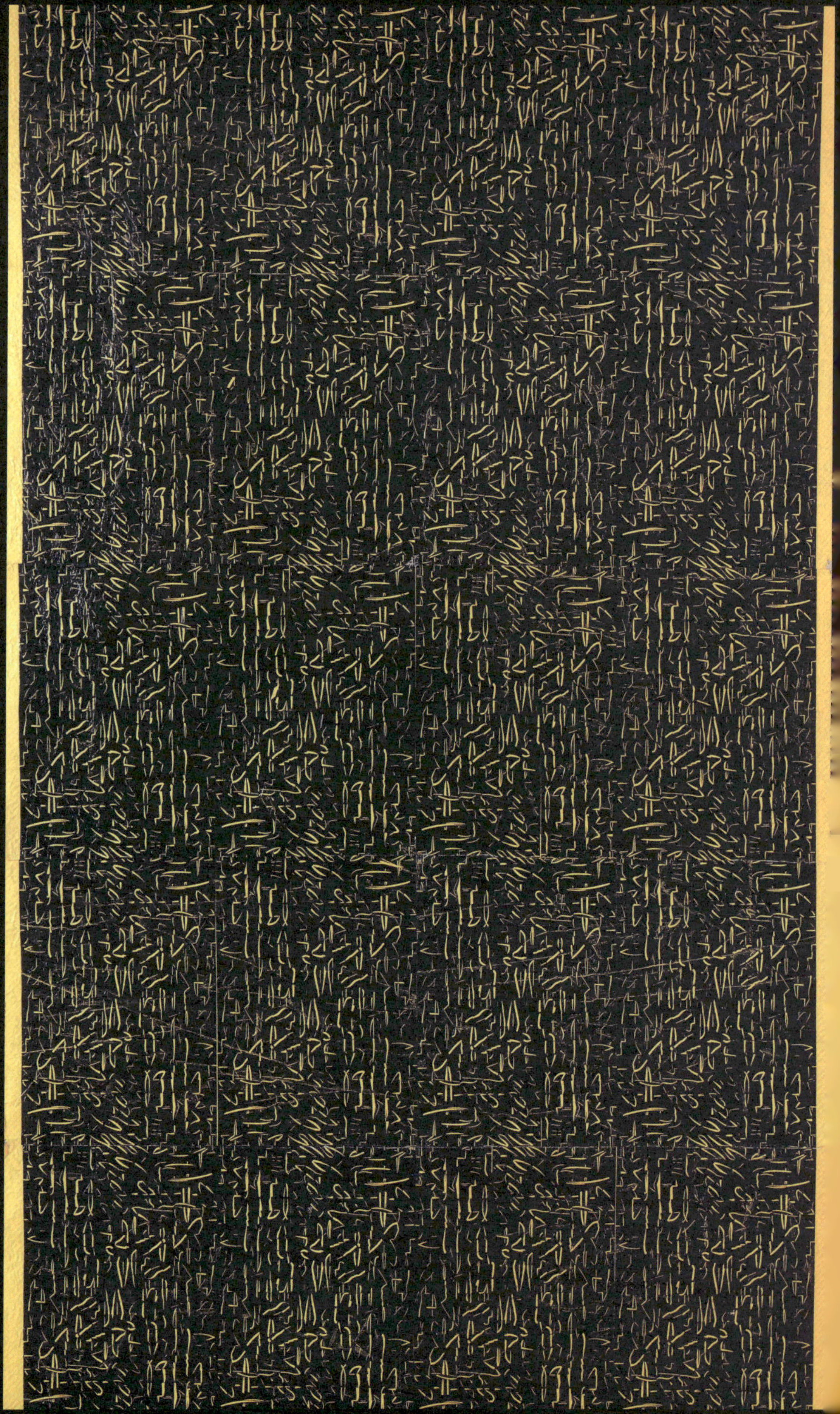

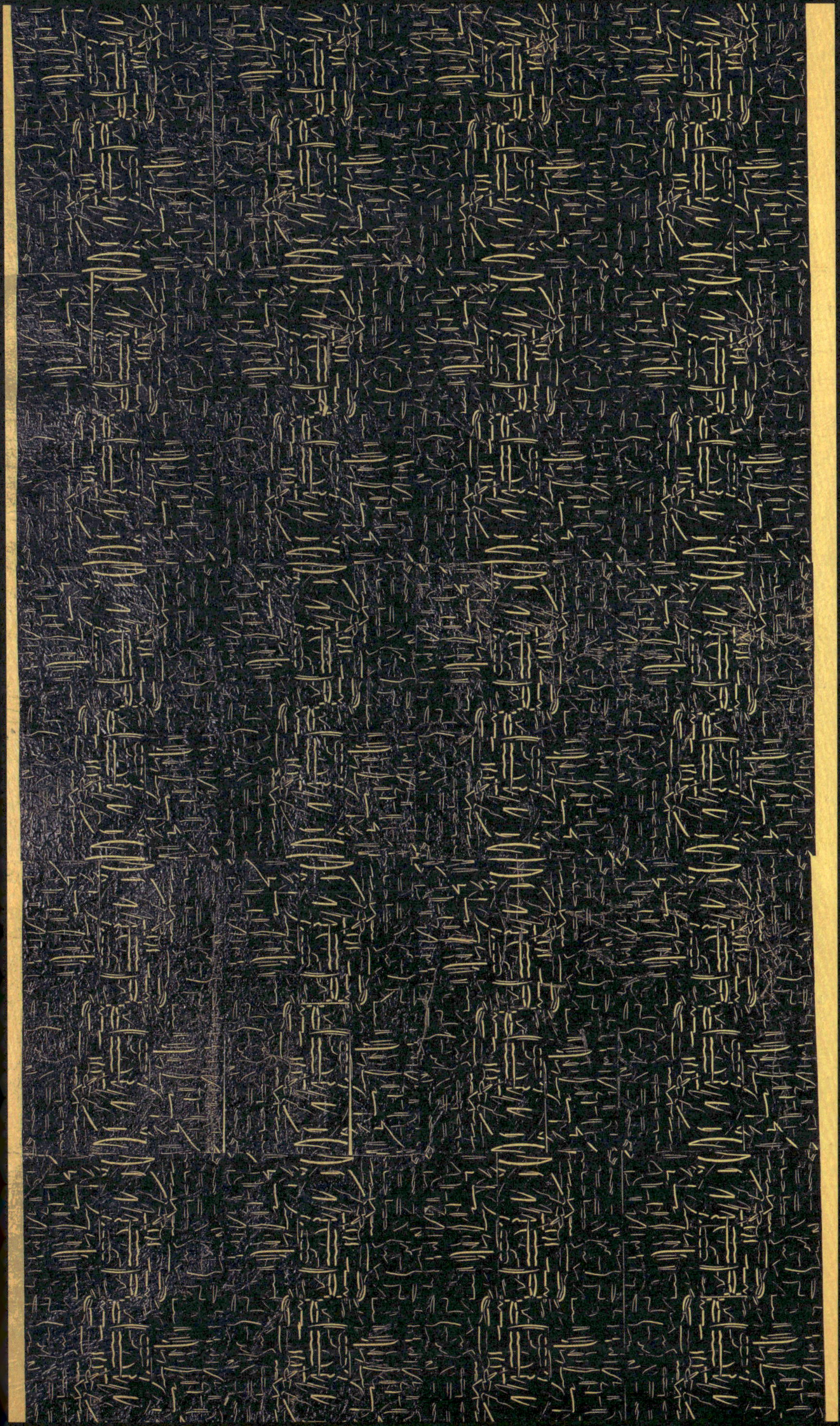

64 Reflex Blue on White — Patterns of Paradise 3 Collection of Prentenkabinet Museum Plantin-Moretus, Antwerp

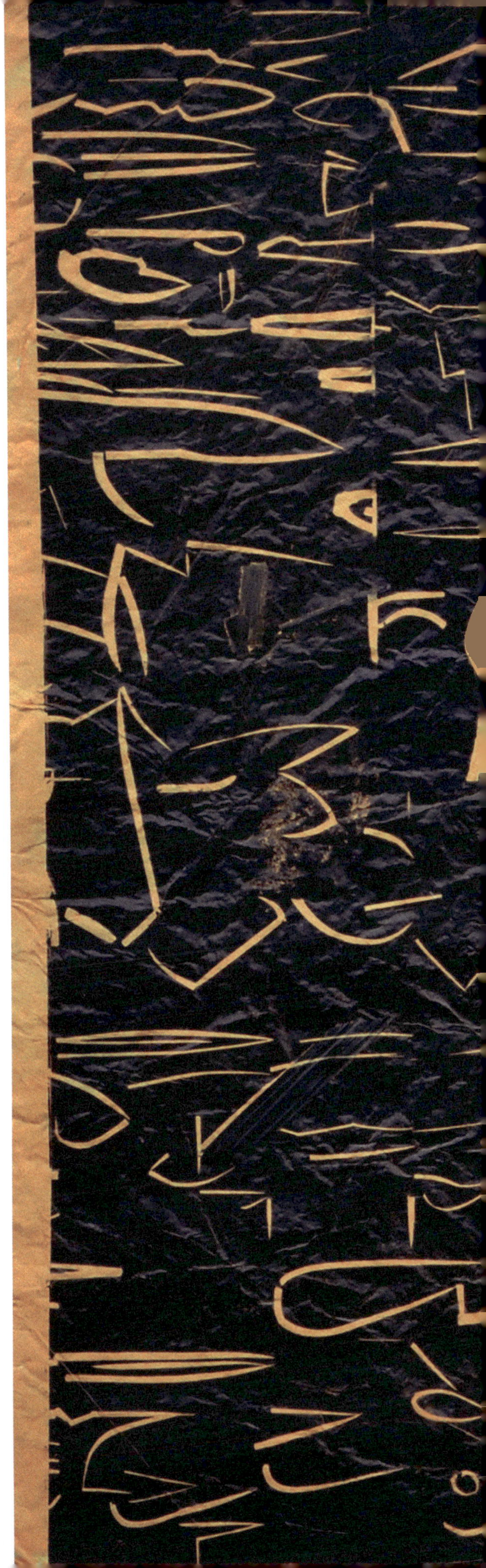

Reflex Blue on Saffron • artist's proof (detail) — Patterns of Paradise

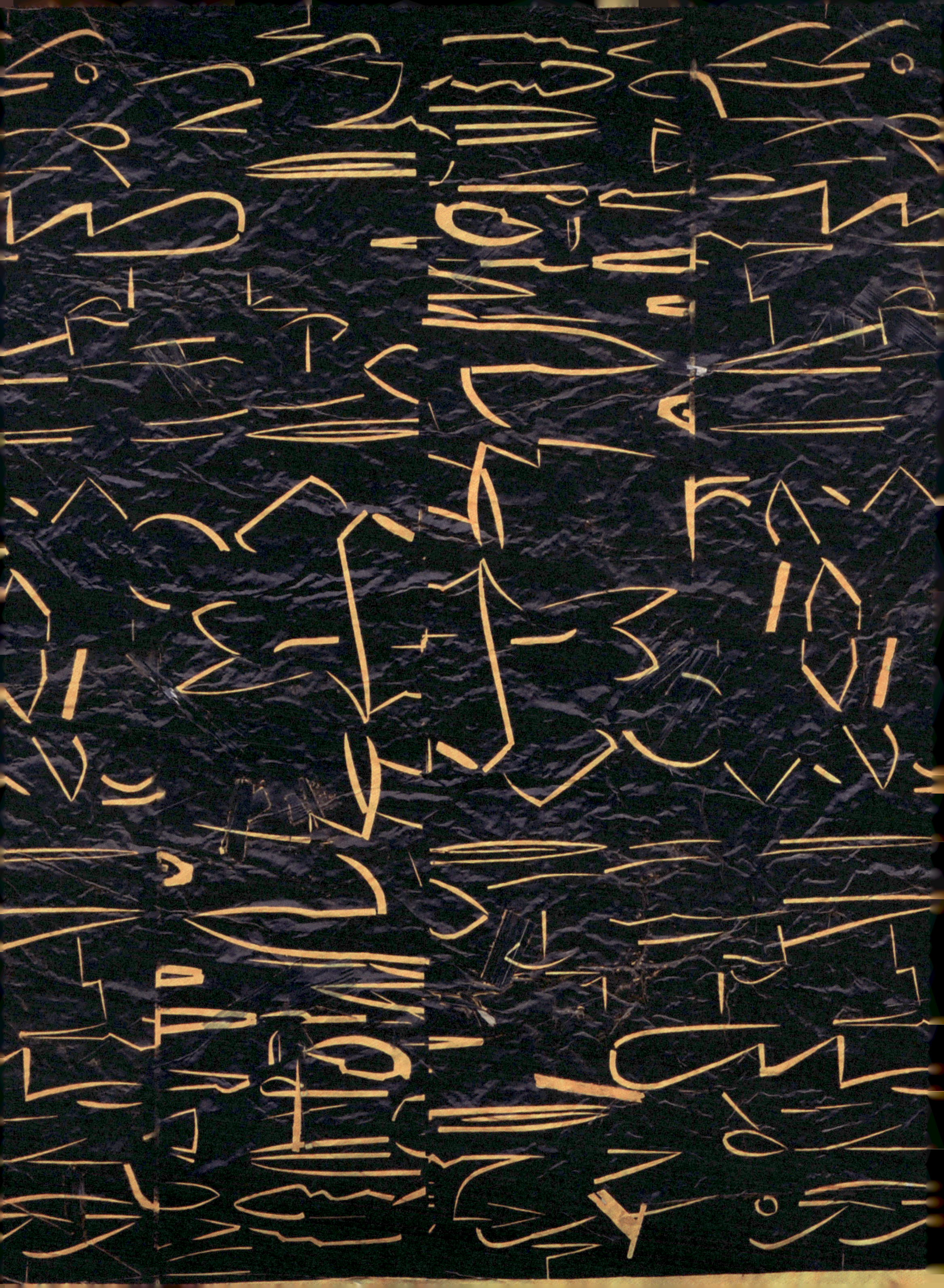

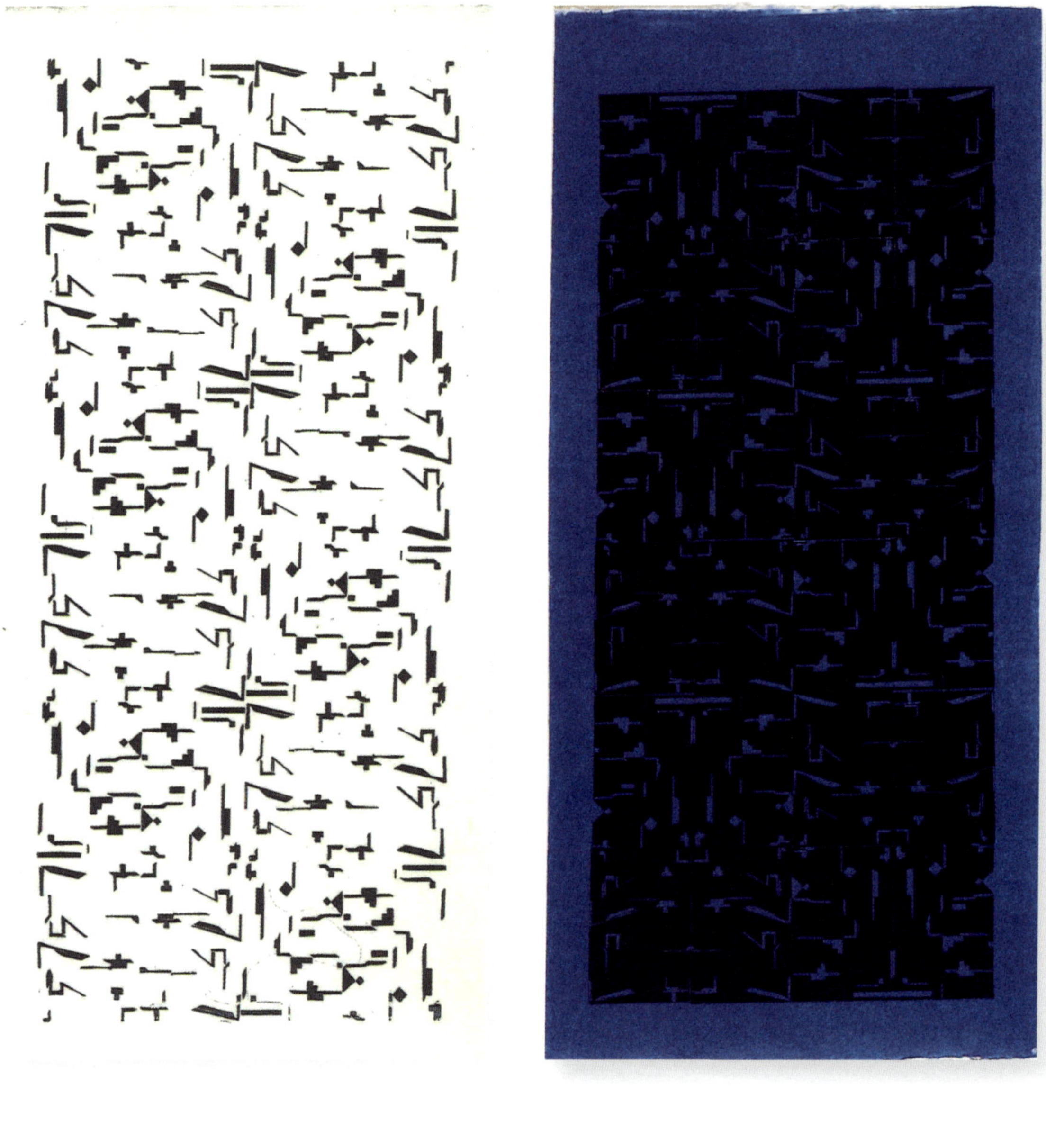

 Kemper meets Chladni 1a & 1b

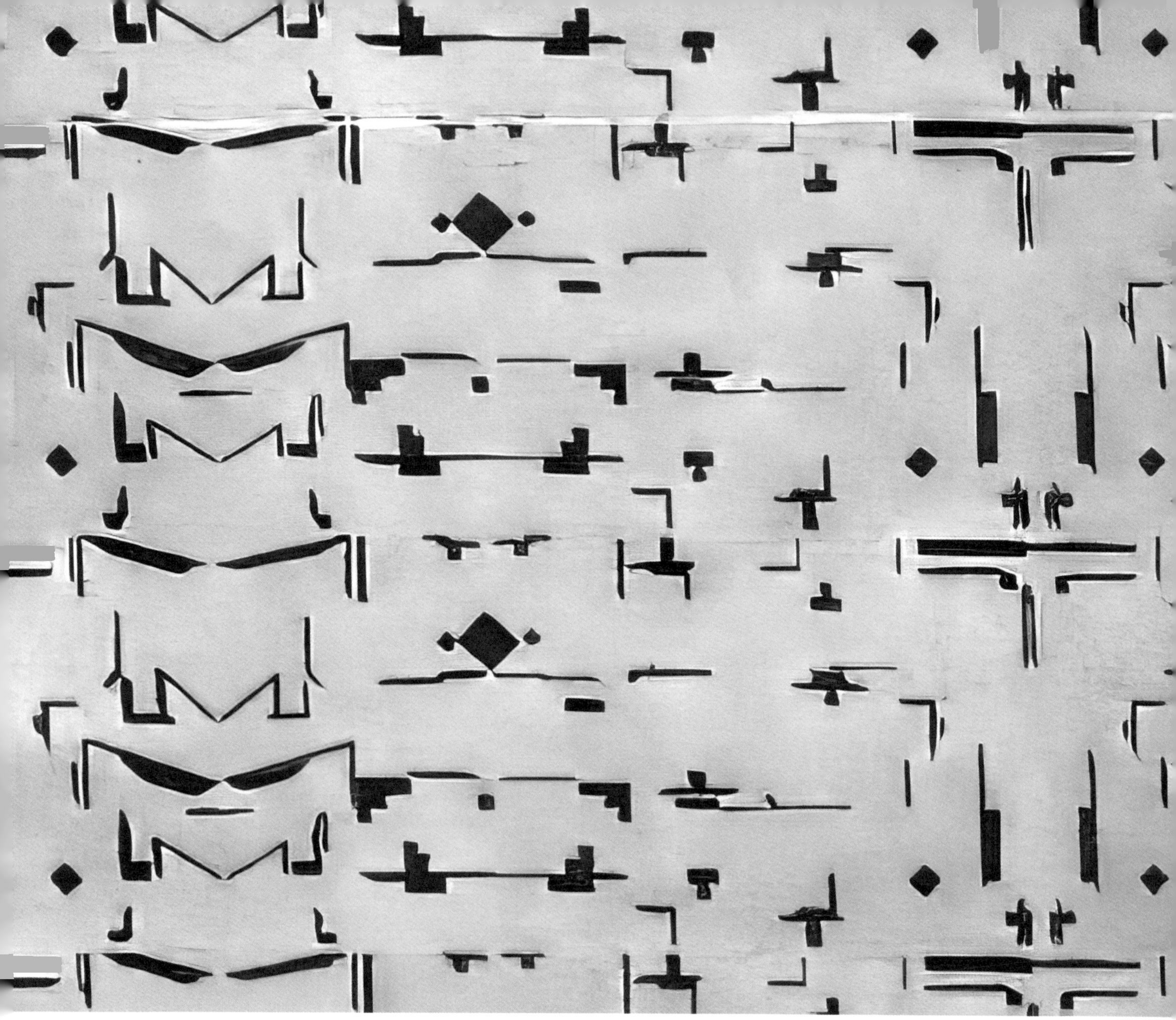

Kemper meets Chladni (detail)

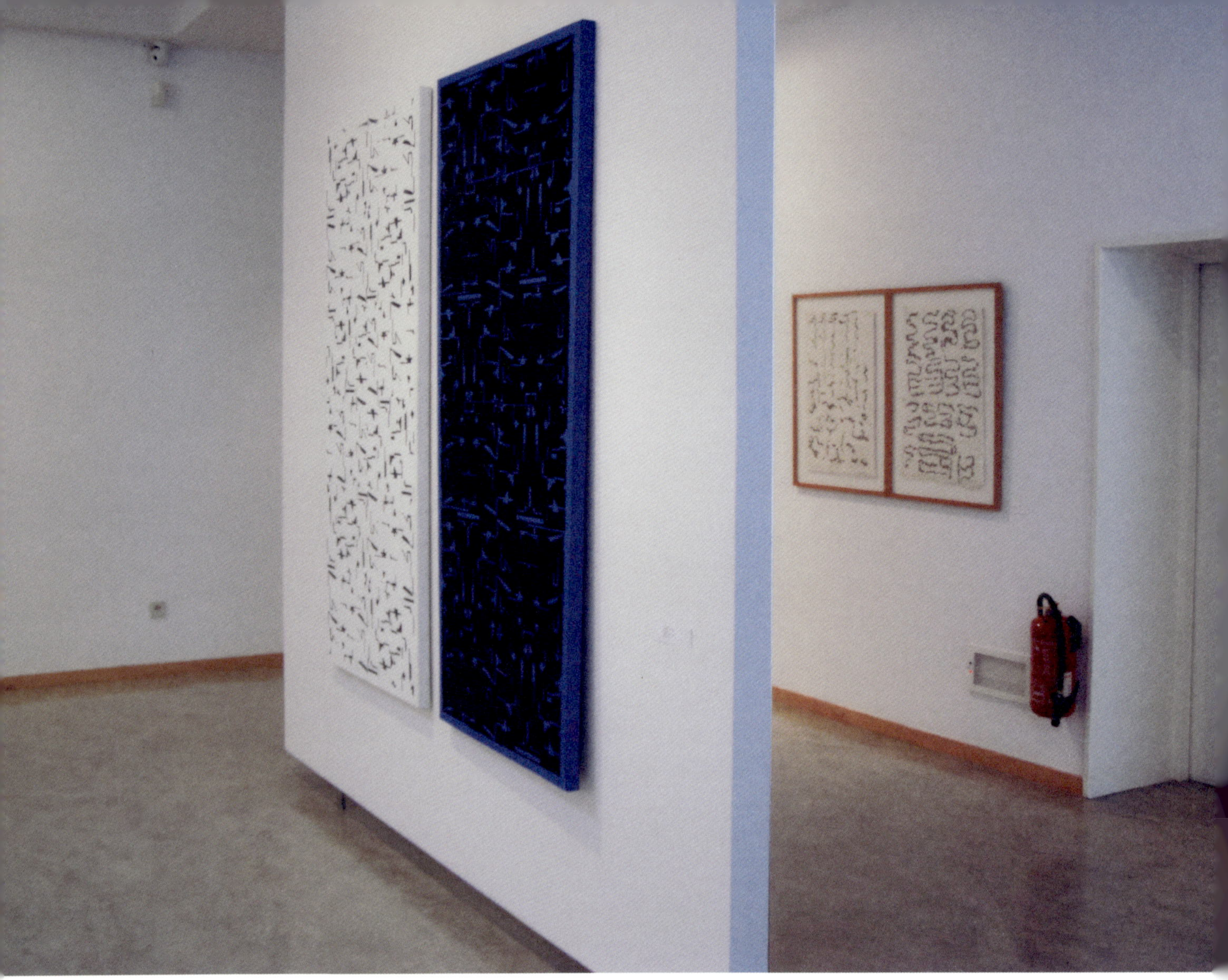

 Kemper meets Chladni, exhibition 'Survey', exhibition view

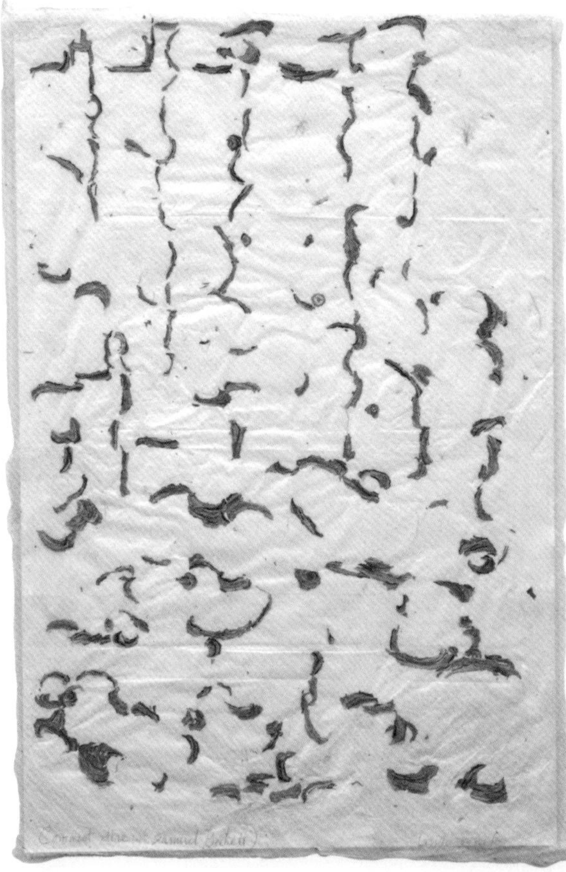

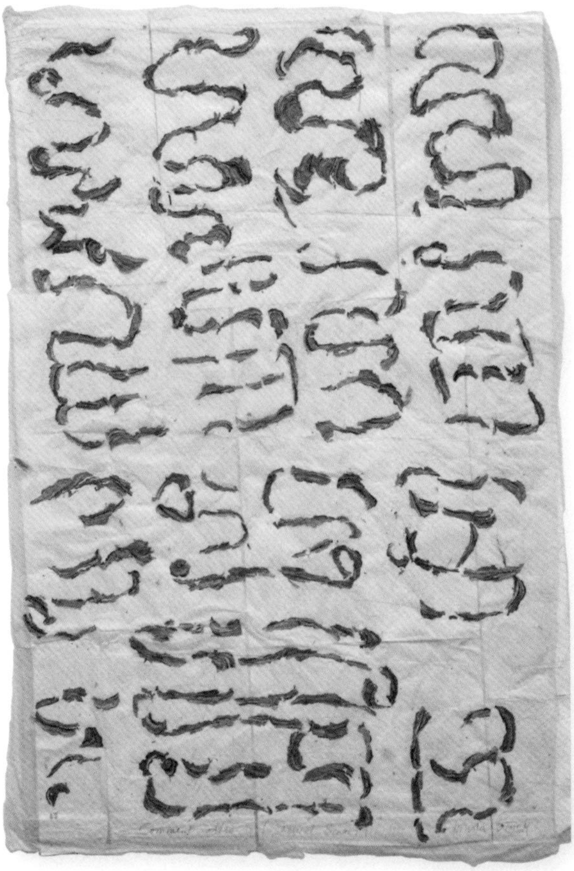

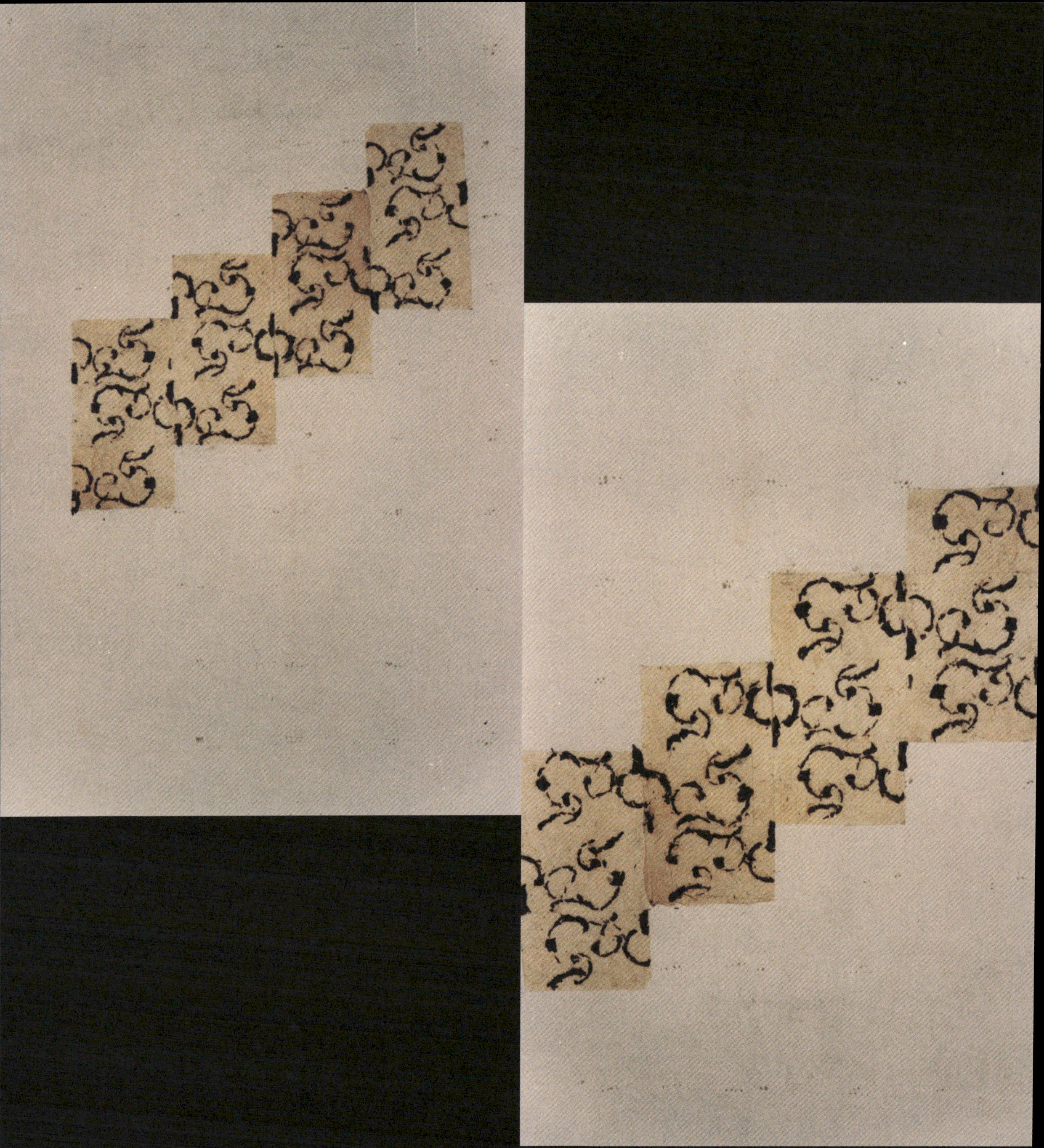

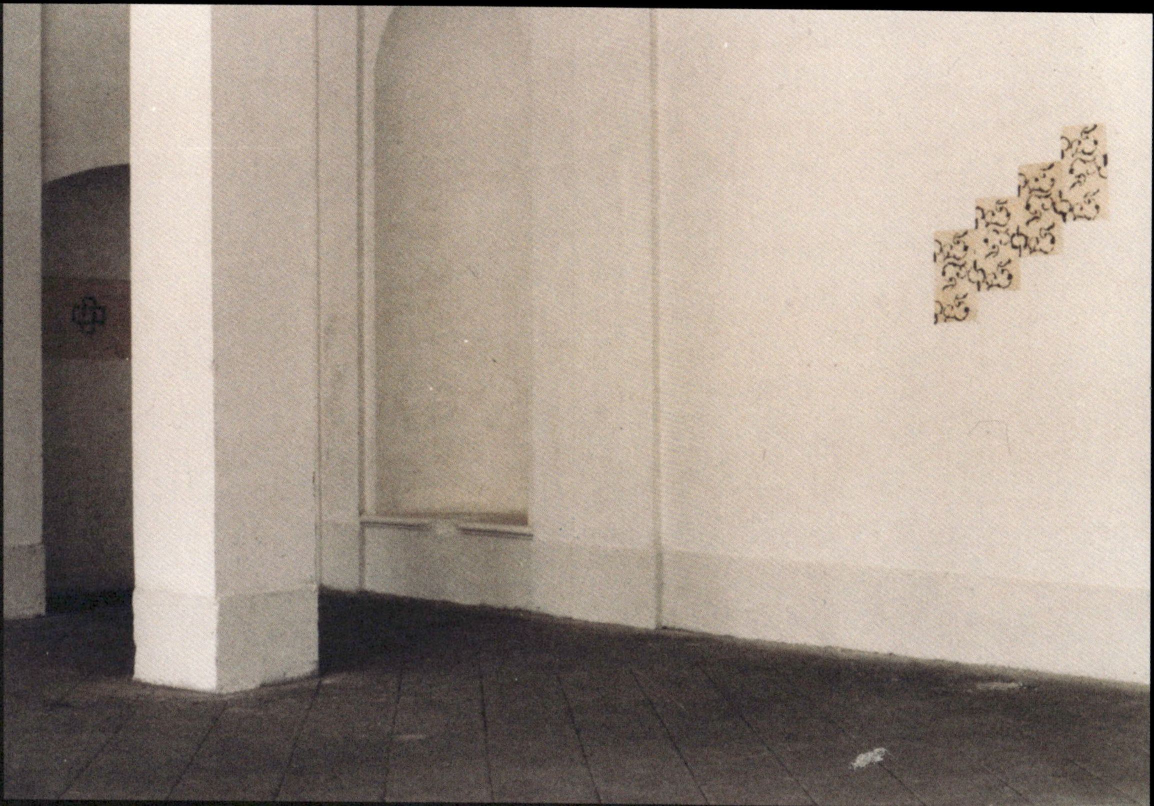

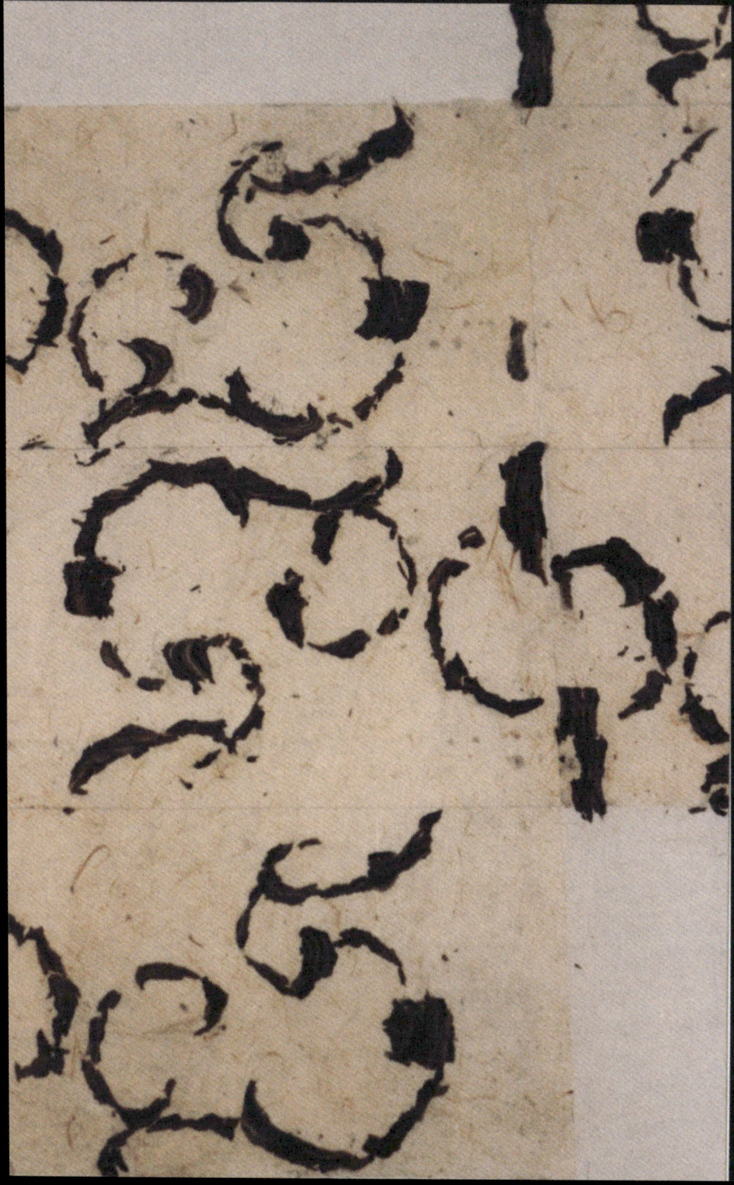

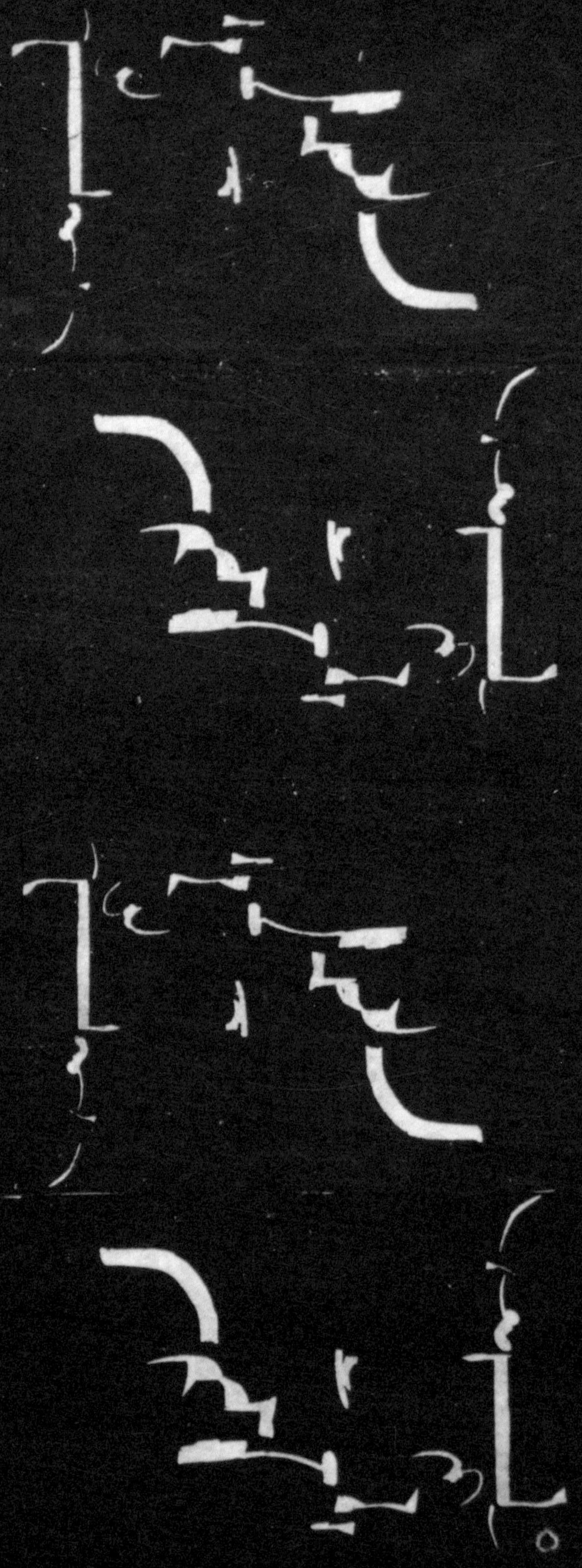

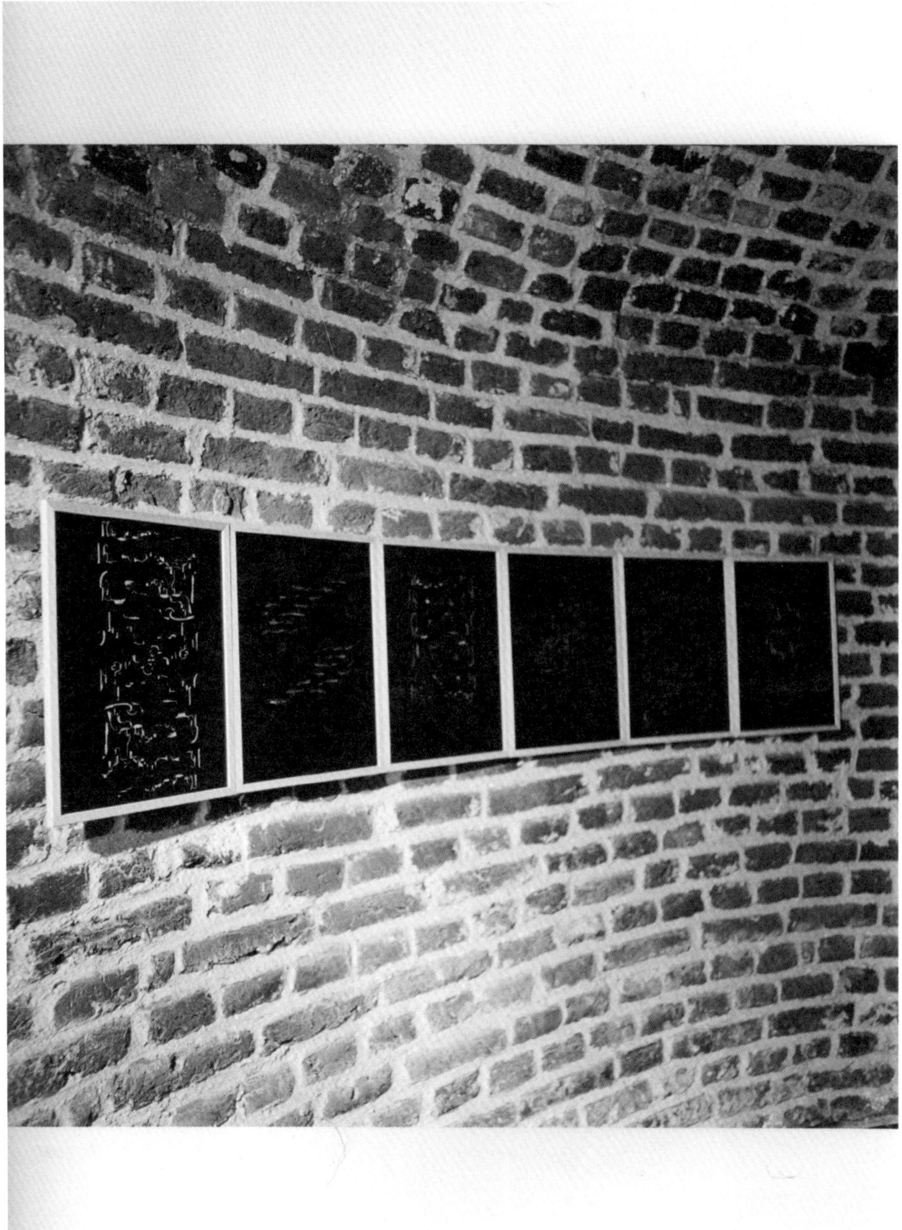

Exhibition 'Papier als Middelpunt', tower in the Castle of Grand Commandery Alden Biesen

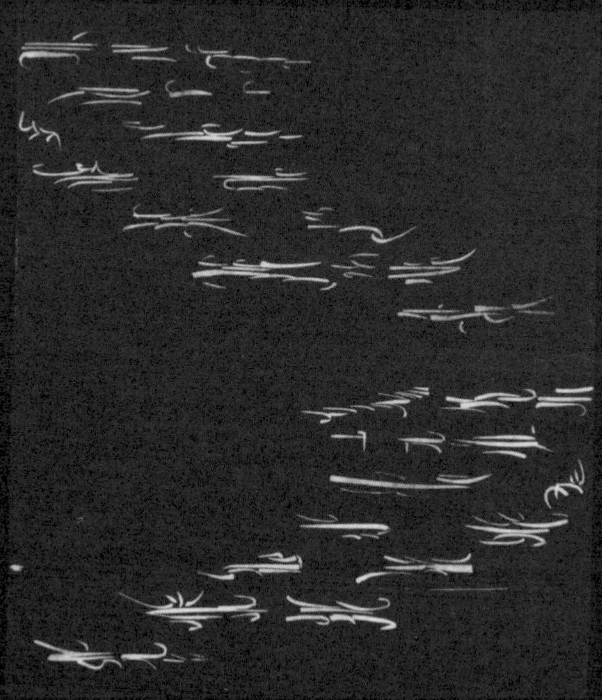

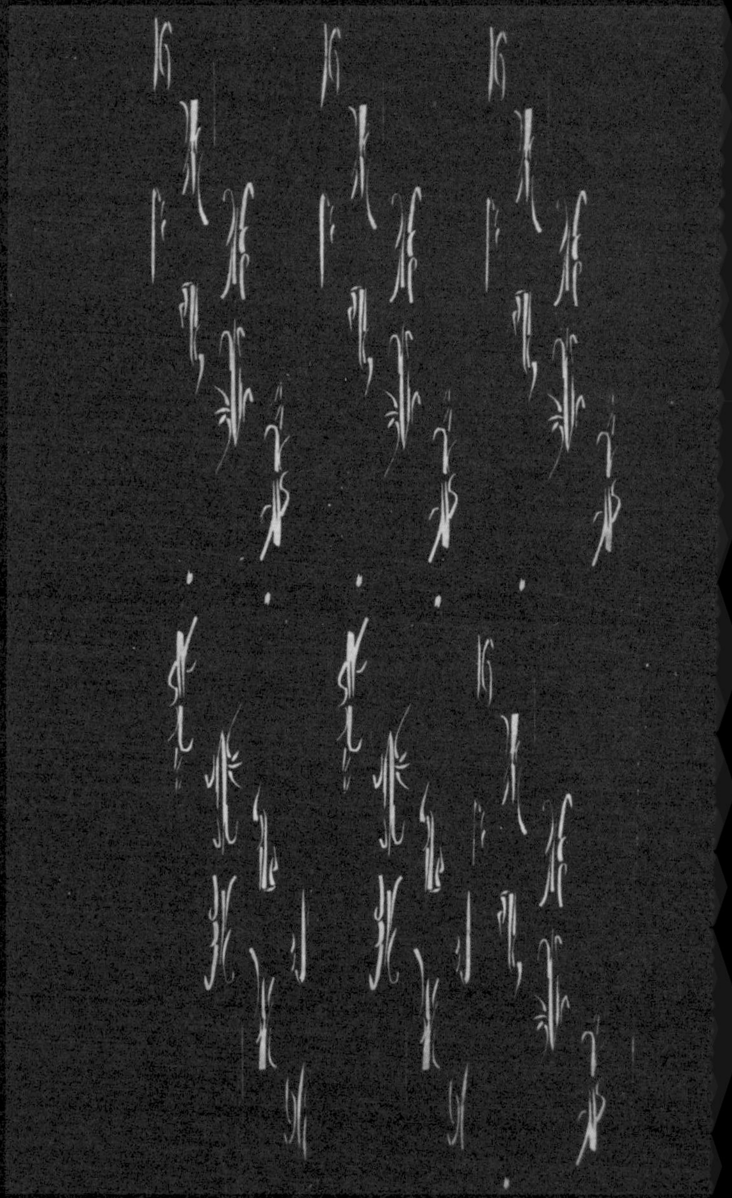

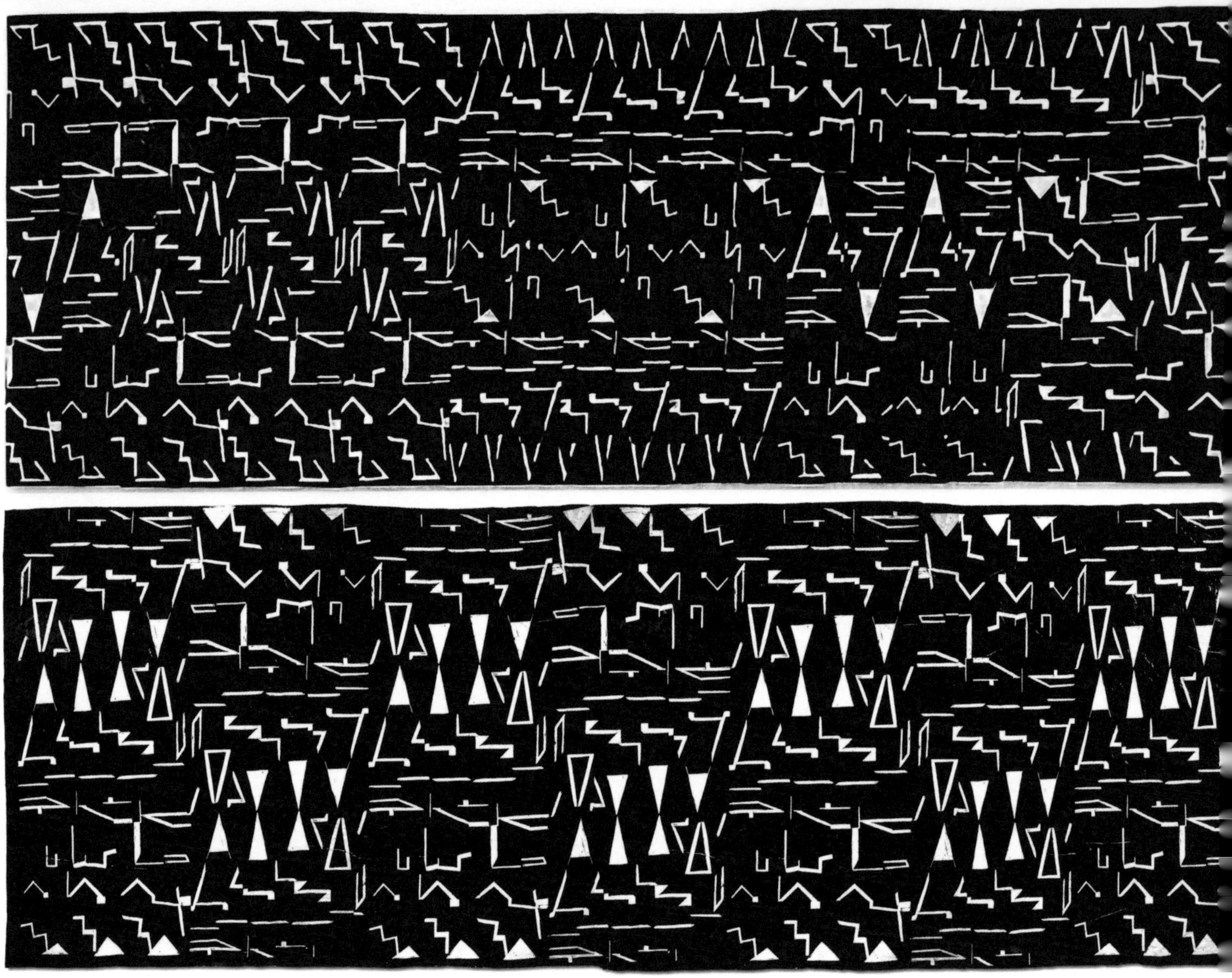

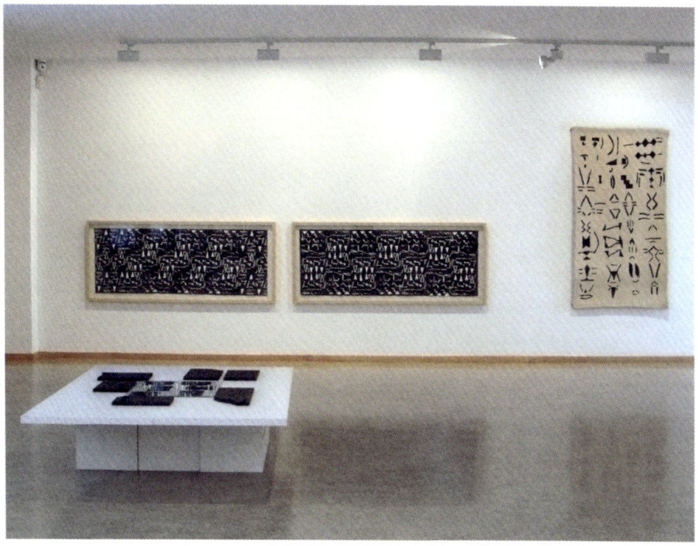

Exhibition 'Survey', exhibition view, Sint-Jorispoort, Elzenveld, Antwerp, Belgium

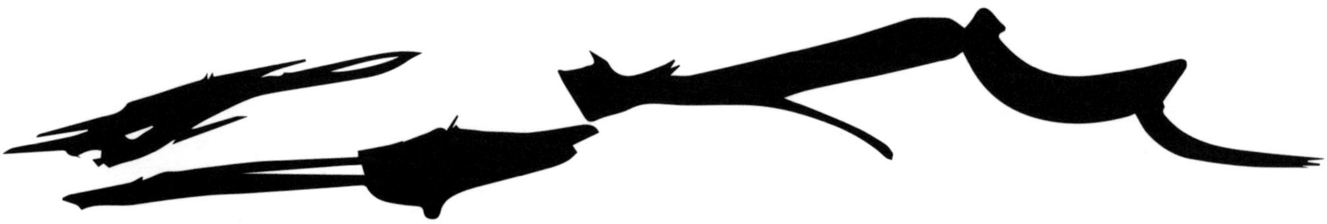

III. We meet it, but no one sees its face. We follow it, but no one sees its back. (Laozi)

Men ontmoet het, maar niemand ziet zijn gelaat.
Men volgt het, maar niemand ziet zijn rug. (Laozi)

Essay by Paul Vandenbroeck

"It may look like nothing. A few curves, a straight line, a point. How come it takes me so much time to bring these together until they are properly in place? Right there and nowhere else?

I have to make sure that they occupy the right space, that they understand each other."

Paul VANDENBROECK

Illuminare Research Centre, KU Leuven
Salon Radical, Kortrijk

We meet it, but no one sees its face.
We follow it, but no one sees its back.

— Laozi

Predictive Memories

THE LABOURING TRAIN.

"Memories from the nursery, which overlooked the railway verge, where only freight trains would pass. These also ran at night, and there must have been a slight hill near our house, as the trains used to act really odd there, as if they could not get over an obstacle and had to make more of an effort. To my ears, it sounded like rhythmic music that would stop for brief moments, tried again repeatedly, then suddenly: the moment of relief. Full steam ahead. They were still steam trains back then. *Choo-choo choo-choo choo-choo choo-choo choo-choo, Dedede Eièèèèèè*, like they were going downhill and then trying again to get up the hill. Yay, it's away, *a kind of happy victory of overcoming the obstacle*, I must not have applauded, but that feeling was there." [1]

BACKWARDS YET FORWARDS.

"During the day, I was captivated by the locomotive's wheels, three in total, with something pulling them along. Off-and-on, but still moving forward, like the Echternach procession."

SLOW SHAPING OF BEAUTY.

"With not only amazement, but also great admiration, I would sit for hours watching how snow crystals would slowly but steadily be drawn on the nursery windows in unlikely beautiful patterns, with the cold making them grow further each time."

1 I recently asked the artist about memories from her early childhood. I have faithfully reproduced them here.

UNSTOPPABLE PROGRESS IN ENERGISED DIVERSITY.

"Fanfare: in those days, there were brass bands for a whole number of festive occasions. That had a profound impact on me. It moved me so much as a child, watching with tears in my eyes, stomping my boots on the cobblestones. The drums, the trumpets! I don't remember if there were majorettes back then. I must not have considered them important enough, as they did not come into *the picture*. It was the *rhythmic advance* to the beat of the drums." [2]

ALLOWING PATTERNS TO EMERGE.

"Game: we would place nails on the seats of wooden chairs, moving a magnet underneath to get *everything moving...*"

PATTERNS, CHANGING SHAPES AND COLOURS.

"A kaleidoscope, a cardboard tube with cut glass. How you could *duplicate*, *combine* anything in the environment and how, depending on what you were pointing at, you could conjure *brilliant patterns*. I still have it here in my studio: the *rainbow hour*. The late afternoon sun shines on the crystal chandelier hanging from the ceiling, casting rainbow-like patterns, spread out all over the walls and other objects."

2 "I once saw a video by Francis Alÿs, recorded in London, which had as much impact on me as the brass bands used to. That video has EVERYTHING: the square formation of the marching guards. The sound of their boots on the cobblestones... the purposeful and growing number. I used this work during a lecture in Japan, as it contains everything I work on as an artist." (LV)

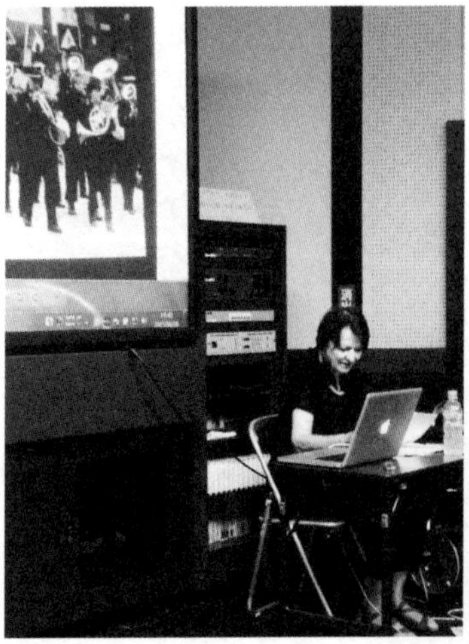

Maan beschijnt de nacht (detail), 530 × 180 mm, woodcut and lino on paper, 2010
Portfolio with Peter Holvoet-Hanssen

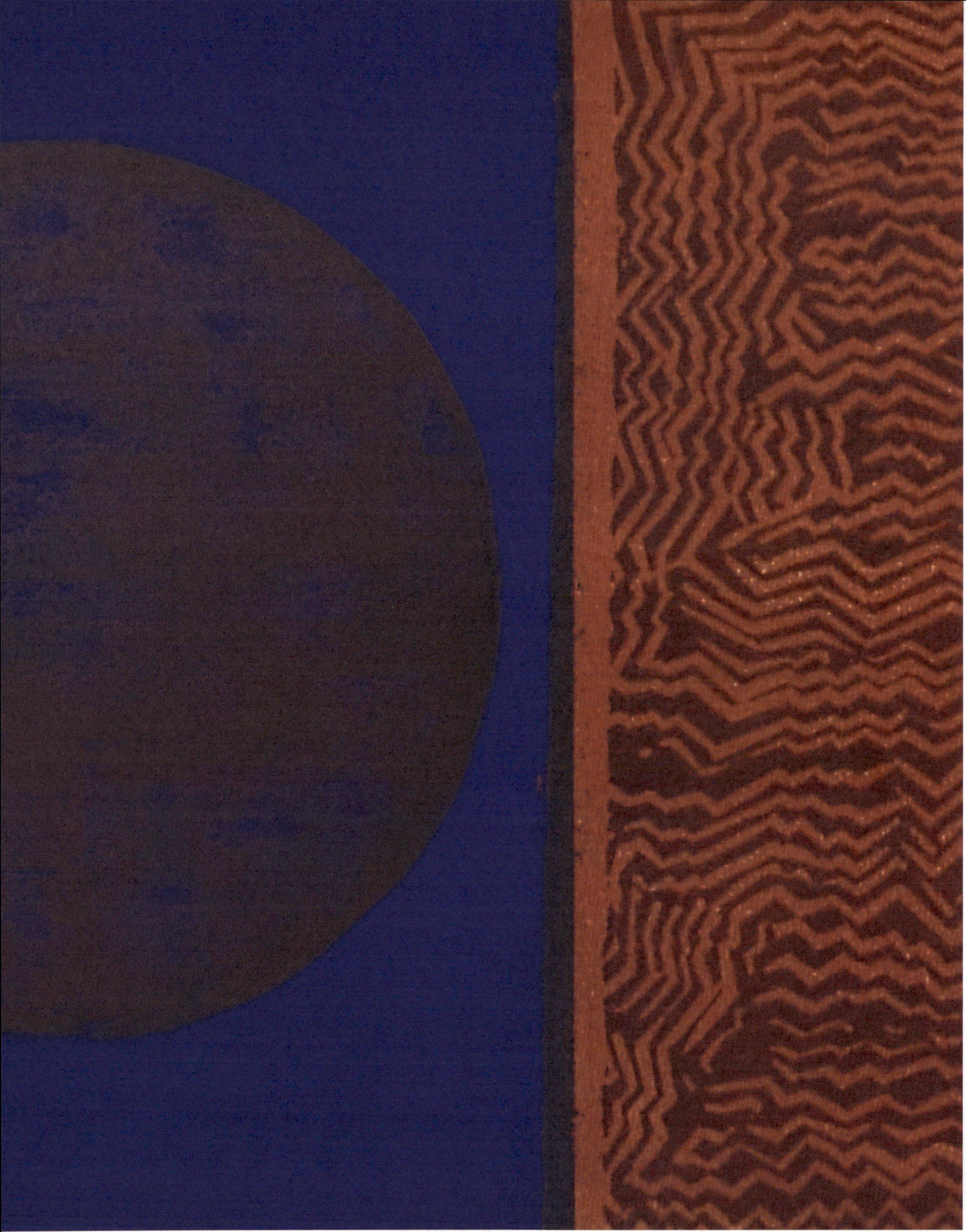

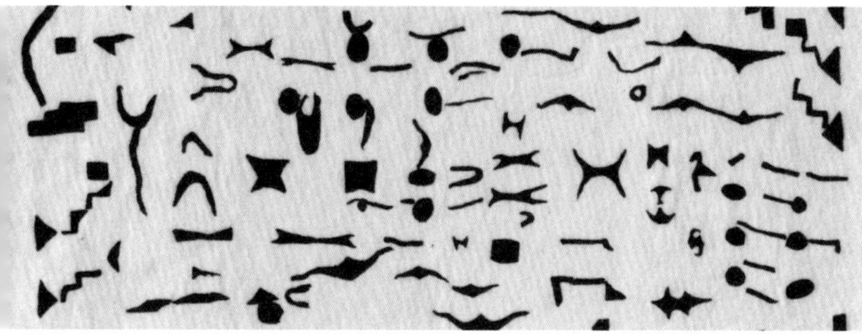

fig. 1

fig. 1 **Harpa Doris — Felt (detail)**

[Antescriptum]

Linda Vinck's work is completely abstract. Nowhere will you find a single recognisable element offering a direct connection. Superficially, the artist fills her field with motif groupings. And yet, the process is not the result of a *horror vacui*, even when the whole field is already filled. In fact, some works leave room for *blank* spaces.

Titles

The titles of Linda Vinck's works are references to a place, an experience, a perception. They have acted, if you will, as something for the artist to hang her hat on.

Sometimes, she would name her series after an animal (*Harpa Doris*, a type of sea snail found on the Cape Verde Islands, among others, whose home displays endlessly varied patterns) or a place on the Cape Verde Islands, such as *Kebra Kanela* (a beach on the island of Santiago, whose name means 'Break your leg' in the local Creole language) or *Salamansa* (a beach on the island of São Vicente).

Two styles

Linda Vinck's oeuvre follows a dual path. On the one hand, we have the *free* compositions, showcasing non-geometric forms. On the other, we have the more *constrained* works, featuring geometric components. This division is not an absolute one, with geometric forms also featuring within the more free style, and vice versa.

Her *free style* works include: the early linocuts and later dry-needle etchings (1983, 2004); *Zonder titels* (1985–1991), *Zonder titels* (1988), the large series *Zonder titels* (1991), *Anthiagrammes* (1994), *Correntes* (2000–2001), *Towards the Ocean* (2001), *Kebra Kanela* (2004), *Salamansa* (2004), *Harpa Doris* (2006) and *Transformation* (2007).

Examples of her more constrained, geometric style include: *Anthiapolis* (1996), *Kemper meets Chladni* (1998), *Genetic Process* (2004–2024) and *Bugaku* (2021).

There are a number of printed series from 2008–2013 that do not conform to either of the aforementioned categories: *Concentric Circles* (2008), *Circles* (2008–2009), *Look and listen* (2010), *Lichtpuntjes* (2010), *Patterns* (2010), *Reminiscence* (2010), *Maan beschijnt de nacht* (2010), *De inslag* (2010), *Return* (2010), *Locomotion* (2012) and *Interactions* (2012–2013).

The years 1986–1993 also saw the creation of remarkable abstract paintings, which remind me of South Africa in their colour and design.

Polymorph

Technically, Vinck's oeuvre is polymorphic in nature, spanning across linocuts or lino-assemblages on paper (including Zerkall, Chinese rice paper, various Japanese papers, handmade Nepalese paper, layered paper), on fleece or canvas, felt-printing, dry-needle etching, woodcut on Gampi paper or canvas, woodcut combined with screen printing, paintings (acrylic on canvas or layered

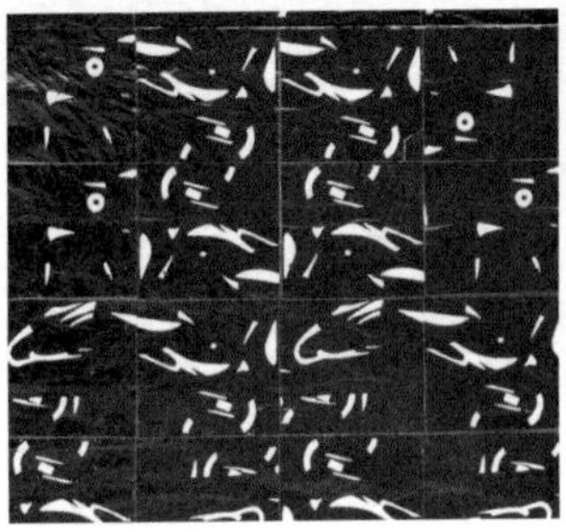

fig. 2

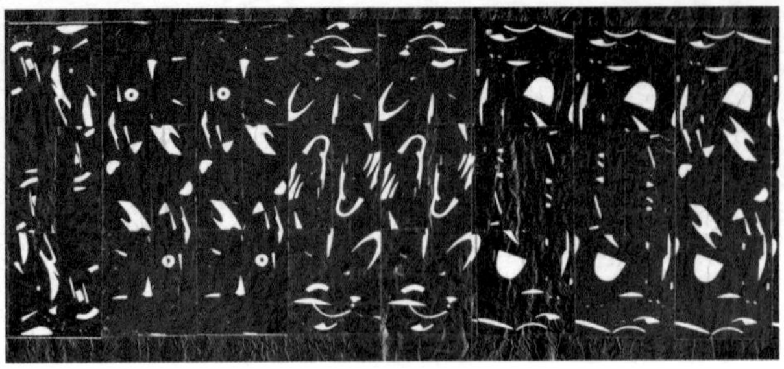

fig. 3

fig. 2 **Oceanography 1 (detail)**
fig. 3 **Oceanography 3 (detail)**

paper) and, more recently, sculptures. The tactile dimension also plays an important role, with both the aforementioned 1986–1993 series of paintings and numerous linocuts executed on a medium consisting, for instance, of various sheets of paper glued together (often Japanese paper varieties, sometimes handmade by the artist). The edges of these mediums are usually ragged or not well-defined. The surfaces on larger works (or sometimes of the paintings from the 1986–1993 period) comprise a hilly landscape – this becomes abundantly clear when shining a light over it – as seen with the etchings of Hercules Seghers. The sometimes slightly undulating and 'wavering' edges of these collages – for that is what they are in their early stages – render such works similar to fabrics made on traditional wooden looms.

Organic Abstractions

Linda Vinck's works, however radically abstract, have their roots in sensory and meta-sensory perception. The artist has always been fascinated by the physical world: the sounds of the ocean, the tweeting of birds, the rolling of the waves, the movements of a school of fish or other sea creatures, the rhythms of natural phenomena. And since the *self* also belongs to the world, her attention has equally been focused on unremitting sensations within the *self*: breath, heartbeat, rhythms. It is not *images*, rather patterns and energies that mark life, that are inseparable from it.

These energies are usually not drawn or painted, rather taking shape through the long and laborious process of linocut, the basis for much of Vinck's work. This is a technique that requires the utmost concentration. It is far from a modern piece of technology.

A technique such as etching is relatively forgiving: using the etching needle, one draws into the wax layer on the copper plate. If the artist makes a mistake, an additional layer of wax can be used to eliminate the error. The techniques practised by Linda Vinck, such as dry needle and linocut, serve to directly manipulate a hard and uncorrectable material. This requires a steady hand and an adaptable approach. While using the burin to cut a narrowing or widening line in the copper plate, one should not hesitate for even a fraction of a second, or the line will reveal said hesitation. And while copper sheet is flat and stable, linoleum, on the other hand, is pliable and unstable. Even with masters like Frans Masereel, we sometimes still see the outliers that the artist has tried to make the best of. Evidence of an extremely supple and determined hand is typical of Linda Vinck's work.

Her larger works are also collages on varying principles. Multiple modules are used as a base. A module can be divided or trimmed. Each print from a lino module may have differences, deviations and colour variations. Through a quiet, meditative process, the whole is composed. However, before composing the whole, there is the intensive work of bringing a module into being.

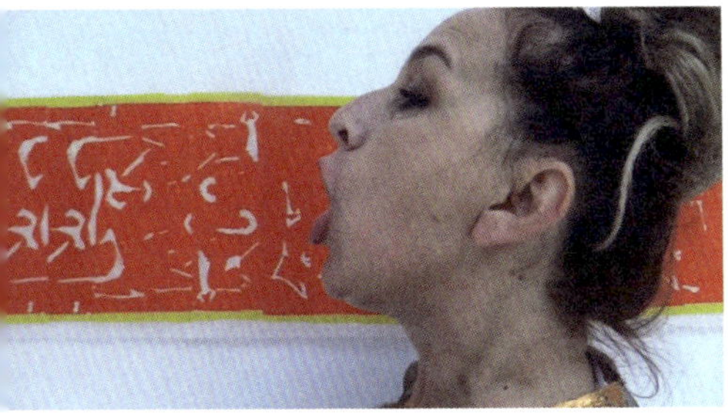

g. 4

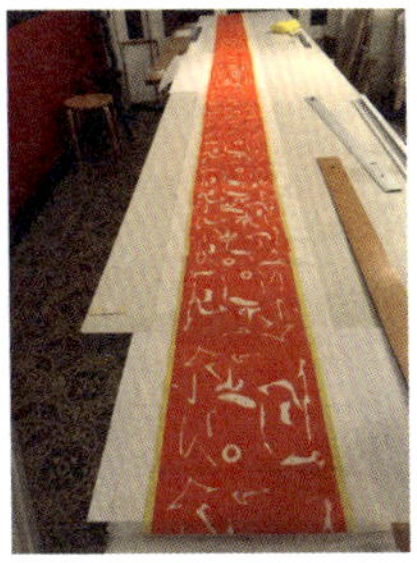

fig. 5

fig. 4 Red Oxygen, performance, Pé Vermeersch, 2020
fig. 5 Transformation 2 (Red Oxygen), woodcut on Gampi paper, 2009

In Linda Vinck's work, there is little hint of hierarchy: we see more of a collaboration, sometimes playful, a multitude of participants throughout the space. Here, there is an analogy with Pé Vermeersch's work in dance[3], where even the smallest part of the body can be mobilised, the breath can be driven by the smallest action and can lend it an essential *fullness*. But open space, silence, waiting and motionlessness can also be essential.

Back and forth: from form design to original psychocorporal process and vice versa

The basic aesthetic forms – a broken, swerving, curved line, just to name a few of the thousands of possibilities – and their compositions do not come from nowhere. They are related to the primordial movements or creations on the boundary between body matter and 'psyche' in its different *forms*. While these are partially decorative, they are crucial in the development of psychic activity and aesthetic creation. Form is never simply form.

It could be argued that the creation of works of art entails a lengthy path, arising from unconscious impulses, passing through a body-bound labour process, and becoming an autonomous end product, which – in the case of the visual arts – is no longer body-bound and, moreover, can attain a very high status as an important emanation from within a given culture. A work of art harbours a combination that is at once *basic* and abstracted. *It is akin to and has grown out of the most inaccessible psychocorporal impulses, while at the same time being light years away from them.*

Every aesthetic form, even without any recognisable reference to the world, is a manifestation of one of the original psychocorporal processes or events. They do not emerge, at least not directly, from the 'world', rather form an alphabet with which 'to read the world'. They are also transmodal: the artist has made them cross over into a creation that can be perceived by the senses.

The effect of the aesthetic form: not derivation, but a source

Pictograms are termed formal signifiers[4]. These are tangible or psychically-tangible images of something happening, not visible, phantasmatic images. If one had to express them in language form, they would only cover a verb or a subject-and-verb. This subject is not a person, rather a form or a piece of a body, or a space. There is no story, only a transformation of an appearance or trait, a transformation that takes place

3 Pé Vermeersch is a dancer/choreographer with her company Radical HeArts. She collaborated with Linda Vinck on *Ademrood* (Rouge Respirant/Red Oxygen), Brussels, 2020 and *Blauw — Teken van de Nacht* (Blue — Sign of the Night), 2023.

4 Didier ANZIEU, *Le moi-peau*, Paris, Bordas, 1985 & 1995; from the same author, see also: id., *Le moi-peau*, in *Nouvelle revue de psychanalyse*, 1974, pp. 195-208; id., *La peau: du plaisir à la pensée*, in *L'attachement*, ed. id. et al, Geneva, Delachaux & Nestlé, 1974.

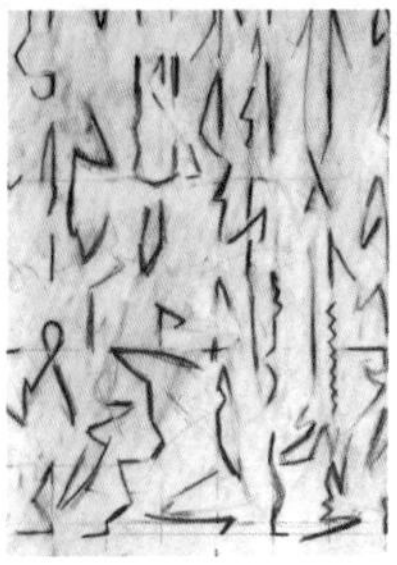

fig. 6

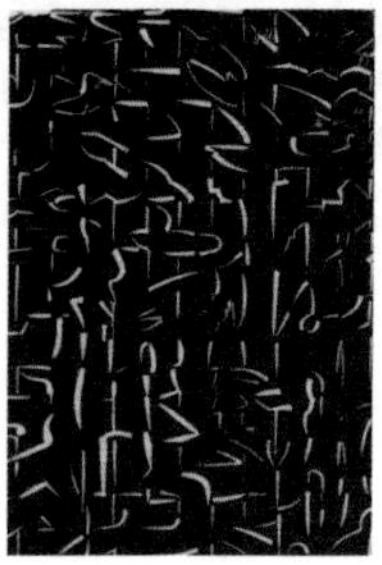

fig. 7

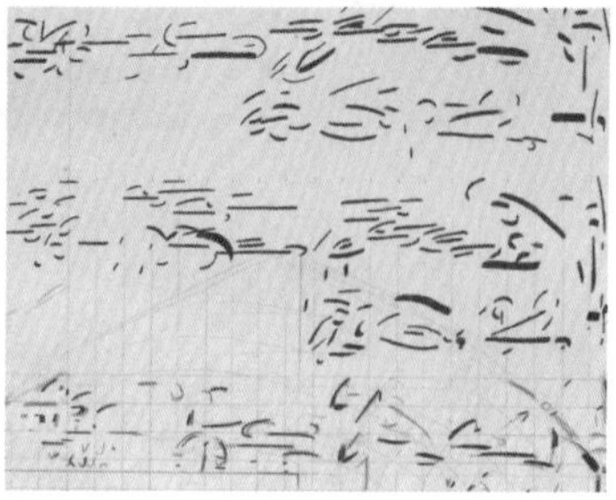

fig. 8

fig. 6 Pencil drawing
fig. 7 From Matrix series
fig. 8 Formation of modules

within or outside one's own body. It involves, for example, contraction, undulation, breathing, swirling, falling, deflating, being pulled away, piercing, exploding, crumbling, tearing. There are also processes such as incorporating or superimposing, curling or deflecting, something seeking something else, cutting off, doubling, changing direction, leaving traces, opening/closing, coinciding and removing.

A pictogram is an image of the 'bodily thing', of the 'complementary object-zone' or of the *meeting zone*, a primary image through which the psyche processes its *encounters with the other* and gives form to each encounter experience between itself and the world.

Walking on a knife edge

Some art historians point to similarities between the work of Linda Vinck and Henri Michaux (1899–1984), or *informal art* more broadly. This is wrong, as both are fundamentally different. So-called informal art mostly arose from an altered state of consciousness (someone like Michaux used *mezcal* to activate the creative process). The result was usually a *horror vacui*, a canvas filled with characters crowding each other out. This applies equally to Jackson Pollock (1912–1956) *cum suis*, to artists who leapt from an existence on the rural margins to modern artistry, such as Sa'id Ouarzaz or Mohamed Tabal[5] in Morocco, or to some Australian *Aboriginal* artists in similar circumstances[6]. They cannot get away from the dichotomy of order or chaos.

Informal art is not based on controlled deliberation. By this I absolutely do not mean that art is or should be based on rational control, nor on its absence.

Linda Vinck's oeuvre eludes this dichotomy. It does not follow the principles of *order* (centre/periphery, axes/mirror/symmetry, framing), but neither does it lose itself in the pseudo-freedom of phallocentric chaos.

Comparing with North African fabrics: traditionally, there is no border (except in urban carpet work), sometimes a middle axis (in whole or in part), but there is always space wherein one can go in all directions and where one can do what is deemed necessary, with possibly one element, to render the composition a success.

Something analogous can take place in dance: for a dancer/choreographer like Pé Vermeersch, small movements, variations, slowing down, speeding up, can prove essential for a performance. But these are never wholly at random, neither consciously contemplated nor thoughtlessly produced.

In Linda Vinck's work, this approach requires all the more mental and physical strength, as her so-often used medium, the linocut, is a

5 Paul VANDENBROECK, *De kleuren van de geest. Dans en trance in Afro-Europese tradities*, Ghent, Snoeck-Ducaju, 1997, *with many illustrations of works by e.g. Ouarzaz and Tabal (298 pages, 200 illustrations).*

6 Judith RYAN & Geoffrey BARDON, *Mythscapes. Aboriginal art of the desert from the National Gallery of Victoria*, Victoria, National Gallery of Victoria, 1989; Judith RYAN & Kim AKERMAN, *Images of power. Aboriginal art of the Kimberley*, Victoria, National Gallery of Victoria, s.d.

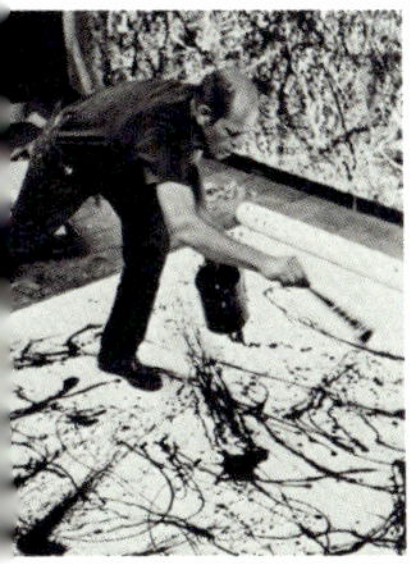

j. 9

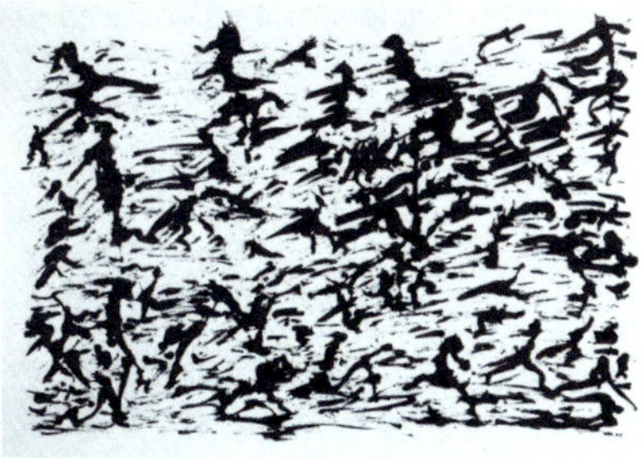

fig. 10

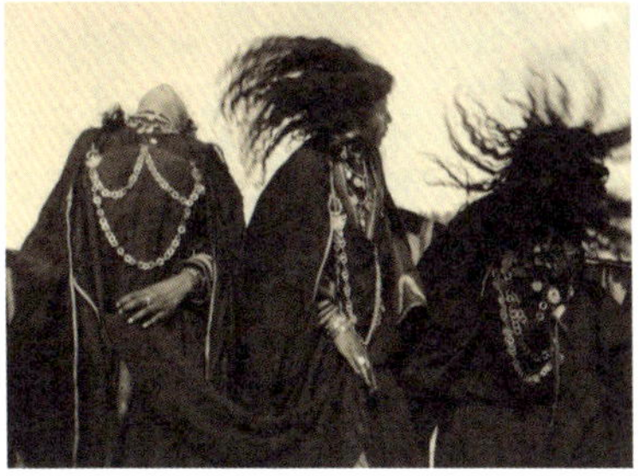

fig. 11

fig. 9 Jackson Pollock painting in his studio in East Hampton, New York, 1950
fig. 10 Henri Michaux, Peinture à l'encre de chine, 1967
fig. 11 Hair dance, DOUZ (Tunisia), c. 1950, unknown photographer

very stubborn material. Carving smooth, subtle shapes into the tough material requires an enduring, controlled approach. Balancing their mutual incorporation requires an emotionally charged energy, which has to be unwavering in nature, or the elements "do not understand each other well", as the artist puts it.

The process behind Linda Vinck's larger works is particularly slow in nature, especially due to the difficulties imposed by her chosen medium, requiring patience in the composition of the whole (often a form of collage), as well as a high level of attention to achieve the right depth of colour. In this sense, there is an analogy with weaving, at least its free forms, as seen in Iran (the *gabbeh*) or Morocco. Weaving and knotting a carpet according to one's own inspiration is a laborious and lengthy task. What's more, the inspiration must cannot be permitted to fade, or the work will lose its aesthetic power.

Without fail, both in her oeuvre and in said textile art, great risks need to be taken. Inspiration needs to persist over a long and strenuous period of time, under pain of dull results. This psychocorporal state cannot possibly be the result of a conscious act of will, nor is it gratuitous in nature. It is only by occupying an in-between state, akin to walking a tightrope or walking on a knife-edge for an extended period of time, that this becomes achievable. And this goes hand in hand with another paradox: spontaneous creation does not come free, either.

Earlier, we talked about another paradox: a work of art harbours a combination of both the *basic* and the *abstract*. This paradox partly lies in the (in)accessibility and physicality in which it takes root. It is rooted in and has grown out of the most inaccessible psycho-corporeal impulses, light years away from them.

Participating in the *Way*

Deeper reflections on the aforementioned 'neither conscious nor unconscious' can be found in Taoism.

Awareness of the need for the aforementioned paradoxes is nothing new, at least within Eastern traditions. Chinese and Japanese artists, poets and scholars have been trying to formulate this insight for a millennium, especially through the experience of the *Tao* and from the practice of Zen (Chinese *Ch'an*).

The *Tao* (i.e. the Way) cannot be talked about. Just as God is a hyper-essence for which all human cognitive categories are inadequate, so "the Way that can be talked about is not the Way, and the name of it that can be named is not its true name" (*Tao Te Ching*)[7]. The Way is a dynamic field, in which everything is/will be according to innumerable rhythms. Wisdom and creative power can only become fully developed when one becomes one with the movements of the Way, expanding and condensing, coming and going.

7 **Paul VANDENBROECK, *The leap and paradoxical space of intuitive creation and imagination in religious and mystical tradition*, in *INTUITION*, exh. cat., Venice, Fondazione Musei Civici di Venezia & The Axel & May Vervoordt Foundation, Venice, Palazzo Fortuny, 2017, pp. 86-100.**

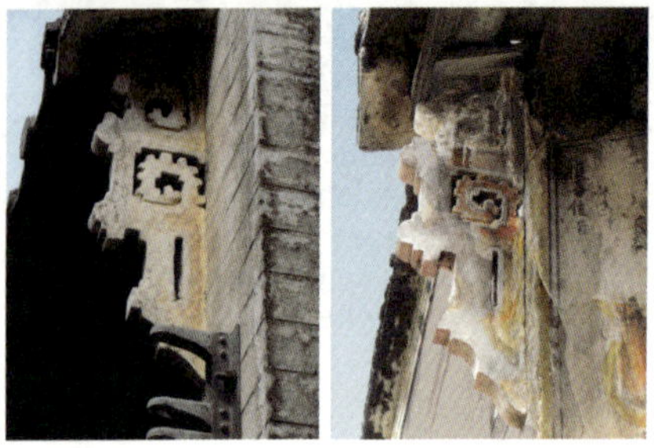

fig. 12

fig. 12 China's roof pillars ornamentation

Hsun Tsu-yung, in his book *The Ferry Boat of Painting*: "In the process of composing the painting, a spiritual breath must come and go without hindrance."[8]

For Su Tung-p'o, the true artist is not so much concerned with the literal likeness of forms, rather is focused on evoking the *inner rhythm* that pulses through them, which is then transmitted to the viewer[9]. (This is eminently applicable to Vinck's compositions, created after prolonged study of numerous natural phenomena and societies of organisms: T*owards the Ocean*, *Anthiagrammes*, *Anthiapolis* or *Birdsongs*).

"It looks like nothing…" (LV). By ridding oneself of ego-driven urges, the obstructions that prevent one from participating in the Way are cleared. Doing so makes it seem as if one is doing nothing. It is not passivity, rather unison with the flowing energies of the Way[10]. 'To not do' is not the same as passivity, fatalism or laziness. It occurs in a prepared body, and from that preparation 'it' happens.

Ching Hao (10th century): *"Chi* (breath, inspiration) arises when the artist's spirit/mind *does not intervene* in the movement of the brush which, as it were, creates the painting of its own accord, without fear."[11]

"When the intuition (of the artist) becomes one with the unfathomable reality and the brushwork approaches the depths of the unconscious… their creation will be boundless… Their thoughtless thought shall permeate the tip of his brush…"

This state is fully paradoxical: without-thinking but highly lucid in the here-and-now, free of doing but extremely purposeful. This also applies to the performative arts, in moments where the sublime is achieved. The artist then reaches a state of transcendence, akin to that seen in clairvoyance and trance-like states. "It is in the empty room that comes the light" (Chuang Tzu[12]). It is in this non-space that the creative spark emerges[13].

Being at one with the Way[14], in defiance of the principle of 'not-doing', does not amount

8 Chang CHUNG-YUAN, *Creativity and Taoism: a study of Chinese philosophy, art, and poetry*, New York, Harper, 1970, p. 212.

9 CHUNG-YUAN, 1970, p. 210.

10 The ostensible act of 'doing nothing' (wu wei) is illustrated by the image of the stone above the surface of the water: to end up at the place on the bottom where it wants/needs to be, it suffices to drop into the right place. Without any effort, it lands.

11 CHUNG-YUAN, 1970, p. 213.

12 *Chuang Tzu: Taoist philosopher and Chinese mystic*, ed. Herbert GILES, London, George Allen & Unwin, 1961.

13 Arthur WALEY, *Zen Buddhism and its relation to art*, London, 1922; Yasuichi AWAKAWA, *Zen paintings*, Tokyo, Kodansha, 1970; Shinichi HISAMATSU, *Zen and the fine arts*, Tokyo, Kodansha, 1971; Sylvan BARNET & William BURTO, *Zen paintings*, Tokyo, Kodansha, 1982; Helmut BRINKER, *Zen in the art of painting, Japanese monks, 1600–1925*, New York, Abrams, 1989; Helmut BRINKER & Hiroshi KAWAZAWA, *Zen: masters of meditation in images and writings*, Zürich, Artibus Asiae Publishers, 1996; John STEVENS, *Zenga: brushstrokes of enlightenment*, New Orleans, Museum of Art, 1990.

14 The goal of the WAY is not 'nirvana' or 'mystical' ascension. "Fetching water and cutting wood – therein lies the wonderful WAY". This was seen no differently by the medieval mystics of the Christian tradition when they said that the deepest mystical experience should be put aside if it can help a poor person beg for soup.

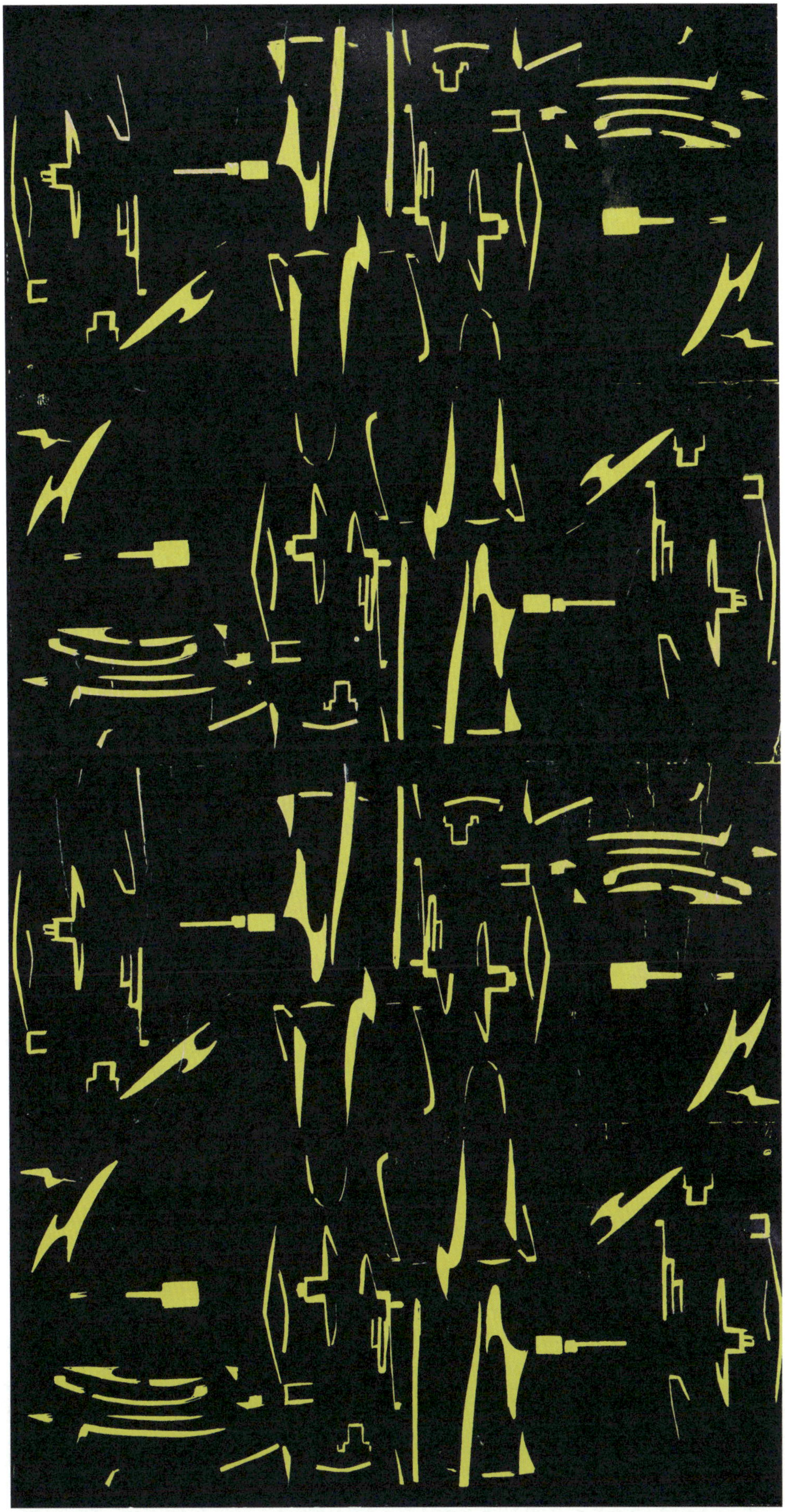

Arquipélago 5, 800 × 420 mm, lino assemblage on layered paper, 2004

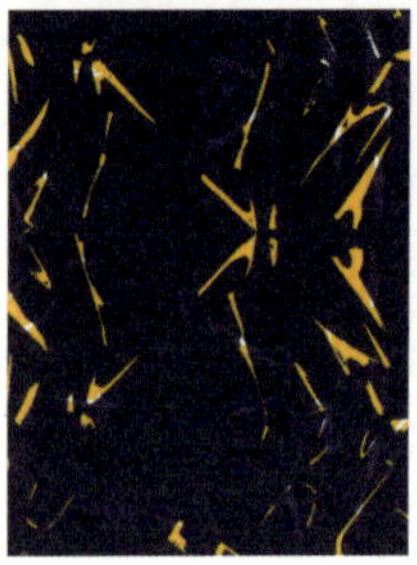

fig. 13

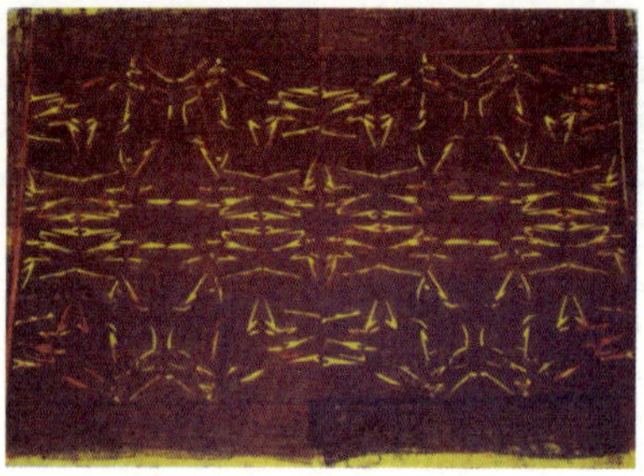

fig. 14

fig. 13 **Correntes, 90 mm × 163 mm, linocut on paper, linocut, handprinted / painted on canvas, 2000**

fig. 14 **Correntes, linocut, handprinted / painted on canvas, 2001**

to mere passivity. It is only an apparent inertia, which leads to the birth of something new and valuable. The aesthetic power in form is not achieved through *conscious* action. If the form is a product of the *conscious* mind, it will only be a creation. Only if the artist works from a field with which they are not consciously engaged, but delves into depths that are barely attainable, will the artwork have *depth*. Paradoxically, the aesthetic act is only possible through an entering / reactivation of an unconscious activity that works *tangentially*, of an unconscious knowing, which at the same time carries within it a summum of lucidity. The artist creates in a paradox of lucid higher purpose and of near-conscious action that is not rationally or cognitively framed. If the latter does occur, the artwork will not exude inspiration, rather remain a reasoned end product. This idea of lucidity has nothing to do with an intellectual and intentional insight or action.

A wide range of artists, scientists and philosophers have already argued that their deepest discoveries / creations emerged out of nowhere, independently of everyday consciousness. Einstein: "tapping into God's thoughts"[15], Poincaré: "the insight... must be diametrically opposed to that which one consciously defends"[16], Bill Viola: "Artists have long known that the most interesting things emerge from zones of limited and unclear information, so-called gaps in their knowledge. That is the moment of engagement, or, for the viewer, of participation in the work of art."[17]

It is clear from the above that the work of art, worthy of the name, was created on the edge of a knife: not controlled by will, yet not out of control; not aimlessly passive, yet not consciously engaged; not conscious exploring, rather high lucidity.

15 Denis BRIAN, *Einstein: a life*, New York, John Wiley & Sons, 1996, p. 129.

16 Rollo MAY, *Courage to create*, New York, Bantam Books, 1983.

17 Bill VIOLA, *Reasons for knocking at an empty house. Writings 1973–1994*, London, Thames & Hudson, 1998, p. 71.

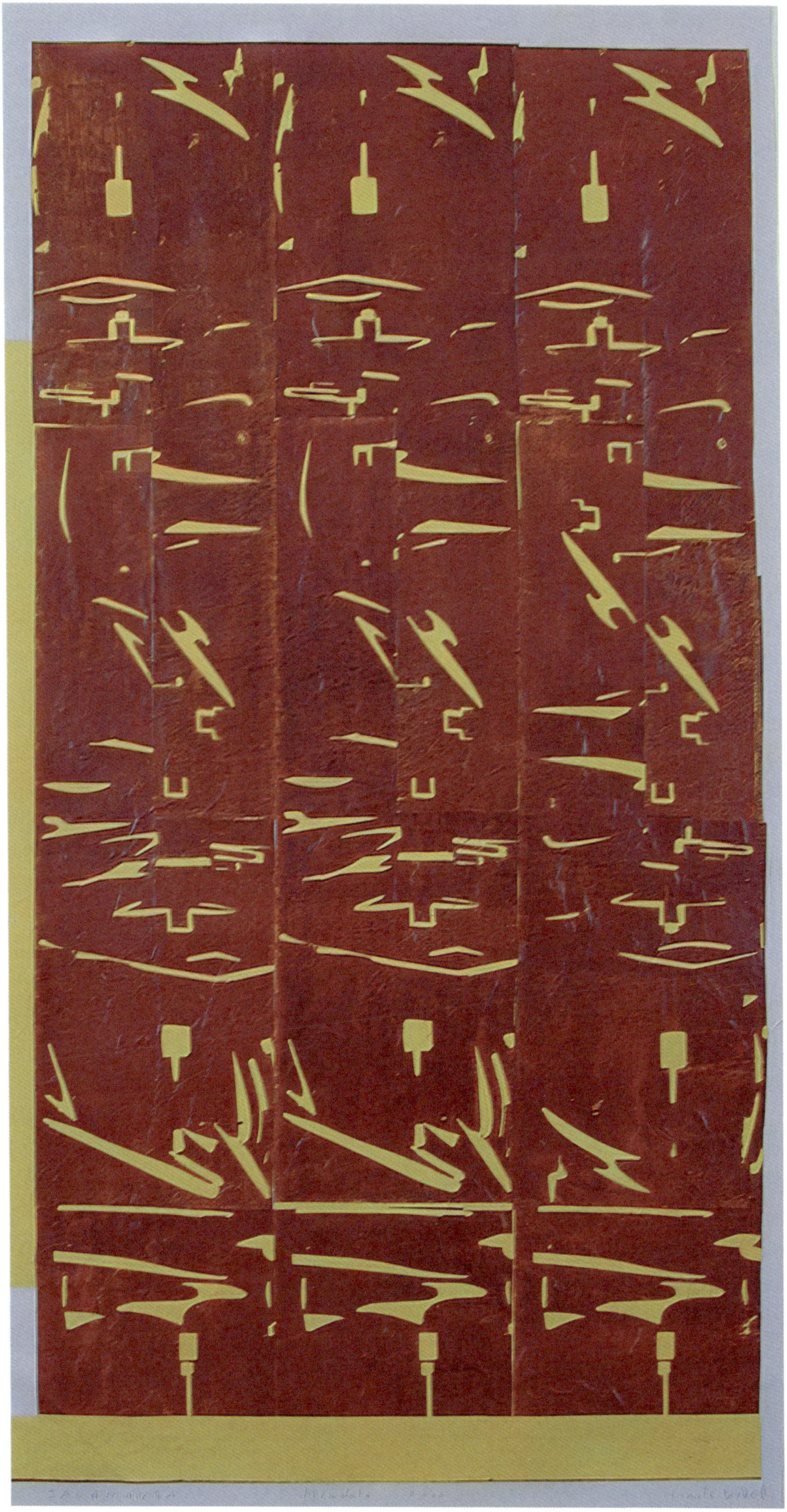

Salamansa 5, Funaná, 840 × 430 mm, lino assemblage, 2004–2019

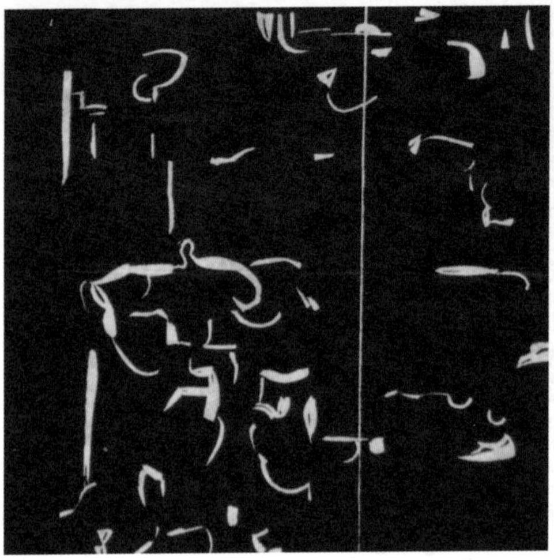

Anthiagramme (detail)

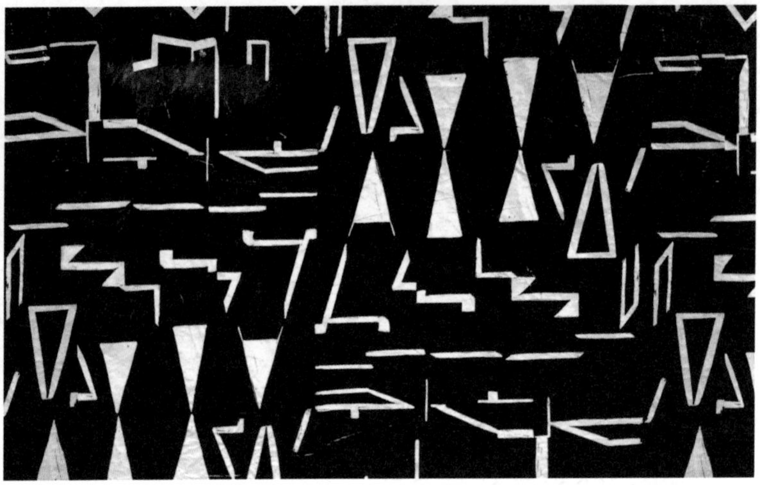

Anthiapolis 2 (detail)

Excursion I: Anthiagrammes

In my eyes, one of the most subtle sequences in Vinck's oeuvre are her *Anthiagrammes*. The word originates from *Anthias anthias*, a small fish that lives in the East Atlantic and the Mediterranean, between 15 and 200 metres deep, usually among rocks and coral. During the day, it hides in hollows or caves. At night, it feeds on zooplankton, smaller crustaceans and fish. *Anthias* is a protogynous hermaphrodite, with all individuals born female. Whenever a male dies, one of the larger females transforms into a male. As such, they possess a clear insight into their community.

The group (or perhaps some members?) ceaselessly evaluates its composition, its needs, before certain individuals then decide to change gender.

Excursion II: Anthiapolis

The considerably larger works within the *Anthiapolis series* (*Anthiapolis*, i.e. city of Anthias) evoke a totally different effect: no dreamlike, often undulating or curved features, rather a busy world in straight, often hacking, incisive lines, with small formations of triangles in between. While the complex remains full of dynamic changes, it is *more ruthless*, a harsher society where there is no hesitation.

Excursion III: Bugaku

Bugaku is a traditional Japanese performance, originally performed only for the highest nobility at the imperial court. Its history is said to go as far as 12 centuries back in time. Its performance was subject to extremely stringent rules, described in manuals. Every action was performed in slow, controlled, precise and *regal* fashion. The dancers would wear expensive attire, often with masks. The performances would explore encounters between humans and divine or supernatural beings, famous battles and mythical events. In terms of content, Bugaku comprises a mixture of Shinto and of Buddhist, Chinese, Korean and even Indian and Southeast Asian influences.

The sense of spatial proportions between all participants is crucial: the distances are fixed by tradition and cannot be changed at will by the performers. Movements and actions are tight, measured and geometrically defined.

Linda Vinck's *Bugaku* seems to reflect this aesthetic. A similar rigour in design and composition, incidentally, is also inherent in other series such as *Anthiapolis*, *Kemper meets Chladni*, and the series being currently (2024) prepared at the Frans Masereel Centrum in Kasterlee. In the vein of Japanese *Bugaku*, the artist has come to incorporate a three-dimensional, performative aspect to her strict style.

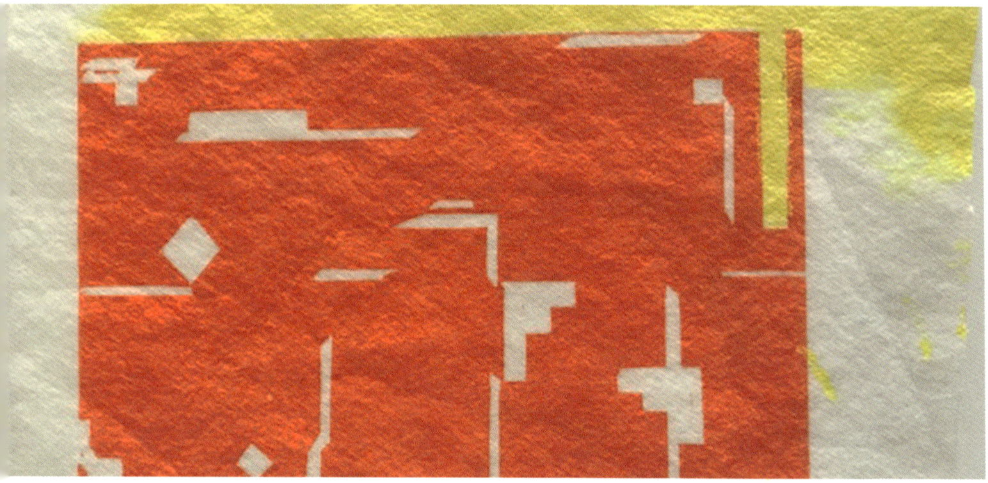

ugaku

Excursion IV: Birdsongs

In 'Birdsongs', we find a series of smaller works. For hours, the artist would listen to the twittering of various bird species. These works could be seen as scores from another world, in which certain melodic and / or rhythmic sequences are not blindly repeated, rather constantly shapeshifting and / or resonating.

These usually small works could only have been created through transmodal means: translating and resonating with sounds towards a visual composition. Other artists have also been affected by the 'art of birds', usually composers or musicians within the auditory field.

Of particular note here is Olivier Messiaen (1908–1992). Messiaen's greatest inspiration was the beauty of God's creation, especially the twittering of birds. Messiaen[18] would regularly visit nature to record birdsong, incorporating it in many of his compositions. Works the likes of *Abîme des Oiseaux* (from the *Quatuor pour la fin du temps*)[19] and *Oiseaux exotiques* speak for themselves. He even went on to score a wide array of birdsong for piano (*Catalogue d'oiseaux*). In one of his last orchestral works (*Éclairs sur l'Au-delà...*) he predominantly incorporated the sounds of Australian bird species. While the songs produced by the birds could be made into a score, Messiaen opted not to do so. His observations of birdsong have been pulled through a number of processing filters, allowing them to take on a new and more complex aesthetic form. For Messiaen, birdsong not only possessed idyllic and lovely connotations. He composed the *Abîme des Oiseaux* (Abyss of Birds), as part of his *Quatuor pour la fin du temps* (Quatuor for the End of Time). The observation of birdsong therefore served Messiaen to create compositions about terrible earthly, religious and transcendental experiences.

His birdsong-based compositions are never literal transcriptions. Even works with titles that refer directly to birds are sound poems that serve to co-create the moment, the landscape, the colours and the atmosphere.

Messiaen is an artist of a *modernist* nature. However, birdsong has also led to aesthetic resonance in very *archaic*, tribal communities. Take, for example, the Kaluli in Papua New Guinea, where instruments are limited to

18 Harry HALBREICH, *L'œuvre d'Olivier Messiaen*, Paris, Fayard, 2008; Peter HILL & Nigel SIMEONE, *Messiaen*, New Haven–London, Yale University Press, 2005; Vincent BENITEZ, *Olivier Messiaen: A Research and Information Guide*, New York–London, Routledge, 2018.

19 Anthony POPLE, *Messiaen: Quatuor pour la fin du temps*, Cambridge: Cambridge University Press, 1998; Rebecca RISHIN, *For the End of Time: The Story of the Messiaen Quartet*, Ithaca NY, Cornell University Press, 2003.

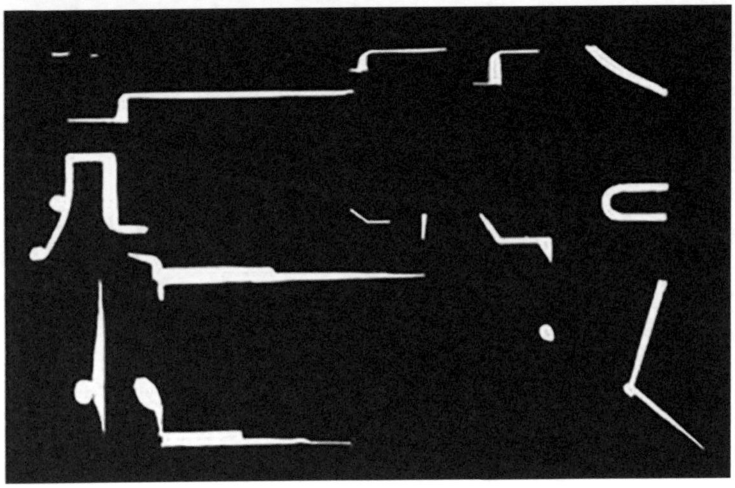

Birdsong 3b Kobalt Blue (detail)

drums and rattles, no melodic instruments in sight. Essential is the playing of moving arrangements on top of a solid rhythmic foundation. The aesthetic Kaluli canon favours densely packed, overlapping, intertwined, alternating sounds (*dulugu ganalan*, i.e. 'lifting/overlapping tone')[20]. The use of drums and rattles avoids unison or single sound, instead striving for a dense wall of sound, internally highly fluctuating and varied, which intensifies until the climax, and which has to take possession of the musician and listeners in mind as well as body (just as the vibrations of today's *techno*, *drum & bass*, which literally serve to take possession of the body).

One particular bird plays a starring role in all this: the *tibodai* (Pitohui cristatus). This one first calls *bo...bo...bo*, then *tibo...tibo...tibo*, finally *dowo dowo dowo*. The drum acts as this *bird*'s voice (the Kaluli only knew rhythm instruments). Both the drum and the metaphysical *tibodai* carry multiple meanings.

Thus, the Kaluli see their music as a projection of the rainforest, helping to deal with and interpret their heaviest emotional experiences. These musical structures – largely created through collective processes – are then exploited as a code for humankind and the world around them. The accumulation of rhythmic and tonal structures in Kaluli music serves as a metaphor for their view of the world: through these patterns, one must find their *inner* self, the 'inner reflection'[21].

It is perhaps easier to understand how birdsong would inspire the musician more than the visual artist. In the latter case, as with Linda, having a degree of *transmodal* ability is essential, being able to filter auditory input into a visual aesthetic without falling into an attempt of parity.

20 Steven FELD, *Aesthetics as iconicity of style; or, Lift-up-over-sounding: Getting into the Kaluli Groove*, in Yearbook for Traditional Music, 1988, pp. 74-113.

21 Steven FELD, *Sound as a symbolic system: the Kaluli drum, in The varieties of sensory experience*, ed. David HOWES, Toronto – London, Toronto U.P., 1991, pp. 79-99.

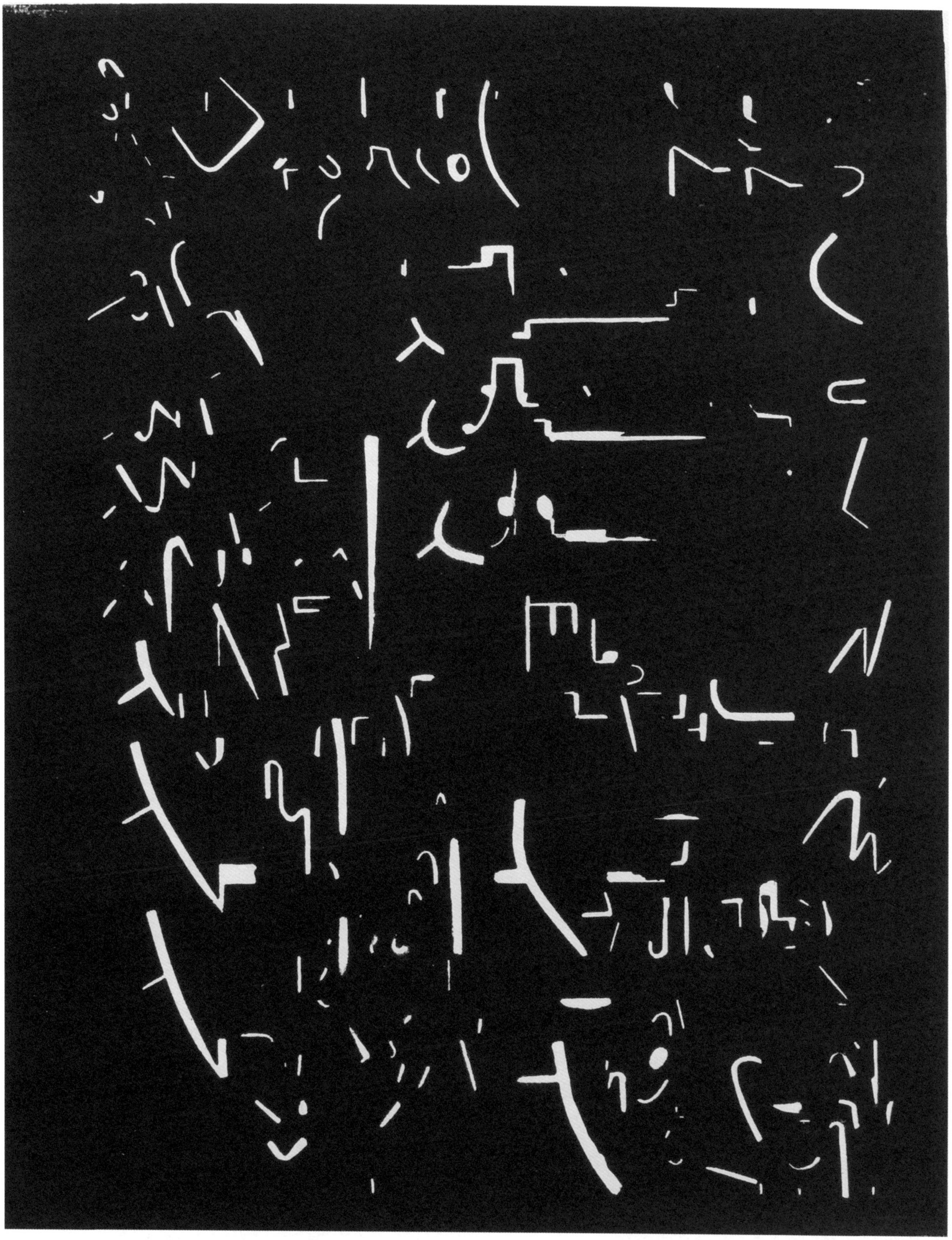

Birdsong 2, 310 × 245 mm, linocut, 2019

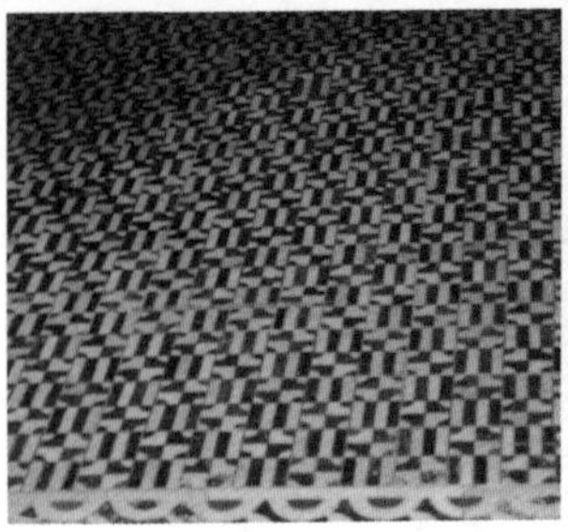

fig. 15

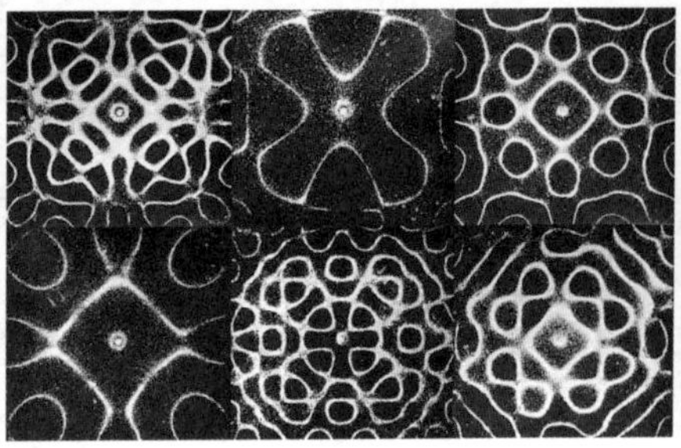

fig. 16

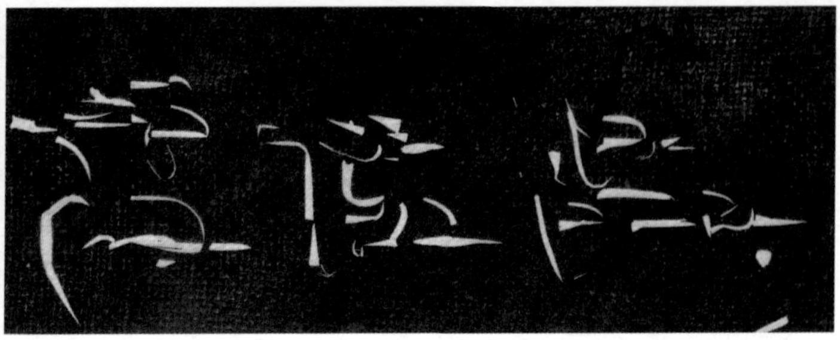

fig. 17

Variations and Resonances

Linda's larger compositions seem, superficially, to consist of repeating segments. On closer inspection, this observation is incorrect. Each sequence shows variations, shifts and changes. As compositions, they are analogous to, say, musical variations. Musical variations are themselves an ancient process: even archaic tribal cultures, however limited in their available instrument, liked variation, even if they repeated one *cantilene*, sequence or verse over and over. Ancient and Eastern music took calibrated melodic themes (*nomos* in Ancient Greece, *raga* in India, *maqam* in Islam) as a prelude to improvised elaborations with ingenious techniques of variation. In Gregorian chant, originally improvised variation must have played a significant role, with the Alleluia psalm verses, for instance, relying on the principle of variation.

A *variation*[22] is generally the one-off or repeated repetition of a musical idea in a slightly different form from the original. This may involve a theme, a character, a harmonic progression, a rhythm or metre, or a combination of these elements. A thematic variation is possible by adding or omitting notes to a melody (e.g. through embellishments), octaving or doubling with other intervals of a melody, changing notes or intervals within a melody, of rhythm or metre, of instrumentation or setting, or of accompaniment. Symmetry can belong to this[23], as well as retrograde. In a broad sense, variation is a compositional process by which a musical fact undergoes a change when repeated. In a narrower sense, variation is a musical form consisting of a theme and transformed repetitions of said theme.

Counterpoint

Counterpoint (doctrine of polyphonic writing) allows various melodic voices to develop above one another. Contrapuntal compositions emerged around 1500, such as the *ricercare* (literally translated: 'searching'). A lot of Linda Vinck's compositions are visual *ricercari*. *Ricercare* is an instrumental composition from the Renaissance and Baroque periods, wherein various motifs are tried out through *varying* imitations. The *ricercare* is considered a precursor to the *fugue*, where the pumping bass, the flight, the opposition, the lifting, and the intensifying accumulation of layers are so important. The *basso ostinato*, a pattern shaped by the bass line, carries the musical structure.

The fugue

The *fugue* ('flight') is based on the principle of equality of the different voices/lines. Also essential is the ever-varying repetition. The musical genre is an aesthetic processing of the idea of pursuit, the chasing, the flight, the imminent act of being caught.

Flight and pursuit, as in hunting (there was also a musical genre literally called *caccia*, i.e. 'hunting'[24]), are the guiding principles

22 **J. MÜLLER-BLATTAU, *Gestaltung — Umgestaltung. Studien zur Geschichte der musikalischen Variation*, 1950.**

23 **O. JANDER, *Rhythmic Symmetry in the 'Goldberg Variations'*, in *The musical quarterly*, 1991.**

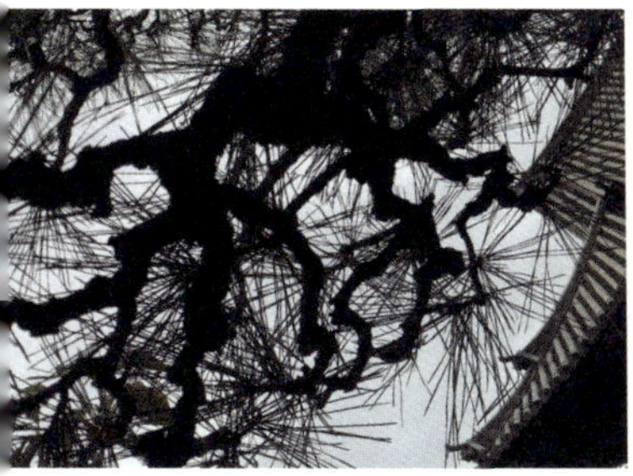

fig. 18

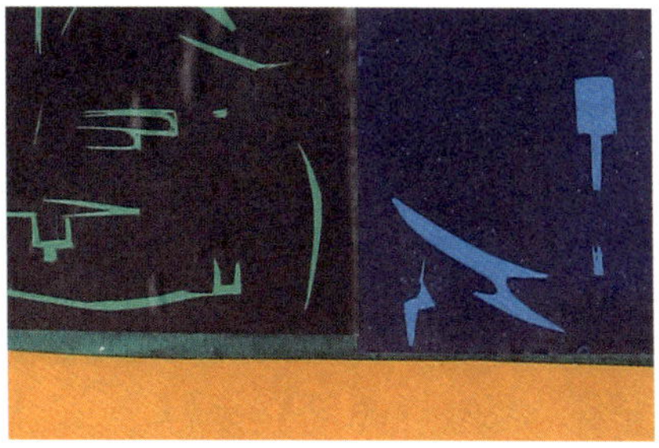

fig. 19

fig. 15 Tile floor in the Mosque of the Barber, Karouan, Tunisia
fig. 16 Chladni's plates
fig. 17 Variation, handcrafted Nepalese paper
fig. 18 Japanese tree, travel archive, Kanazawa, 2019
fig. 19 Salamansa 1a (detail)

of the composition. A subconscious aspect of emotionality – such as a vague and lingering anxiety, which may not have been expressible due to notions of social *decorum* – is ultimately expressed in an aesthetic structure, the complexity of which may be an expression of the processing and sublimation process.

Analogies between appearance dimensions in the world

While resonance often walks along the senses, it is also primarily trans-sensory in nature. It is not necessarily a *sensory* inspiration that resonates. Resonance occurs between individuals through sense perceptions, or between individuals along or across senses in a kind of heart-to-heart contact. Resonance is also possible between (an element or state in) the 'world' and one's own psyche[25]. While resonance involves letting sounds reoccur, this new sound will not be a copy of the first. We mentioned the resonance between musician and listener. In fact, resonance has traditionally been taken *literally* as an artistic, even therapeutic tool. Capturing and participating in resonance forms the basis of many therapeutic rituals, such as the possession rituals that aim at healing an individual through music, dance and trance. Such practices have long existed across a wide variety of cultures. In the past, we have studied some of them, particularly in their North African and ancient European contexts[26].

As such, they tried to make the universe more comprehensible, bringing it in unison. Considering the universe as a macrocosm, in this system, humankind was a miniature version of it, a microcosm (literally 'small world').

In essence, resonance denotes the resounding of the vibration inherent in all moods, energies, affects, pathologies. This reverberation was beneficial, laid the foundation of deep contact.

Modern science shuns such realities, but from the experiences of everyday life, we know how interpersonal sympathy 'resonates' and antipathy 'dissonates'. Resonance is the 'co-vibration' of a matter by the capture and action of a vibration from elsewhere. Now when

24 *In European 17th and 18th-century painting, there were an extensive number of representations of hunting, and still lifes of hunting spoils.*

M. SASS, *Hunting grounds for painters: The killing of animals and the artistic domination of nature*, in *Netherlands Yearbook for History of Art*, 2021; S. JABLONSKI, *Acts of violence: Rubens and the hunt*, 2004; C. GIRARD, *Rococo Massacres: Hunting in Eighteenth-Century French Painting*, 2014; S. THOMSON, *The continuity of the hunt theme in palace decoration in the eighteenth century in France*, 1981

25 Today's globalisation, which already began *in nucleo* in the 15th century but is growing exponentially due to today's media and improved mobility, will bring about a superlative resonance. Never before did people have access to such a variety of inputs. For example, the first European exhibition of indigenous art from Mexico took place at the Nassau Palace on Brussels' Coudenberg as early as 1520 – see Paul VANDENBROECK, *Amerindian art and ornamental objects in royal collections. Brussels, Mechelen, Duurstede, 1520–1530*, in *America. Bride of the sun: 500 years Latin America and the Low Countries*, exhib. cat., Antwerp, KMSKA, 1992, pp. 99-120.

26 Paul VANDENBROECK, *De kleuren van de geest. Dans en trance in Afro-Europese tradities*, Ghent, Snoeck-Ducaju, 1997.

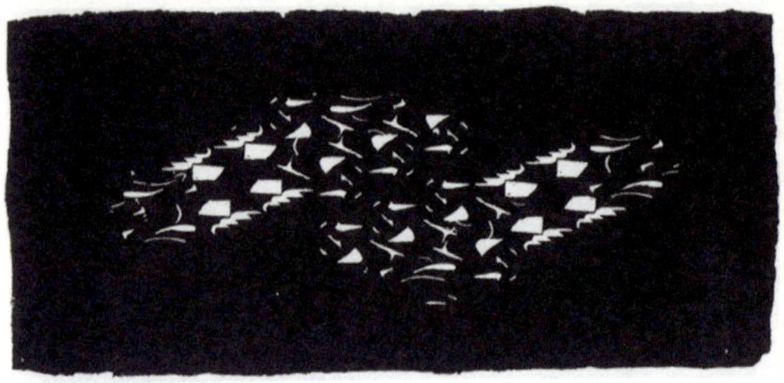

fig. 20

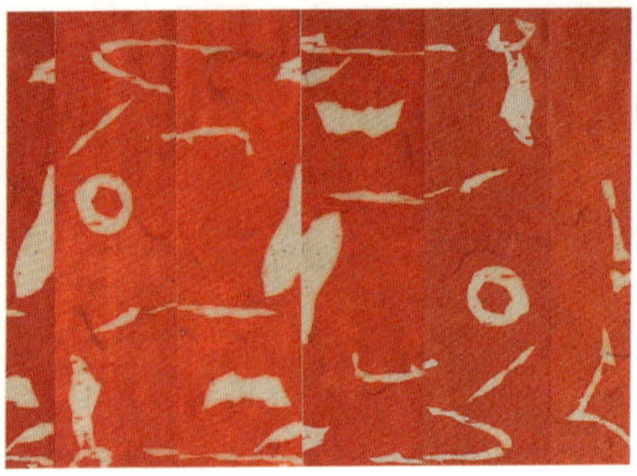

fig. 21

fig. 20 **Oceano — Felt, 1550 × 720 mm, felt on felt 2006**

fig. 21 **Transformation (detail)**

a celestial body vibrates like a string, other celestial bodies must co-resonate: the 'harmony of the spheres'... A similar resonance occurs between individuals.

Resonance is not the same as identification, i.e. seeing oneself in others. Resonance is an answer that co-sounds, that contains echoes of the 'question' but possesses unmistakable uniqueness.

While hearing provides the 'model' of resonance, the latter extends across other sensory and aesthetic fields. There is rhythmic, spatial-kinetic, colouristic and visual resonance. Aesthetic works in one culture resonate invariably through other creations.

Conclusion

The artist is not a machine without agency archiving 'the world'. Unconscious affinities with observed phenomena must be present in order to choose – albeit unconsciously – what one will choose to process, by which we mean to give partly external, partly internal events an unchangeable aesthetic form, work that is perhaps not unrelated to the coming to terms with oneself throughout life. What's more, work can also be taken literally, as Linda Vinck's creations progress through a process of prolonged dedication. Her techniques are also layered, complex, requiring relentless concentration as well as effort.

I end this review of Linda's work with a personal anecdote. In 2002, I was living in a state of absolute crisis. One day, an acquaintance invited me to join her that evening to visit an artist friend of hers in Mortsel. Once there, both ladies became embroiled in an animated conversation. However, I heard none of it. Some of Linda's larger works stood against the wall. I was absorbed in it in the most profound way. The deep tone backgrounds, the seemingly endless rhythms and movements in the patterns, while perhaps repetitive to a superficial observer (but never are), transported me to vast spaces, just as one's heart can rejoice by observing the swooping flight of a flock of birds, guided by an unknowable coherence...

Lost for words, I surmised that these joyful works had been created even in times of mourning and suspense. And yet, Linda Vinck's works always have an uplifting power, without telling one known story or depicting anything that we know. That evening, a door within my cramped mind began to open a crack. As such, that first encounter with Linda Vinck's work became an unforgettable moment for me.

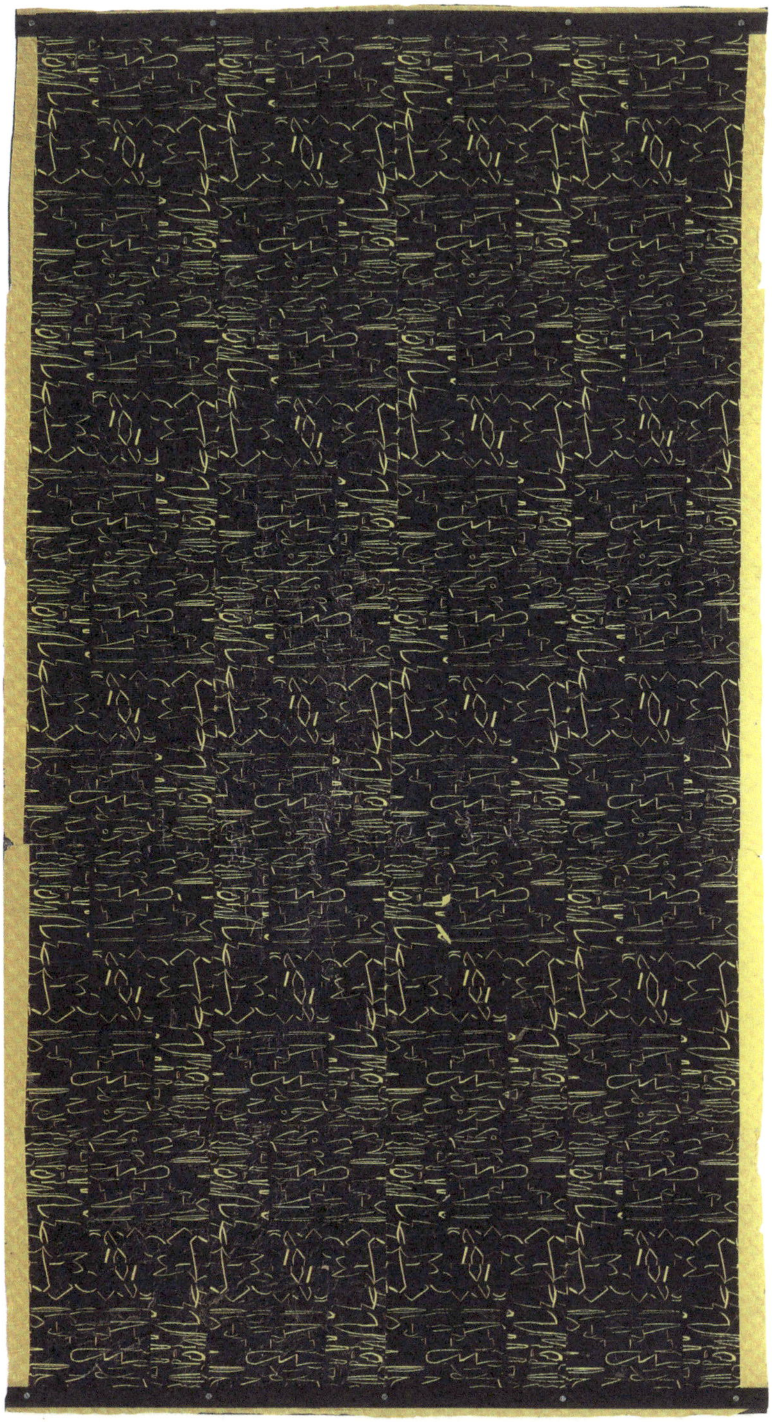

Patterns of Paradise 4, 2350 × 1300 mm, 1992

"Het lijkt alsof het niets is. Enkele draaiingen, een rechte lijn, een punt. Hoe is het mogelijk dat het me zoveel tijd kost om hen bijeen te brengen tot ze op hun juiste plaats staan? Dáár en nergens anders?

Ik moet zorgen dat hun ruimte klopt, dat ze zich goed verstaan onder mekaar."

Paul VANDENBROECK

Illuminare Research Centre, KULeuven
Salon Radical, Kortrijk

Men ontmoet het, maar niemand ziet zijn gelaat.
Men volgt het, maar niemand ziet zijn rug.

— Laozi

Voorspellende herinneringen

DE LIJDENDE TREIN.

"Herinneringen uit de kinderkamer, die uitkeek op de spoorwegberm waar enkel goederentreinen langskwamen. Die reden ook 's nachts en er moet een heuveltje geweest zijn ter hoogte van ons huis, want de trein deed daar heel raar, alsof hij ergens niet over geraakte en meer moeite moest doen. Het klonk in mijn oren als ritmische muziek die even stopte, herhaaldelijk terug probeerde, en ineens: de opluchting: volle gas vooruit. Het waren toen nog stoomtreinen: sissend en schokkend, *TSJe, TSJe, tsj, tsj, tsj Tttsjssss TSJOUKK tsjoeéééék, Dèdède Eièèèèèè*, alsof hij bergaf ging en dan opnieuw proberen het bergje op te geraken, Jeeej weg is hij, *een soort vrolijke overwinning van het obstakel*, ik zal wel niet geapplaudisseerd hebben, maar dat gevoel was er wel." [1]

ACHTERUIT EN TOCH VOORUIT.

"Tijdens de dag waren het de locomotiefwielen die ik heel fascinerend vond, drie in aantal en iets dat ze verder deed rijden, aantrekken. Iets weg-en-weer maar dan toch vooruit, zoals de processie van Echternach".

LANGZAME VORMING VAN SCHOONHEID.

"Met verbazing en vooral grote bewondering uren zitten kijken naar hoe er op de ramen in de kinderkamer traag maar zeker en in onwaarschijnlijk mooie patronen sneeuwkristallen op de ruiten getekend werden, en de koude ze deed groeien, telkens verder".

1 Onlangs vroeg ik de kunstenares naar herinneringen uit haar vroege kindertijd. Ik heb ze hier getrouw weergegeven.

ONSTUITBARE VOORTGANG IN ENERGETISCHE VERSCHEIDENHEID.

"Fanfare: in die tijd waren er bij veel feestelijke gelegenheden fanfares. Dat had een diepe impact op mij. Dat ontroerde mij als kind zozeer dat ik met tranen in de ogen toekeek. Het stampen van de botten op de kasseien. De trommels, de trompetten! Ik herinner me niet of er toen al majorettes waren. Ik zal ze niet belangrijk gevonden hebben, want ze kwamen niet *in the picture*. Het was *het ritmische vooruitgaan* op maat van de trommels ."[2]

HET LATEN TOT STAND KOMEN VAN PATRONEN.

"Spelletje: wij gooiden nageltjes op het zitvlak van houten stoelen, en bewogen eronder met een magneet om *alles in beweging te brengen*..."

PATRONEN, VERANDEREND VAN VORM EN KLEUR.

"Een kaleidoscoop, een kartonnen kokertje met geslepen glas. Hoe je iets in de omgeving kon *verdubbelen, combineren* en hoe je er, naargelang waarop je richtte, *schitterende patronen mee kon toveren*. Dat heb ik hier in mijn atelier nog steeds: het *regenbooguur*. De kristallen luchter aan het plafond waar de late namiddagzon op schijnt, waardoor we overal op de muren, op voorwerpen, heel ruimtelijk dus, regenboogvlakjes te zien krijgen."

2 "Ik zag ooit een video van Francis Alÿs, opgenomen in Londen, die evenveel impact op me had als de fanfares vroeger. In die video zit ALLES: de vierkante formatie van de marcherende guards. Het geluid van hun laarzen op de kasseien ... het doelgerichte en groeiende aantal. Ik gebruikte dit werk als hebbende alles waarmee ik als kunstenaar bezig ben in een lezing in Japan." (LV)

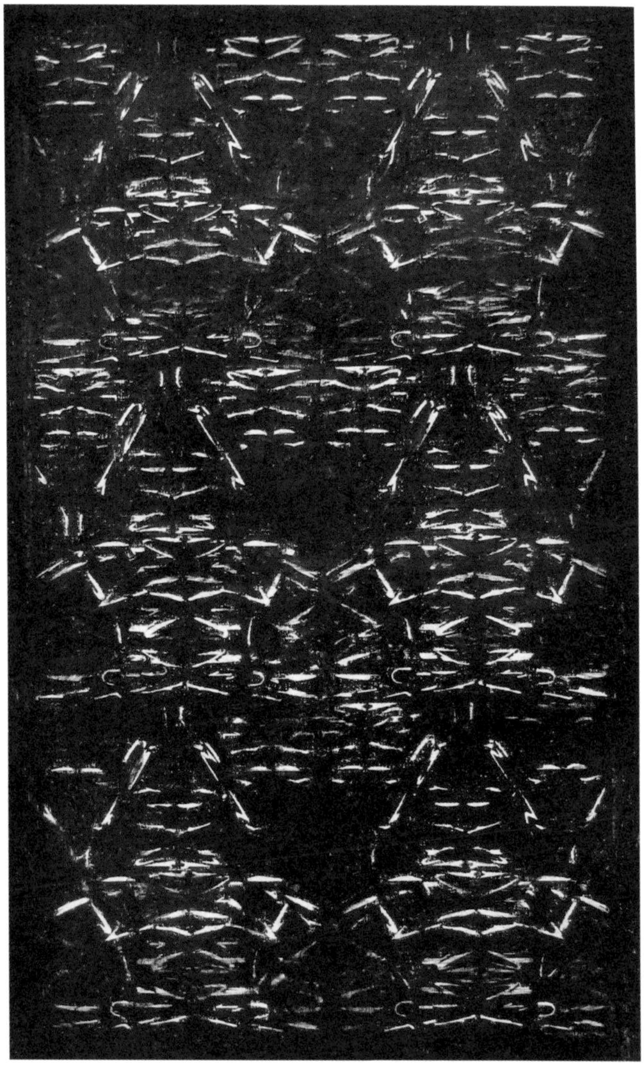

Correntes 1, 570 × 920 mm, linocut, handprinted/painted on canvas, 2000

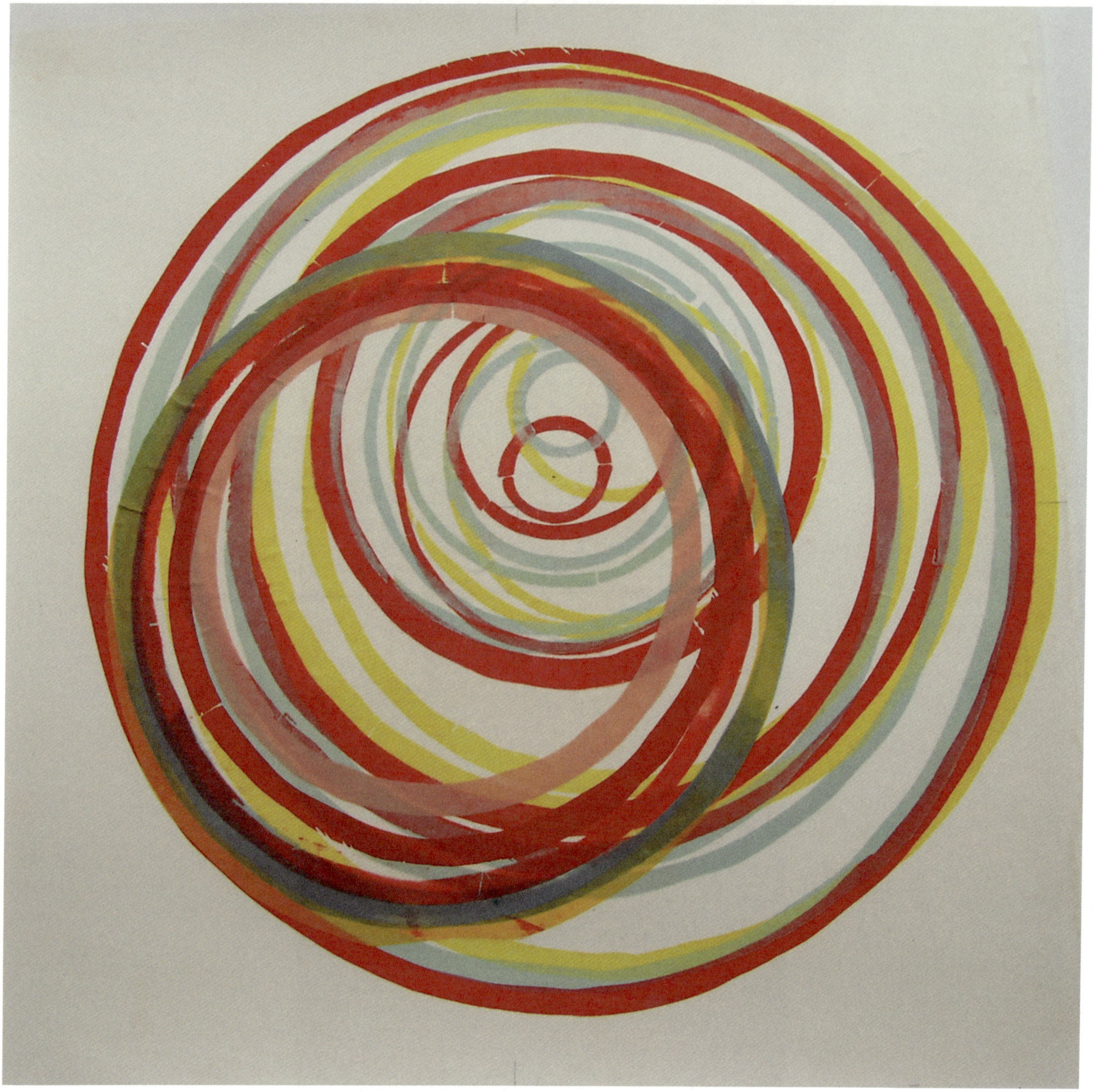

 Concentric Circles, 380 × 380 mm, woodcut printed on Gampi paper, 2009

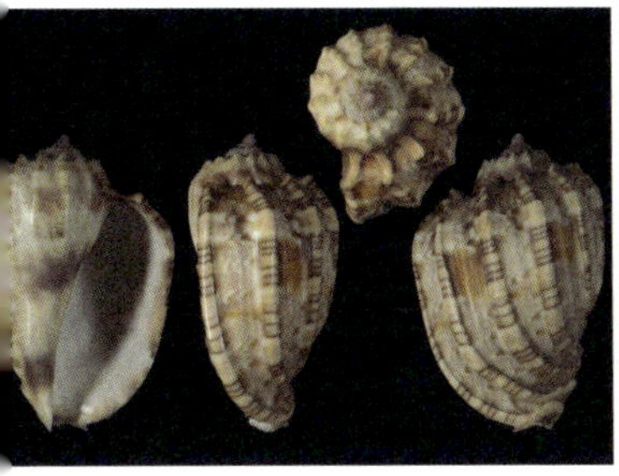

fig. 1

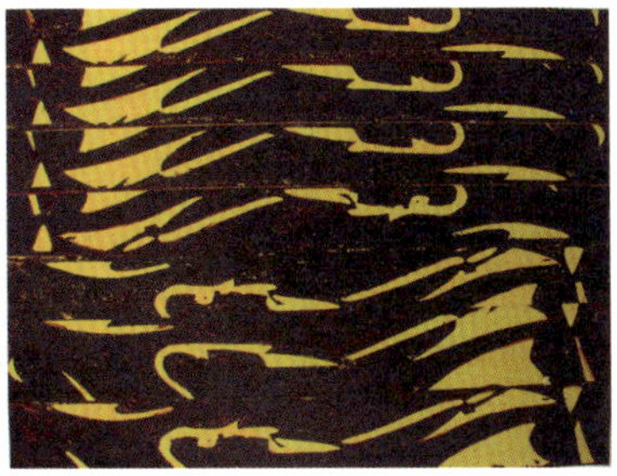

fig. 2

fig. 1 **Harpa Doris, sea snails**
fig. 2 **Kebra Kanela, 400 × 300 mm, linocut on Zerkall paper, 2004**

[Antescriptum]

Linda Vincks werk is volledig abstract. Nergens is er één element dat herkenbaar is, een rechtstreeks aanknopingspunt biedt. Oppervlakkig beschouwd vult de kunstenares haar veld met motiefgroepen. Toch is het procédé geen gevolg van een *horror vacui*, zelfs niet wanneer heel het veld reeds gevuld is. Sommige werken laten overigens ruimte voor *lege* gebieden.

Titels

De namen van Linda's werken zijn een verwijzing naar een plaats, een ervaring, een waarneming. Ze zijn, zo men wil, een kapstok voor de kunstenares geweest.

Soms verkreeg een reeks een naam van een dier (*Harpa Doris*, een soort zeeslak die men o.a. aan de Kaapverdische Eilanden vindt en waarvan het huisje eindeloos gevarieerde patronen vertoont) of van een plaats op de Kaapverdische Eilanden, zoals *Kebra Kanela* (een strand op het eiland Santiago, waarvan de naam in het lokale Creools "Breek je been" betekent) of *Salamansa* (een strand op het eiland São Vicente).

Twee stijlen

Linda Vincks oeuvre volgt een dubbel pad: enerzijds zijn er de *vrije* composities met niet-geometrische vormen, anderzijds de meer *strakke* werken met geometrische bestanddelen. Absoluut is deze scheiding niet: ook in de vrije stijl kunnen geometrische vormen figureren, en omgekeerd.

Tot de vrije stijl kunnen gerekend worden: de vroege lino's en latere droge-naald-etsen (1983–2004); *Zonder titel* (1985–1991), *Zonder titel* (1988), *Zonder titel* (1991), *Anthiagrammes* (1994), *Correntes* (2000–2001), *Towards the Ocean* (2001), *Kebra Kanela* (2004), *Salamansa* (2004), *Harpa Doris* (2006) en *Transformation* (2007).

Voorbeelden van de strakkere, geometrische stijl: *Anthiapolis* (1996), *Kemper meets Chladni* (1998), *Genetic Process* (2004–2024) en *Bugaku* (2021).

Uit 2008–2013 stammen enkele gedrukte reeksen die aan geen van beide voornoemde opties beantwoorden: *Concentric Circles* (2008), *Circles* (2008–2009), *Look and listen* (2010), *Lichtpuntjes* (2010), *Patterns* (2010), *Reminiscence* (2010), *Maan beschijnt de nacht* (2010), *De inslag* (2010), *Return* (2010), *Locomotion* (2012) en *Interactions* (2012–2013).

In de periode 1986–1993 ontstonden ook opmerkelijke abstracte schilderijen, die mij in hun kleur en vormgeving aan Zuid-Afrika doen denken.

Polymorf

Technisch is Vincks oeuvre polymorf: linosnedes of lino-assemblages op papier (o.a. Zerkall, Chinees rijstpapier, diverse Japanse papiersoorten, handgeschept Nepali-papier, gelaagd papier), op vlieseline of op canvas, viltdruk op vilt, droge-naald-etsen, houtsnede op Gampipapier of op canvas, houtsnede in combinatie met zeefdruk, schilderijen (acryl op canvas of gelaagd papier) en recent ook sculpturen.

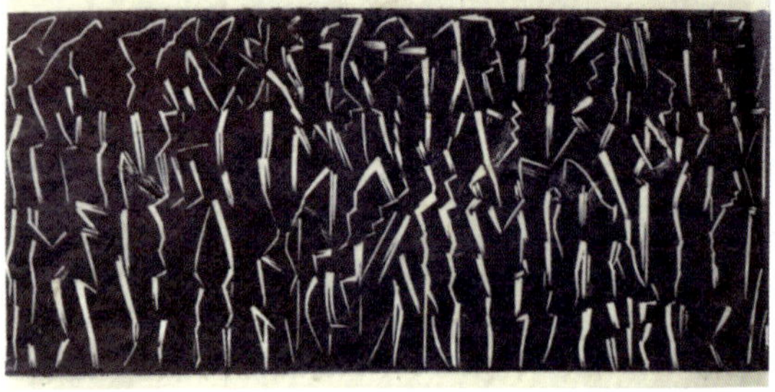

fig. 3

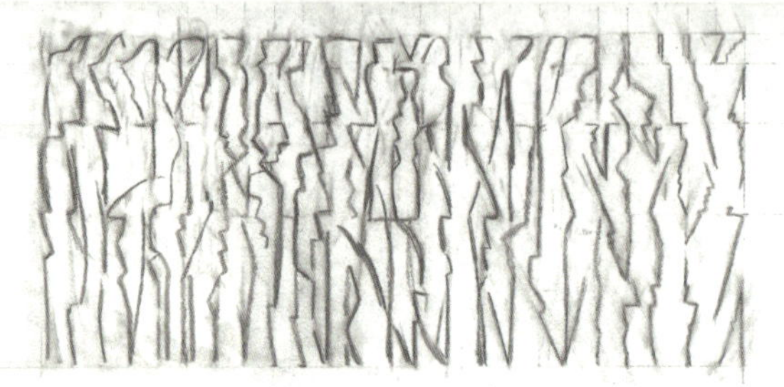

fig. 4

fig. 3 Module for Meditation on Peace
fig. 4 Drawing of modules for Meditation on Peace

Wezenlijk is ook de tactiele dimensie: zowel de voornoemde reeks schilderijen uit 1986–1993 als talloze lino's zijn uitgevoerd op een drager die bijvoorbeeld bestaat uit diverse, op mekaar gelijmde vellen papier (vaak Japanse papiervariëteiten, soms door de kunstenares handgeschept papier). De randen van deze dragers zijn doorgaans rafelig of niet strak afgelijnd. Het oppervlak van de grotere werken (of soms ook van de schilderijen uit de periode 1986–1993) is – en met scherend licht wordt dit overduidelijk – een geaccidenteerd landschap, zoals Hercules Seghers ze etste. De soms licht golvende en 'weifelende' randen van deze collages – want dat zijn ze in hun beginstadia – maken dat zulke werken dicht bij weefsels staan die op traditionele houten weefgetouwen zijn vervaardigd.

Organische Abstracties

De werken van Linda Vinck, hoe radicaal abstract ook, hebben hun wortels in de zintuiglijke en metazintuiglijke waarneming. Steeds was de kunstenares gefascineerd door de fysieke wereld: de geluiden van de zee, het zingen van de vogels, het aanrollen van de golven, de bewegingen van een school vissen of andere zeewezens, de ritmes van natuurverschijnselen. En aangezien het *ik* ook tot de wereld behoort, ging haar aandacht evenzeer uit naar onophoudelijke gewaarwordingen in het *zelf*: adem, hartslag, ritmes. Geen *beelden* maar patronen en energieën die het leven tekenen, er onlosmakelijk eigen aan zijn.

Die energieën worden meestal niet getekend of geschilderd, maar krijgen gestalte doorheen een lang en moeizaam proces: een groot deel van Vincks werk is gebaseerd op de linosnede. Dit is een techniek die een summum van concentratie vereist. Het is ook geen hedendaagse techniek.

Een techniek als etsen is relatief vergevingsgezind: met de etsnaald tekent men in de waslaag op de koperplaat. Als de kunstenaar zich vergist, kan een bijkomend laagje was de fout wegwerken. De technieken die Linda Vinck beoefent, zoals droge naald en linosnede, bewerken rechtstreeks een hard en niet-corrigeerbaar materiaal. Dat vereist een vaste hand en een soepele geest. De burijn, die in de koperplaat een versmallende of verbredende lijn snijdt, mag geen fractie van een seconde aarzelen, of de lijn zal de aarzeling onthullen. En terwijl een koperplaat nog vlak en stabiel is, is linoleum plooibaar en instabiel. Zelfs bij meesters als Frans Masereel zie je soms de uitschieters waarvan de kunstenaar nog het beste tracht te maken. Een uiterst soepele en vastberaden hand is eigen aan het werk van Linda Vinck.

Haar grotere werken zijn tevens collages volgens wisselende principes. Meerdere modules worden als basis gebruikt. Een module kan verdeeld of bijgeknipt worden. Elke afdruk van een linomodule kan verschillen, afwijkingen en kleurvariaties vertonen. In een rustig, als het ware meditatief proces wordt het geheel samengesteld, maar vóór het componeren van het geheel, is er de intensieve arbeid om een module tot stand te laten komen.

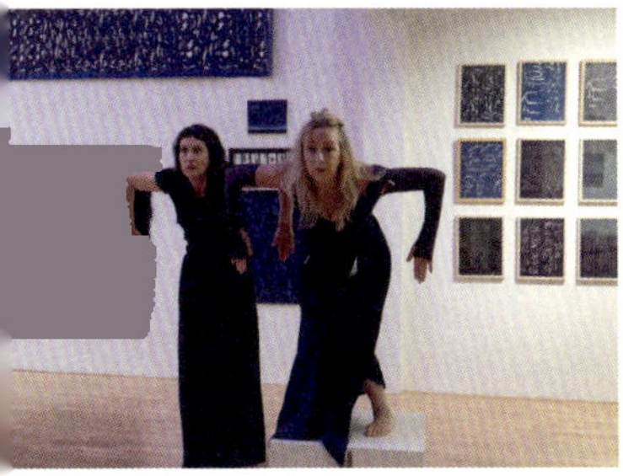

g. 5

fig. 5 **Pé Vermeersch and Mira Walschot, dance performance for the exhibition *Blauw — Teken van de nacht* (Blue — Sign of the Night): with a collection of Tunisian textiles from Paul Vandenbroeck, paintings by Koen Broucke, linographs by Linda Vinck and drawings by Pé Vermeersch, November 2023**

In het werk van Linda Vinck is er bezwaarlijk sprake van hiërarchie: er is meer een samenwerken, soms speels, van een veelheid van deelnemers doorheen de ruimte. Hier is er een analogie met het danswerk van Pé Vermeersch[3]: tot het kleinste element van het lichaam kan gemobiliseerd worden, de adem kan gestuwd worden door de kleinste handeling en kan daaraan een wezenlijke *volheid* verlenen. Maar ook de open ruimte, de stilte, het afwachten, de roerloosheid kunnen essentieel zijn.

Heen en Weer: van vormgeving naar originaire psychocorporele processen, en omgekeerd

De esthetische basale vormen – een gebroken, zwenkende, gebogen lijn, om maar slechts enkele van de duizenden mogelijkheden te vermelden – en hun composities komen niet uit het niets. Ze staan in verband met de primordiale bewegingen of scheppingen op de grens tussen lichaamsmaterie en 'psyche' *vormen*. Deze zijn in genen dele decoratief maar cruciaal in de ontwikkeling van de psychische activiteit en de esthetische schepping. De vorm is nooit louter vorm.

Men zou kunnen stellen dat de creatie van het kunstwerk een lange weg bevat: het ontstaat uit onbewuste pulsies, loopt door een lichaamsgebonden arbeidsproces, en wordt een autonoom eindproduct, dat – in het geval van de beeldende kunsten – niet meer lichaamsgebonden is en bovendien een zeer hoge status kan bereiken als belangrijke emanatie van een cultuur. In een kunstwerk huist een combinatie die tegelijk *basic* en geabstraheerd is. *Het is verwant aan en gegroeid uit de meest ontoegankelijke psychocorporele pulsies en is er tegelijk lichtjaren van verwijderd*.

Elke esthetische vorm, ook zonder enige herkenbare verwijzing naar de wereld, is als het ware een manifestatie van één der originaire psychocorporele processen of gebeurtenissen. Ze komen niet voort, althans niet rechtstreeks, uit de 'wereld', maar zullen een alfabet vormen 'om de wereld te lezen'. Ze zijn ook transmodaal: de kunstenaar heeft hen de oversprong naar een zintuiglijk waarneembare schepping doen maken.

De affectgeladenheid van de esthetische vorm: geen derivaat, maar een bron

Pictogrammen worden vormelijke betekenaars genoemd[4]. Het gaat hier om voelbare of psychisch-tastbare beelden van iets wat gebeurt, geen zichtbare, fantasmatische beelden. Indien men ze in taal zou moeten uitdrukken, zouden ze slechts een werkwoord of een onderwerp-en-werkwoord beslaan. Dit onderwerp

3 Pé Vermeersch is danseres/choreografe van haar gezelschap Radical HeArts. Ze werkte met Linda Vinck samen voor *Ademrood* (Rouge Respirant/Red Oxygen), Brussel, 2020, en voor *Blauw — Teken van de Nacht* (Blue — Sign of the Night), 2023.

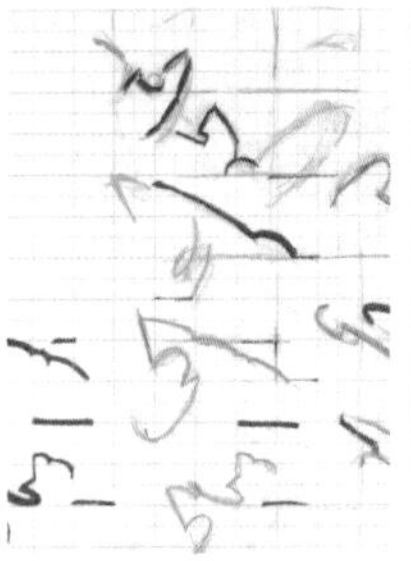

fig. 6

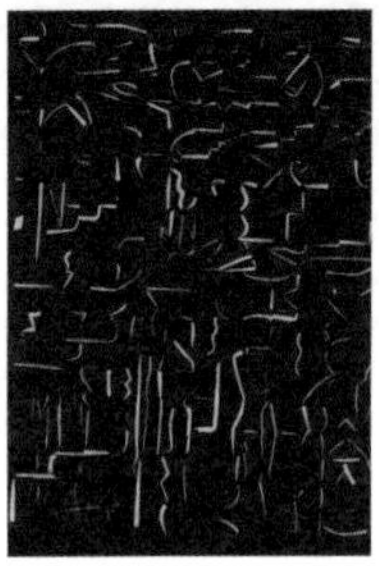

fig. 7

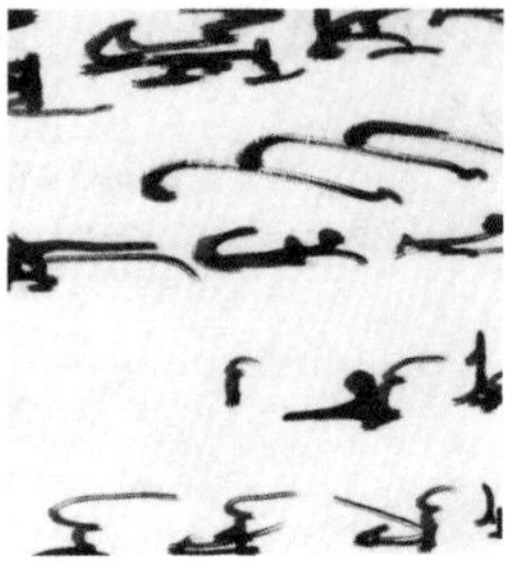

fig. 8

fig. 6 Preparatory work
fig. 7 From Matrix series
fig. 8 Working rhythms

is geen persoon maar een vorm of een stuk van een lichaam of een ruimte. Er is geen verhaal, maar slechts een omvorming van een verschijning of een eigenschap, omvorming die in of buiten het eigen lichaam plaatsvindt. Het gaat om – bijvoorbeeld – samentrekking, golving, ademing, werveling, val, leeglopen, weggerukt worden, doorboring, ontploffing, verbrokkeling, verscheuring. Er zijn ook bewerkingen als in- of boven-elkaar-geplaatst-worden, krullen of afbuigen, iets dat iets anders zoekt, afsnijding, verdubbeling, richting-verandering, sporen nalaten, opening / sluiting, samenvallen, verwijdering.

Een pictogram is een beeld van het 'lichamelijke ding', van de 'complementaire object-zone' of van de *ontmoetingszone*, een primair beeld waardoor de psyche haar *ontmoetingen met de ander* verwerkt en aan elke ontmoetingservaring tussen zichzelf en de wereld vorm verleent.

Lopen op het scherp van het mes

Sommige kunsthistorici wijzen op overeenkomsten tussen het werk van Linda Vinck en Henri Michaux (1899–1984) en de *informele kunst*. Ten onrechte, want beiden zijn ten gronde verschillend. De zogenaamde informele kunst ontstond veelal uit een gewijzigde staat van bewustzijn (iemand als Michaux gebruikte *mezcal* om het scheppingsproces te activeren). Het resultaat was doorgaans een *horror vacui*, een oppervlakte gevuld met mekaar verdringende tekens. Dit geldt eveneens voor Jackson Pollock (1912–1956) *cum suis*, voor kunstenaars die een sprong maakten van een bestaan in de rurale marge naar het moderne kunstenaarschap, zoals Sa'id Ouarzaz of Mohamed Tabal[5] in Marokko, of voor sommige Australische *Aboriginal* kunstenaars in gelijkaardige omstandigheden[6]. Zij komen niet los van de dichotomie: orde of chaos.

De informele kunst is niet gebaseerd op een beheerst overleg. Hiermee wil ik absoluut niet zeggen dat kunst op rationele beheersing gestoeld is of moet zijn. Maar evenmin op de afwezigheid van beheersing.

Het oeuvre van Linda Vinck ontsnapt aan die dichotomie. Het laat zich niets gelegen aan de principes van de *orde* (middelpunt / periferie, assen / spiegeling / symmetrie, omkadering) maar verliest zich evenmin in de pseudovrijheid van de fallocentrische chaos.

Vergelijkend met Noord-Afrikaanse weefsels: traditioneel is er geen boord (behalve in stedelijke tapijten), soms een middenas (geheel of gedeeltelijk), maar steeds is er ruimte waarmee men alle kanten uit kan en waar men met eventueel één element kan doen wat men nodig vindt, om de compositie te doen slagen.

Iets analoogs kan plaats vinden in de dans: voor een danseres / choreografe als

4 Didier ANZIEU, *Le moi-peau*, Paris, Bordas, 1985 & 1995; van dezelfde auteur, zie ook: id., *Le moi-peau*, in *Nouvelle revue de psychanalyse*, 1974, pp. 195-208; id., *La peau: du plaisir à la pensée*, in *L'attachement*, ed. id. e.a., Genève, Delachaux & Nestlé, 1974.

5 Paul VANDENBROECK, *De kleuren van de geest. Dans en trance in Afro-Europese tradities*, Gent, Snoeck-Ducaju, 1997, *met vele illustraties van het werk van bv. Ouarzaz en Tabal (298 blz., 200 ill.).*

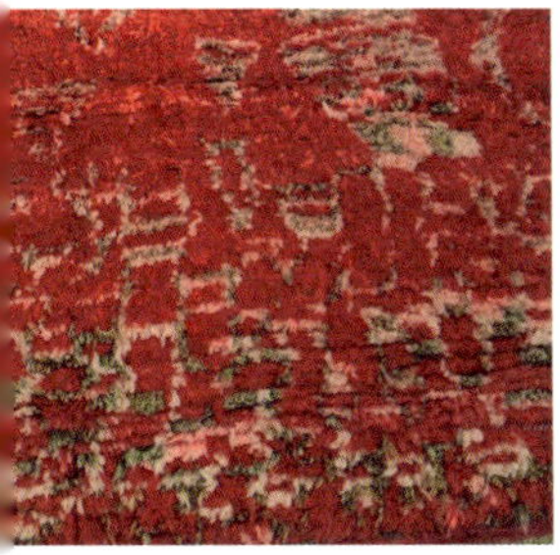

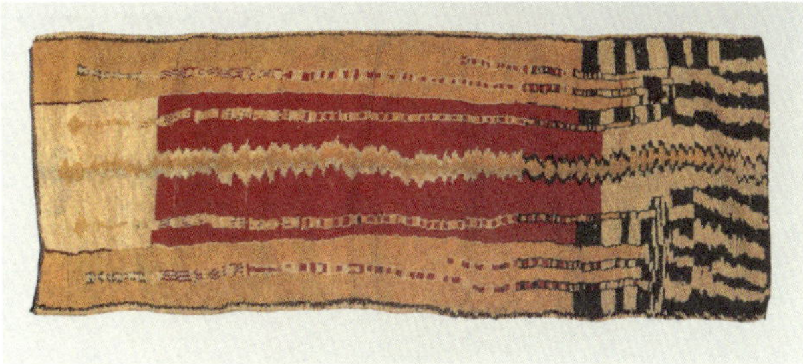

fig. 9 fig. 10

fig. 9 Anonymous weaver, ca. 1970. Knotted carpet (detail). Haouz of Marrakech, Morocco.

fig. 10 Knotted carpet. Marrakech, Morocco, ca. 1950-60 – from '*Berber women and their art / AZETTA*', Paul Vandenbroeck, Ludion, 2000

Pé Vermeersch, kunnen kleine bewegingen, variërend, vertragend, versnellend, essentieel zijn in een performance. Maar nooit in het wilde weg, en dat wil zeggen: noch bewust overdacht, noch onnadenkend voortgebracht.

In het werk van Linda Vinck vereist deze aanpak des te meer mentale en fysieke kracht, aangezien haar zo vaak gebruikt medium, de linosnede, een zeer hardnekkige materie is. Het insnijden van soepele, subtiele vormen in het taaie materiaal vereist een blijvend beheerste energie. Het afwegen van hun onderlinge plaatsing vereist een gevoelsgeladen energie, die nooit mag verzwakken, of de elementen "verstaan zich niet goed onder mekaar", zoals de kunstenares het verwoordt.

Het wordingsproces van Linda Vincks grotere werken duurt lang: door de moeilijkheidsgraad van het medium, door het geduldige samenstellen van het geheel (vaak een vorm van 'collage'), door de aandacht, gewijd aan de juiste kleurdiepte. In die zin is er een analogie met de weefkunst, tenminste met de 'vrije' vormen ervan, zoals in Iran (de 'gabbeh') of Marokko. Een tapijt weven en knopen volgens de eigen inspiratie is een moeizame en langdurige arbeid; bovendien mag de 'ingeving' niet wegebben, of het werk verliest zijn esthetische kracht.

Zowel in haar oeuvre als in genoemde textiele kunst moeten grote risico's zonder falen genomen worden. Inspiratie moet over een lange en inspannende periode aanhouden, op straffe van een saai resultaat. Deze psychocorporele staat kan onmogelijk het resultaat van een bewuste wilsact zijn, maar evenmin is ze gratuit. Het is maar in een tussen-in-staat, dat dit langdurig koorddansen of lopen op het scherp van het mes haalbaar is. En dit gaat samen met een andere paradox: spontaan scheppen is evenmin kosteloos.

Eerder hadden we het nog over een andere paradox: in een kunstwerk huist een combinatie die tegelijk *basic* en geabstraheerd is. In deze paradox ligt deels de (on)toegankelijkheid en lichamelijkheid waarin het wortelt. Het is verworteld in en het is gegroeid uit de meest ontoegankelijke psychocorporele pulsies en het staat er lichtjaren van verwijderd.

Deel hebben aan de *Weg*

Diepere reflecties over het voornoemde 'noch bewust, noch onbewust' vinden we terug in het Taoïsme.

Het besef van de noodzaak van voornoemde paradoxen is niet nieuw, tenminste niet in de Oosterse tradities. Chinese en Japanse kunstenaars, dichters en geleerden hebben dit inzicht al een millennium geleden trachten te formuleren. Vooral vanuit de ervaring van de *Tao* en vanuit de praktijk van de Zen (de Chinese *Ch'an*).

Over de *Tao* [= de Weg] kan niet gesproken worden. Zoals God een hyperessentie is

6 Judith RYAN & Geoffrey BARDON, *Mythscapes. Aboriginal art of the desert from the National Gallery of Victoria*, Victoria, National Gallery of Victoria, 1989; Judith RYAN & Kim AKERMAN, *Images of power. Aboriginal art of the Kimberley*, Victoria, National Gallery of Victoria, s.d.

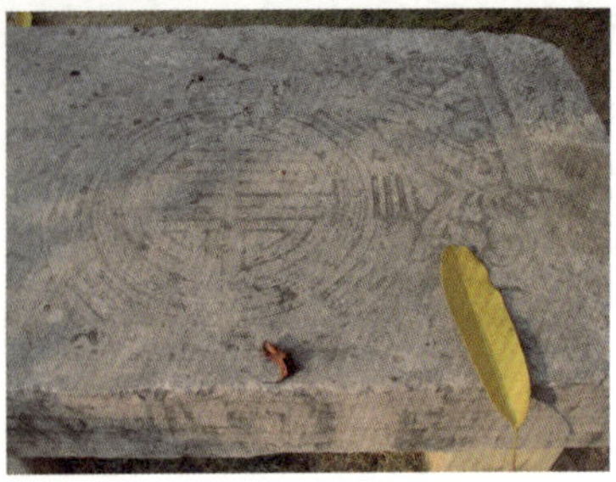

fig. 11

fig. 11 **Stone with symbols of I Tching, Book of Change**

waarvoor alle menselijke cognitieve categorieën ontoereikend zijn, zo is "de Weg waarover verteld kan worden niet de Weg en de naam ervan die genoemd kan worden is niet de echte naam" (*Tao te ching*[7]). De Weg is een dynamisch veld, waarin alles wordt/verwordt volgens ontelbare ritmes. Wijsheid en ook scheppingskracht kunnen pas ten volle ontwikkelen wanneer men als het ware één wordt met de bewegingen van de Weg, uitdeinend en verdichtend, komende en gaande.

Hsun Tsu-yung, in zijn boek *De overzetboot der schilderkunst*: "In de opbouw van het schilderij moet een spirituele adem komen en gaan zonder gehinderd te worden."[8]

Voor Su Tung-p'o is de ware kunstenaar niet zozeer bekommerd om de letterlijke gelijkenis der vormen, maar is hij gericht op het oproepen van het *innerlijke ritme* dat daarin pulseert, en overgedragen wordt op de toeschouwer[9]. [Dit is bij uitstek van toepassing op Vincks composities, ontstaan na langdurige studie van bepaalde natuurfenomenen en samenlevingen van organismen: *Towards the Ocean*, *Anthiagrammes*, *Anthiapolis* of *Birdsongs*].

"Het lijkt alsof het niets is..." (LV). Door zich te ontdoen van egogebonden driften worden de obstructies, die beletten deel te hebben aan de Weg[10], opgeruimd. Door zich daarvan te ontdoen lijkt het, alsof men niets doet. Het is geen passiviteit, maar eenklank met de stromende energieën van de Weg. Het 'niet-doen' is niet hetzelfde als passiviteit, fatalisme, of luiheid. Het geschiedt in een voorbereid lichaam, en vanuit die voorbereiding gebeurt 'het'.

Ching Hao (10e eeuw): "*Chi* (adem, bezieling) ontstaat wanneer de geest/het verstand van de kunstenaar *niet tussenbeide komt* in de beweging van het penseel dat als het ware uit zichzelf het schilderij schept, zonder angst."[11]

"Wanneer de intuïtie [van de kunstenaar] één wordt met de ondoorgrondelijke werkelijkheid en de penseelvoering in de buurt komt van de diepten van het onbewuste... zal zijn schepping grenzeloos zijn... Zijn gedachteloze gedachte doordringt de punt van zijn penseel..."

Deze staat is ten volle paradoxaal: zonder-denken maar hoog-lucide in het hier-en-nu, zonder-doen maar uiterst doelgericht. Dit geldt trouwens ook voor de performatieve kunsten, op ogenblikken dat het sublieme bereikt wordt. De kunstenaar bereikt dan een staat van zijns-transparantie, analoog aan wat er gebeurt bij helderziendheid en trance. "Het is in de lege

7 Paul VANDENBROECK, *The leap and paradoxical space of intuitive creation and imagination in religious and mystical tradition*, in *INTUITION*, exh. cat., Venice, Fondazione Musei Civici di Venezia & The Axel & May Vervoordt Foundation, Venice, Palazzo Fortuny, 2017, pp. 86-100.

8 Chang CHUNG-YUAN, *Creativity and Taoism: a study of Chinese philosophy, art, and poetry*, New York, Harper, 1970, p. 212.

9 CHUNG-YUAN, 1970, p. 210.

10 Dat schijnbare nietsdoen (wu wei) wordt geïllustreerd door het beeld van de steen boven het wateroppervlak: om terecht te komen op de plaats op de bodem waar hij wil/moet zijn, volstaat het, zich op de juiste plaats te laten vallen. Zonder enige moeite komt hij terecht.

11 CHUNG-YUAN, 1970, p. 213.

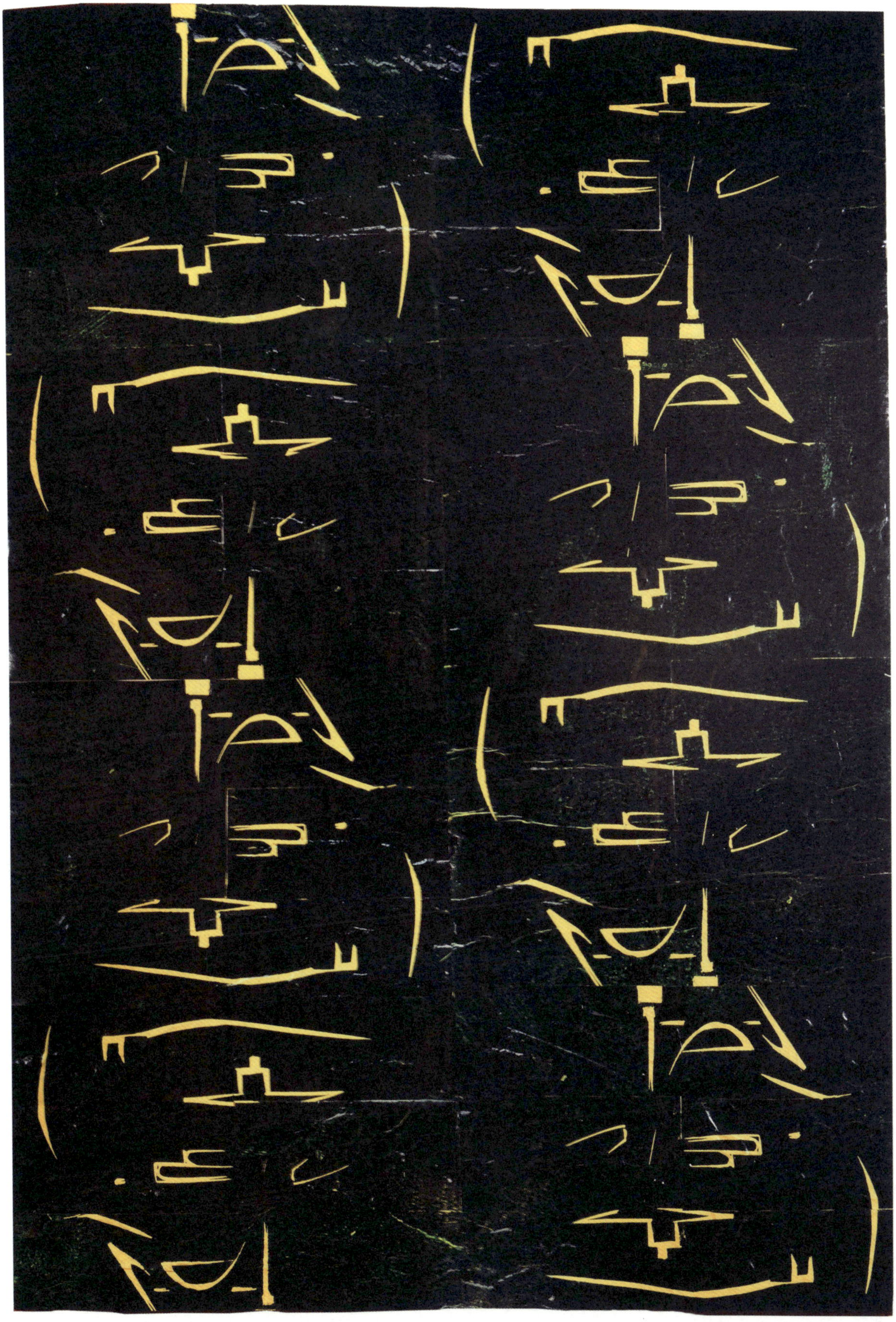

Arquipélago 1, MAS, 565 × 395 mm, lino assemblage on layered paper, 2004

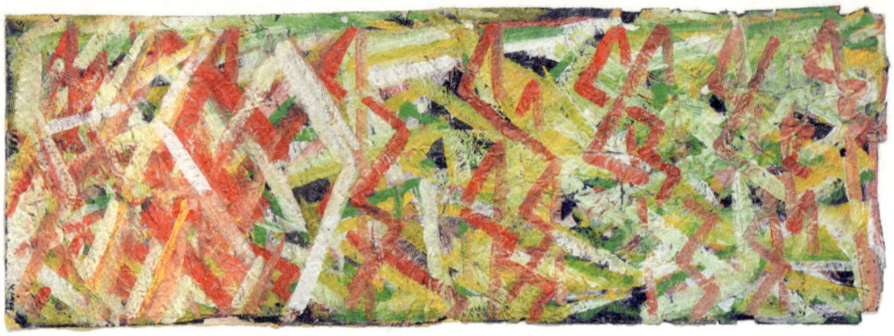

fig. 12 **Cross Roads 5**
1425 x 500 mm, painting,
acrylic on layered paper, 1989

fig 12.

kamer dat het licht wordt" (Chuang Tzu[12]). Het is in deze niet-ruimte dat de scheppende vonk overspringt[13].

Het leven in eenklank met de Weg[14], in weerwil van het beginsel van het 'niet-doen', komt dus niet op loutere passiviteit neer. Het is slechts een schijnbare inertie, die wel degelijk tot de geboorte van iets nieuws en waardevols leidt. De esthetische kracht in de vorm wordt niet bereikt door *bewuste* actie. Als de vorm een product is van de *bewust* werkende geest, zal hij maar een maaksel zijn. Slechts als de kunstenaar werkt vanuit een veld waarmee hij/zij niet bewust bezig is, maar zinkt tot in een laag die nauwelijks bereikbaar is, zal het kunstwerk *diepgang* bezitten. Paradoxaal genoeg is de esthetische act pas mogelijk door een betreden/reactiveren van een niet-[bewuste-]activiteit die toch *raak* werkt, van een niet-[bewust-]weten, dat tegelijk een summum van lucididiteit in zich draagt. De kunstenaar schept in een paradox van lucide hoogste doelgerichtheid en van naast-bewust handelen, dat niet rationeel-cognitief ingekaderd wordt. Als dit laatste toch gebeurt, zal het kunstwerk geen bezieling uitstralen, zal het een beredeneerd product blijven. De lucididiteit waarover sprake heeft niets vandoen met een intellectueel en intentioneel inzicht/handelen.

De meest uiteenlopende kunstenaars, wetenschappers en filosofen hebben reeds gesteld dat hun diepste ontdekkingen/scheppingen als het ware van zelf uit het niets oprezen, ver buiten het dagelijkse bewustzijn. Einstein: "tappend uit Gods gedachten"[15], Poincaré: "het inzicht... moet haaks staan op hetgene men bewust verdedigt"[16], Bill Viola: "Kunstenaars hebben al lang geweten dat de interessantste dingen opwellen uit zones van lage en onduidelijke informatie, zogenaamde lacunes in herkenning. Dat is de tijd van de betrokkenheid, of, voor de toeschouwer, van de deelname in het kunstwerk."[17]

Uit het voorgaande blijkt dat het kunstwerk, die naam waardig, is ontstaan op het scherp van het mes: niet door de wil beheerst, niet onbeheerst; niet doelloos passief, niet bewust actief; niet bewust speurend, maar hoogst lucide.

12 *Chuang Tzu: Taoist philosopher and Chinese mystic*, ed. Herbert GILES, London, George Allen & Unwin, 1961.

13 Arthur WALEY, *Zen Buddhism and its relation to art*, London, 1922; Yasuichi AWAKAWA, *Zen paintings*, Tokyo, Kodansha, 1970; Shinichi HISAMATSU, *Zen and the fine arts*, Tokyo, Kodansha, 1971; Sylvan BARNET & William BURTO, *Zen paintings*, Tokyo, Kodansha, 1982; Helmut BRINKER, *Zen in the art of painting, Japanese monks, 1600–1925*, New York, Abrams, 1989; Helmut BRINKER & Hiroshi KAWAZAWA, *Zen: masters of meditation in images and writings*, Zürich, Artibus Asiae Publishers, 1996; John STEVENS, *Zenga: brushstrokes of enlightenment*, New Orleans, Museum of Art, 1990.

14 Het doel van de WEG is niet het 'nirvana' of het 'mystiek' zweven, integendeel. "Water halen en hout kappen – daarin ligt de wonderlijke WEG". Niet anders zagen het de middeleeuwse mystici uit de christelijke traditie, wanneer ze zeiden dat de diepste mystieke ervaring terzijde moest worden geschoven als dat kan helpen om een soep aan een arme te bedelen.

15 Denis BRIAN, *Einstein: a life*, New York, John Wiley & Sons, 1996, p. 129.

16 Rollo MAY, *Courage to create*, New York, Bantam Books, 1983.

17 Bill VIOLA, *Reasons for knocking at an empty house. Writings 1973–1994*, London, Thames & Hudson, 1998, p. 71.

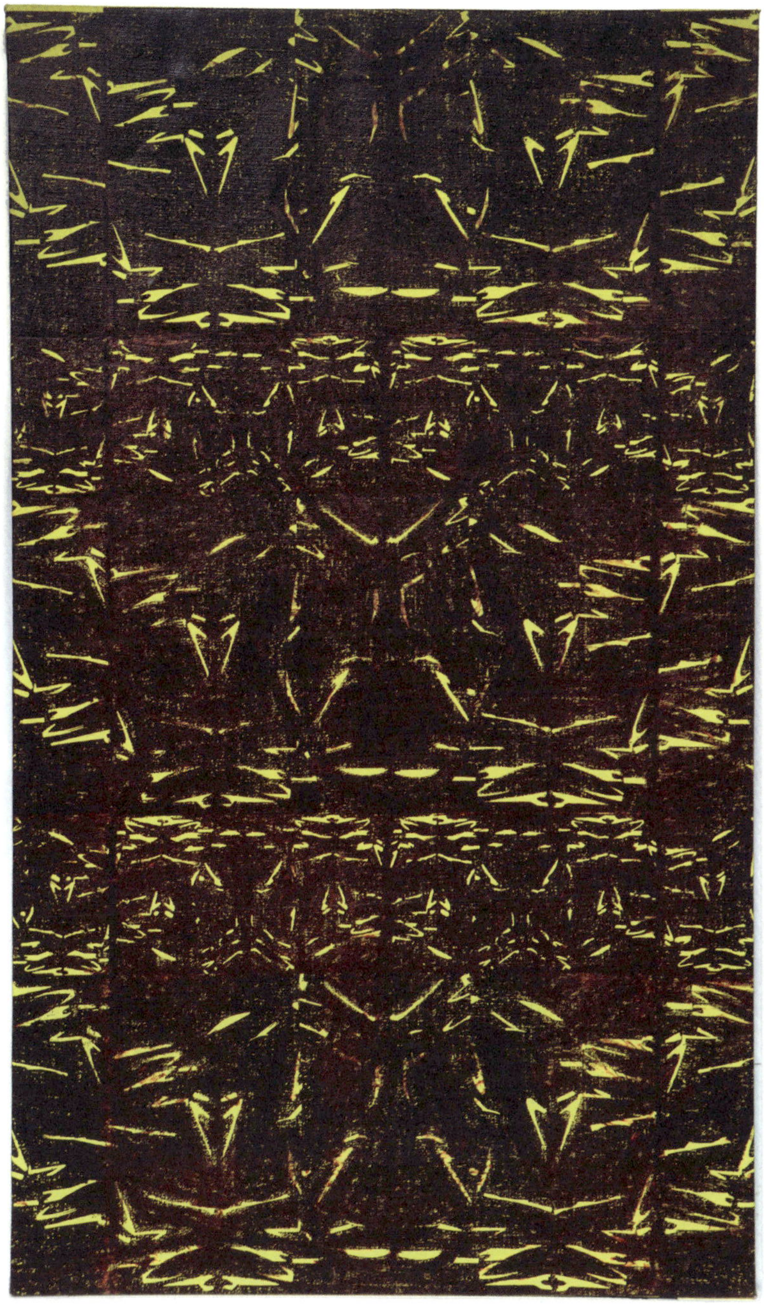

Correntes 7, 670 × 1120 mm, linocut handprinted/painted on canvas, 2000

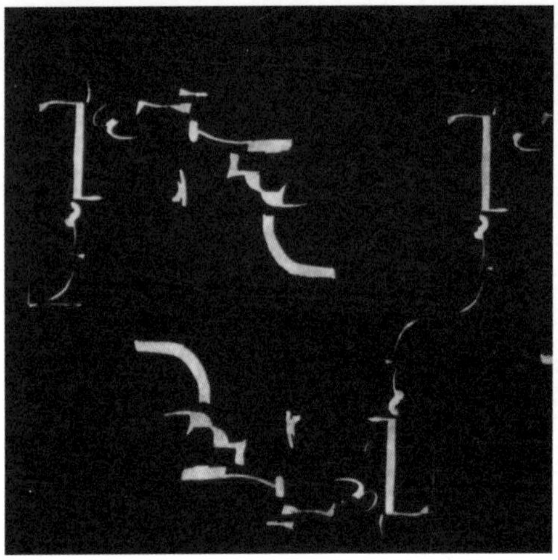

Anthiagramme (detail)

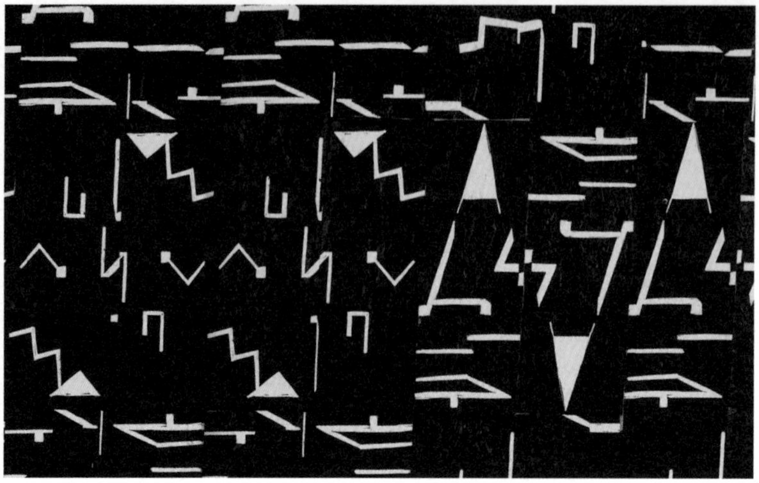

Anthiapolis I (detail)

Excurs I: Anthiagrammes

Eén van de – althans in mijn ogen – subtielste reeksen in Vincks oeuvre zijn de *Anthiagrammes*. Vanwaar de naam? *Anthias anthias* is een kleine vis die in de oostelijke Atlantische Oceaan en in de Middellandse Zee leeft, tussen 15 en 200 meter diep, liefst tussen rotsen en koralen. Overdag schuilt hij in holtes of grotten. 's Nachts voedt hij zich met zoöplankton, kleinere schaaldieren en visjes. *Anthias* is een protogyne hermafrodiet: alle individuen worden als vrouwelijk geboren. Telkens wanneer een mannetje sterft, transformeert één van de grotere vrouwtjes zich tot man. Ze bezitten dus een duidelijk overzicht van hun communauteit.

De groep (of misschien sommige leden?) evalueert onophoudelijk zijn samenstelling en noden en bepaalde individuen beslissen dan, van gender te veranderen.

Excurs II: Anthiapolis

De veel grotere werken uit de *Anthiapolis*-reeks (*anthiapolis* = stad van de anthias) roepen een totaal verschillend affect op: geen droomachtige, vaak van golvingen of krommingen voorziene trekken, maar een wemelende wereld in rechte, vaak hakende, inslaande lijnen, met daartussen kleine formaties van driehoeken. Het complexe geheel blijft vol dynamische wisselingen, maar is *ongenadiger*, een hardere samenleving waar geen aarzeling heerst.

Excurs III: Bugaku

Bugaku is een traditionele Japanse performance die aanvankelijk slechts voor de hoogste adel aan het keizerlijk hof werd opgevoerd. De geschiedenis ervan heet tot twaalf eeuwen terug te gaan in de tijd. De uitvoering ervan was aan uiterst precieze regels, beschreven in handboeken, onderworpen. Elke handeling werd traag-beheerst, precies, *koninklijk* uitgevoerd. De dansers dragen kostbare kledij, en vaak ook maskers. De onderwerpen: de ontmoeting tussen een mens en een goddelijk of bovennatuurlijk wezen; beroemde gevechten; mythische gebeurtenissen. Inhoudelijk is *bugaku* een mix van Shinto en van Boeddhistische, Chinese, Koreaanse en zelfs van Indische en Zuidoost-Aziatische invloeden.

Essentieel is het gevoel voor verhoudingen in de ruimte van alle deelnemers: de afstanden zijn per traditie vastgelegd, en kunnen niet naar willekeur door de performers gewijzigd worden. Ook zijn de bewegingen en handelingen strak, afgemeten en geometrisch bepaald.

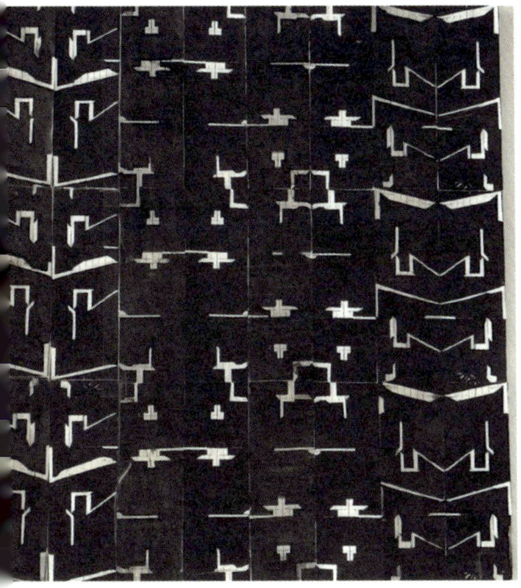

lodules for Bugaku

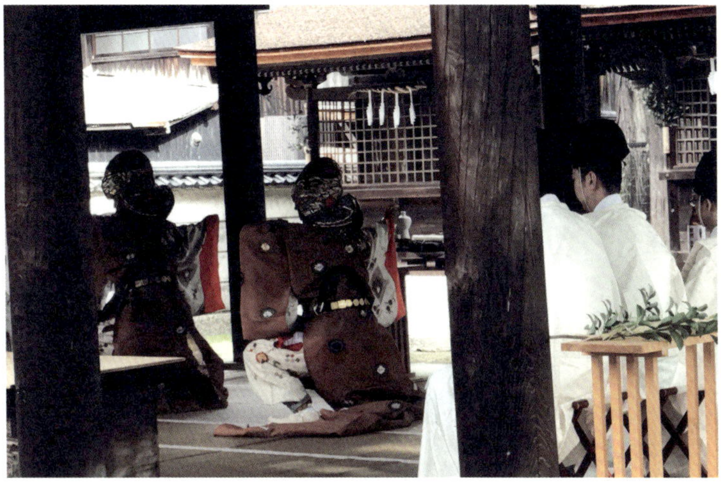

Bugaku dancers

Linda Vincks *Bugaku* lijkt deze esthetiek te weerspiegelen. Een vergelijkbare strengheid in vormgeving en compositie is overigens ook eigen aan reeksen als *Anthiapolis*, *Kemper meets Chladni*, en de nu (2024) in het Frans Masereel Centrum te Kasterlee voorbereide serie. In de Japanse *bugaku* herkende de kunstenares een driedimensionale, performatieve verwant van haar strenge stijl.

Excurs IV: Birdsongs

Een reeks van kleinere werken zijn de 'Vogelgezangen'. Urenlang luisterde de kunstenares naar het gekweel van diverse vogelsoorten. Deze werken zouden als partituren uit een andere wereld kunnen gezien worden, waarin bepaalde melodische en/of ritmische sequensen niet blindelings herhaald worden, maar steeds gedaanteveranderingen en/of resonantie ondergaan.

Deze doorgaans kleine werken konden alleen via transmodaliteit ontstaan zijn: het vertalen van en het resoneren met klanken naar een visuele compositie toe. Andere kunstenaars zijn eveneens door de 'kunst der vogels' getroffen geweest. Het gaat doorgaans om componisten of musici binnen het auditieve veld.

Hier is vooral Olivier Messiaen (1908–1992) te vermelden. Messiaens grootste inspiratiebron was de schoonheid van Gods schepping, met name het gezang van vogels. Messiaen[18] trok regelmatig de natuur in om vogelzang te noteren. In veel van zijn composities heeft hij vogelzang verwerkt. Titels als *Abîme des Oiseaux* (uit het *Quatuor pour la fin du temps*)[19] en *Oiseaux exotiques* spreken voor zich. Hij heeft de zang van een groot aantal vogels getoonzet voor piano (*Catalogue d'oiseaux*). In een van zijn laatste orkestwerken (*Éclairs sur l'Au-delà...*) zijn geluiden van vooral Australische vogelsoorten verwerkt. De gezangen der vogels zouden tot een partituur kunnen worden verwerkt, maar dat heeft Messiaen niet gedaan. Zijn waarnemingen van vogelzang zijn door een aantal verwerkingsfilters getrokken, en zo hebben de vogelgezangen een nieuwe en complexere esthetische vorm aangenomen. Vogelzang bezat voor Messiaen niet alleen idyllische en lieflijke connotaties. Hij heeft de 'Afgrond der vogels' gecomponeerd,

18 Harry HALBREICH, *L'œuvre d'Olivier Messiaen*, Paris, Fayard, 2008; Peter HILL & Nigel SIMEONE, Messiaen, New Haven–London, Yale University Press, 2005; Vincent BENITEZ, *Olivier Messiaen: A Research and Information Guide*, New York –London, Routledge, 2018.

19 Anthony POPLE, *Messiaen : Quatuor pour la fin du temps.* Cambridge: Cambridge University Press, 1998; Rebecca RISHIN, *For the End of Time: The Story of the Messiaen Quartet*, Ithaca NY, Cornell University Press, 2003.

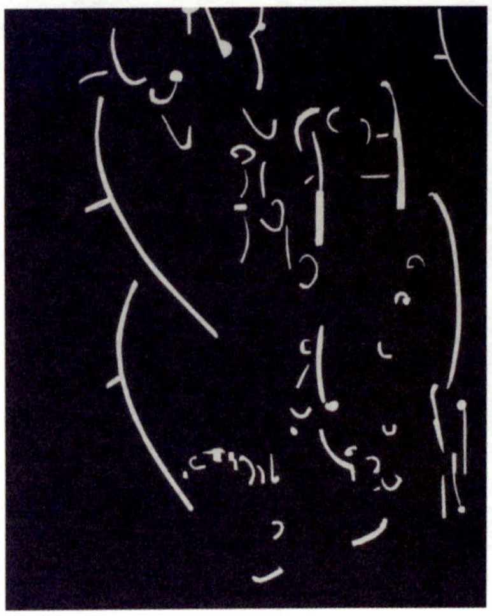

Birdsong 4 (detail)

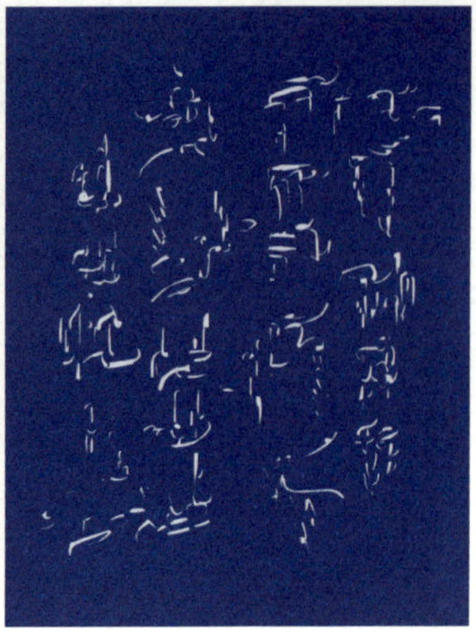

Birdsong 6b Kobalt Blue

in zijn 'Quattuor voor het einde der tijden'. De waarneming van vogelzang diende Messiaen dus tot het scheppen van composities over vreselijk-aardse, religieuze en transcendente ervaringen.

Zijn op vogelzang gebaseerde composities zijn nooit letterlijke transscripties; zelfs de werken met titels die rechtstreeks naar vogels verwijzen zijn klankgedichten die het ogenblik, het landschap, de kleuren, en de atmosfeer mede-opriepen.

Messiaen is een kunstenaar uit de *moderniteit*. Maar ook in zeer *archaïsche*, tribale gemeenschappen heeft vogelzang gevoerd tot esthetische resonantie. Nemen we het voorbeeld van de Kaluli in Papua Nieuw Guinea). De instrumenten zijn beperkt tot trommels en ratels. Melodische instrumenten ontbreken. Essentieel is het spel van de verschuivende ingrepen bovenop een solide ritmische basis. De esthetische Kaluli-canon verkiest dicht-opeengepakte, overlappende, verstrengelde, alternerende klanken (*dulugu ganalan*, 'optillend-overlappende toon')[20]. Drums en ratels vermijden unisono of éénklank, maar streven naar een dichte, inwendig zeer sterk wisselende en afwisselende klankmuur, die verhardt tot aan de climax, die bezit moet nemen van musicus en toehoorders in geest én lichaam (zoals de vibraties van de huidige *techno, drum & bass*, e.d. letterlijk het lichaam moeten in bezit nemen).

Een bepaalde vogel speelt hierin een hoofdrol: de *tibodai* (Pitohui cristatus). Deze roept eerst *bo...bo...bo*, dan *tibo...tibo... tibo*, tenslotte *dowo dowo dowo*. De drum is de stem van deze *vogel* (de Kaluli kenden enkel ritme-instrumenten). Zowel de drum als de metafysische *tibodai* dragen meerdere betekenissen.

Zo zien de Kaluli hun muziek als een projectie van het regenwoud om hun zwaarste emotionele ervaringen te behandelen en te duiden. Deze muzikale structuren – grotendeels in collectieve processen geschapen – worden dan benut als code voor de mens en zijn wereld. De opeenstapeling van ritmische en tonale structuren in de Kaluli-muziek is metaforisch voor hun kijk op de wereld: doorheen de patronen moet men het *binnenste* vinden, de 'innerlijke reflectie'.[21]

Het is misschien gemakkelijker te begrijpen dat vogelzang eerder de musicus dan de beeldende kunstenaar inspireert. In het laatste geval, zoals bij Linda, is het *transmodaal* vermogen essentieel: het filteren van auditieve input naar een visuele esthetica, zonder te vervallen in een poging tot partituur.

20 Steven FELD, *Aesthetics as iconicity of style; or, Lift-up-over-sounding: Getting into the Kaluli Groove*, in *Yearbook for Traditional Music*, 1988, pp. 74-113.

21 Steven FELD, *Sound as a symbolic system: the Kaluli drum*, in *The varieties of sensory experience*, ed. David HOWES, Toronto-London, Toronto U.P., 1991, pp. 79-99.

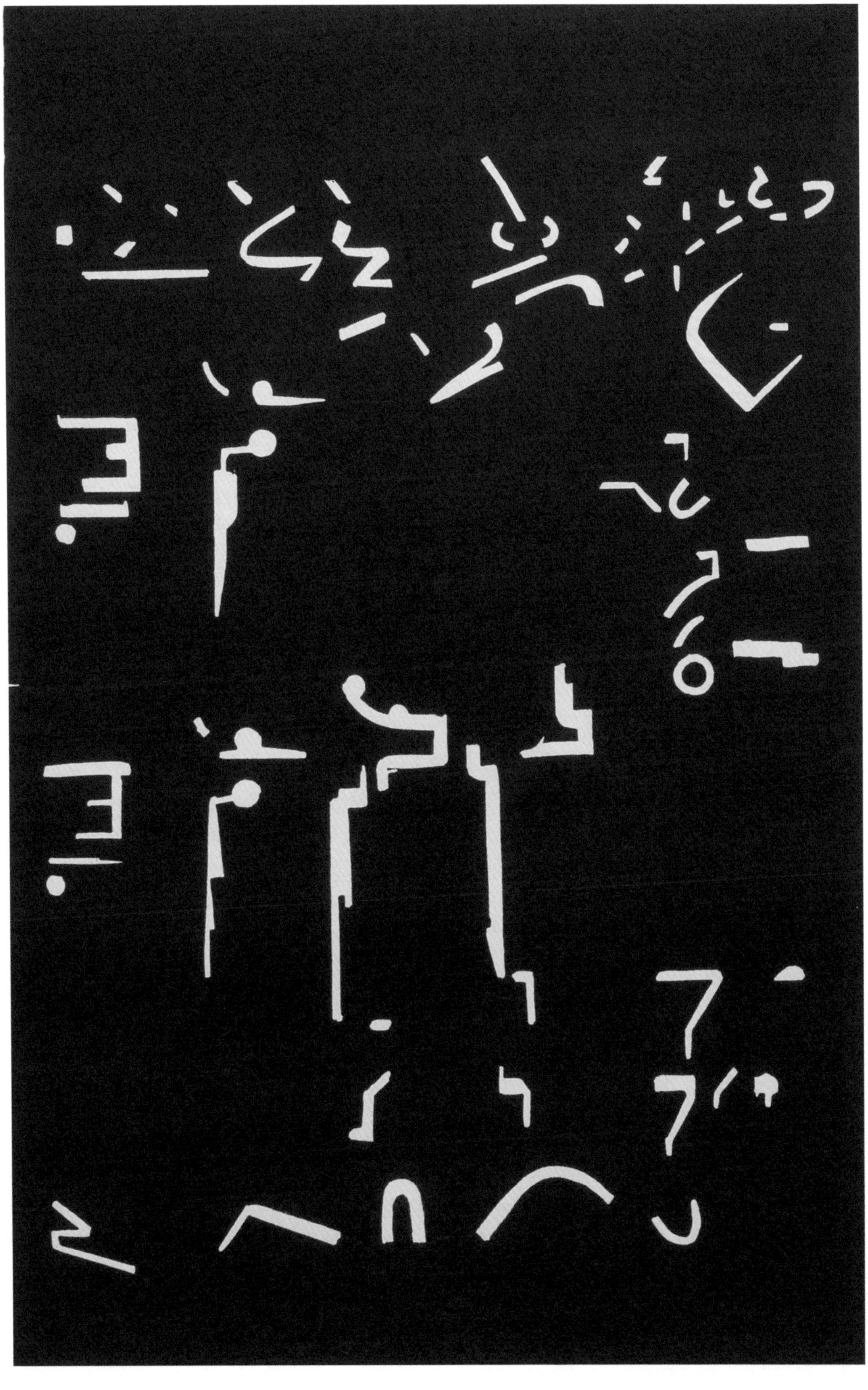

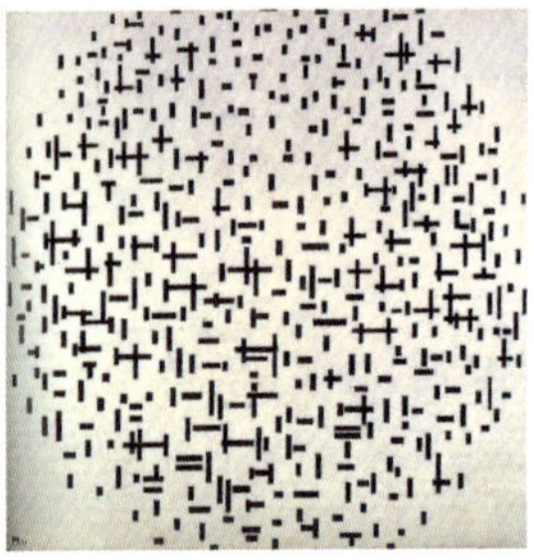
fig. 13

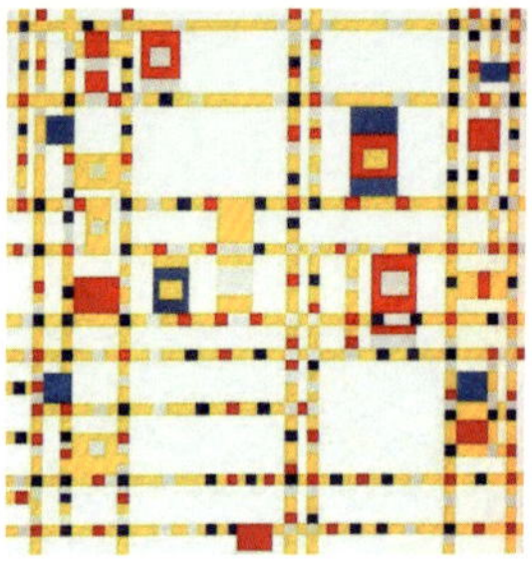
fig. 14

fig. 13 P. Mondrian, 'Compositie in lijn', oil on canvas, 1916–1917

fig. 14 P. Mondrian, 'Broadway Boogie-Woogie', oil on canvas, 1942–1943

Variaties en Resonanties

De grotere composities van Linda lijken, oppervlakkig beschouwd, te bestaan uit elkaar herhalende segmenten. Bij nader toezien is deze waarneming fout. Elke sequens vertoont variaties, verschuivingen, wisselingen. Als compositie zijn ze analoog aan bijvoorbeeld muzikale variaties. Muzikale variaties zijn op zich een oeroud procedé: ook *archaïsche* tribale culturen, hoe beperkt ook in hun instrumenten, hielden van variatie, ook al herhaalden ze talloze malen één cantilene, sequens of vers. De antieke en Oosterse muziek nam geijkte melodische thema's (*nomos* in het Oude Griekenland, *raga* in India, *maqam* in de Islam) als aanloop tot geïmproviseerde uitwerkingen met vernuftige variatietechnieken. In de Gregoriaanse zang moet het oorspronkelijk geïmproviseerde variëren een aanzienlijke rol hebben gespeeld; de 'allelujapsalmverzen' steunen op het beginsel van de variatie.

Een *variatie*[22] is in het algemeen het één- of meermalen herhalen van een muzikaal idee in iets andere vorm dan het origineel. Dat kan een thema betreffen, een karakter, een harmonische progressie, een ritme of metrum, of een combinatie van deze elementen. Een thematische variatie is mogelijk door het toevoegen of weglaten van noten aan een melodie (bijvoorbeeld door versieringen), het octaveren of verdubbelen met andere intervallen van een melodie, het veranderen van noten of intervallen binnen een melodie, van ritme of maatsoort, van instrumentatie of zetting, of van begeleiding. Symmetrie kan hiertoe behoren[23], maar ook retrograde. In ruime betekenis is de variatie een compositieprocédé, waardoor een muzikaal gegeven bij herhaling een wijziging ondergaat. In engere zin is de variatie een muzikale vorm bestaande uit een thema en getransformeerde herhalingen daarvan.

De Contrapunt

De *contrapunt* (leer der meerstemmige schrijfwijze) laat verscheiden melodische stemmen zich boven mekaar ontwikkelen. Contrapuntische composities ontstonden rond 1500, zoals het *ricercare* (letterlijk: het zoeken). Heel wat composities van Linda Vinck zijn visuele *ricercari*. Het *ricercare* is een instrumentale compositie uit de Renaissance en de Barok waarin diverse motieven worden uitgeprobeerd in *variërende* imitaties. Het *ricercare* geldt als voorloper van de *fuga*, waar de pompende bas, de vlucht, de tegenwerking, de opheffing, en de wemelende opeenstapeling der lagen zo belangrijk zijn. De *basso ostinato*, een patroon in de baslijn, draagt de muzikale structuur.

De Fuga

De *fuga* ('vlucht') berust op het beginsel van de gelijkwaardigheid van de verschillende stemmen / lijnen. Essentieel is ook de steeds variërende herhaling. Het muzikaal genre is een esthetische verwerking van de achtervolgingsidee,

22 J. MÜLLER-BLATTAU, *Gestaltung – Umgestaltung. Studien zur Geschichte der musikalischen Variation*, 1950.

23 O. JANDER, *Rhythmic Symmetry in the 'Goldberg Variations'*, in *The musical quarterly*, 1991.

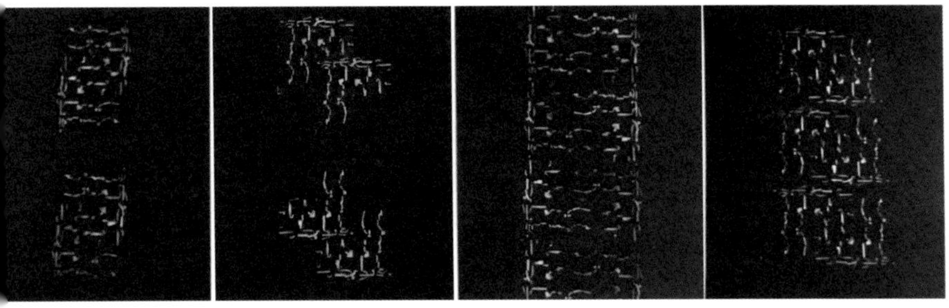

fig. 15 **Anthiagrammes**

. 15

het achternazitten, de vlucht, het dreigende gevangen worden.

De vlucht en de achtervolging, zoals in de jacht (er bestond ook een muzikaal genre dat letterlijk *caccia*, 'jacht', werd genoemd[24]), zijn de leidraad van de compositie. Een onderhuids aspect van de emotionaliteit – zoals een vage en blijvende angst, die wellicht vanwege het *decorum* niet uitdrukbaar was – wordt uiteindelijk vertolkt in een esthetische structuur, waarvan de complexiteit een uitdrukking kan zijn van het verwerkings- en sublimatieproces.

Analogieën tussen de verschijningsdimensies van de wereld

Resonantie wandelt vaak langs de zintuigen, maar is in de eerste plaats ook transsensorieel. Het is niet noodzakelijk een *zintuiglijke* ingeving die resoneert. Resonantie doet zich voor tussen individuen via zintuiglijke waarnemingen, of tussen individuen langs of over de zintuigen heen in een soort kern-kern-contact. Resonantie is ook mogelijk tussen (een element of toestand in) de 'wereld' en de eigen psyche[25]. Resonantie is weer-laten-klinken, maar deze nieuwe klank zal geen kopie zijn van de eerste. We vernoemden de resonantie tussen muzikant en toehoorder. Resonantie is van oudsher zelfs *letterlijk* genomen als artistico-therapeutisch middel. Het opvangen van en deelnemen aan resonantie is een basis van vele therapeutische riten, zoals de bezetenheidsriten die door muziek, dans en trance een heling van een individu beogen. Zulke praktijken bestonden in de meest uiteenlopende culturen. We hebben een aantal ervan, in Noord-Afrika en het oude Europa, eertijds in hun samenhang bestudeerd[26].

Zo trachtte men het universum begrijpelijk te maken en in eenklank te brengen. Beschouwde men het heelal als macrokosmos, dan was de mens in dit systeem een miniatuurversie daarvan, een microkosmos (letterlijk 'kleine wereld').

Basaal is de *resonantie*: het weer-klinken van de trilling, eigen aan alle gemoedstoestanden, energieën, affecten, pathologieën. Deze

24 ***In de Europese schilderkunst van de 17e en 18e eeuw bestond een uitgebreid aantal voorstellingen van de jacht, en stillevens van de jachtbuit.***

M. SASS, *Hunting grounds for painters: The killing of animals and the artistic domination of nature*, in *Netherlands Yearbook for History of Art*, 2021; S. JABLONSKI, *Acts of violence: Rubens and the hunt*, 2004; C. GIRARD, *Rococo Massacres: Hunting in Eighteenth-Century French Painting*, 2014; S. THOMSON, *The continuity of the hunt theme in palace decoration in the eighteenth century in France*, 1981

25 De huidige globalisering, die overigens *in nucleo* reeds in de 15e eeuw inzette maar door de huidige media en mobiliteit een exponentiële groei kent, zal een resonantie in overtreffende trap teweegbrengen: nooit voordien had men toegang tot zulk een verscheidenheid van ingaven. Zo vond de eerste Europese tentoonstelling van indigene kunst uit Mexico reeds in 1520 (!) plaats in het Paleis van Nassau op de Brusselse Coudenberg: zie Paul VANDENBROECK, *Amerindian art and ornamental objects in royal collections. Brussels, Mechelen, Duurstede, 1520–1530*, in *America. Bride of the sun: 500 years Latin America and the Low Countries*, exhib. cat., Antwerpen, KMSKA, 1992, pp. 99-120.

26 Paul VANDENBROECK, *De kleuren van de geest. Dans en trance in Afro-Europese tradities*, Gent, Snoeck-Ducaju, 1997.

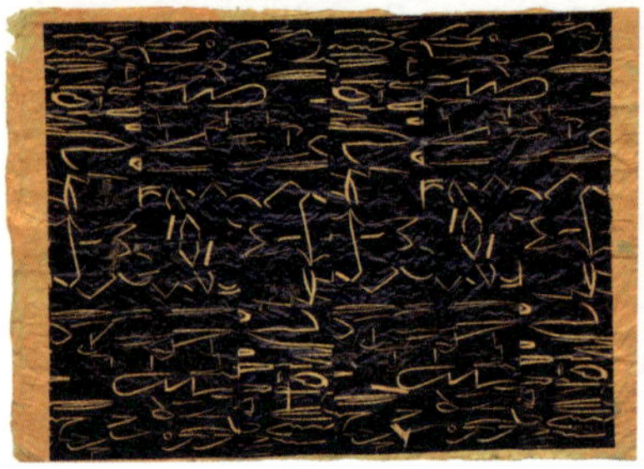

fig. 16

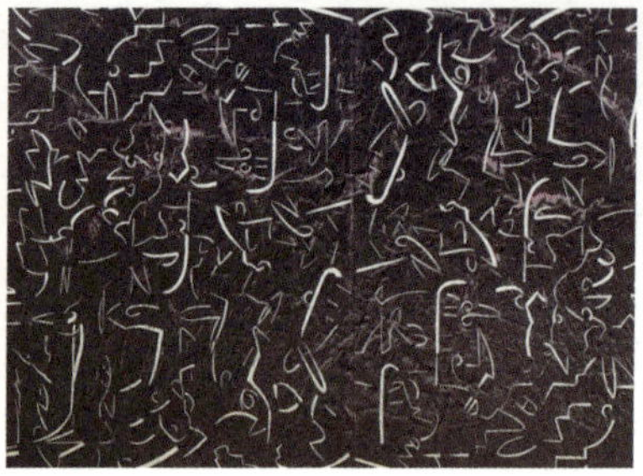

fig. 17

fig. 16 **Half Saffron — Patterns of Paradise**
fig. 17 **Patterns of Paradise (detail)**

weerklank was heilzaam, legde de grondslag van een diep contact.

De moderne wetenschap schuwt dit soort realiteiten, maar uit de ervaringen van het dagelijks leven weten we hoe tussenmenselijke sympathie 'resoneert' en antipathie 'dissoneert'. Resonantie is de 'medetrilling' van een materie door het opvangen en de inwerking van een trilling van elders. Wanneer nu een hemellichaam trilt als een snaar, dan moeten andere hemellichamen co-resoneren: de 'harmonie der sferen'… Een vergelijkbare resonantie doet zich voor tussen individuen.

Resonantie is niet hetzelfde als identificatie, het zich-gelijkschakelen-met. Resonantie is een antwoord dat medeklinkt, dat echo's bevat van de 'vraag', maar onmiskenbare eigenheid bezit.

Hoewel het gehoor het 'model' van resonantie biedt, breidt deze laatste zich uit over andere zintuiglijke en esthetische velden. Er is ritmische, ruimtelijk-kinetische, coloristische, beeldende resonantie. Esthetische werken in een bepaalde cultuur resoneren onophoudelijk in andere scheppingen.

Besluit

De kunstenaar is geen willoos apparaat dat 'de wereld' archiveert: er moeten onbewuste affiniteiten met waargenomen verschijnselen aanwezig zijn, om te kiezen – onbewust – wat men zal verwerken. Verwerken: deels uitwendige, deels inwendige 'gebeurtenissen' een onverwisselbare esthetische gedaante te verlenen, arbeid die misschien niet los staat van het in het reine komen met zichzelf doorheen het leven, Overigens is 'arbeid' ook letterlijk op te vatten Linda Vincks scheppingen groeien door langdurige toewijding. Ook haar technieken zijn gelaagd, complex, vereisen niet-aflatende concentratie én inspanning.

Ik eindig deze bespreking van Linda's werk met een persoonlijk verhaal. In 2002 leefde ik in een staat van absolute crisis. Op een dag nodigde een kennis me uit om mee te gaan die avond naar een vriendin-kunstenares in Mortsel. Eenmaal daar, voerden beide dames een geanimeerd gesprek. Ik hoorde er evenwel niets van. Een aantal grotere werken van Linda stonden tegen de wand. Ik werd erin opgeslokt op de meest weldadige wijze. De achtergronden in diepe tonen, de schier eindeloze ritmes en bewegingen in de patronen, die voor een oppervlakkige beschouwer herhalend lijken, maar dat nooit zijn, voerden me mee in weidse ruimtes, zoals iemands hart kan juichen door het waarnemen van de zwierige vlucht van een zwerm vogels, geleid door een onkennelijke samenhang…

Ik vermoedde woordeloos dat die vreugde schenkende werken zelfs in tijden van rouw en opschorting tot stand waren gekomen. Toch leeft er in Linda Vincks werken steeds een verheffende kracht, zonder dat één gekend verhaal verteld wordt of dat iets, wat we kennen, verbeeldt. Die avond begon een deurtje van mijn verkrampte gemoed op een kier open te staan. Daarom is mij die eerste kennisname met Linda Vincks werk onvergetelijk.

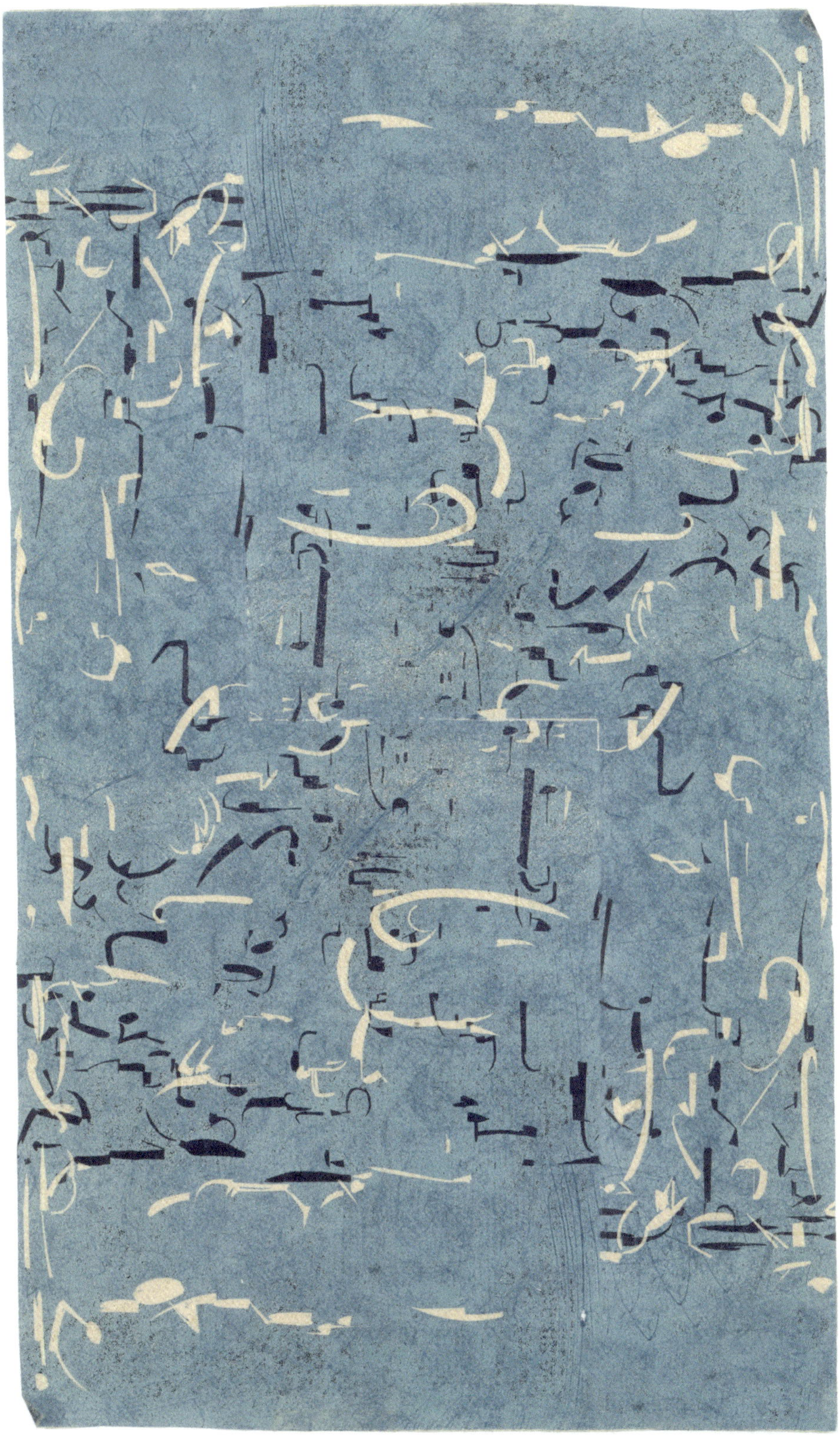

Dialogue — Anthiagramme 10, 236 × 397 mm, linocut on Nepali paper, 2019

This is an artist who, in her endeavour to enumerate and build aesthetic pleasure around patterns, creates one of the most original works in contemporary painting. A lot of contemporary art is enumerative, as I've already emphasised.

But in this particular case, the enumeration, due to its extension, its articulation, and enchantingly spatial impregnation, becomes a narration. It is a narrative art, not in the usual sense of telling a story, but because it narrates almost musical relationships between signs, as waves or fragments of waves, shell motifs, corals, or their stylisations. Since neither the ocean nor what inhabits it is involved in testifying about its past life as an ocean, and of invertebrates: rather it narrates the effort to engender, without any other appetite or general purpose, spatial relationships, I repeat, that fill the world beyond verisimilitudes and often grandiose schemes of ecstasy, which is all that matters to the aesthetic quest to capture.

G.T. Didial, 'Towards the Ocean', Micadinaia, May 2001

IV. Parallel Worlds

Parallelle Werelden

Cabo Verde with essay by Ernest Van Buynder, residencies in South Africa and Japan

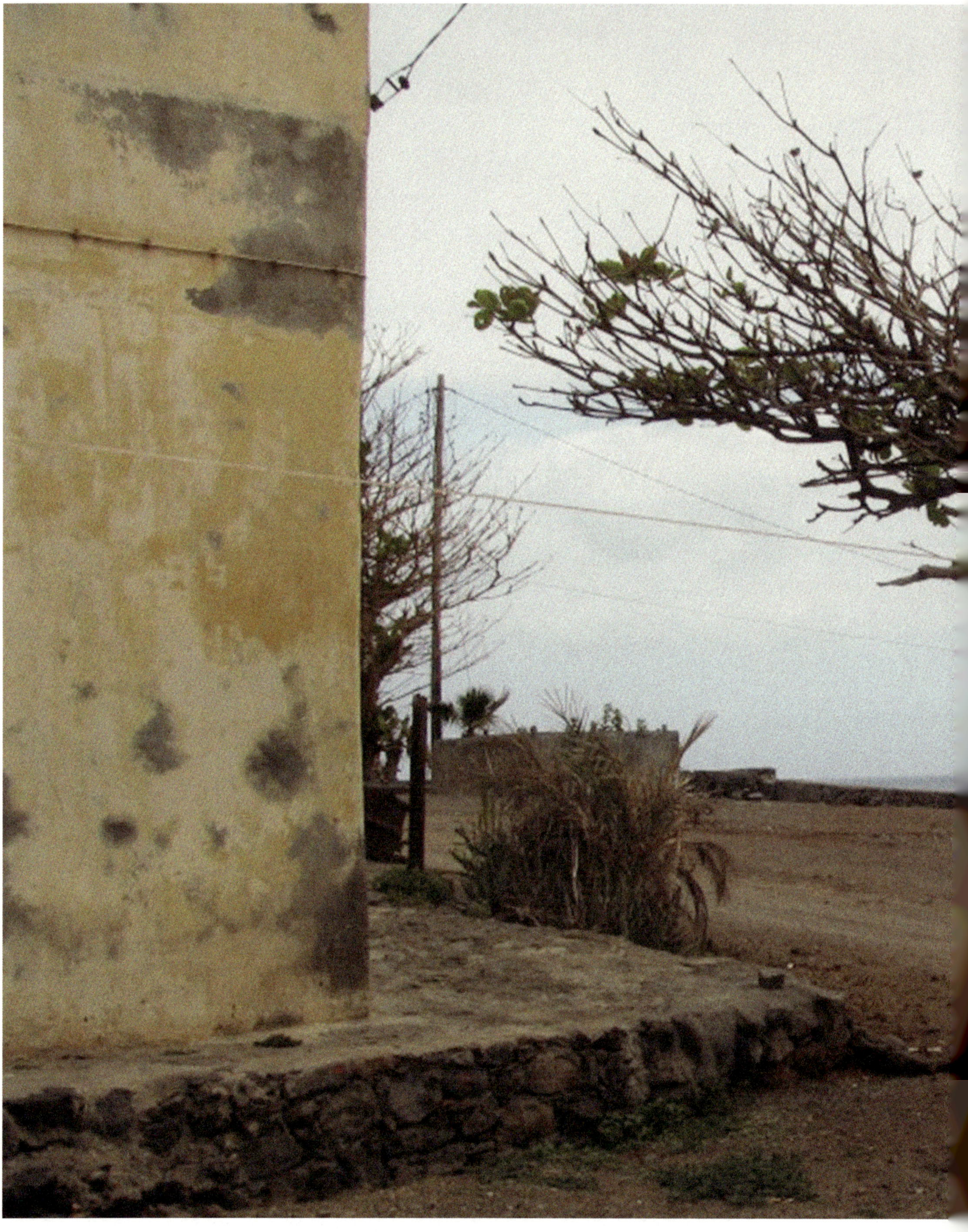

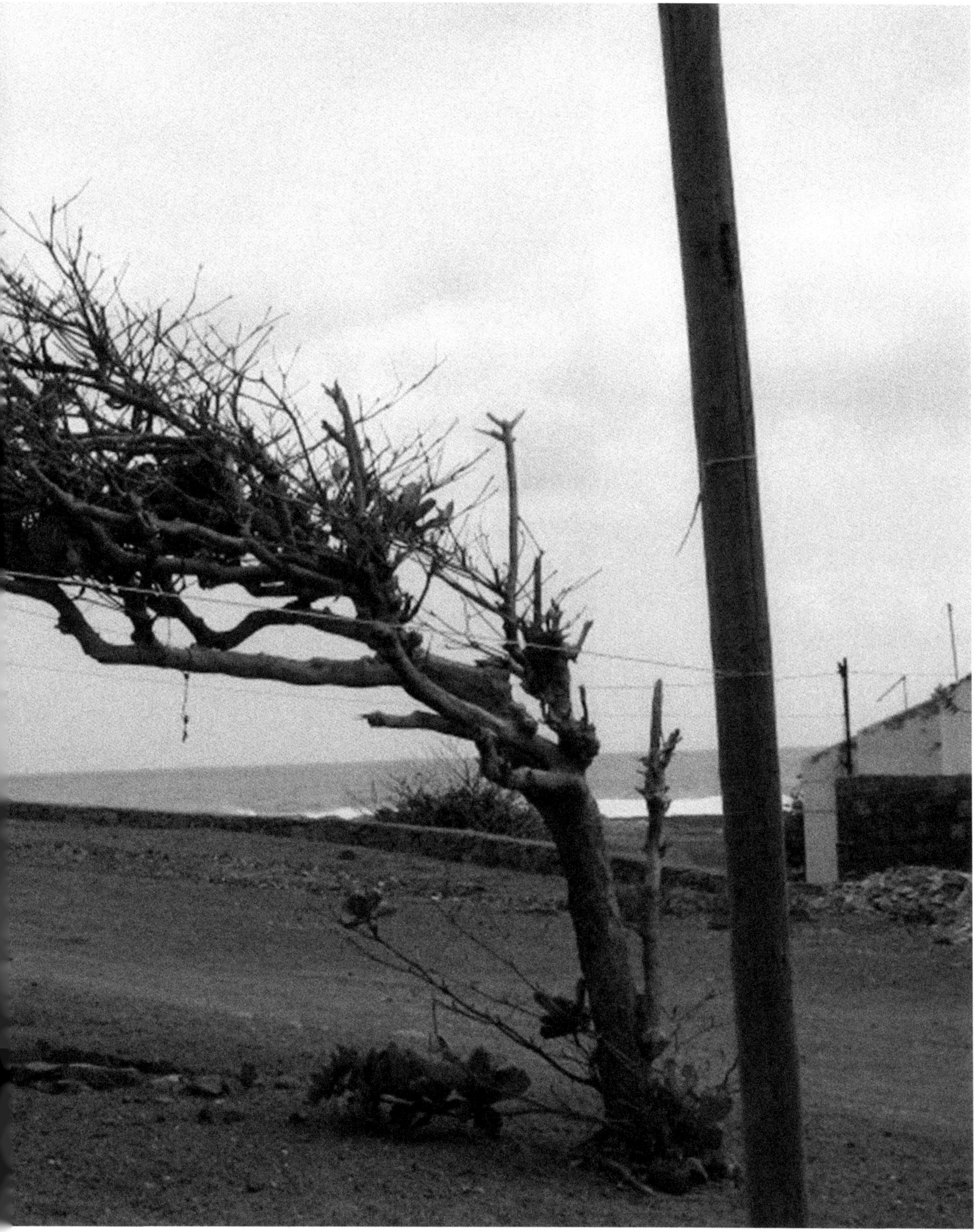

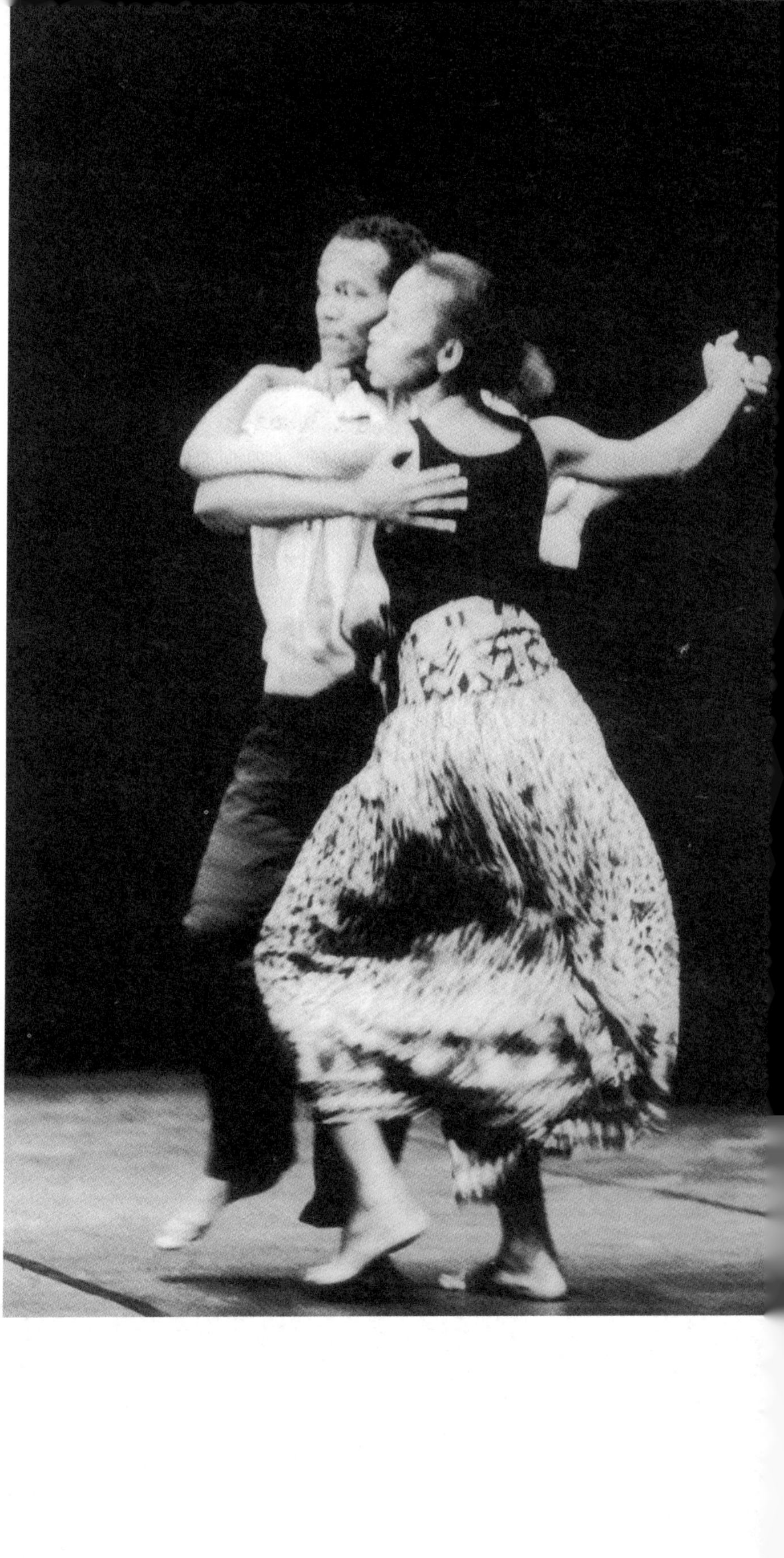

Salamansa 11 (detail)

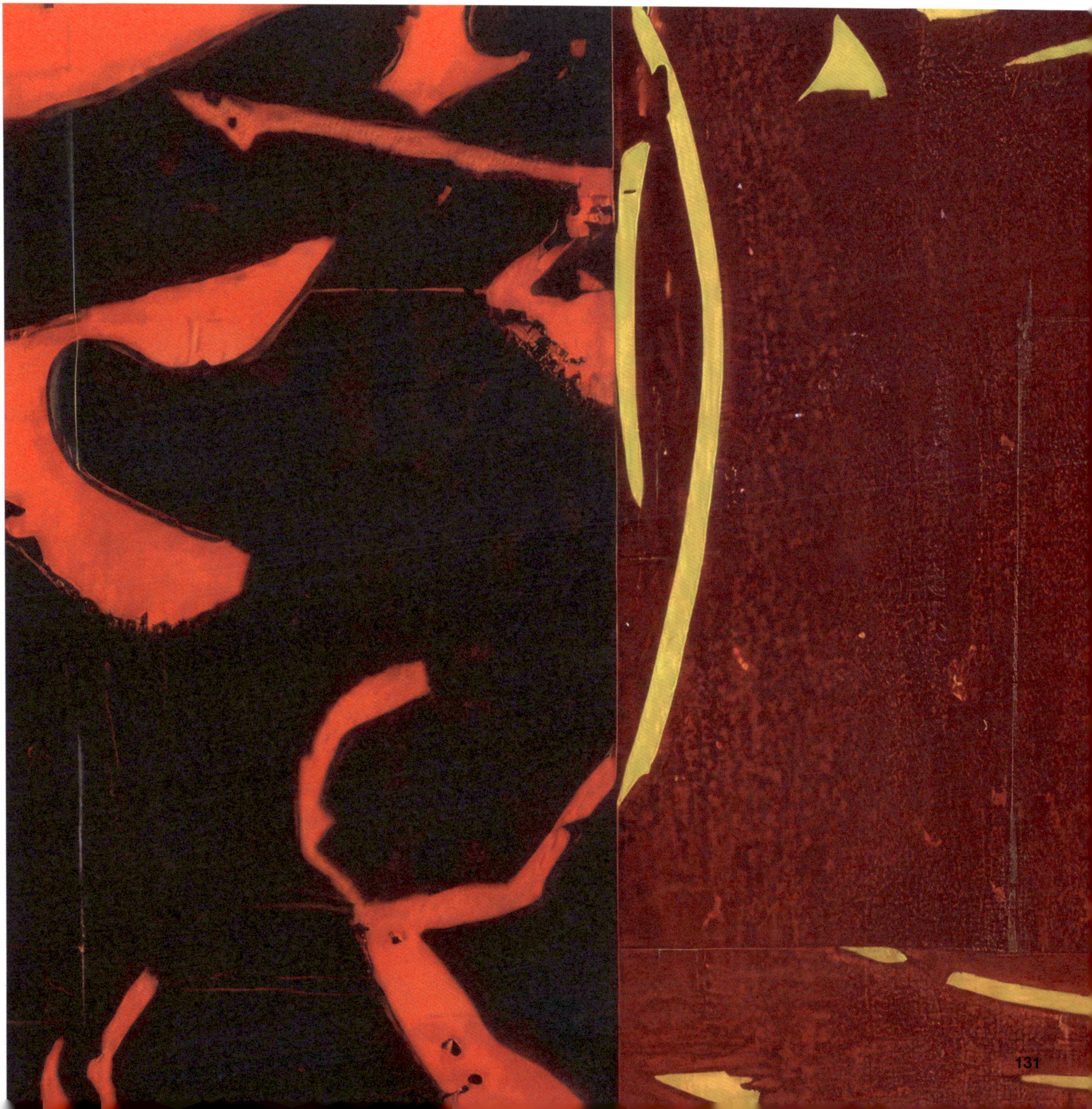

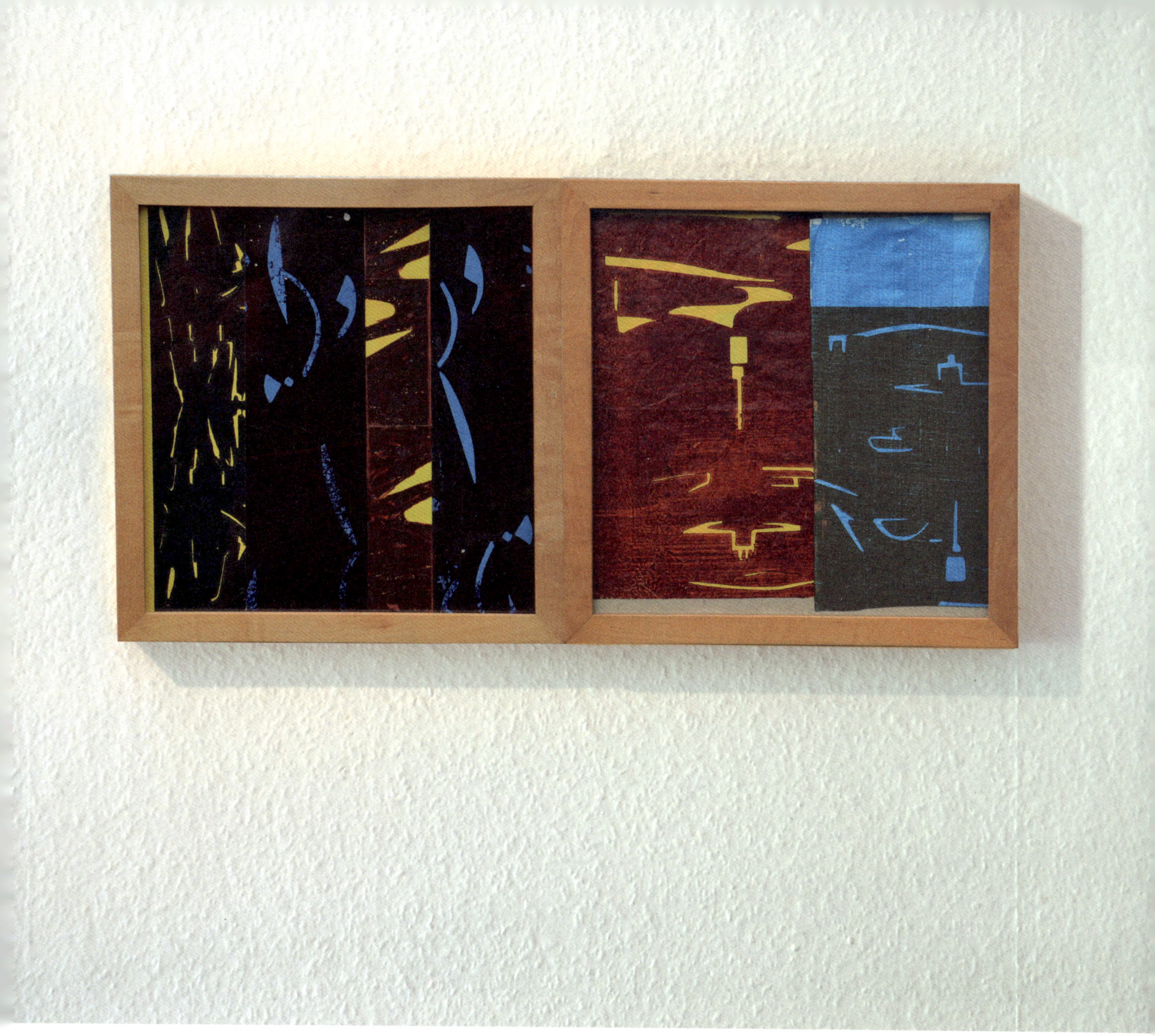

Cabo Verde

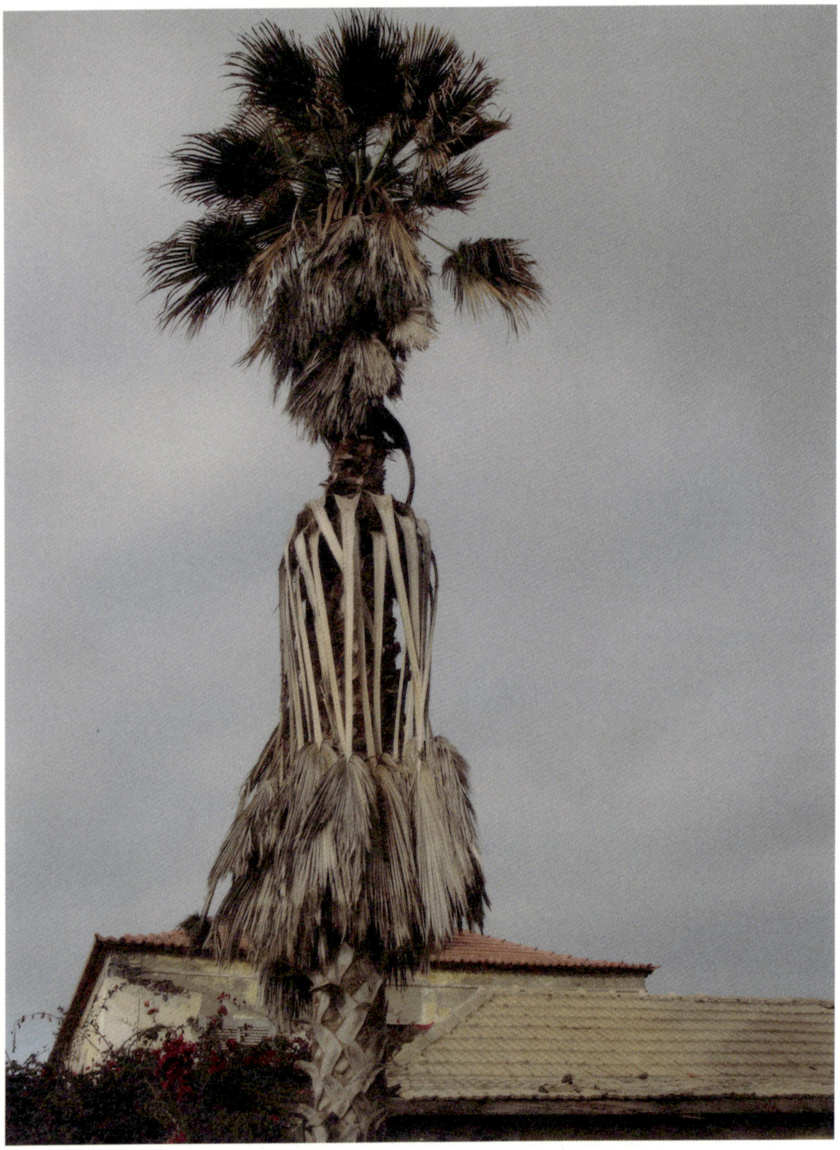

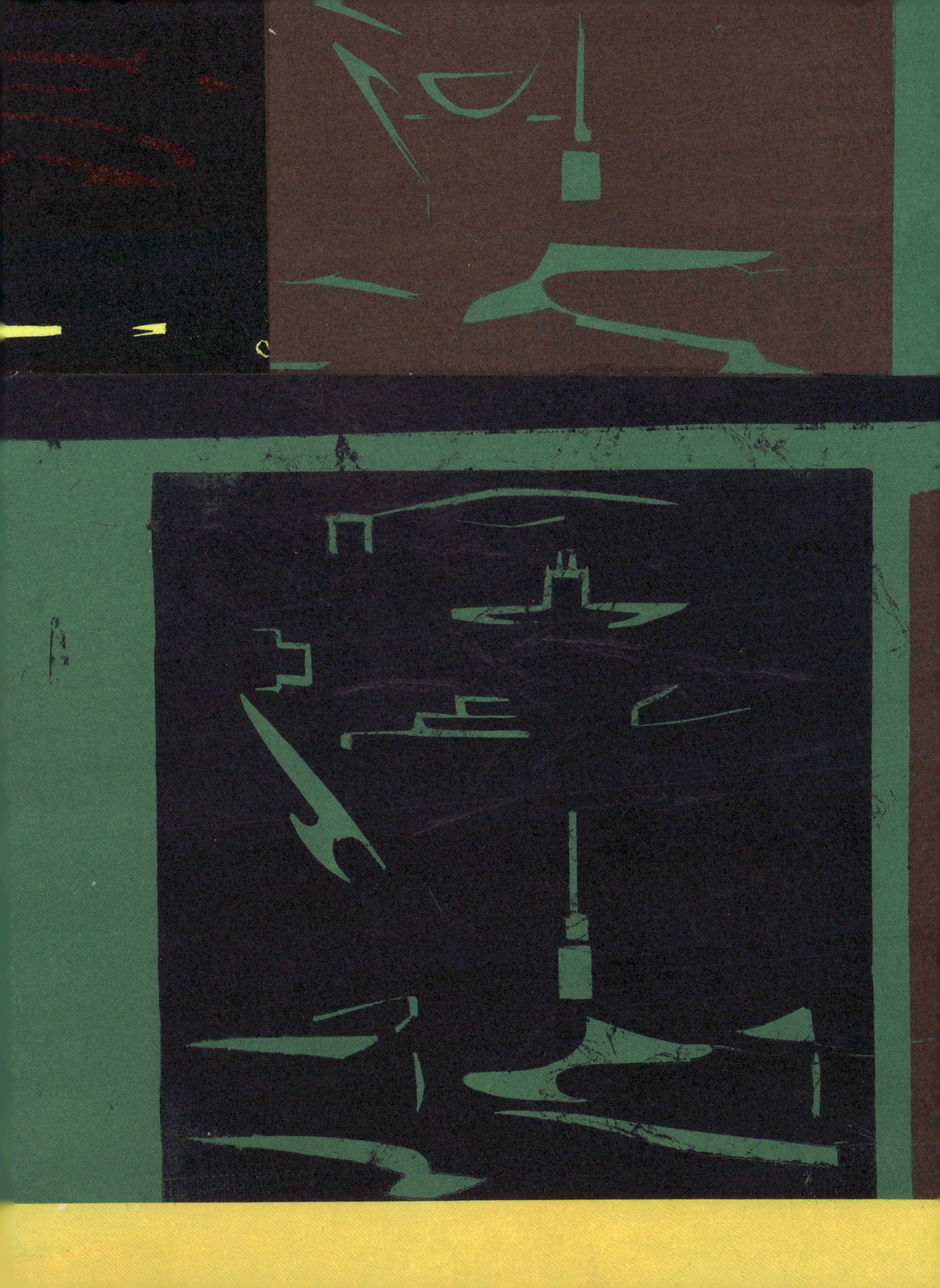

At her 2004 exhibition at Antwerp gallery Wollondilly, Linda Vinck first introduced a new, contemporary art concept to her work: synaesthesia, the interconnection of different sensory spheres. Through her work FUNANÁ, she sought to underline the connection between her visual work, employing a rhythmic use of colour, along with a repetitive and serial character, together with the Cape Verdean musical art of *Funaná*. Linda Vinck lived in Cape Verde between 1998 and 2012. A word of comment.

Here, it is already well established that Cape Verde is a veritable archipelago of music. Perhaps worth remembering that this country only gained independence in 1975, following five centuries of *colonisation*. Consequently, Cape Verdean identity is shaped around that forced encounter between the culture of Portuguese masters and that of African populations. Funaná, as Linda Vinck referred to, represents the end product of an appropriation process by the marginalised black population of an eminently European instrument, the accordion. This instrument was originally intended to replace the harmonium in church services, but was soon used alongside it in traditional folk dances, as well as for birth and wedding celebrations. The accordionist is accompanied by the so-called '*ferrino*' player, who dictates the rhythm by scraping over an iron bar with a kitchen knife. Where there is a singing accompaniment in Creole, it is always centred around use of metaphor. Cape Verdeans are a poetic people. As an accordionist and Funaná player, Linda Vinck also composed odes to the life she is so passionate about through use of lines, symbols and shapes, together with colours.

As quoted in 1989, albeit more relevant than ever today, both in 2004 and through her current work: "*Rhythm has the peculiarity of encompassing both movement (will) and quasi-legal confines (thought). Rhythm is the magnet, the focal plane, the magnetic field. Symbols merge and separate according to principles of attraction and repulsion. Rhythmic patterns form, wherein everything is connected and fits, emerging from a certain intuitive geometry. Unlike analytical works, this requires a synthesising attitude from the viewer*".

End quote.

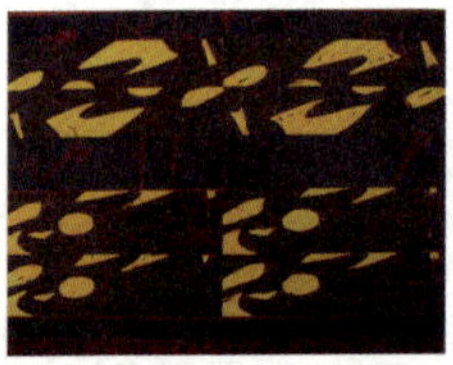

Linda Vinck is an artist who has written her own chapter in the development of modern art in Flanders. Her work situates itself within the evolution of universal (sublime) abstracts in painting. It is not characterised by splashes of *abstract expressionism*, nor linear forms of *constructivism*, rather by the application of symbols on monochrome background, as a pictorial expression of her emotion and temperament, as well as of the transcendental desire to portray '*reality behind reality*' through her craft.

 artwork in text: Kebra Kanela

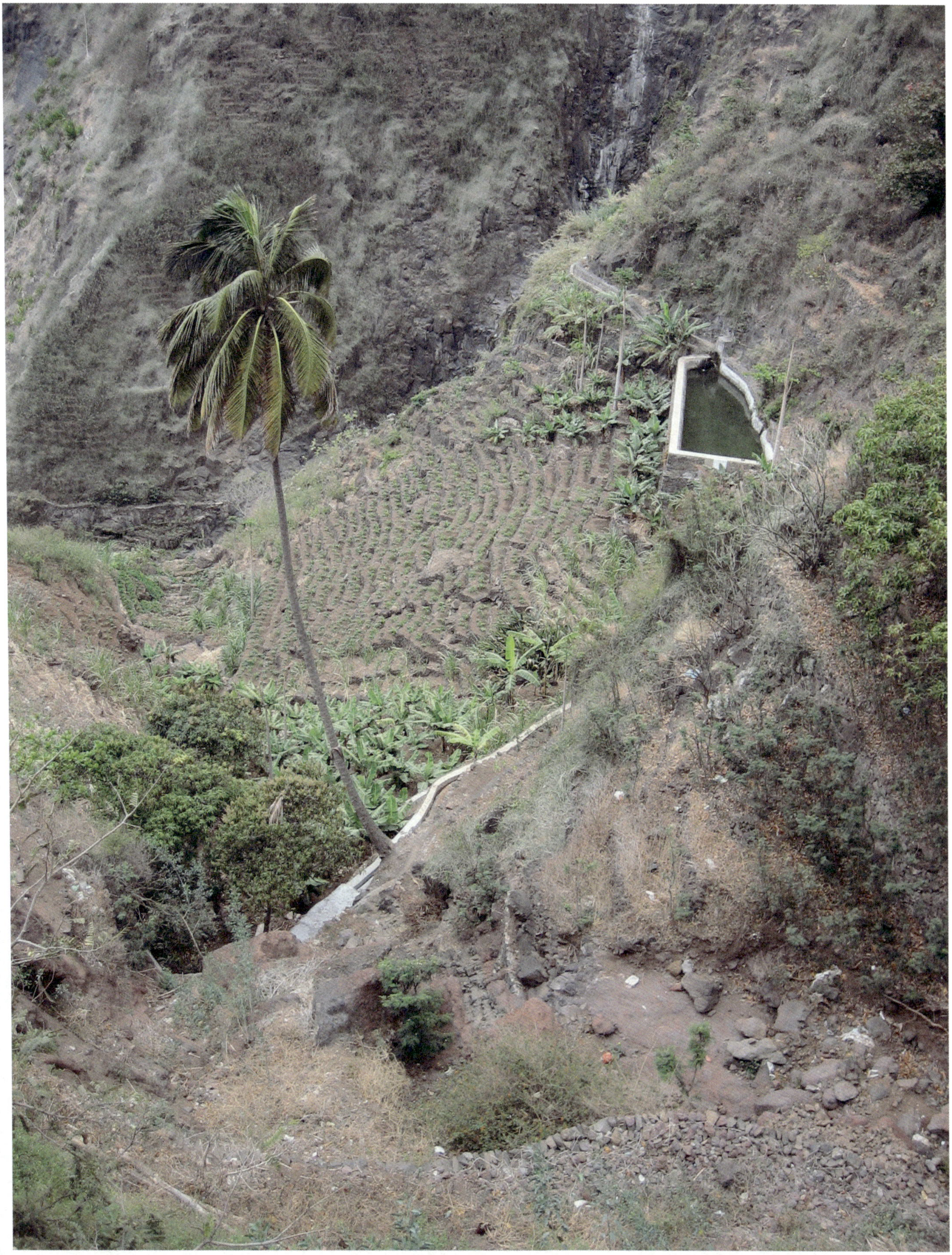

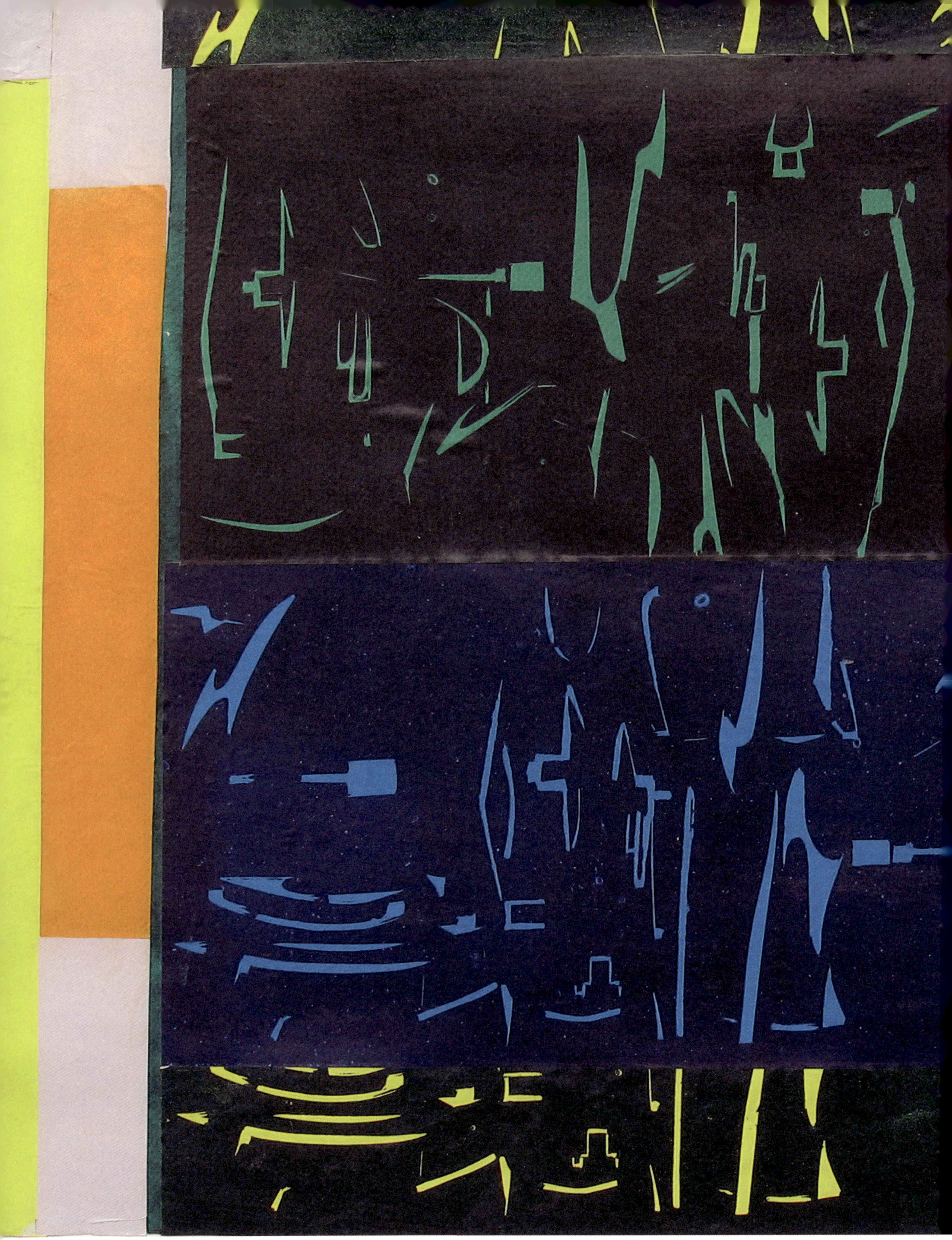

Salamansa groot 1a

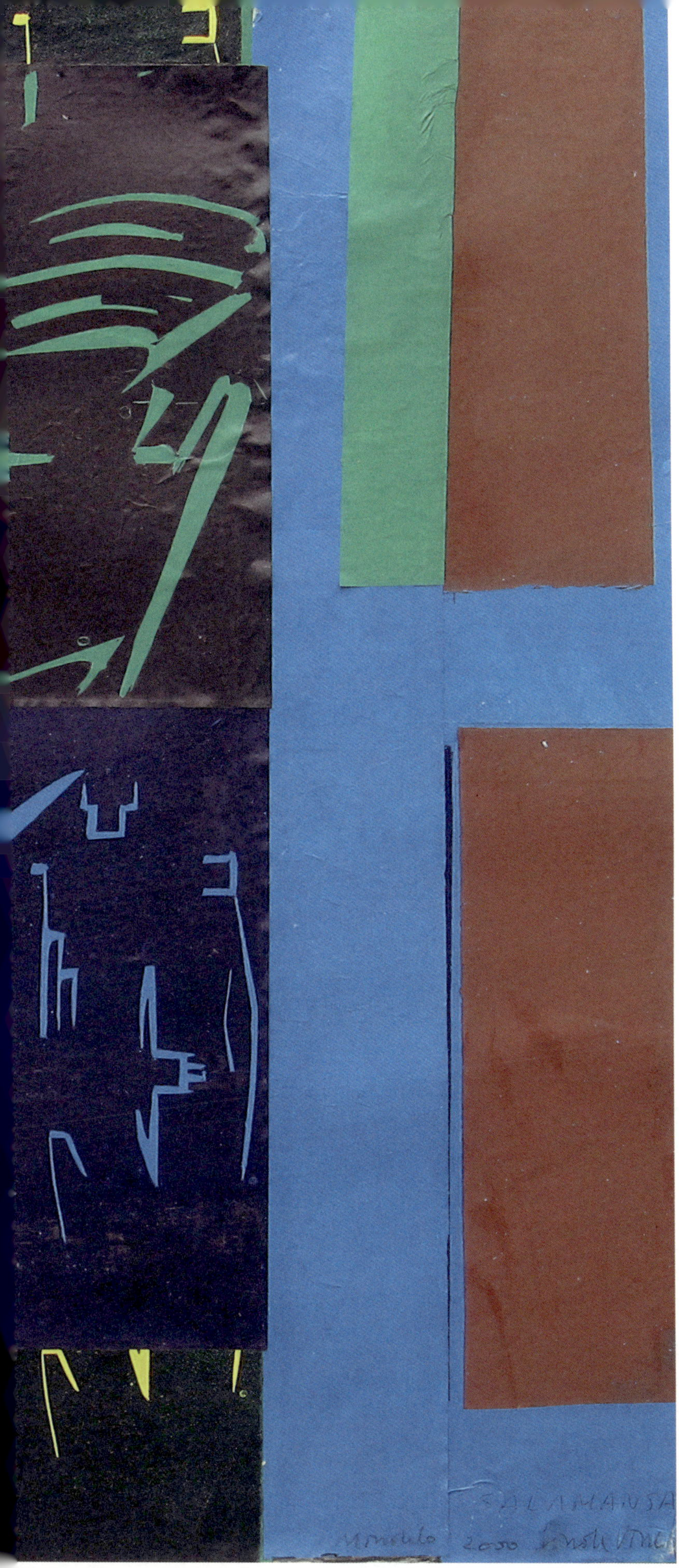

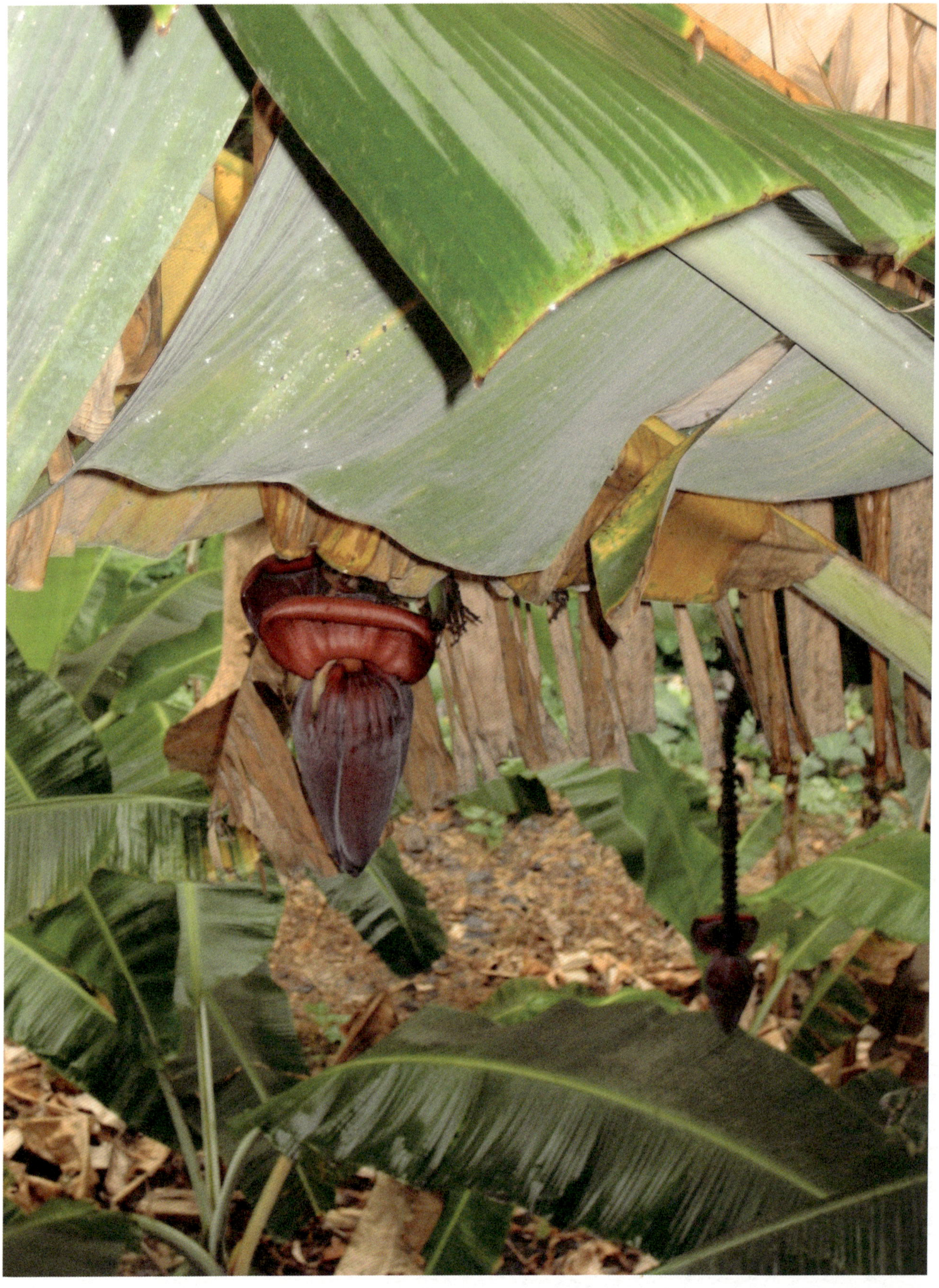

Linda Vinck introduceerde in 2004, met haar tentoonstelling in de Antwerpse galerie Wollondilly een nieuw en actueel kunstbegrip in haar werk: de synesthesie, de verbinding van verschillende zintuigsferen. Met de titel FUNANÁ wilde zij de band tussen haar beeldend werk, met een grote ritmiek aan kleur en vorm, het repetitief en serieel karakter en de muziekvorm *Funaná* uit Kaapverdië onderlijnen. Linda Vinck verbleef in Kaapverdië van 1998 tot 2012. Een woordje commentaar.

Dat Kaapverdië de archipel is van de muziek, is hier reeds goed doorgedrongen. Misschien even herinneren dat dit land pas in 1975 onafhankelijk werd, na vijf eeuwen kolonisatie. De Kaapverdische identiteit is dus gebaseerd op die gedwongen ontmoeting tussen de cultuur van Portugese meesters en die van de Afrikaanse bevolkingsgroepen. Funaná, waar Linda Vinck naar refereerde, is het eindproduct van een toeëigeningsproces, een appropriatie door de gemarginaliseerde zwarte bevolking van een bij uitstek Europees instrument, de accordeon. Dit instrument moest oorspronkelijk het harmonium vervangen in kerkdiensten, maar werd algauw daarnaast ook gebruikt voor populaire bals, geboorte- en huwelijksfeesten. De accordeonist wordt daarbij begeleid door de zogenaamde *ferrino*-speler, die het ritme aangeeft door met een keukenmes op een ijzeren staaf te schrapen. Indien er bij gezongen wordt in het Creools is dit steeds met metaforen. Kaapverdiërs zijn ook een poëtisch volk. Als een accordeoniste, een Funaná-speelster, componeerde Linda Vinck met lijnen, tekens en vormen, met kleuren ook odes aan het leven waarvan zij hartstochtelijk houdt.

Een citaat van haarzelf, geformuleerd in 1989, maar zowel in 2004 als vandaag in haar huidig werk actueler dan ooit:
"Ritme heeft de merkwaardigheid dat het tegelijk beweging (wil) en wetmatigheid (denken) is. Het ritme is de magneet, het beeldvlak, het magnetisch veld. Tekens voegen zich samen en scheiden zich overeenkomstig principes van aantrekking en afstoting. Ritmische patronen vormen zich waarin alles verbonden is en past, ontstaan vanuit een intuïtieve geometrie. In tegenstelling tot een analytische vergt dit werk een synthetiserende instelling van de toeschouwer".
Einde citaat.

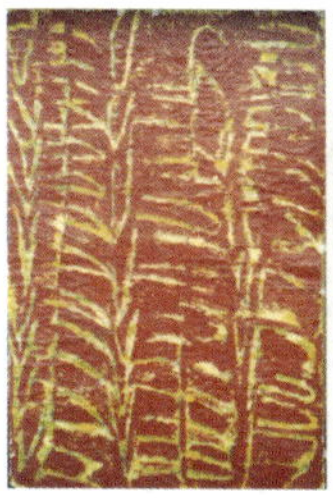

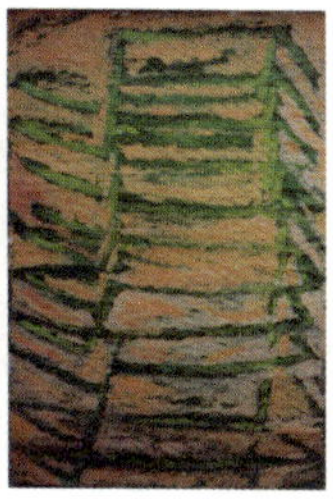

Linda Vinck is een kunstenares die een eigen bladzijde geschreven heeft in de ontwikkeling van de hedendaagse kunst in Vlaanderen. Haar werk situeert zich binnen de evolutie van de universele (sublieme) abstracten in de schilderkunst. Bij haar geen gespetter van het abstract expressionisme, ook geen lineaire vormen van het constructivisme, maar wel het aanbrengen van tekens op een monochrome achtergrond, als picturale uitdrukking van haar emotie en temperament en van het transcendente verlangen via haar handschrift *'de werkelijkheid achter de werkelijkheid'* weer te geven.

artworks in text: Acrylic on layered paper 1 & 2

Cabo Verde

The apprehension of working on enumeration and repetition while focusing on patterns has been developed in African, pre-Columbian or Polynesian art (with wall carpets and textiles), Op Art (Victor Vasarely), and in nature itself.

There is a conspiracy between Hand, Eye and Imagination, listening to the remonstrances and warnings of Reason, while being bewildered, will not have ceased to keep an eye on these accomplices.

 João Vário, from 'Linda Vinck: A special case of enumeration in painting', Antwerp, July 1994

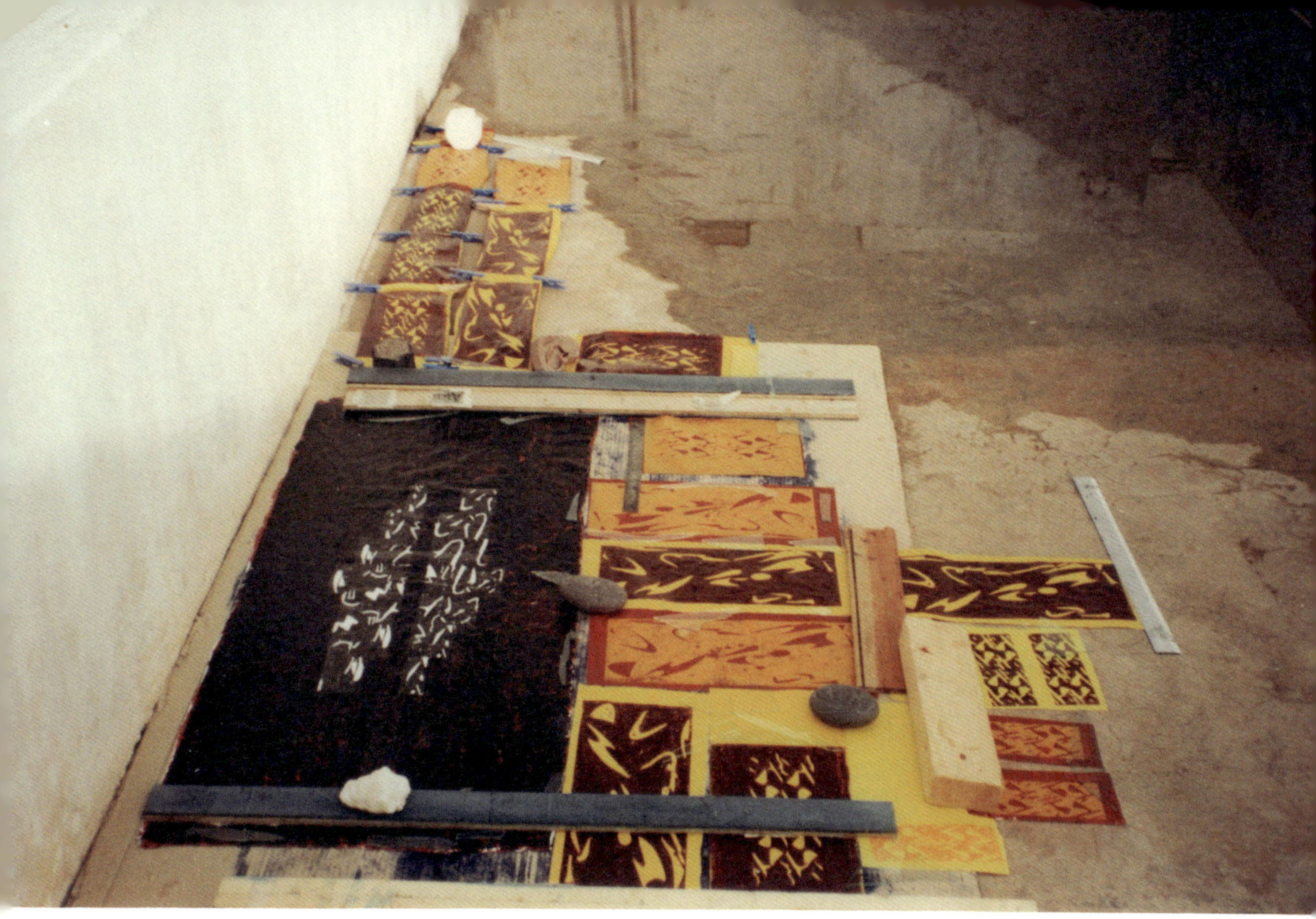

Avenida Baltazar Lopes da Silva n°100, Mindelo, São Vicente Island
Printed artworks drying on the hot sunny roof,
protected from the wind by pebbles and stones, covered by sand coming from the Sahara

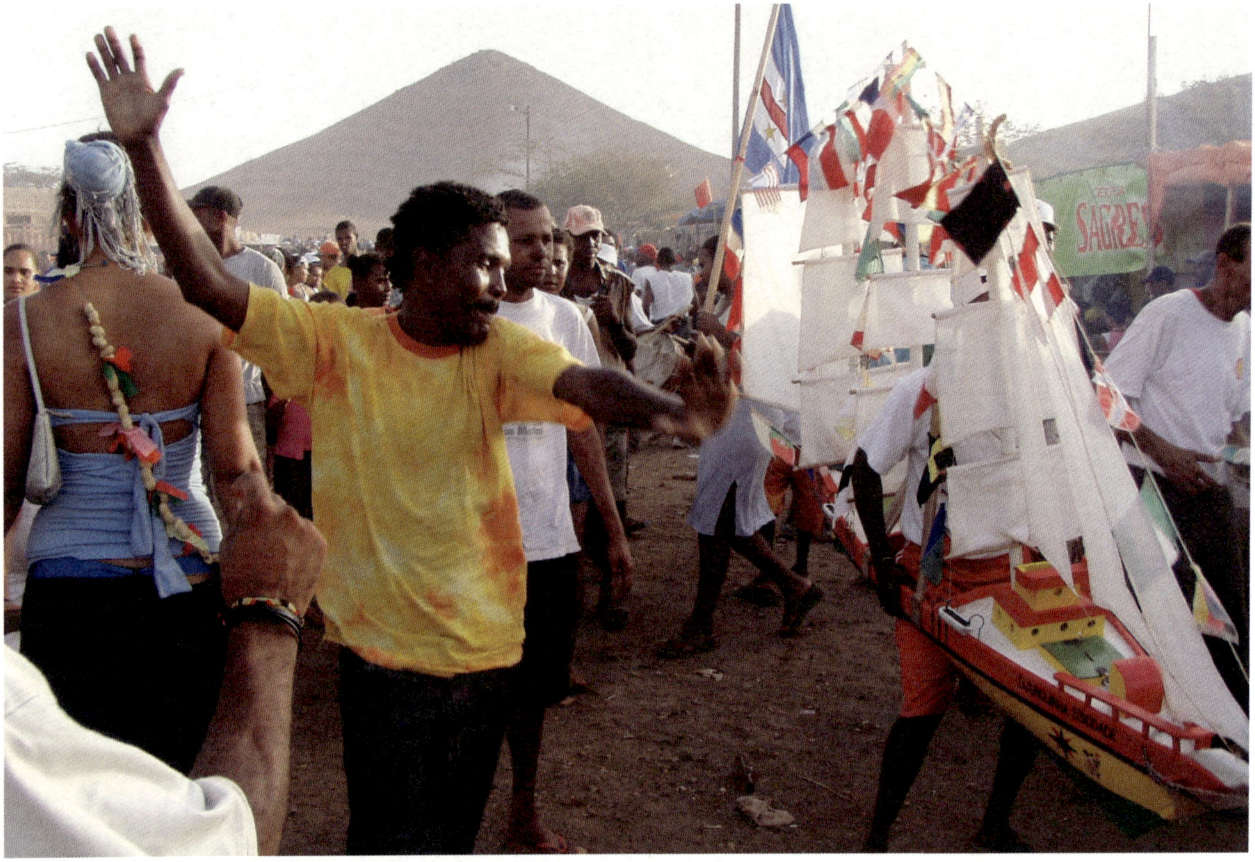

 Festa Kolá San Jon, Ribeira Julião–Mindelo, São Vicente Island

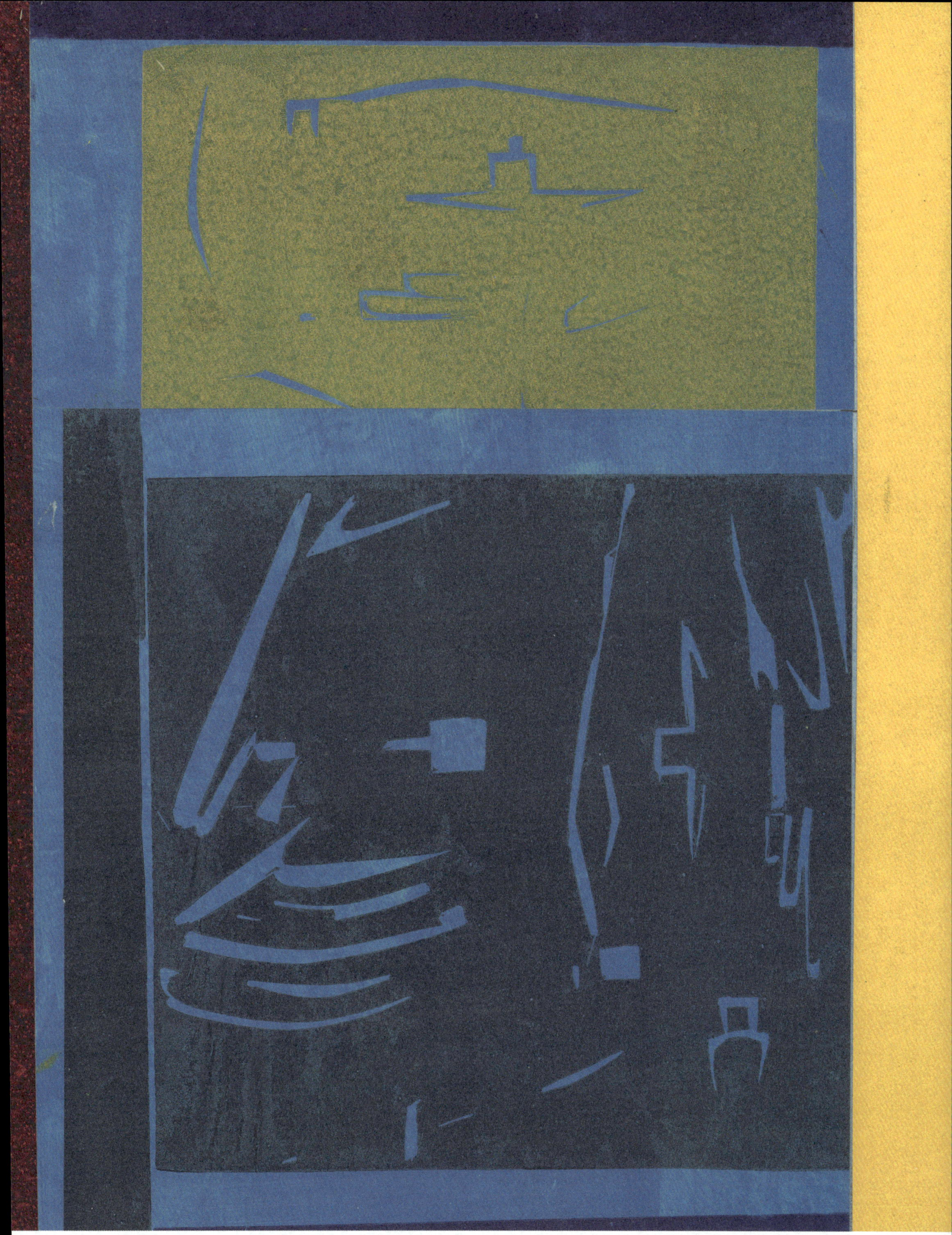

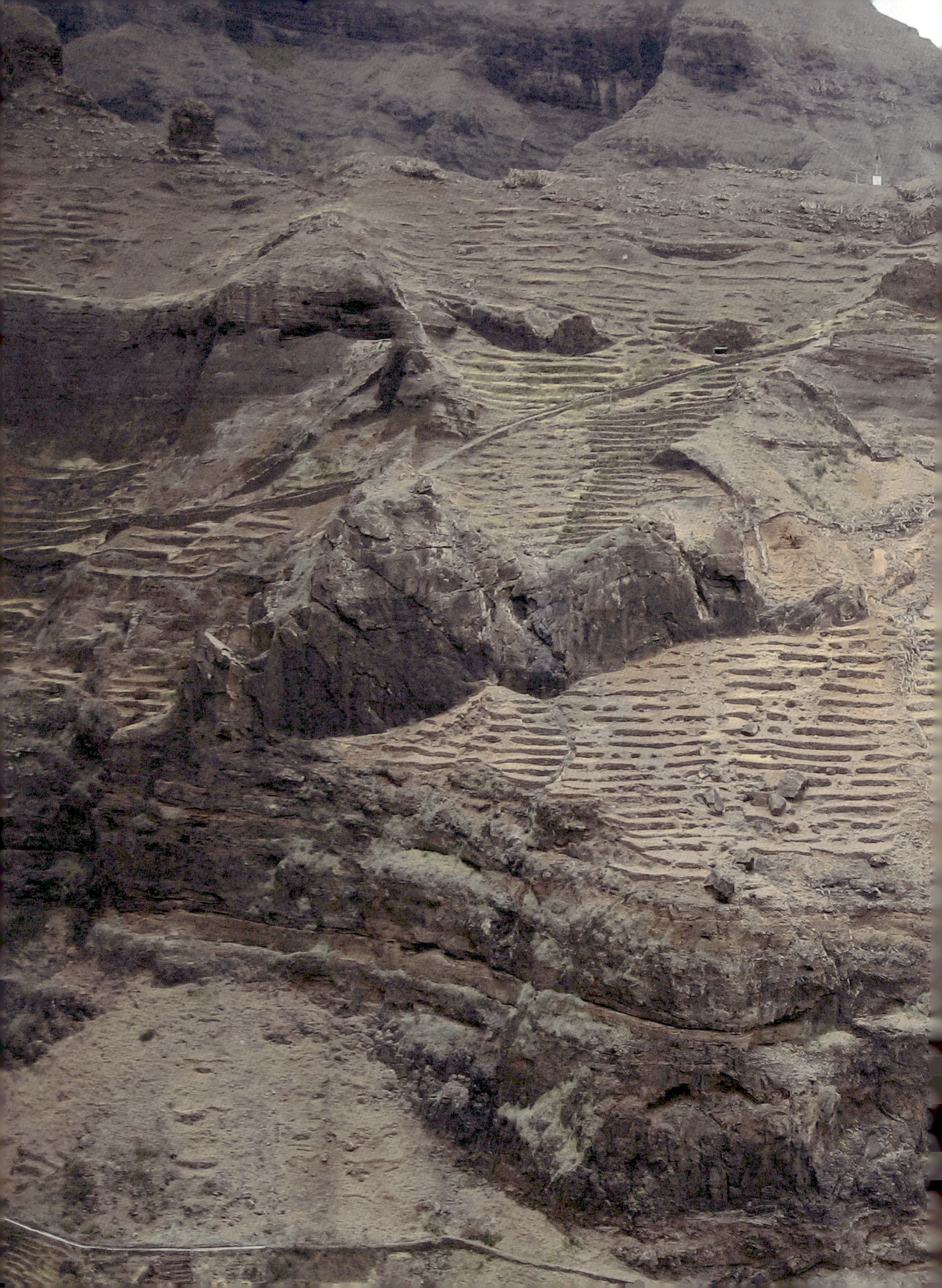

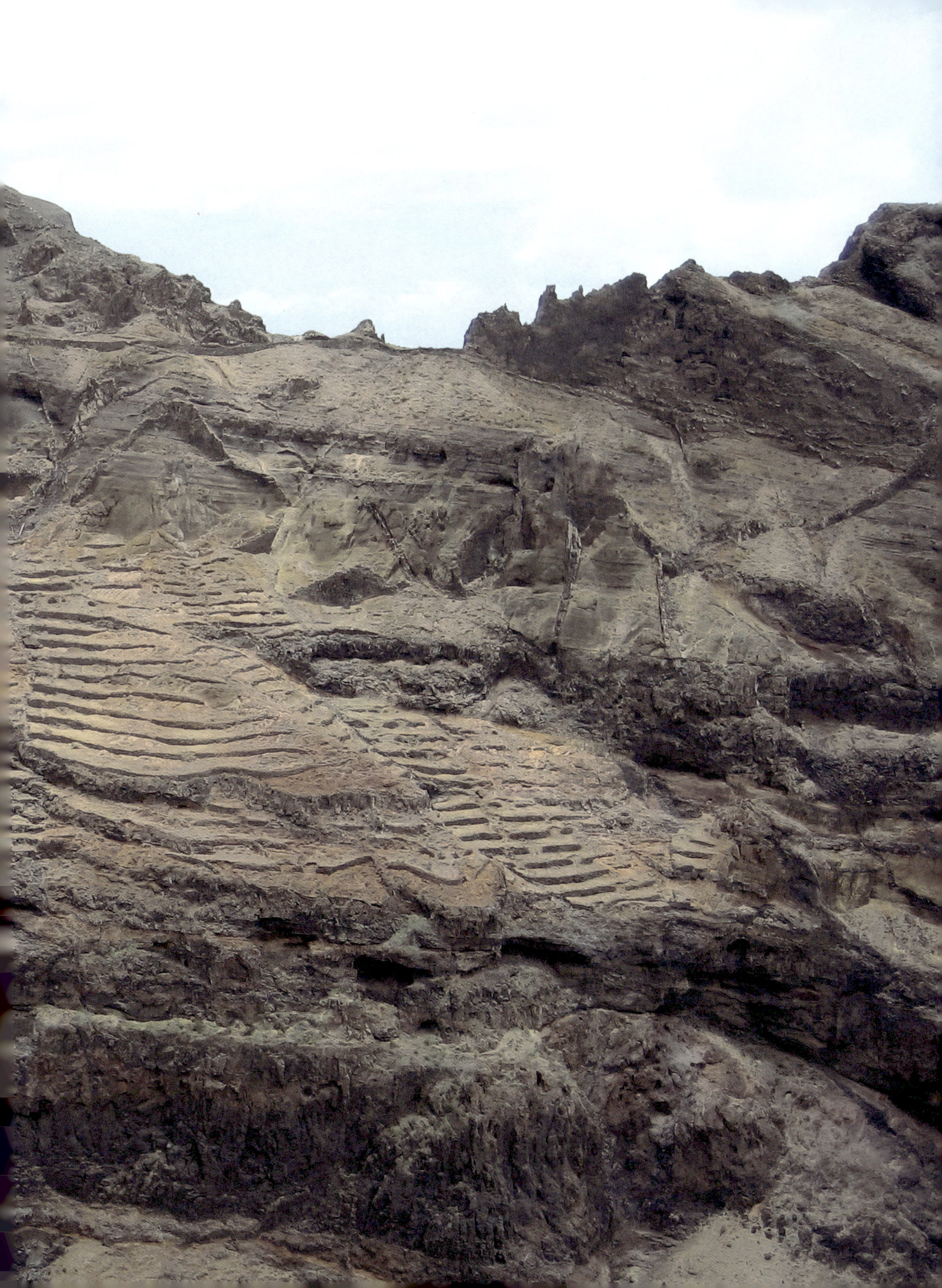

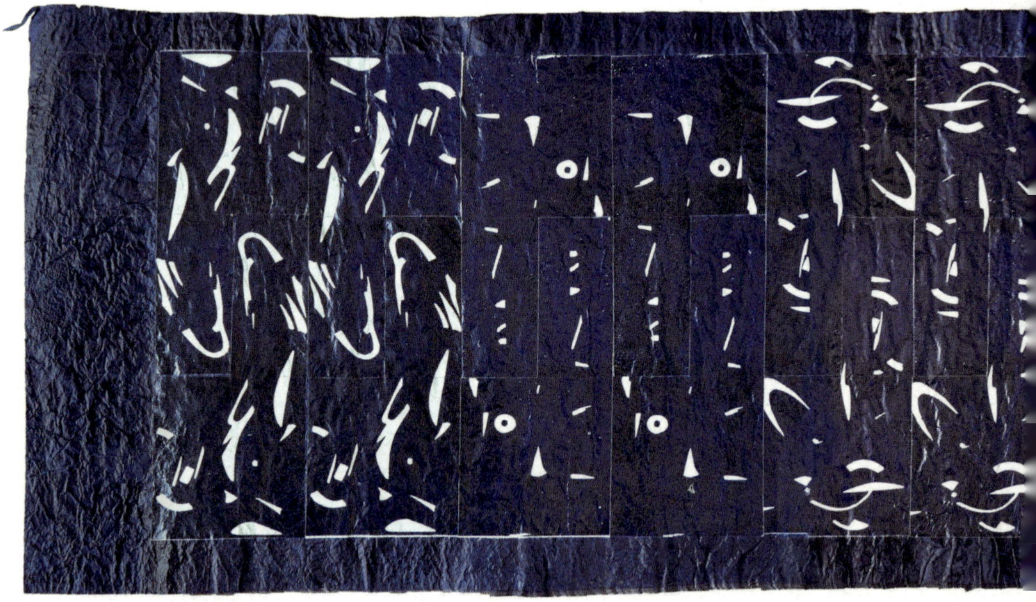

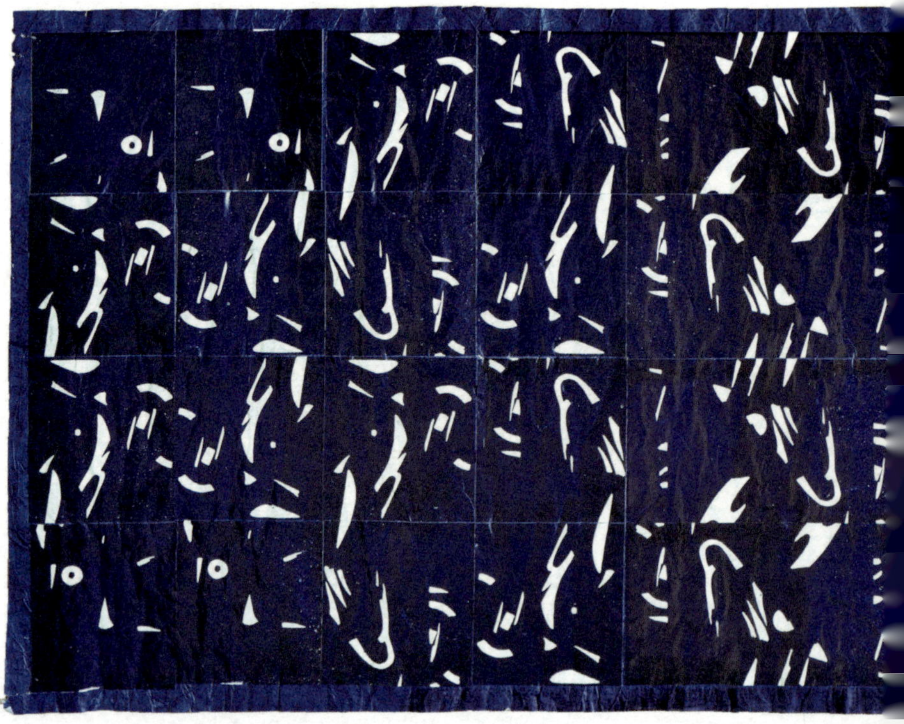

All parts, all fragments of motion relate to one another. They have no meaning on their own. Precisely because they depend on one another, they evoke one another as well. However, the richness of motion emerges not only from the unbelievably high number of motion parts, but also and mainly from the smooth lines they yield. Analyzing a motion is denying its uniqueness. Not linking up the initially analyzed and consequently separated parts turns motion into motion, but rather the merging of what have never been parts.

 Frans Boenders, 'Onherleidbare beweging in de partituren van Linda Vinck', originally published in K&C 92-10

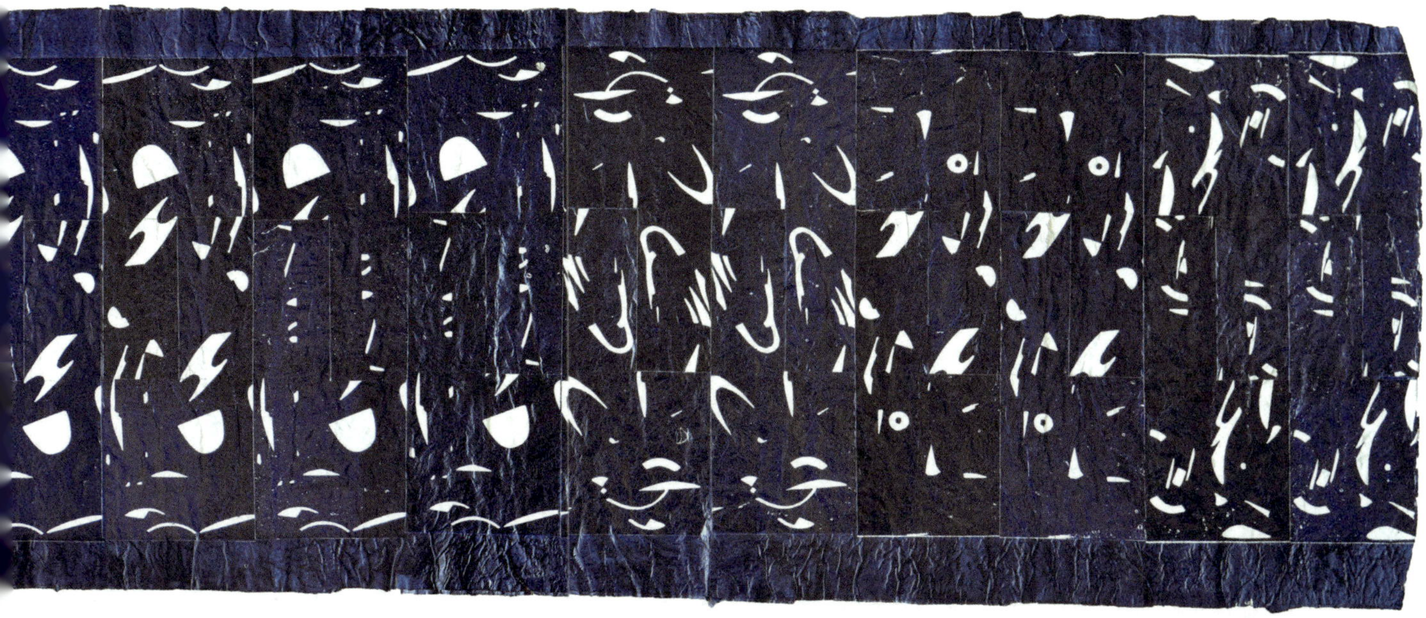

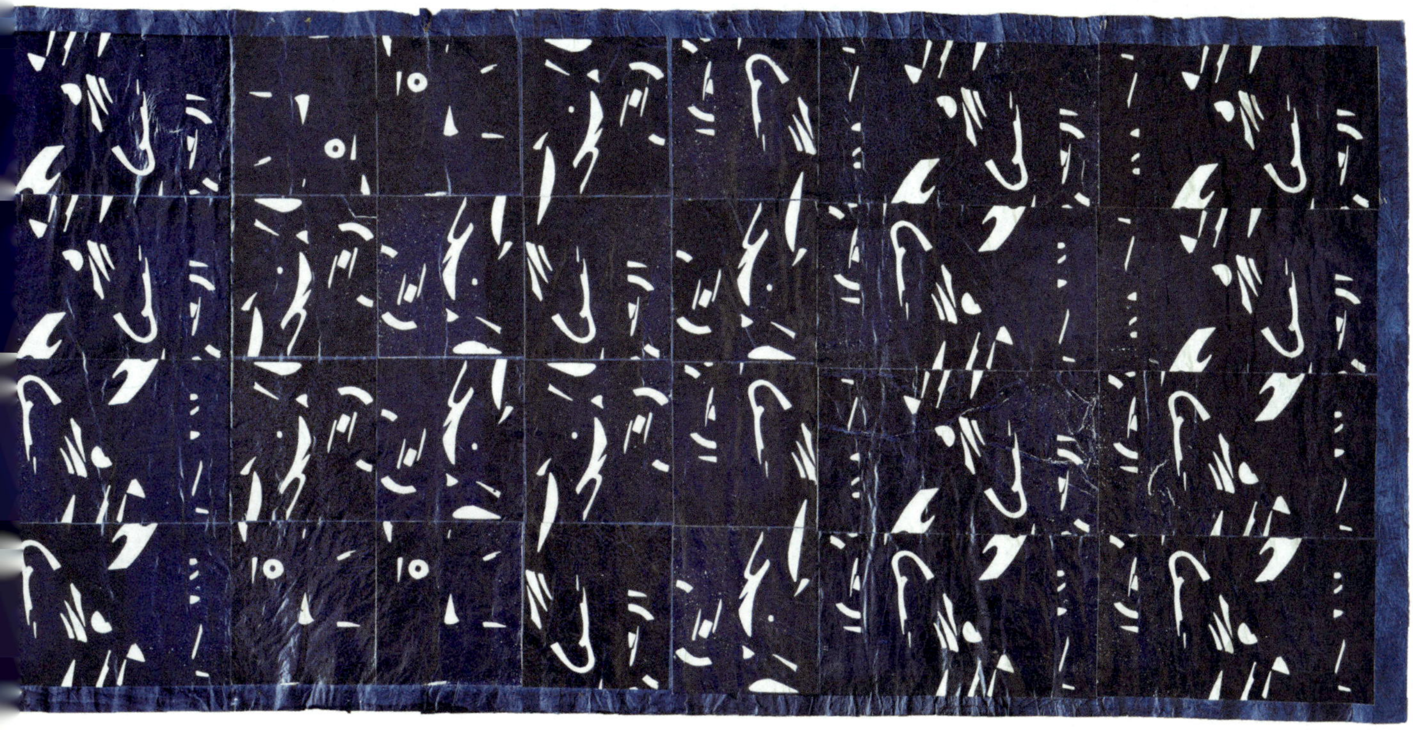

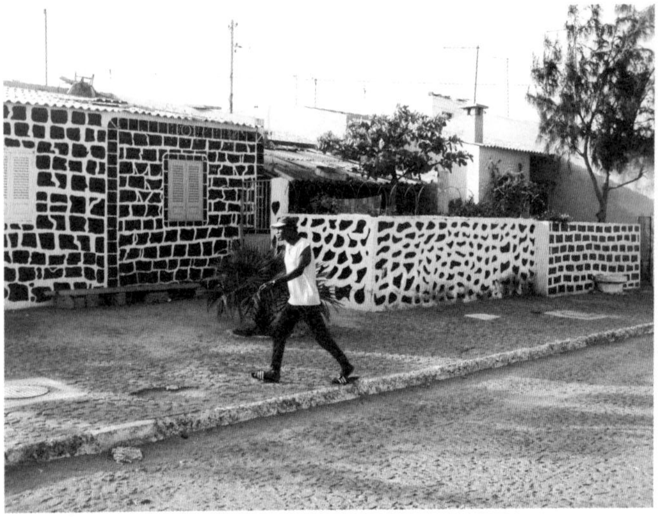

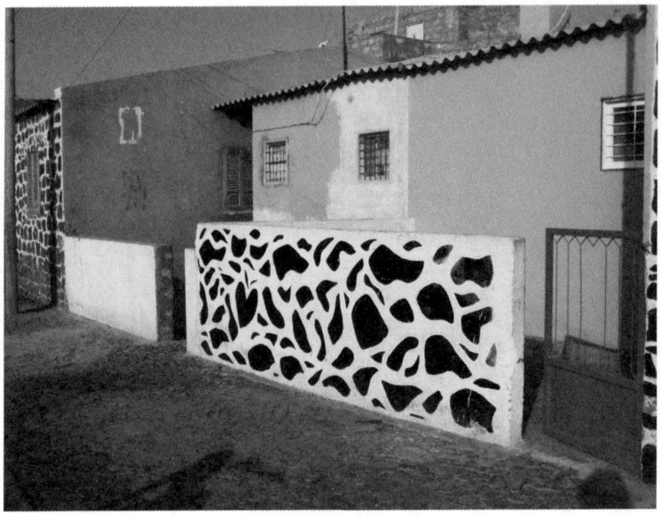

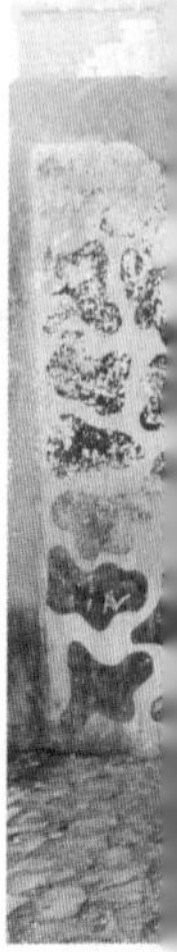

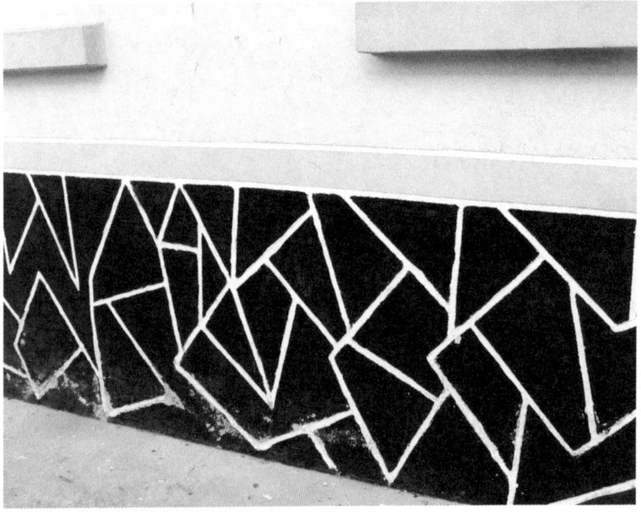

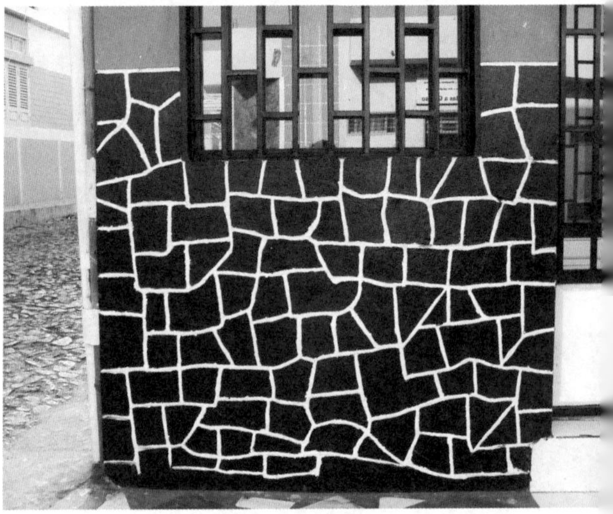

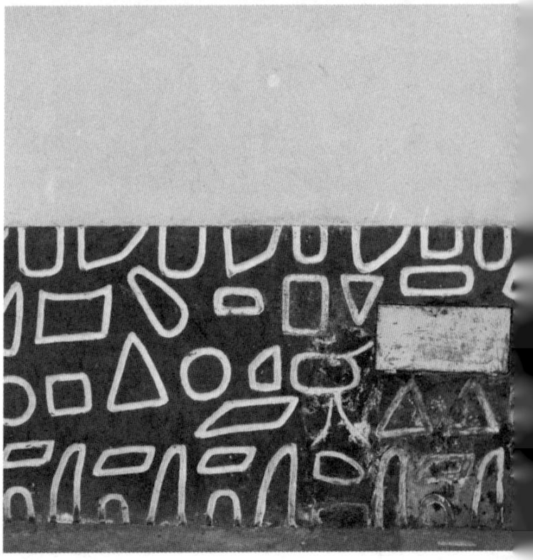

 Walls of Mindelo, São Vicente Island

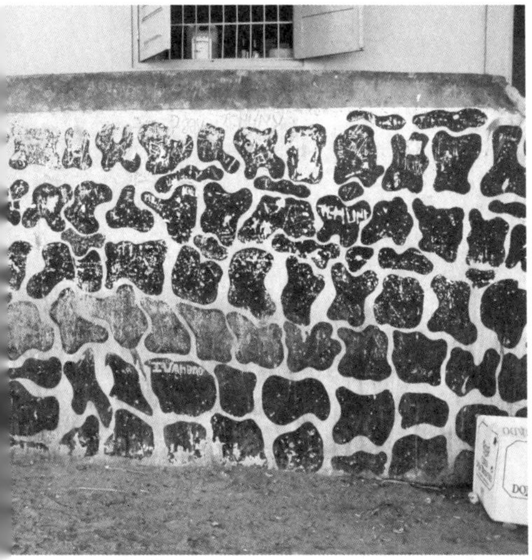

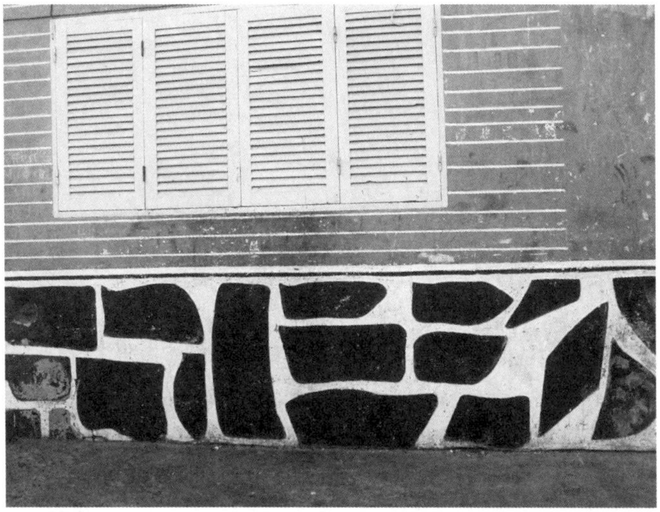

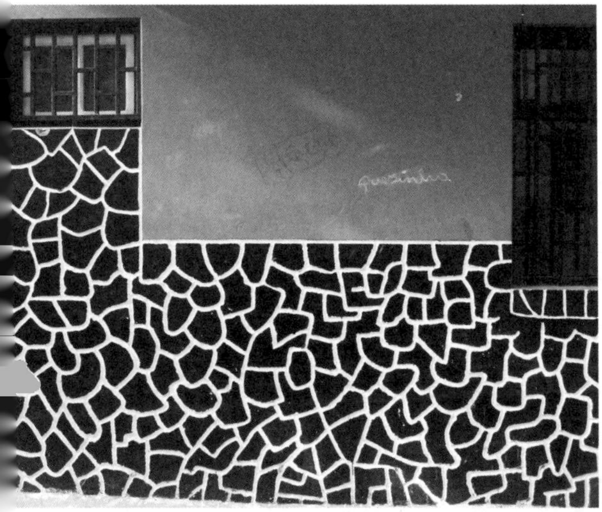

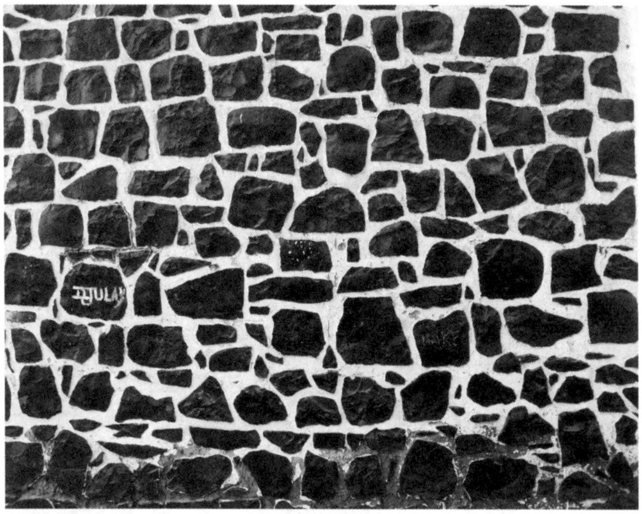

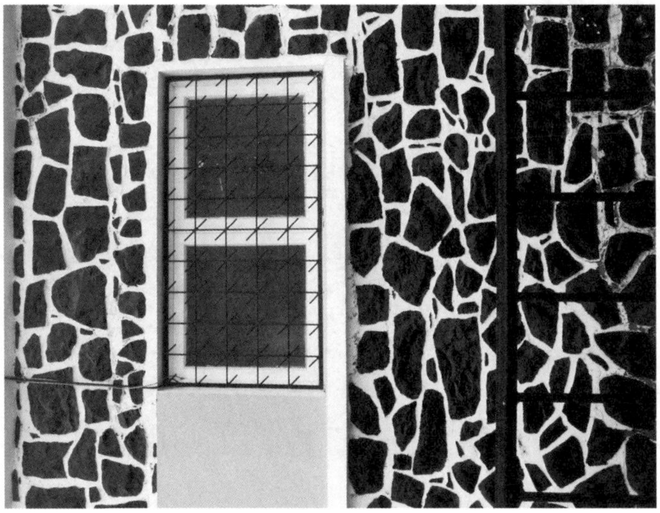

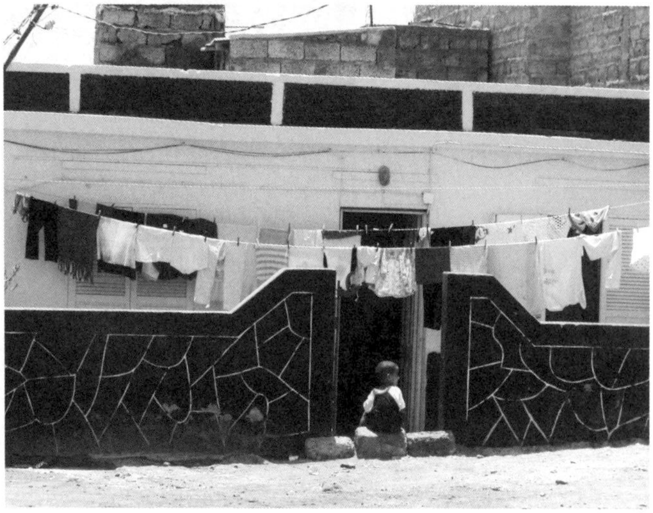

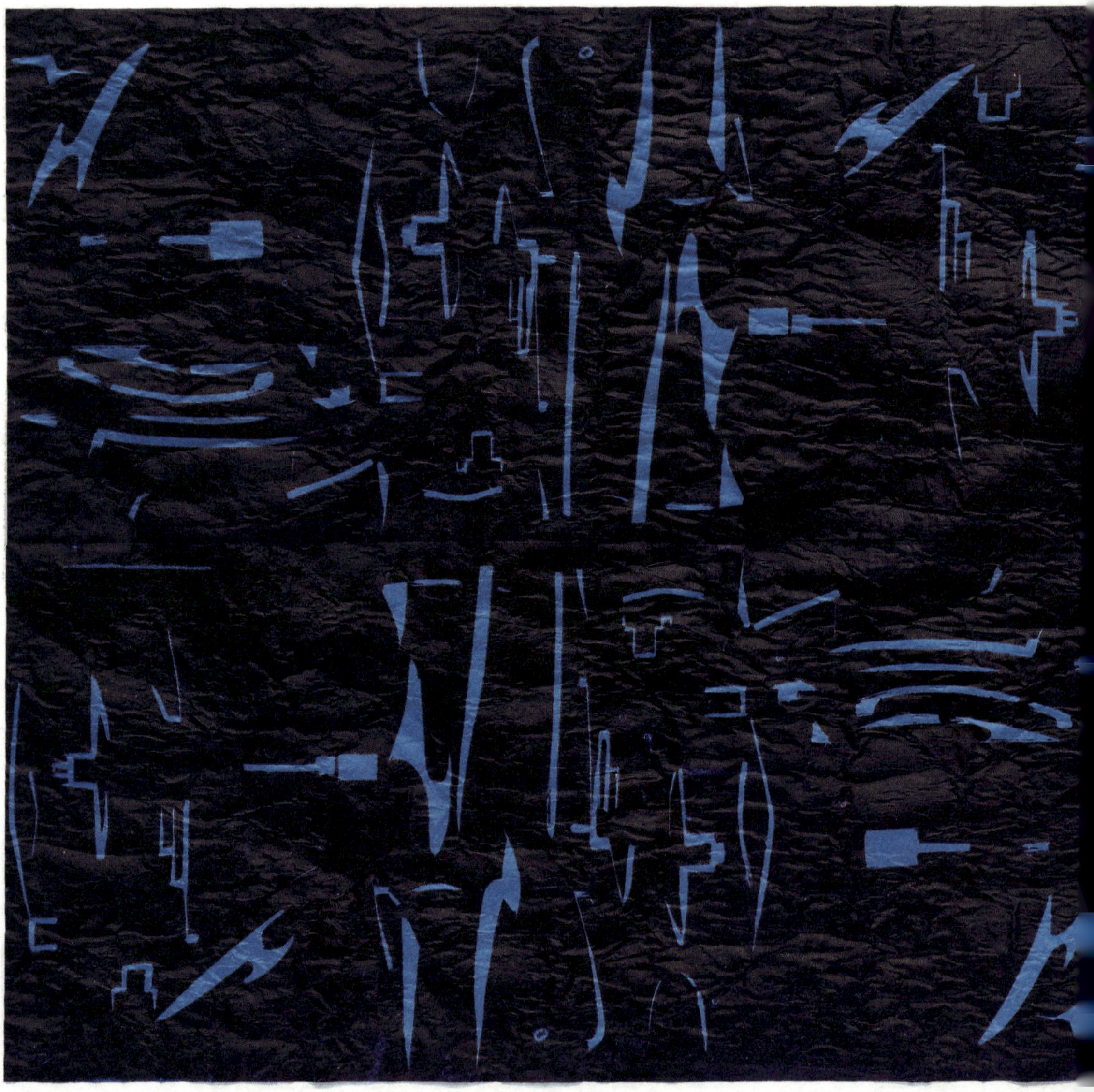

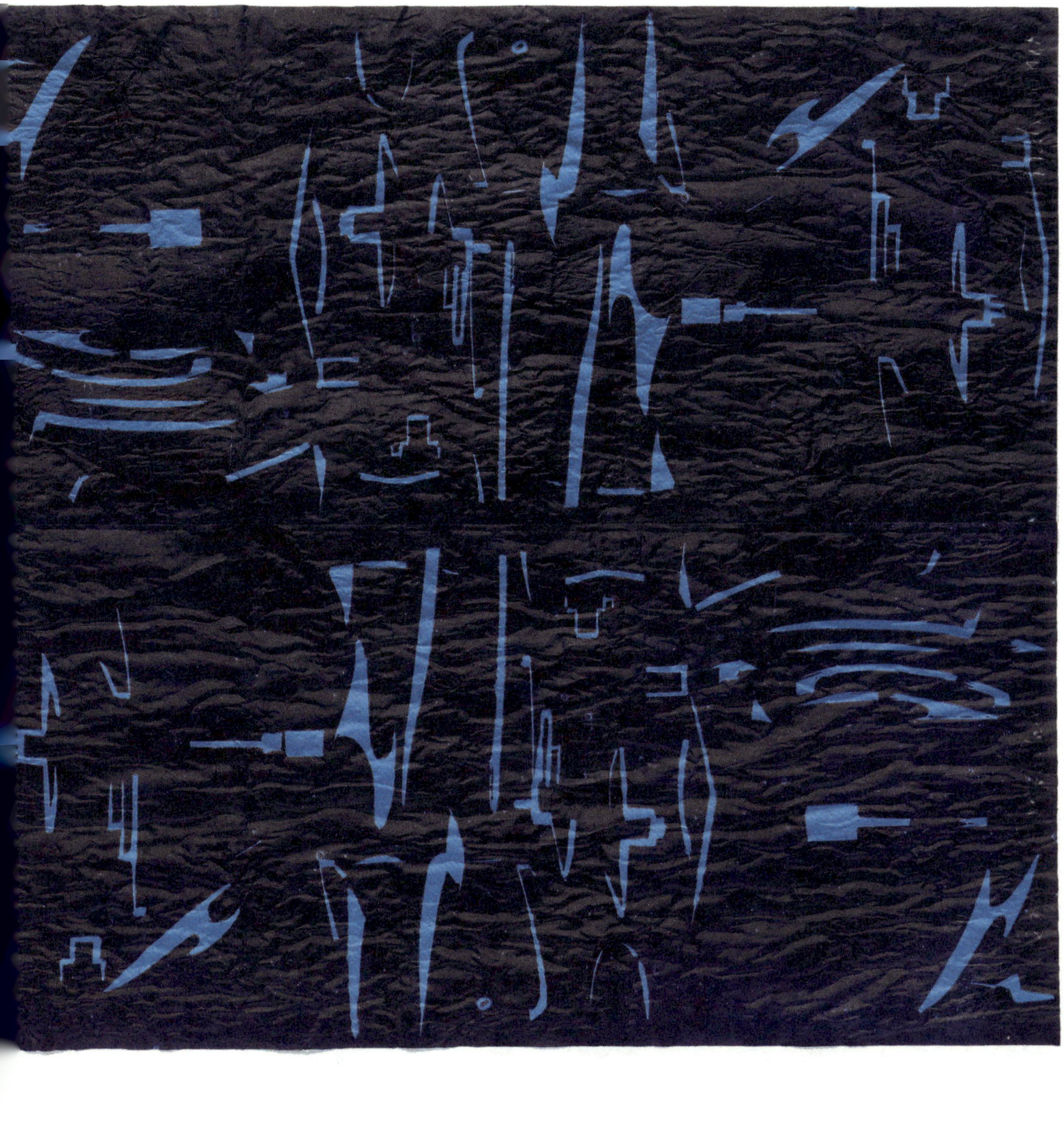

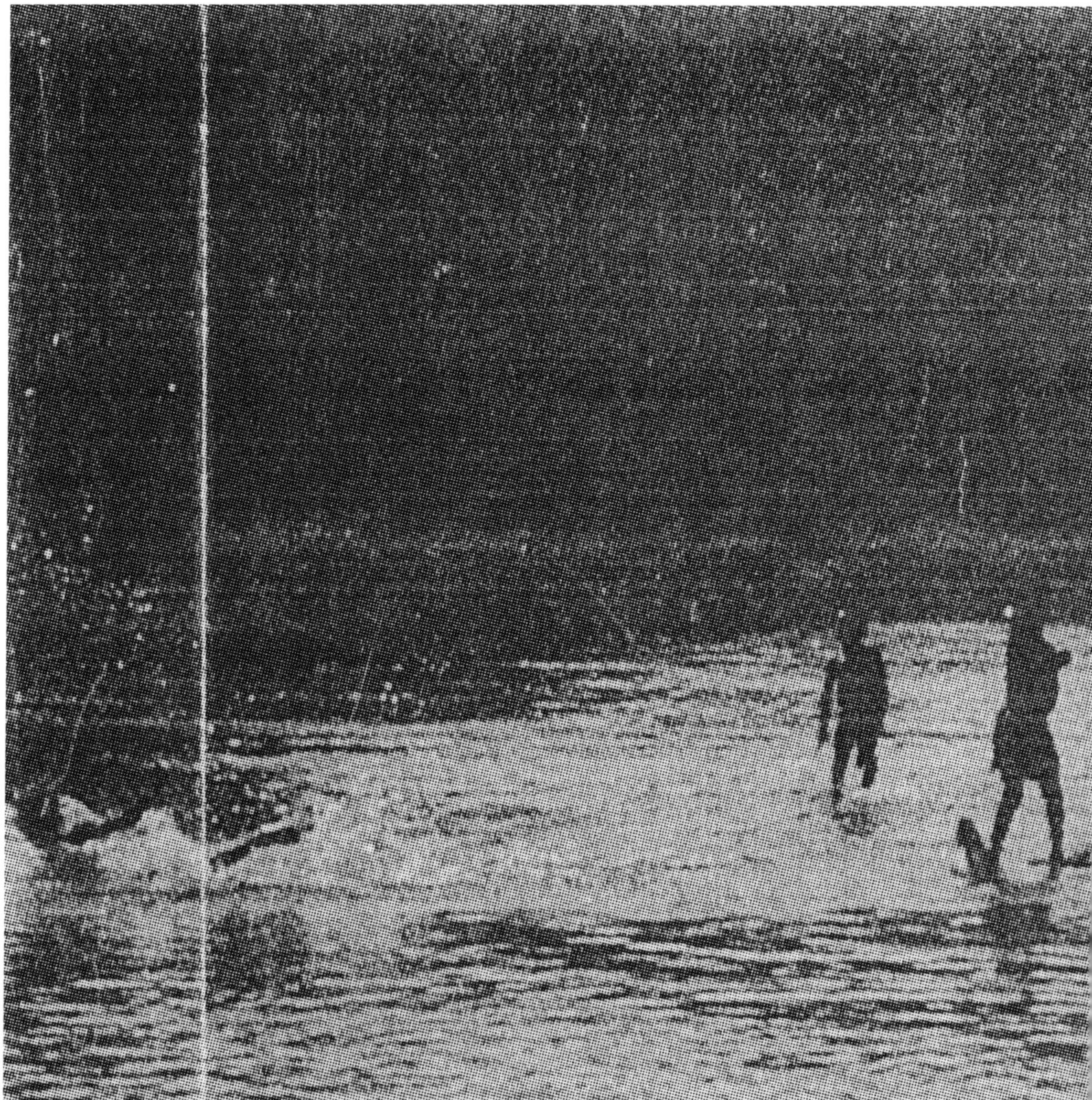

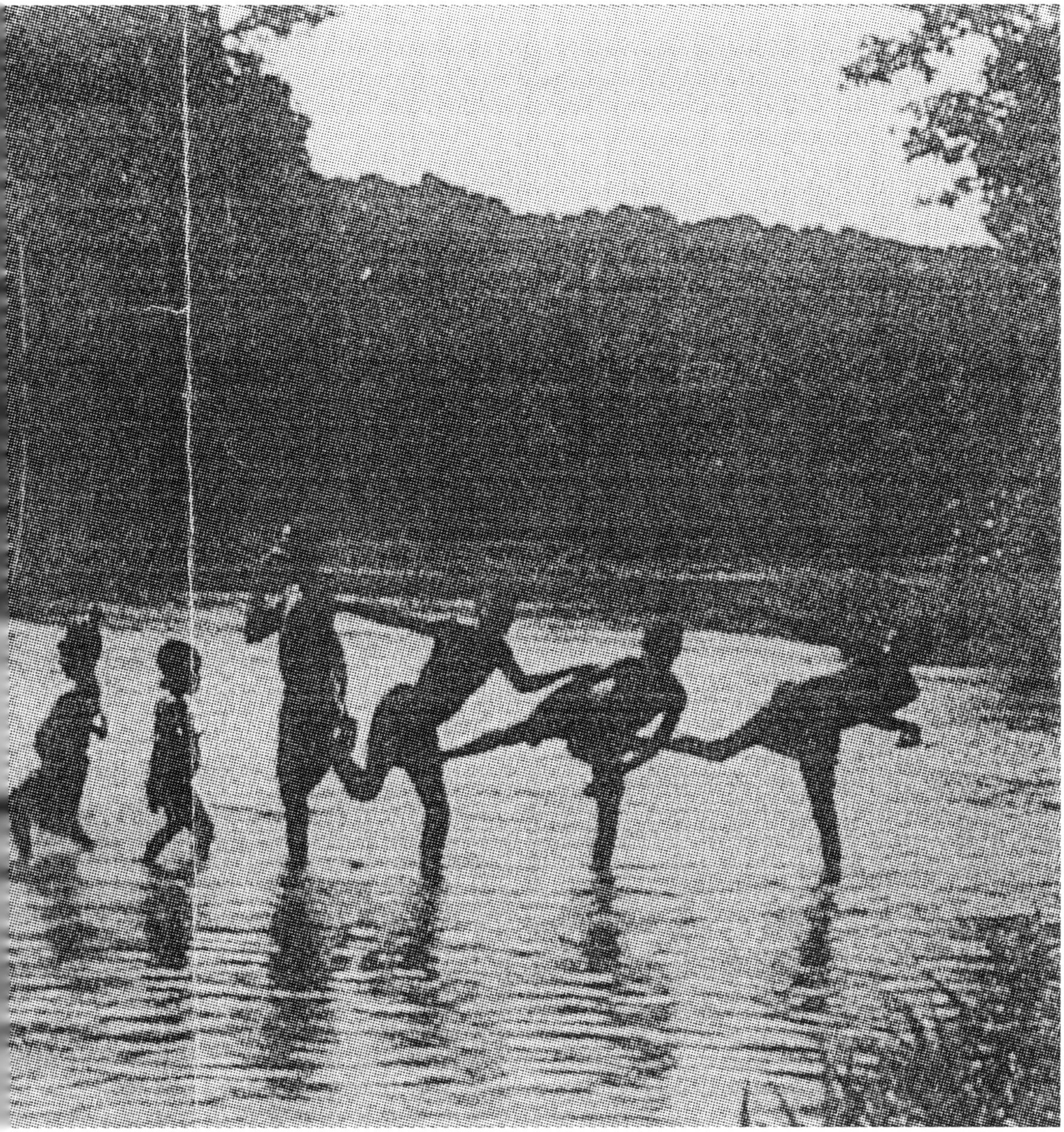

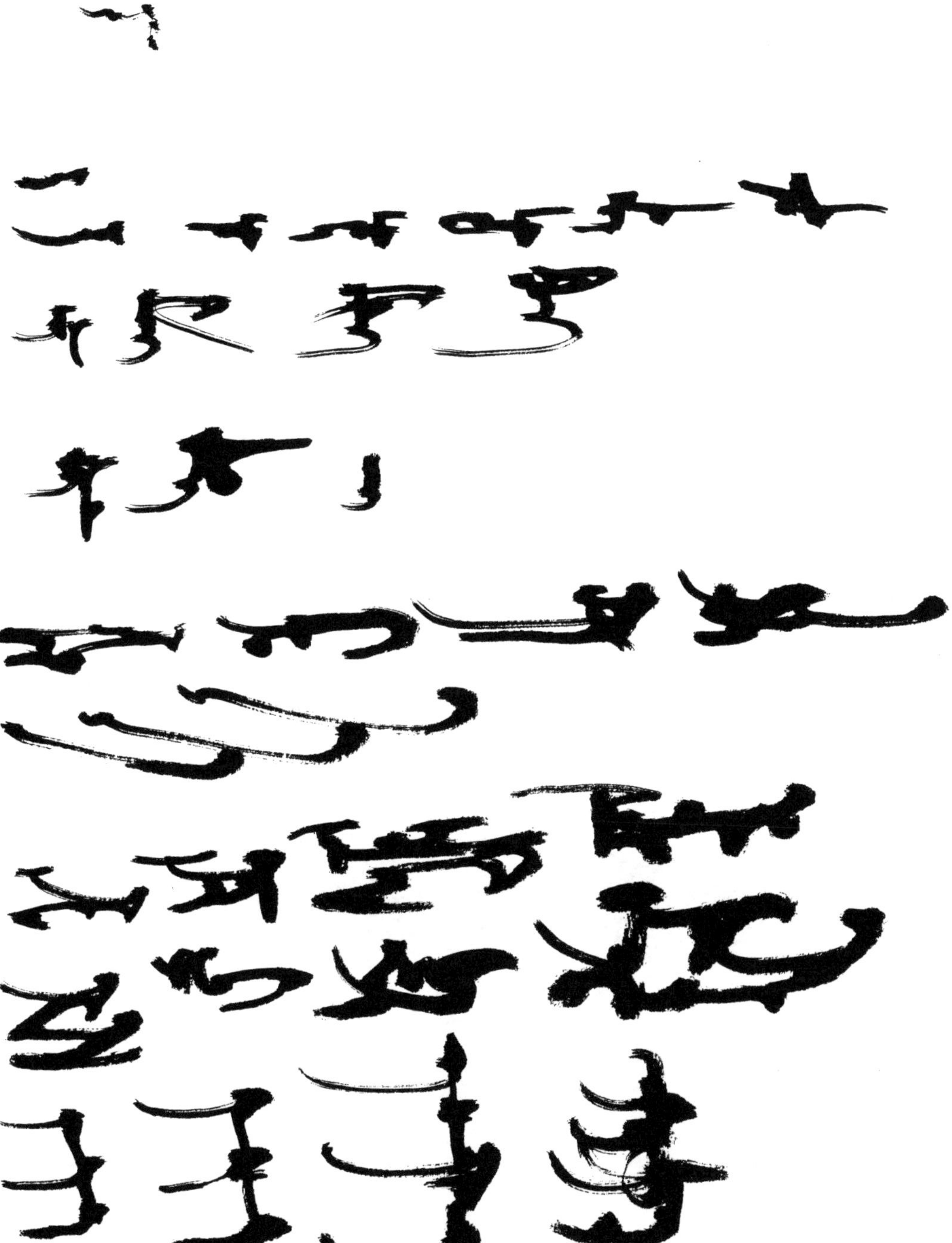

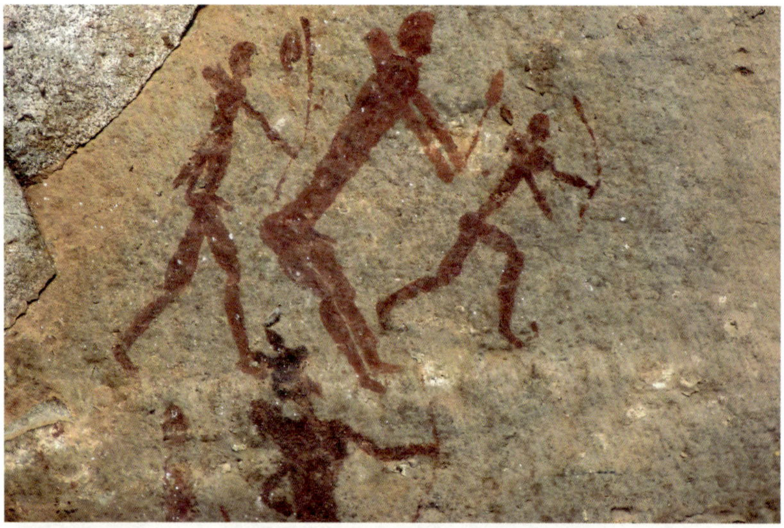

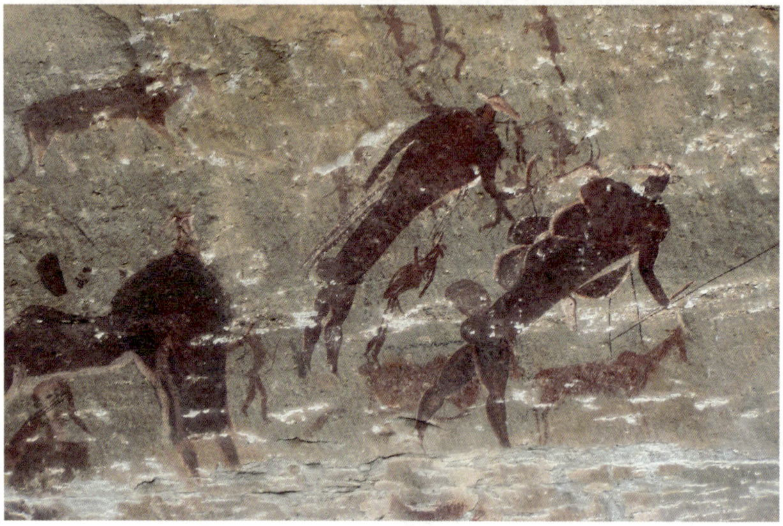

Heart's Patterning

For Linda

the be**a**uty of the **P**rocess
m**a**De visible
rhythm
      sounD
            blooD
turmoiled into inner **P**ower

Deep underw**a**ter Dre**a**ms
surf**a**cing to light **a**nd **a**ir
sIngIng
coDeD meloDies of souls

            w**a**tch
      listen
c**a**tch
he**a**rt's **Pa**tternIng of **Pa**ge

Mavis Smallberg

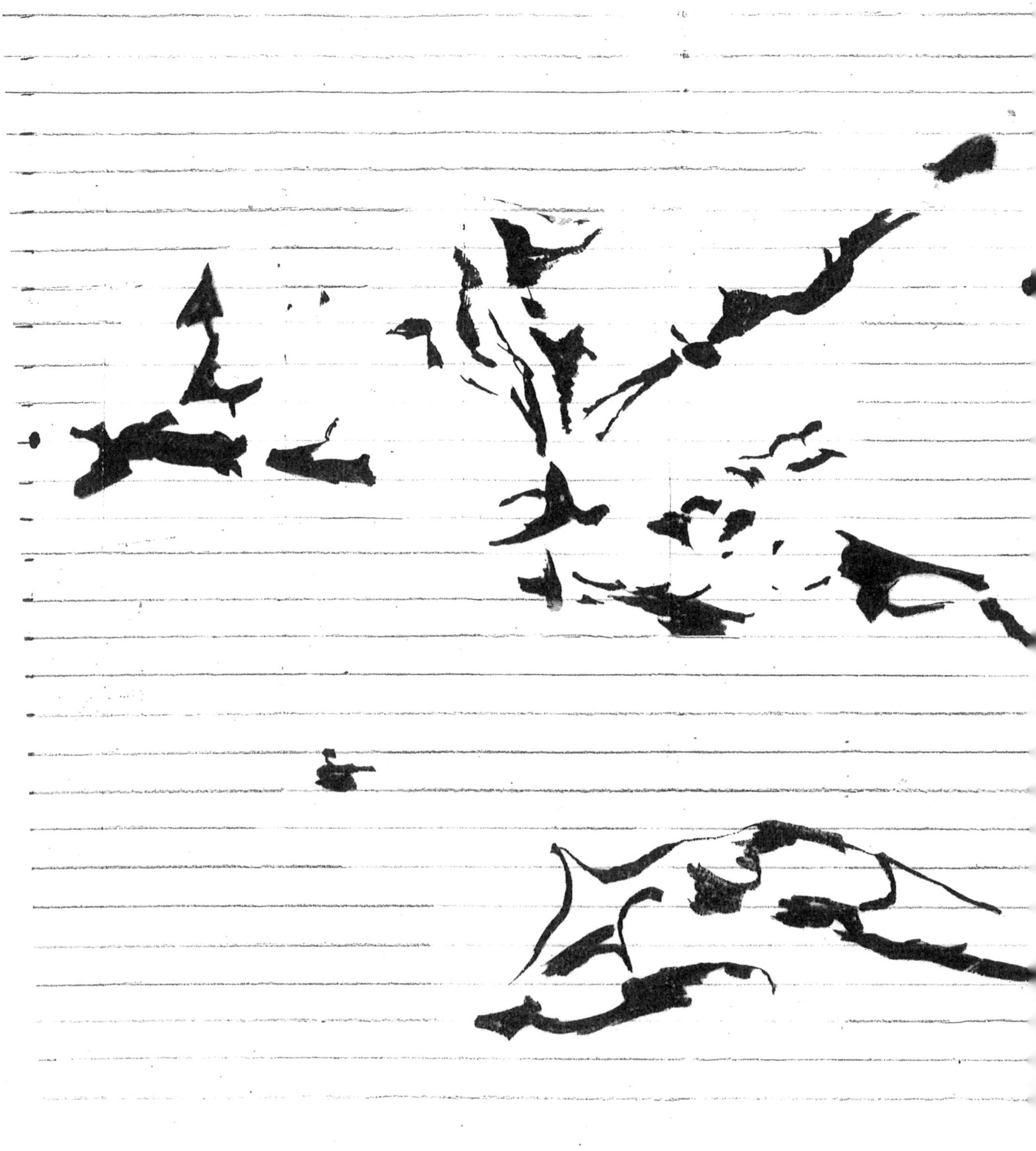

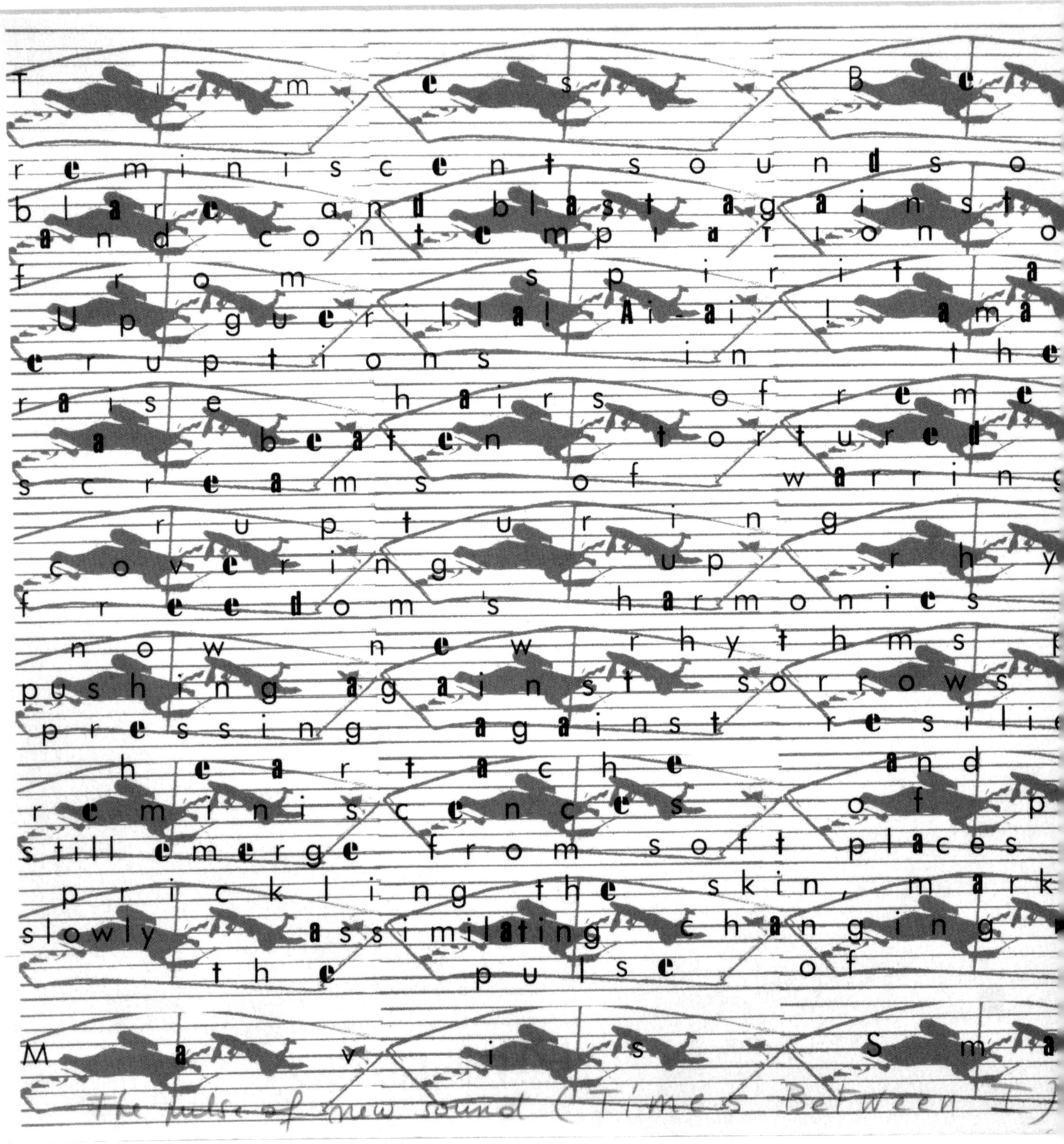
T m e s B e
reminiscent sounds o
blare and blast against
and contemplation o
from spirit a
Up guerilla! Ai-ai! ama
eruptions in the
raise hairs of reme
a beaten tortured
screams of warring
rupturing
covering up rhy
freedom's harmonies
now new rhythms p
pushing against sorrows
pressing against resili
heartache and
reminiscences of p
still emerge from soft places
prickling the skin, mark
slowly assimilating changing
the pulse of
M a v i s S m a
The pulse of new sound (Times Between I)

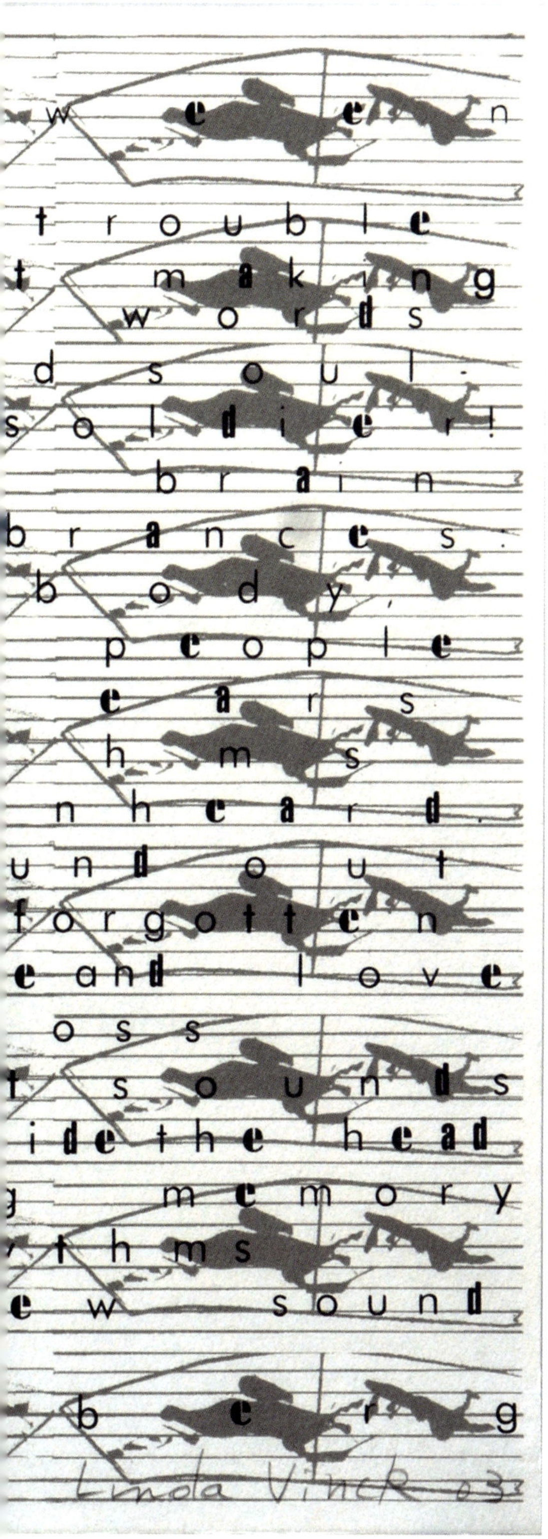

Times Between

reminiscent sounds of trouble blare and blast against art making and contemplation of words from spirit and soul –
Up guerilla, Ai-ai! ama soldier! eruptions in the brain raise hairs of remembrances: a beaten tortured body,
screams of warring people rupturing ears covering up rhythms freedom's harmonies unheard
now new rhythms pound out pushing against sorrows unforgotten pressing against resilience
and love heartache and loss
reminiscences of past sounds still emerge from soft places inside the head prickling the skin,
marking memory slowly assimilating changing rhythms
the pulse of new sound

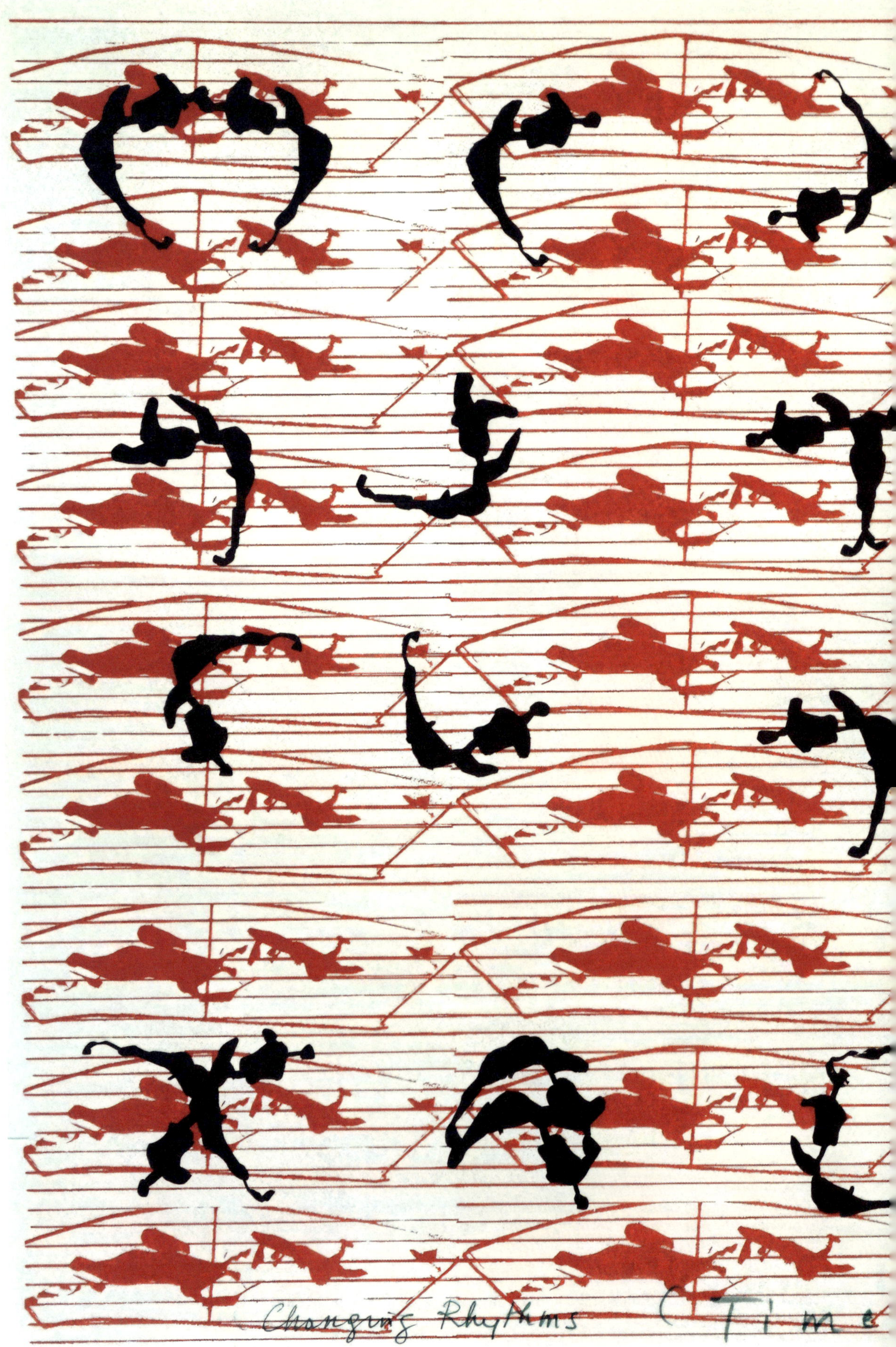
Changing Rhythms (Time

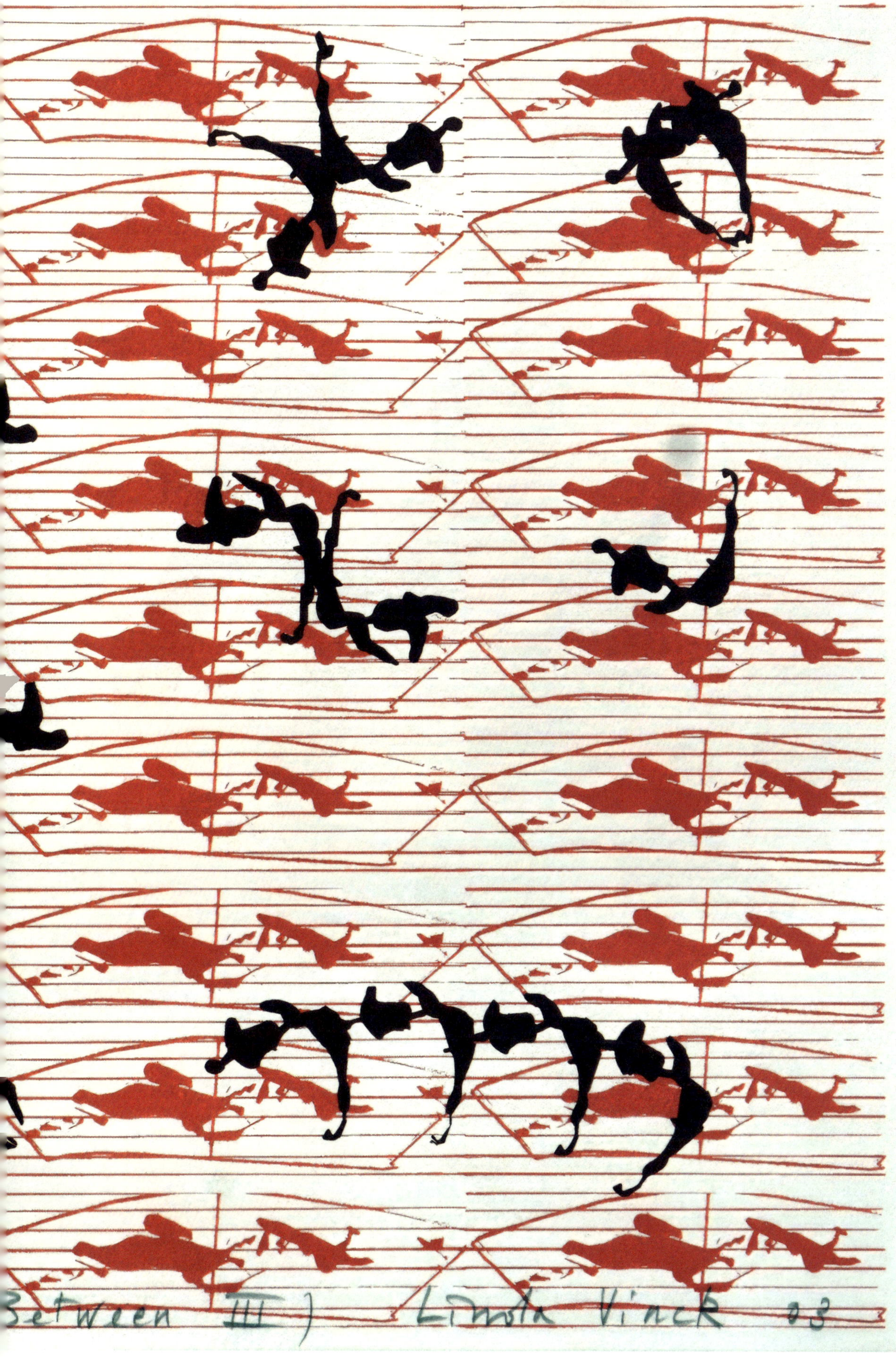
Between III) Linda Vinck 03

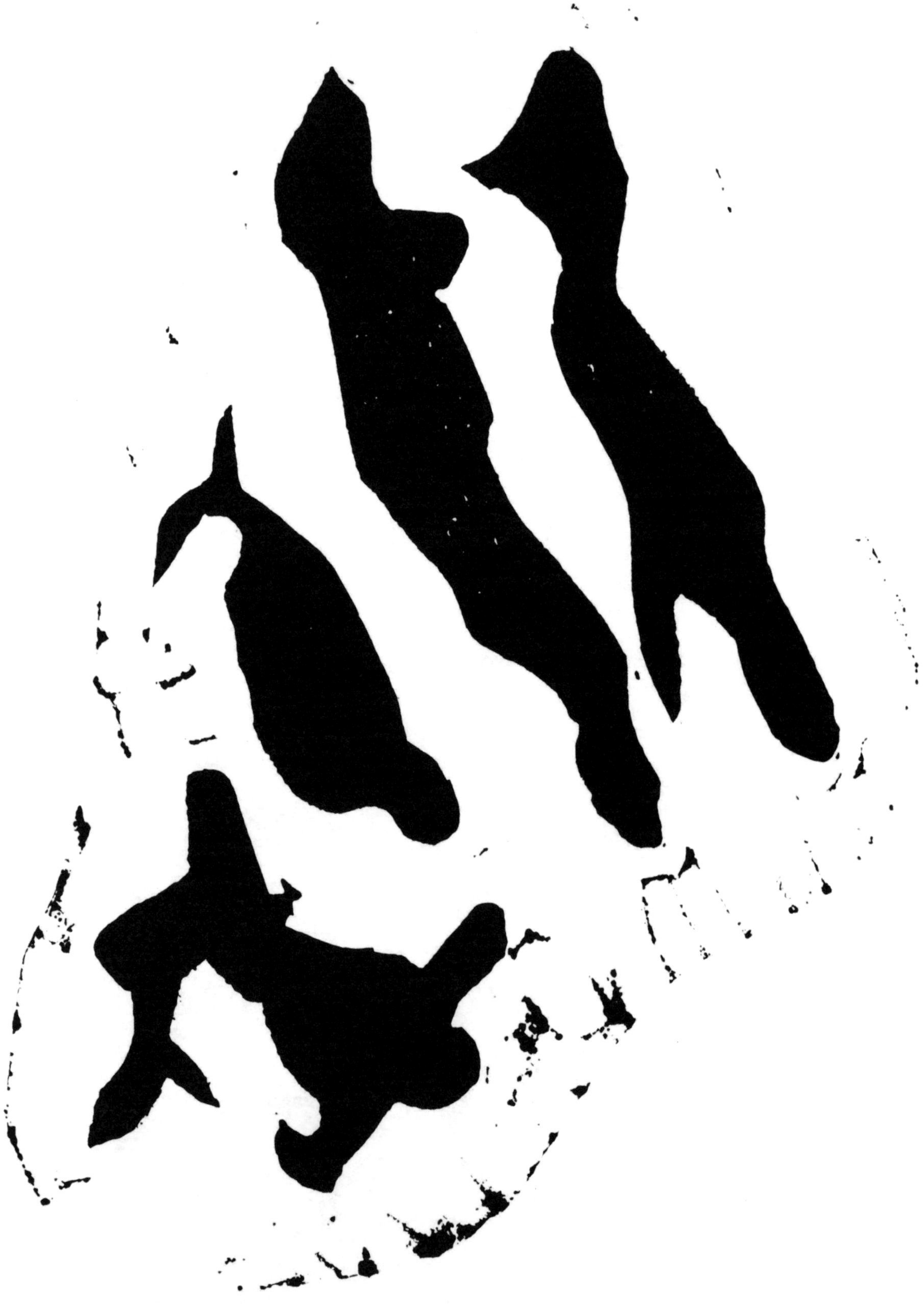

South Africa

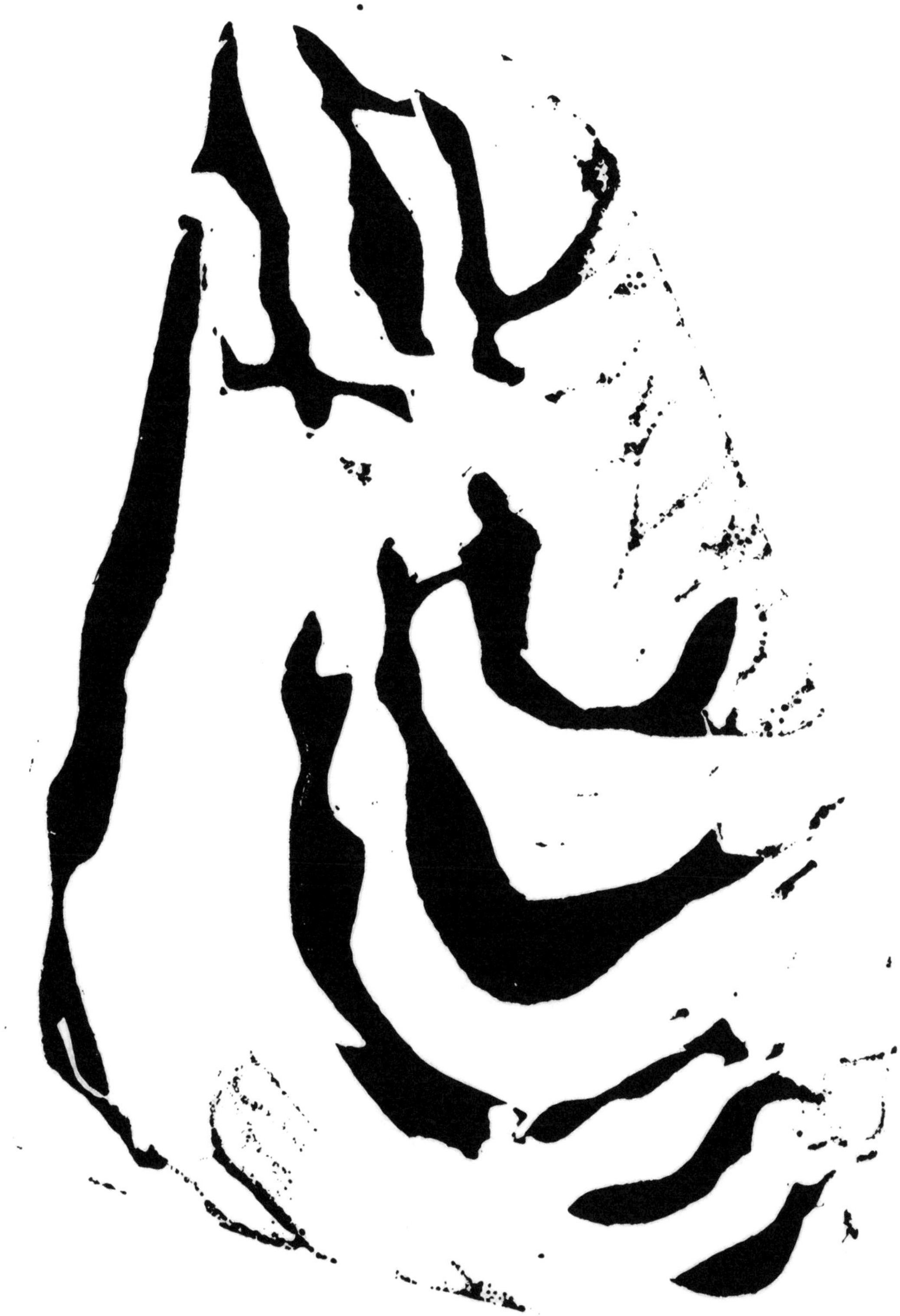

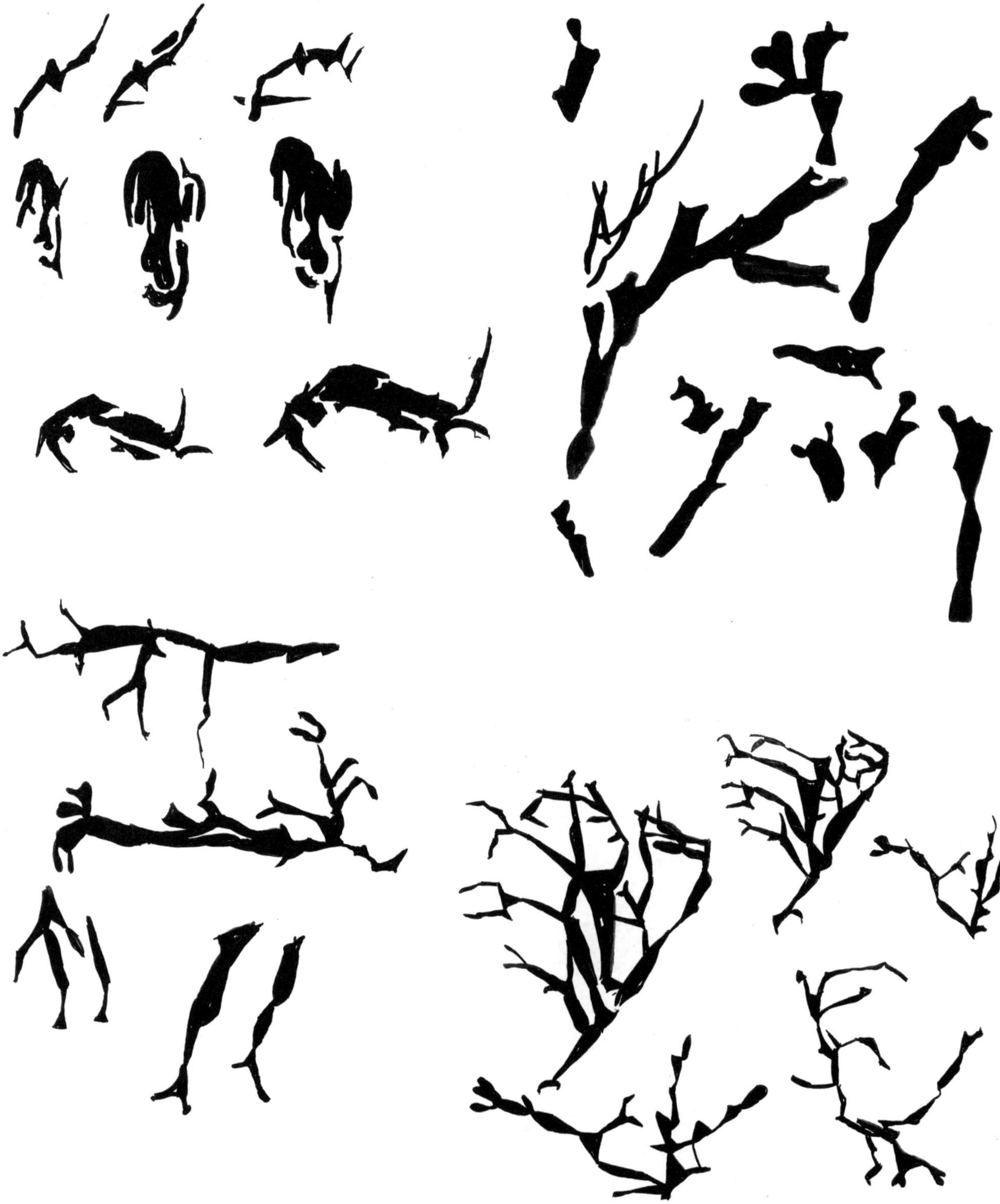

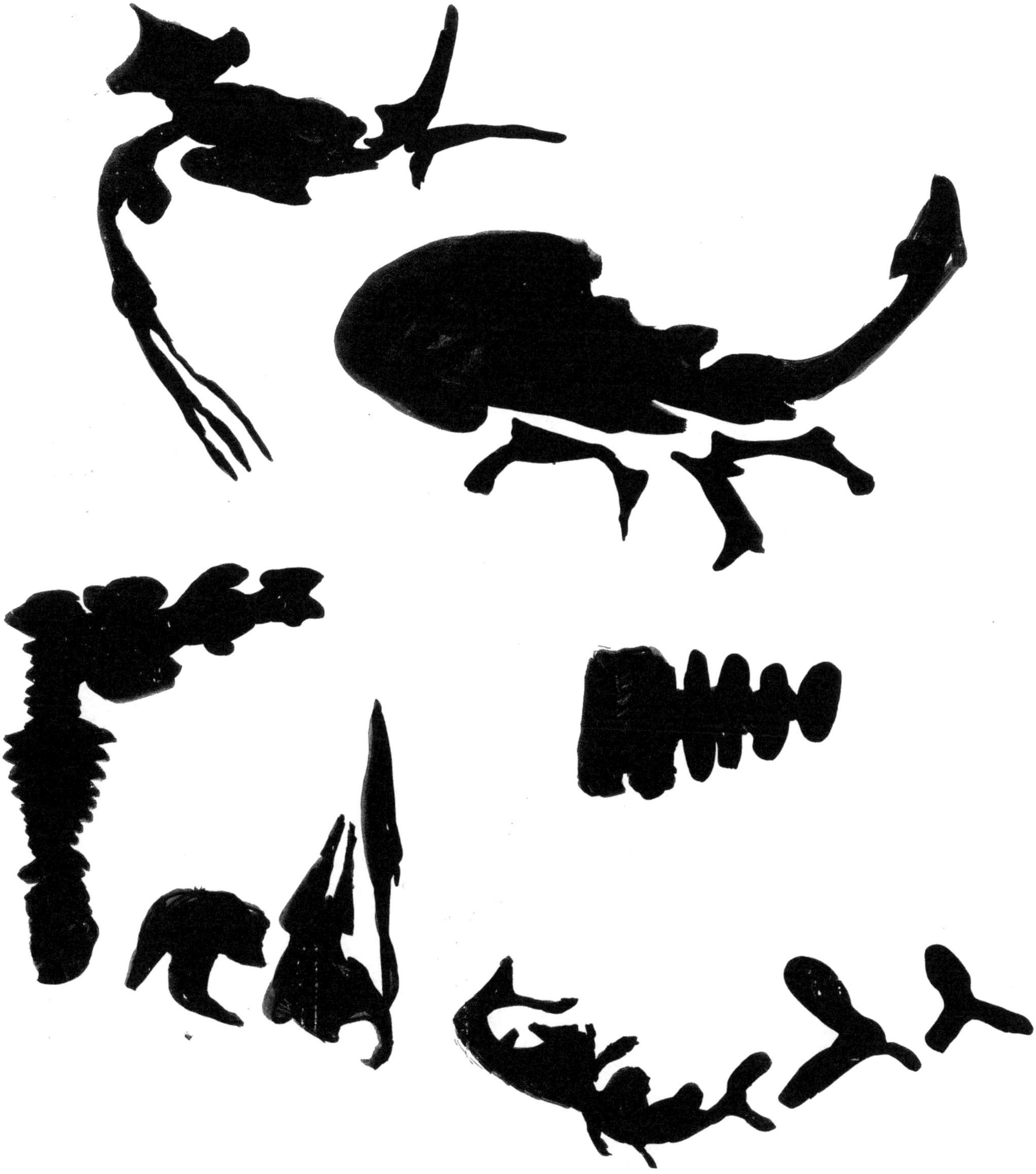

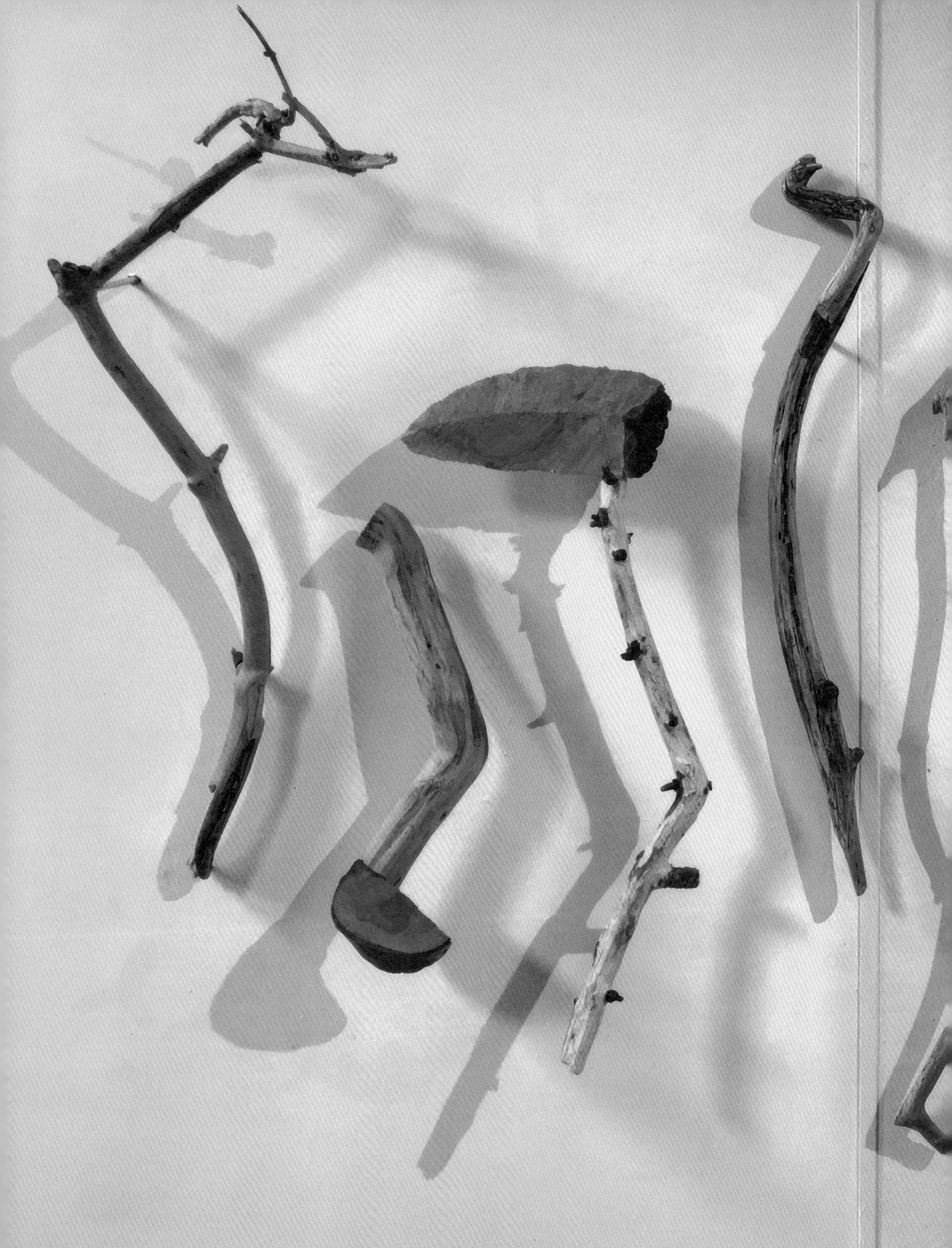

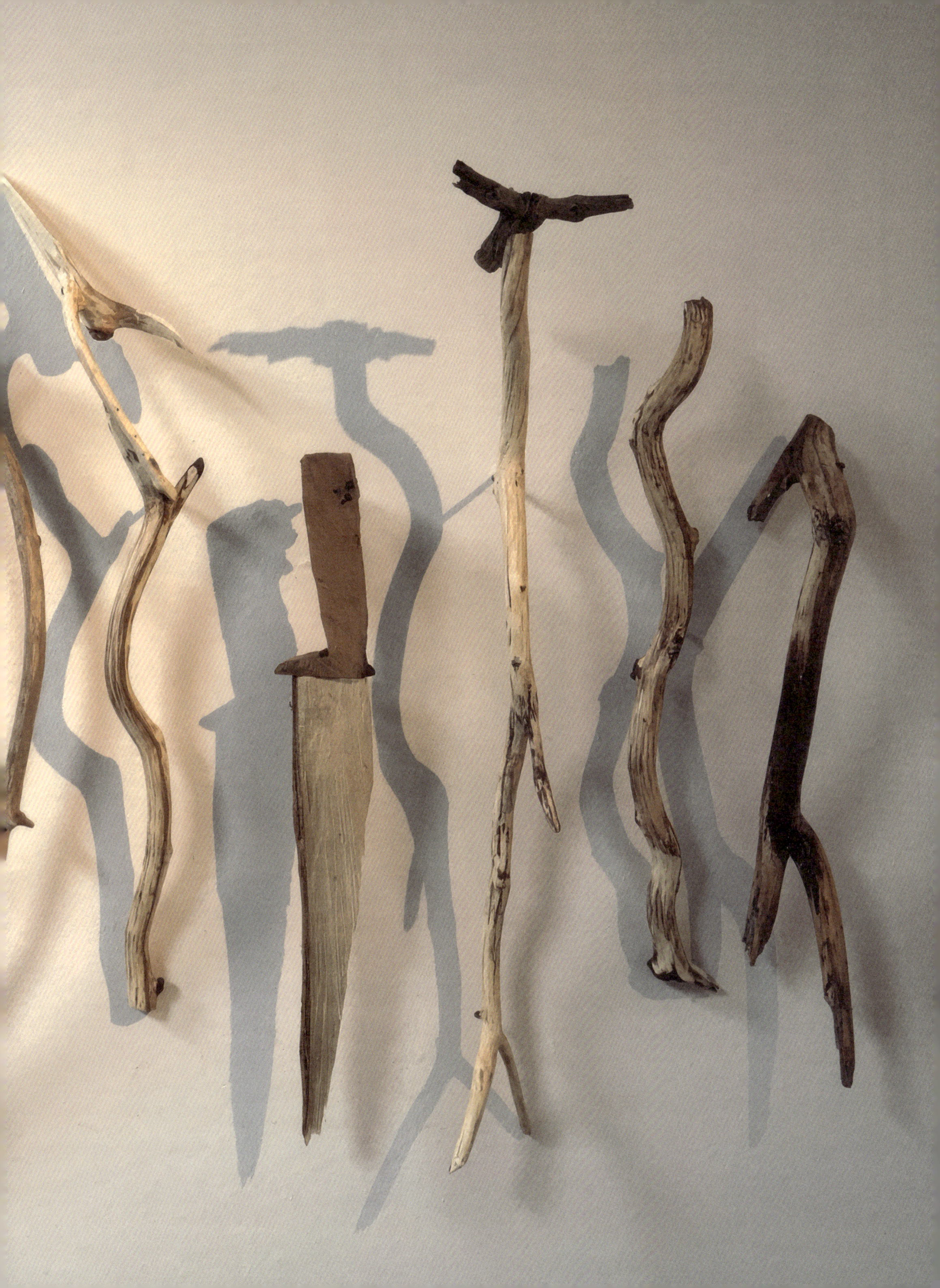

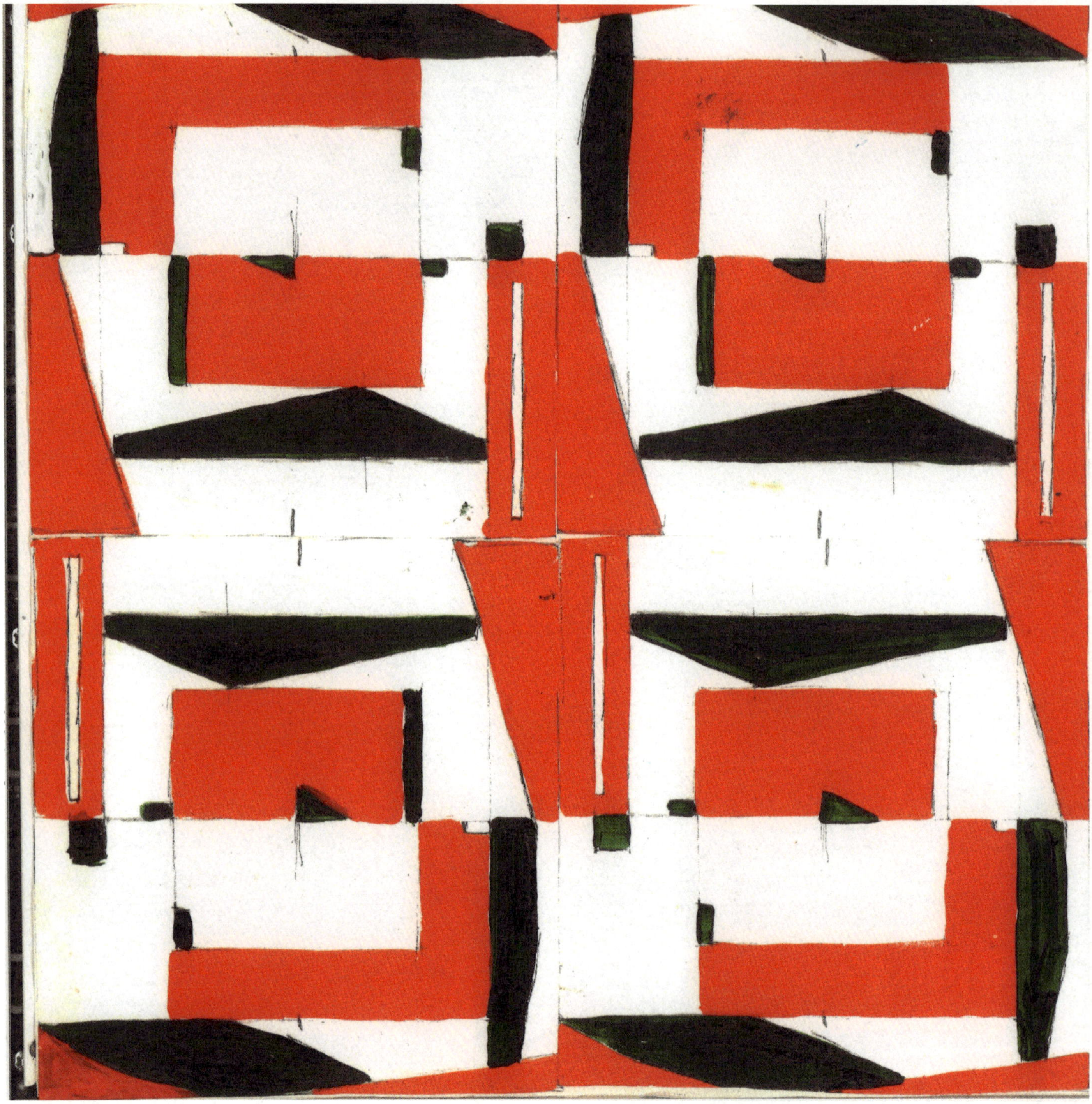

Japan

Linda Vinck produces works of art by combining her delicate sensitivity with influences from the time she spent in Africa. Her rhythmical visual art stimulates the primal memories within us all as humans.

Norimasa Mizutani, Tokyo, 2012

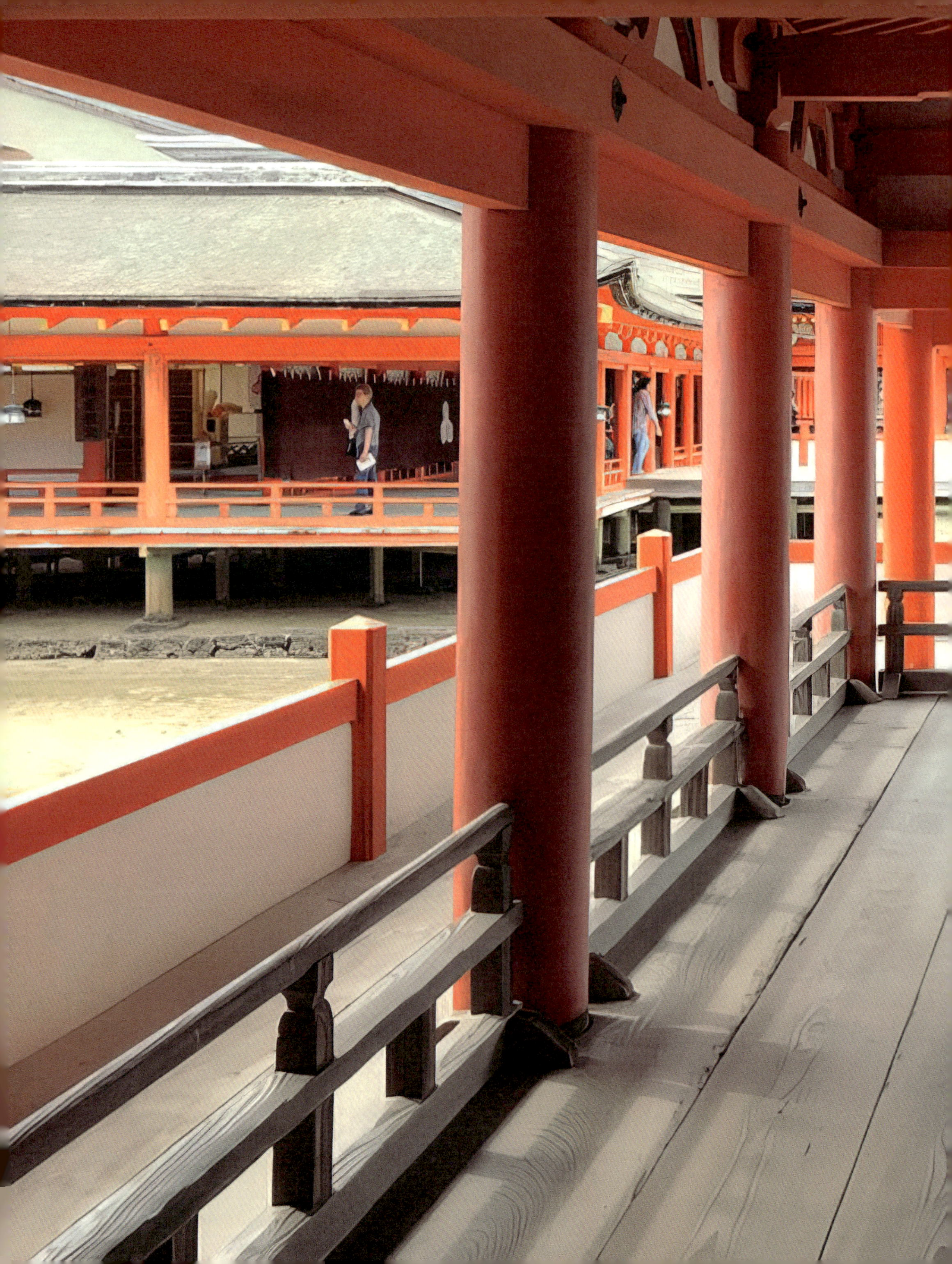

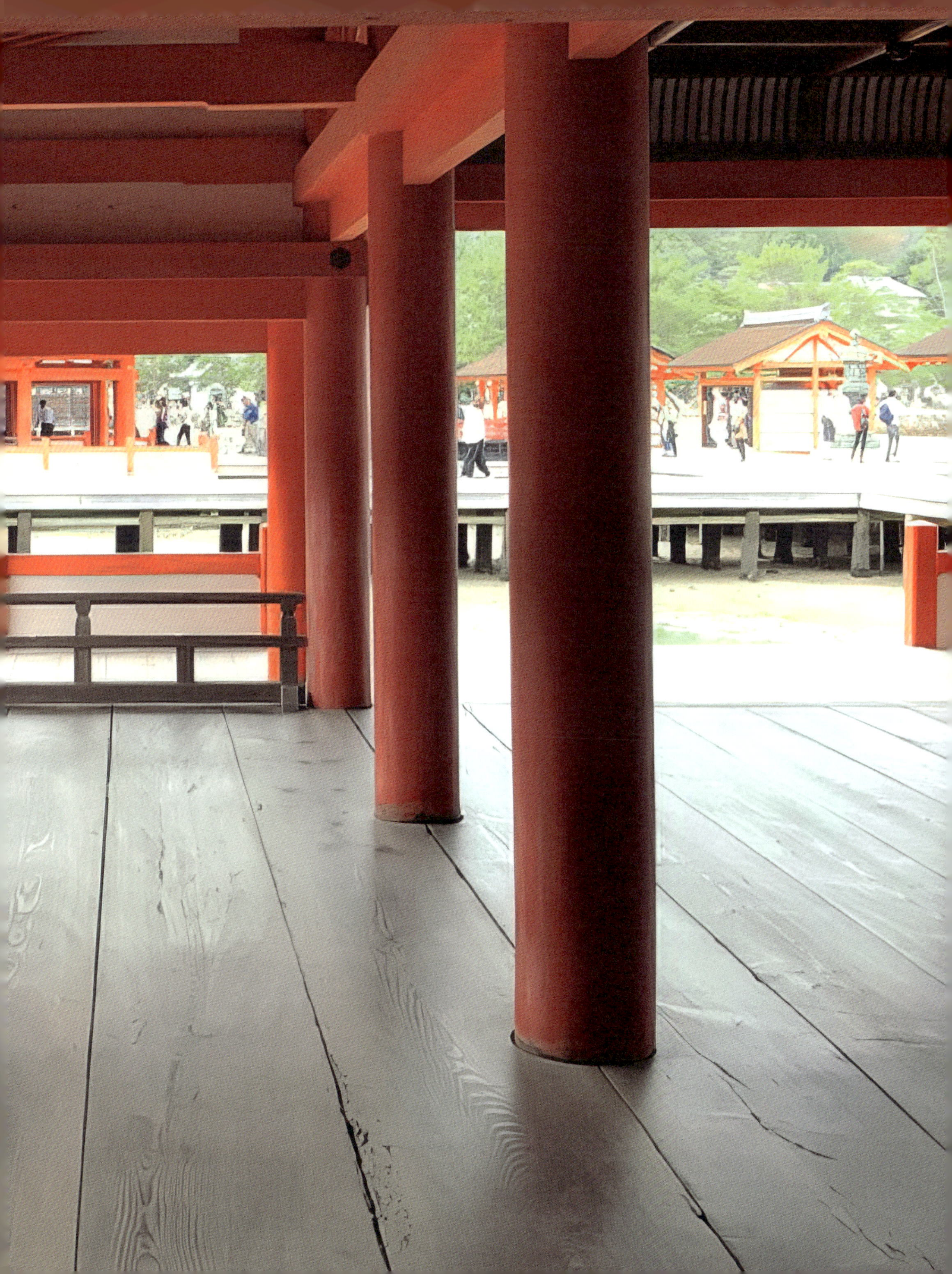

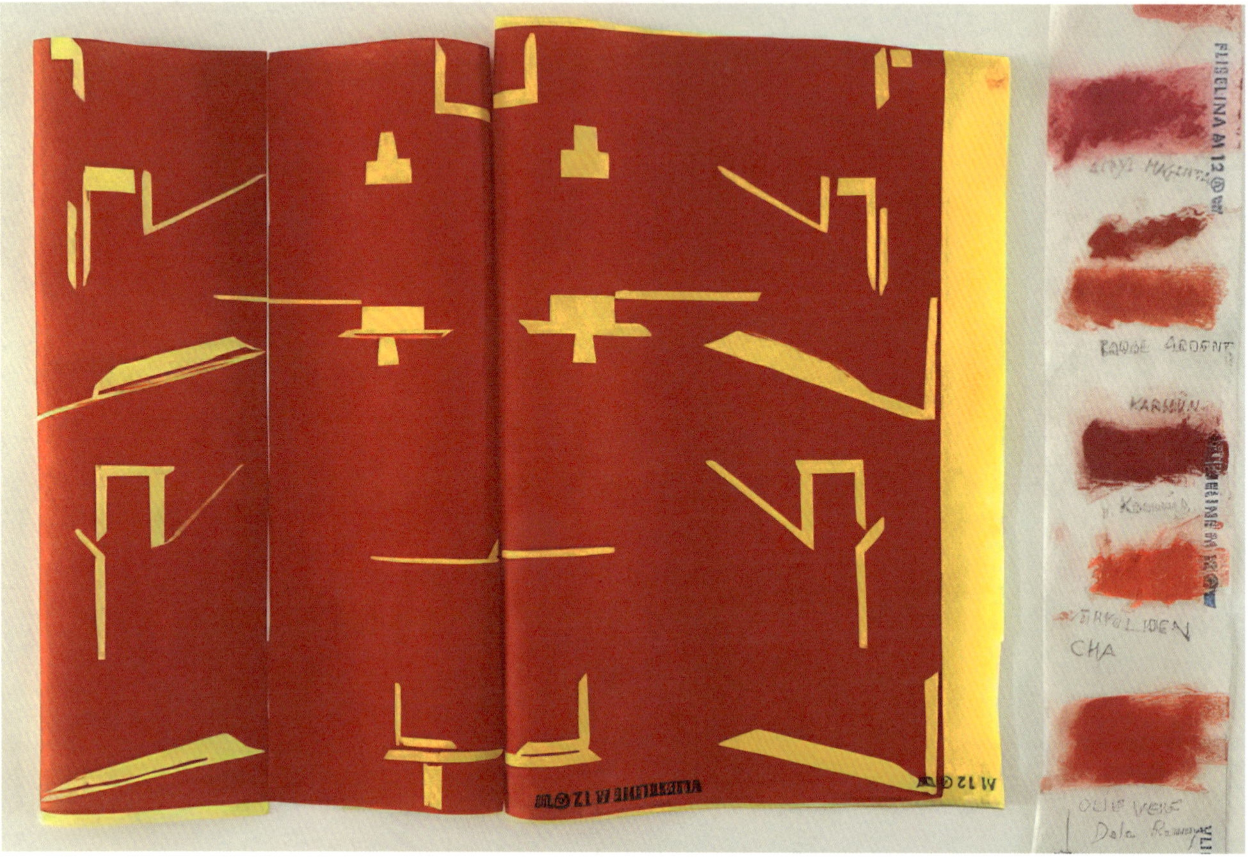

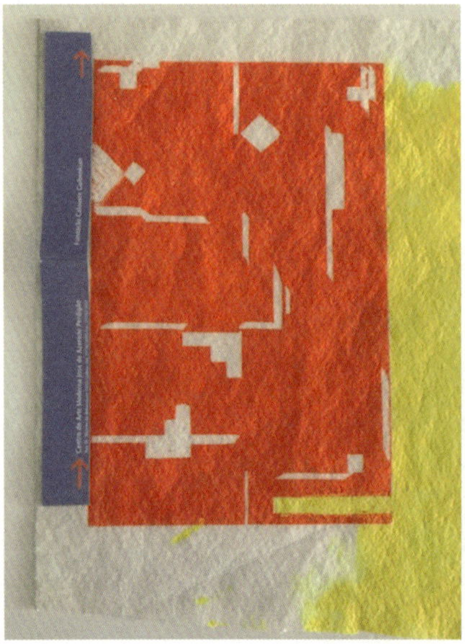

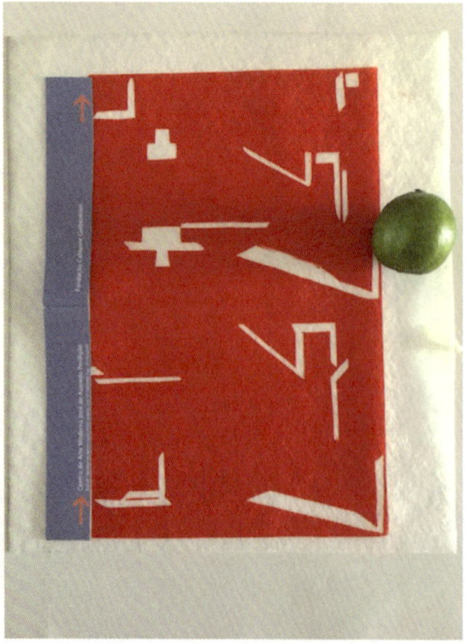

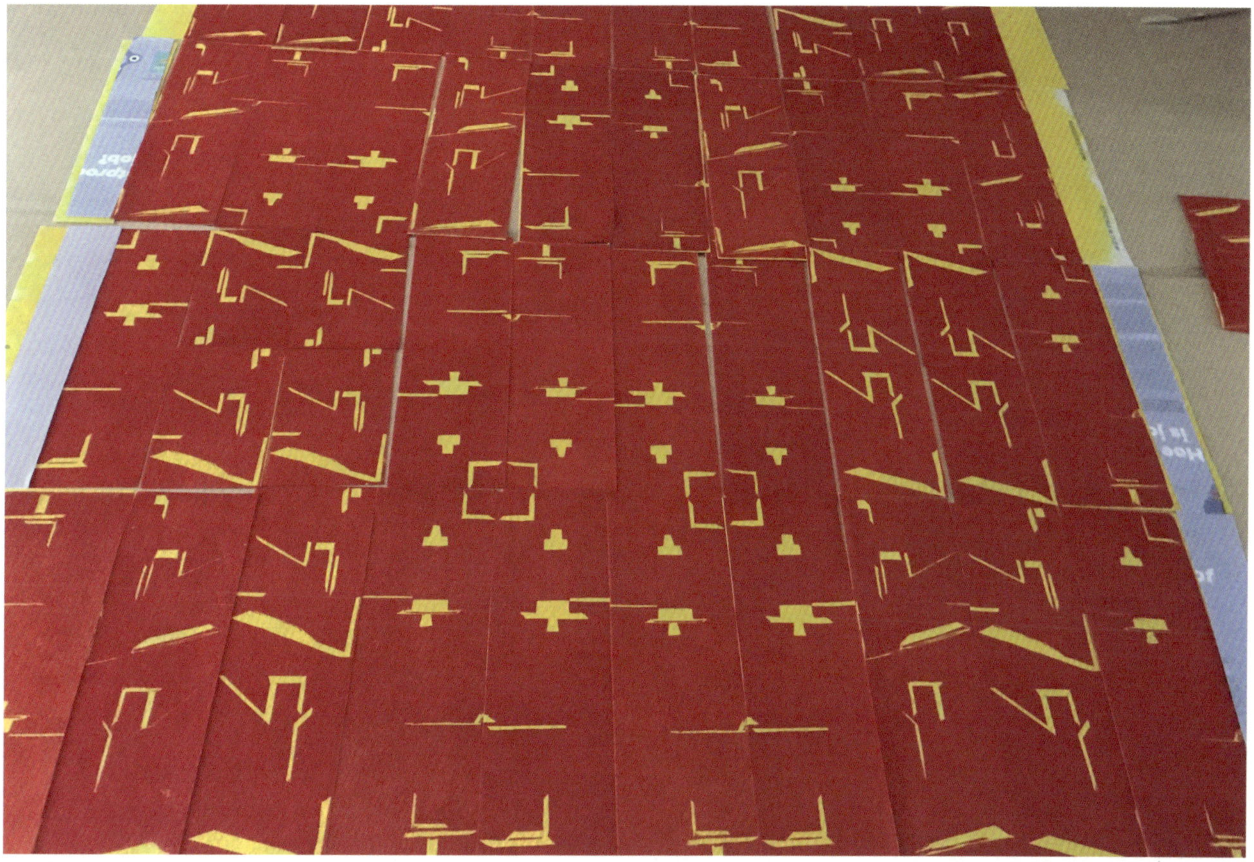

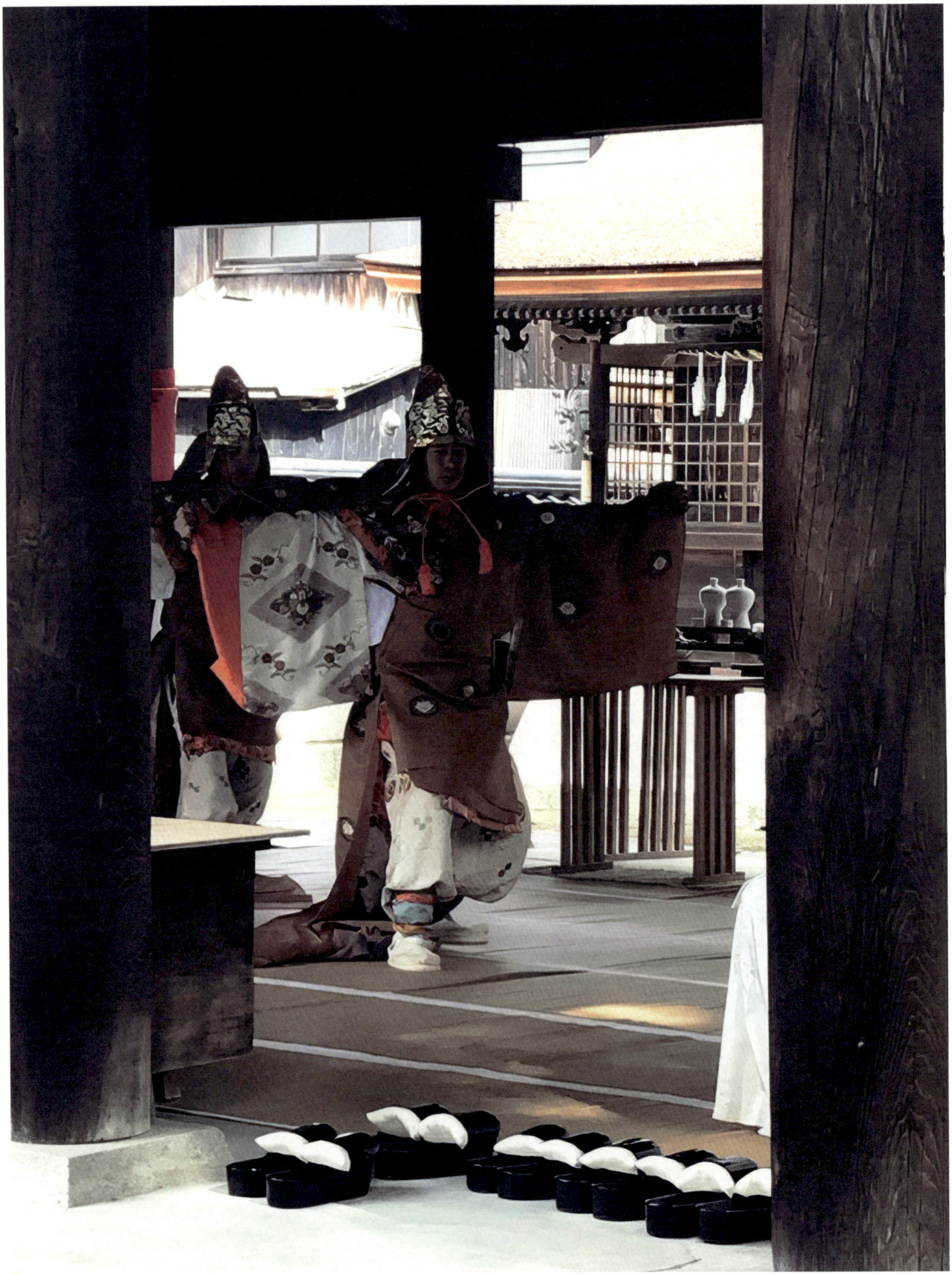

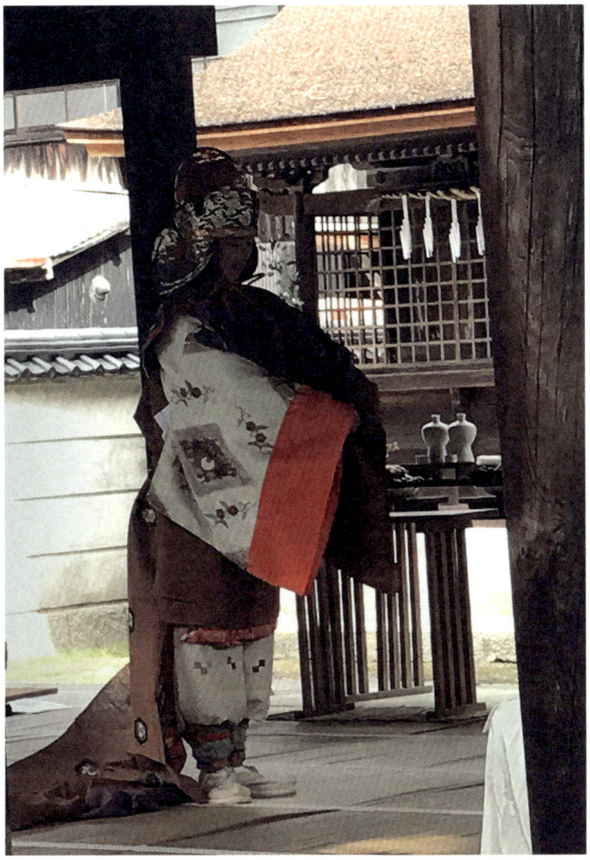

Bugaku *(see also p. 96)* is a traditional Japanese dance performed at the imperial court for over a thousand years. It is characterized by slow, deliberate movements. Bugaku dancers wear costumes made out of precious materials, including expressive masks, and perform highly stylized choreography that often tells stories of ancient legends or rituals.

Although the dance was historically reserved for ceremonies for the elites, Bugaku is still performed today at important cultural and religious events, a testament to the art form's timelessness.

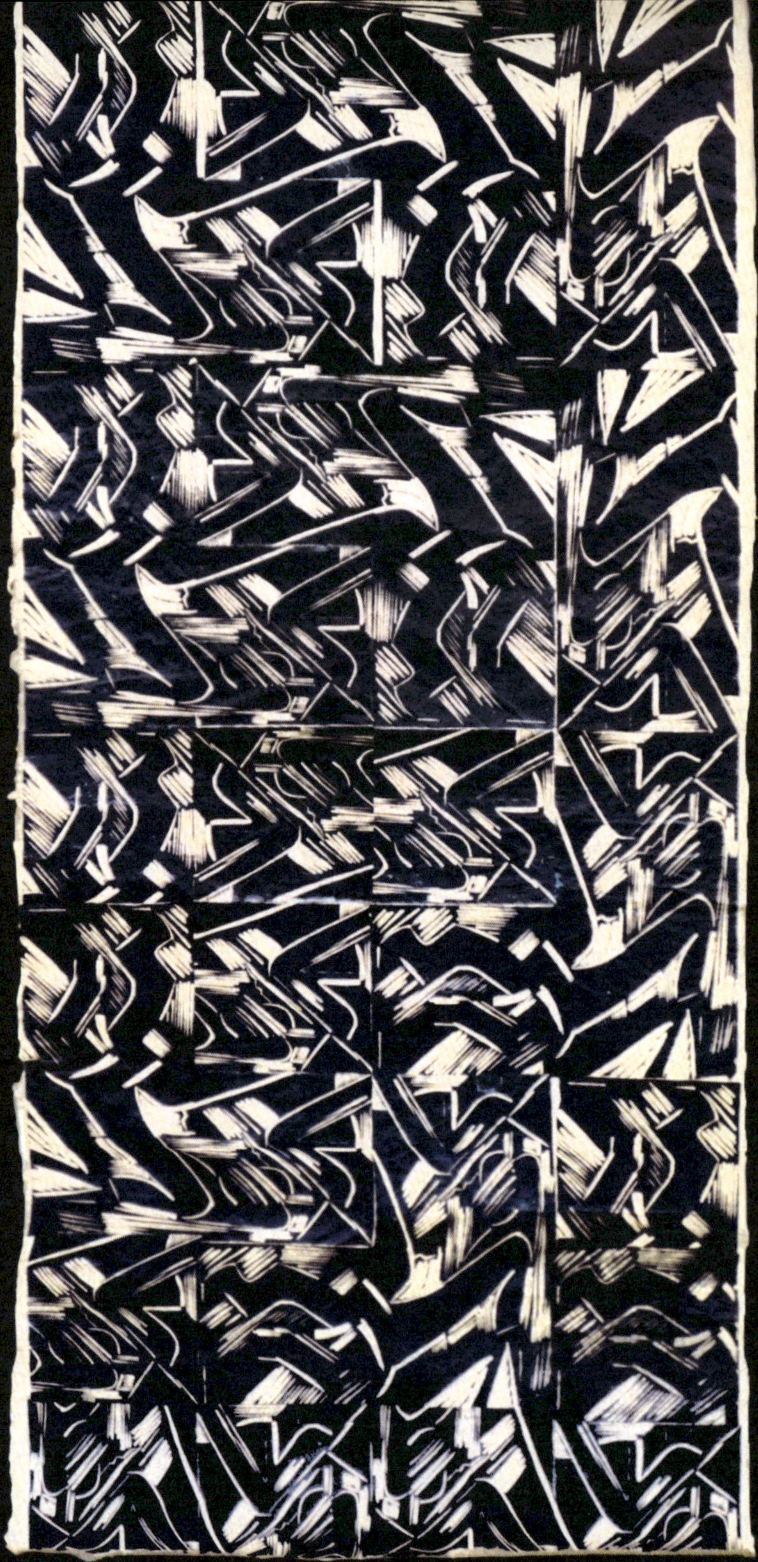

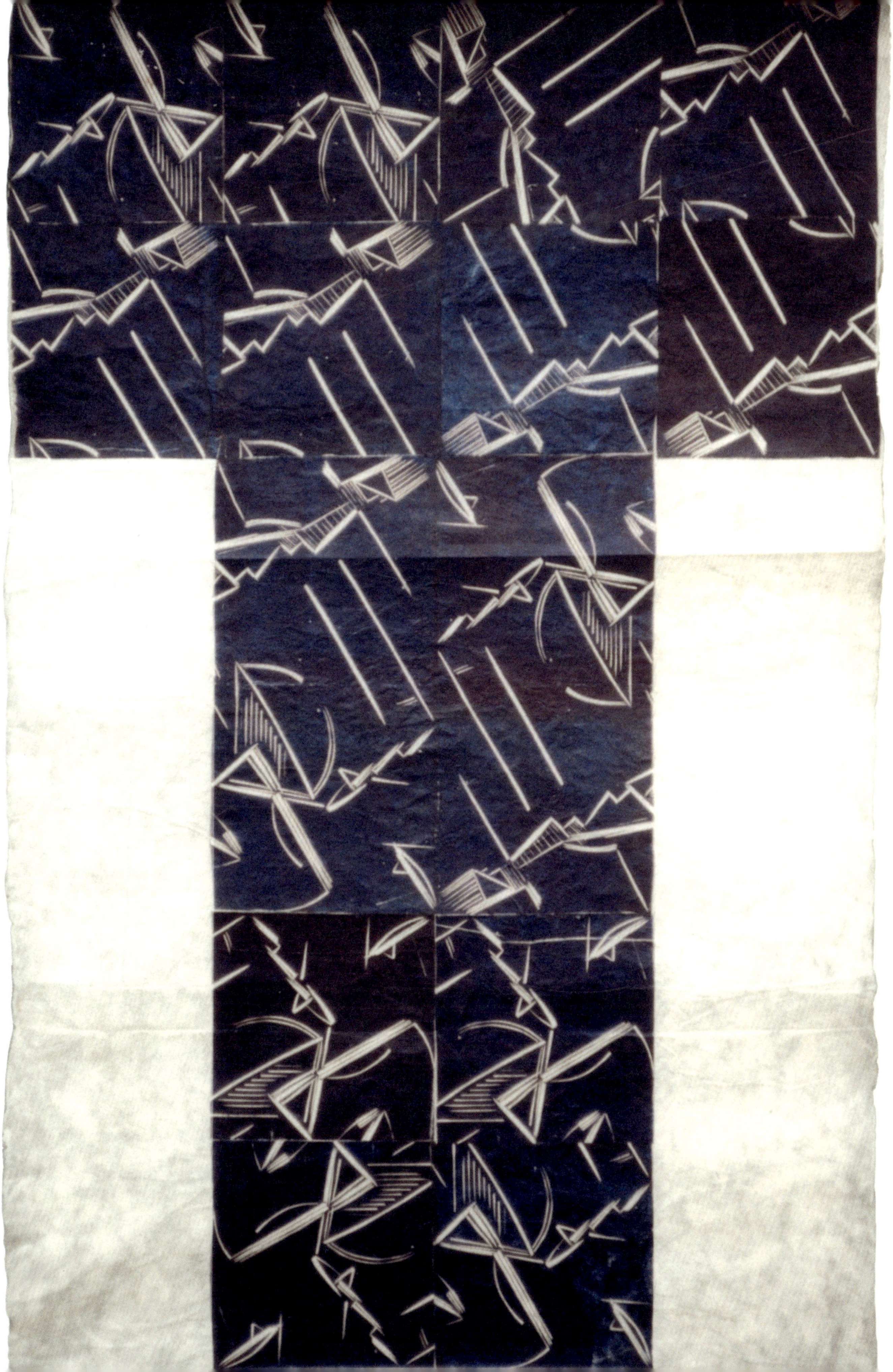

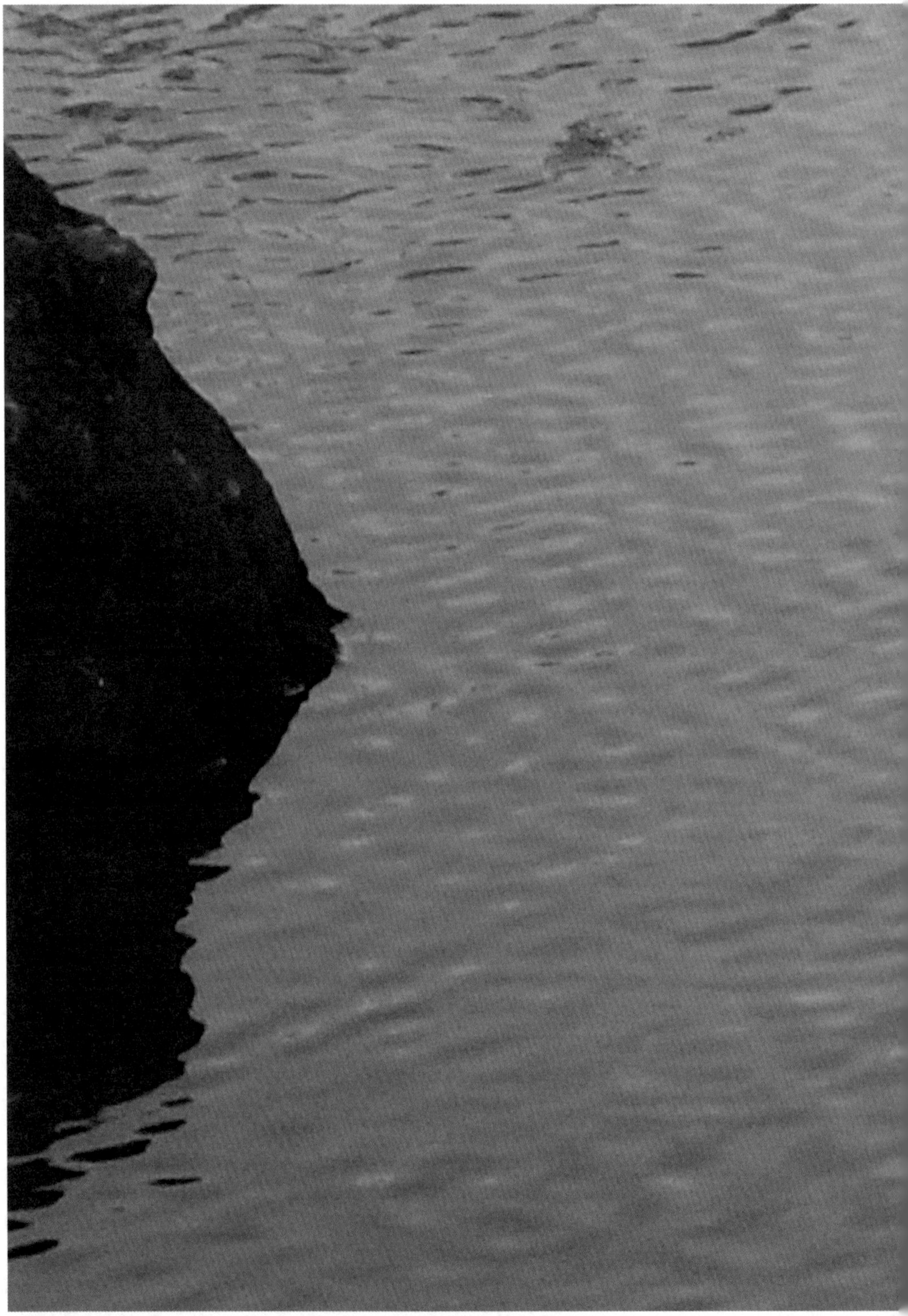

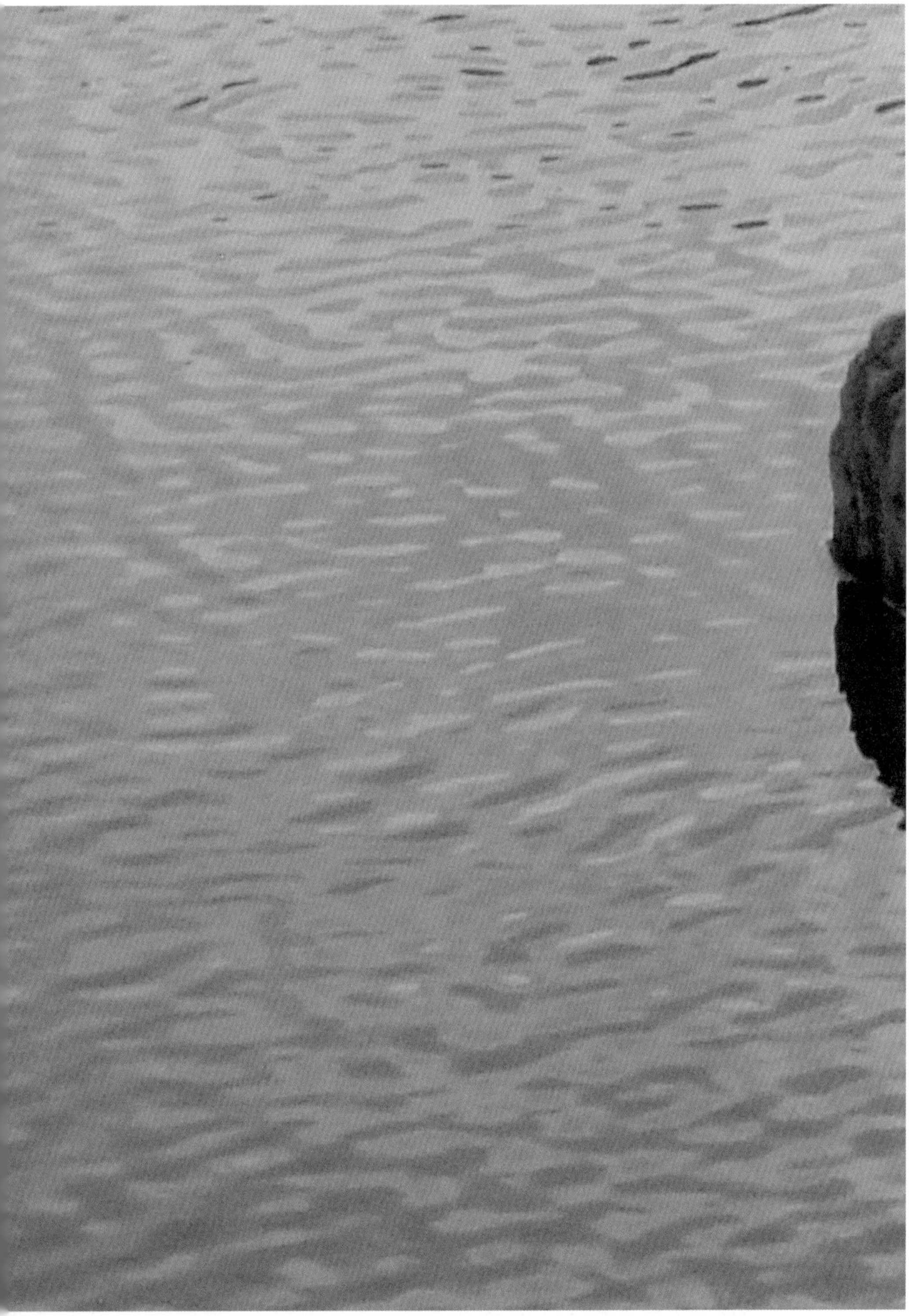

Japan

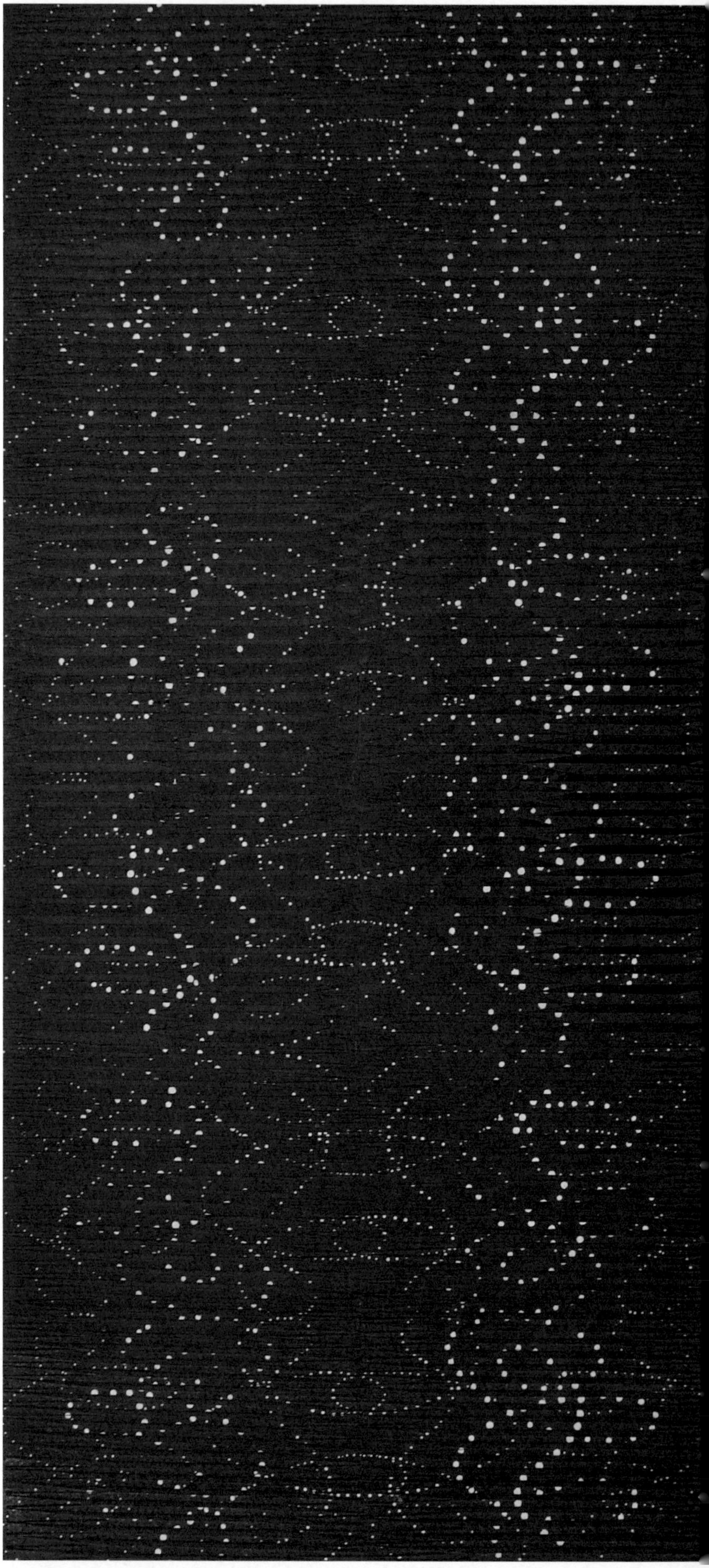

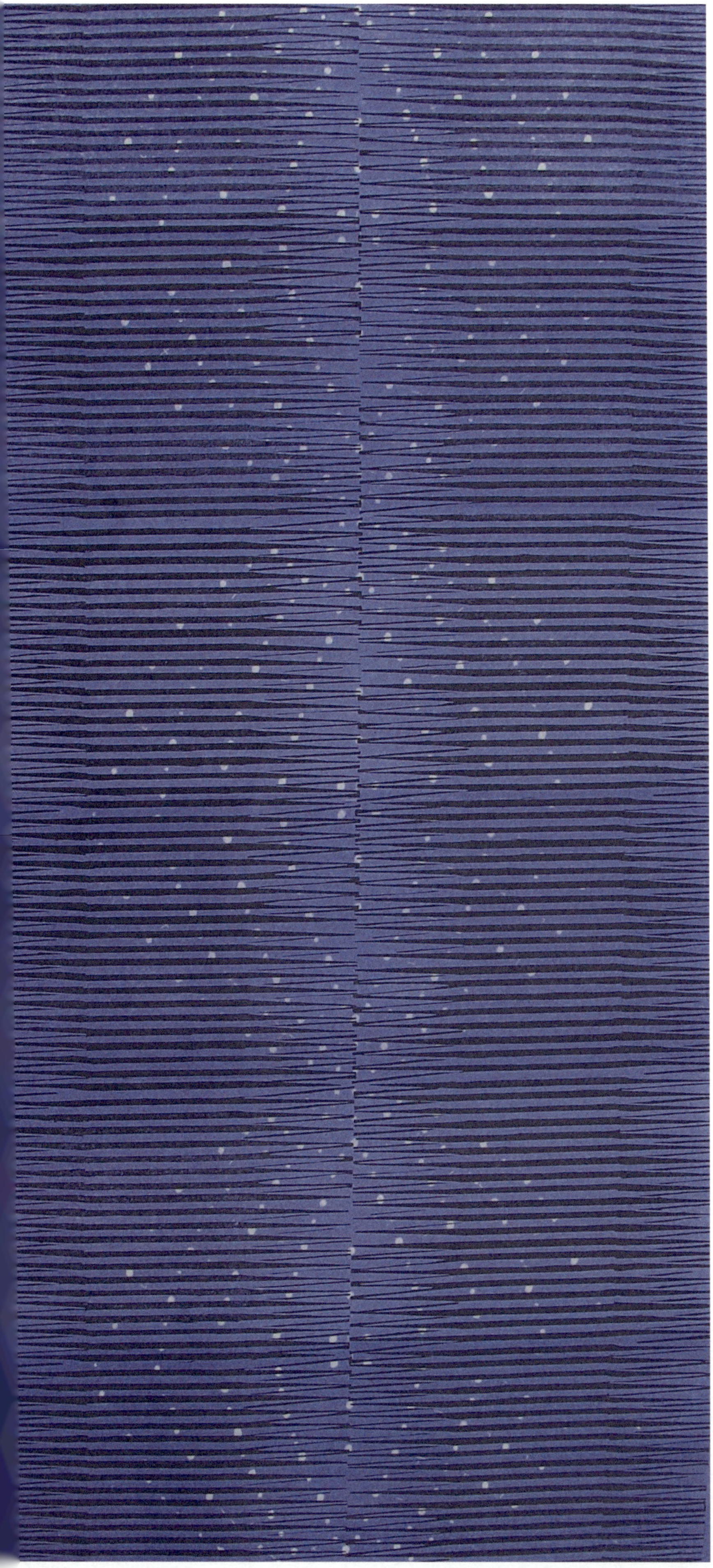

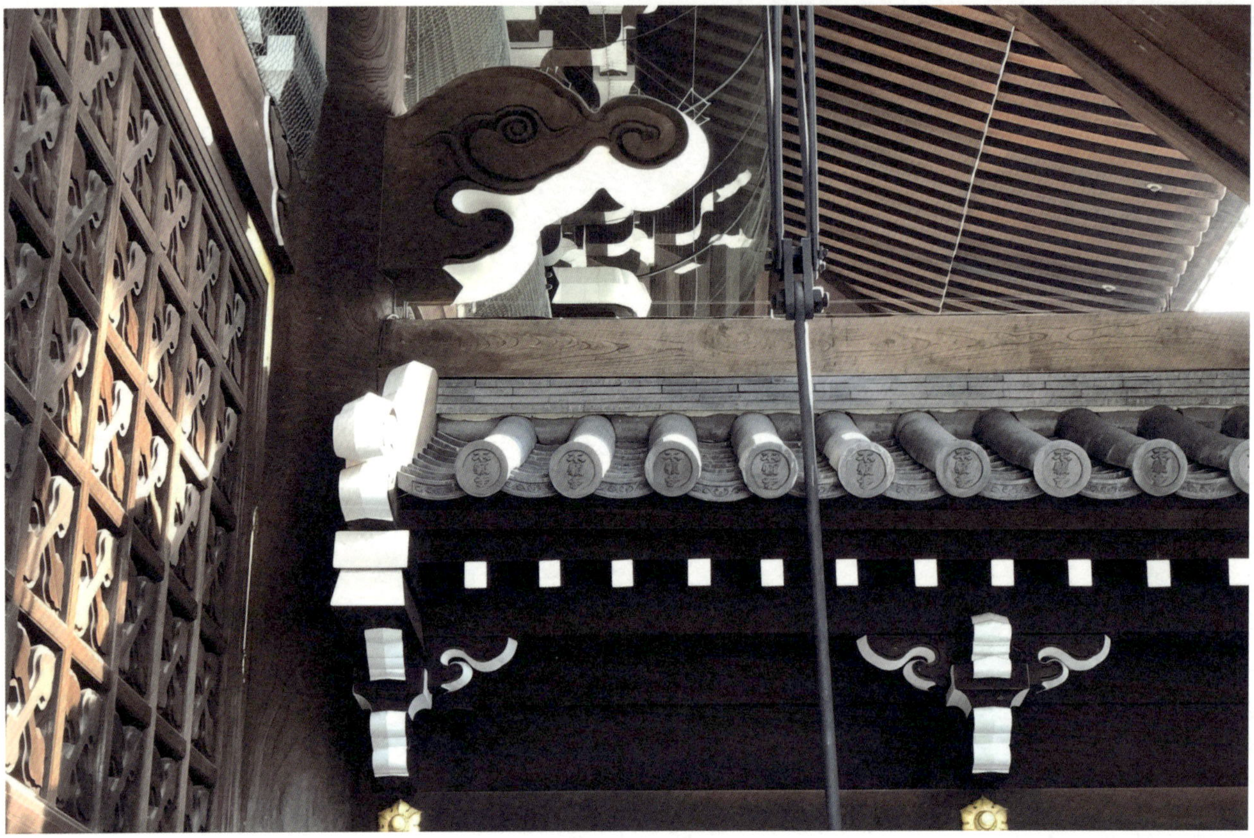

Japan

Birdsong 5 (detail)

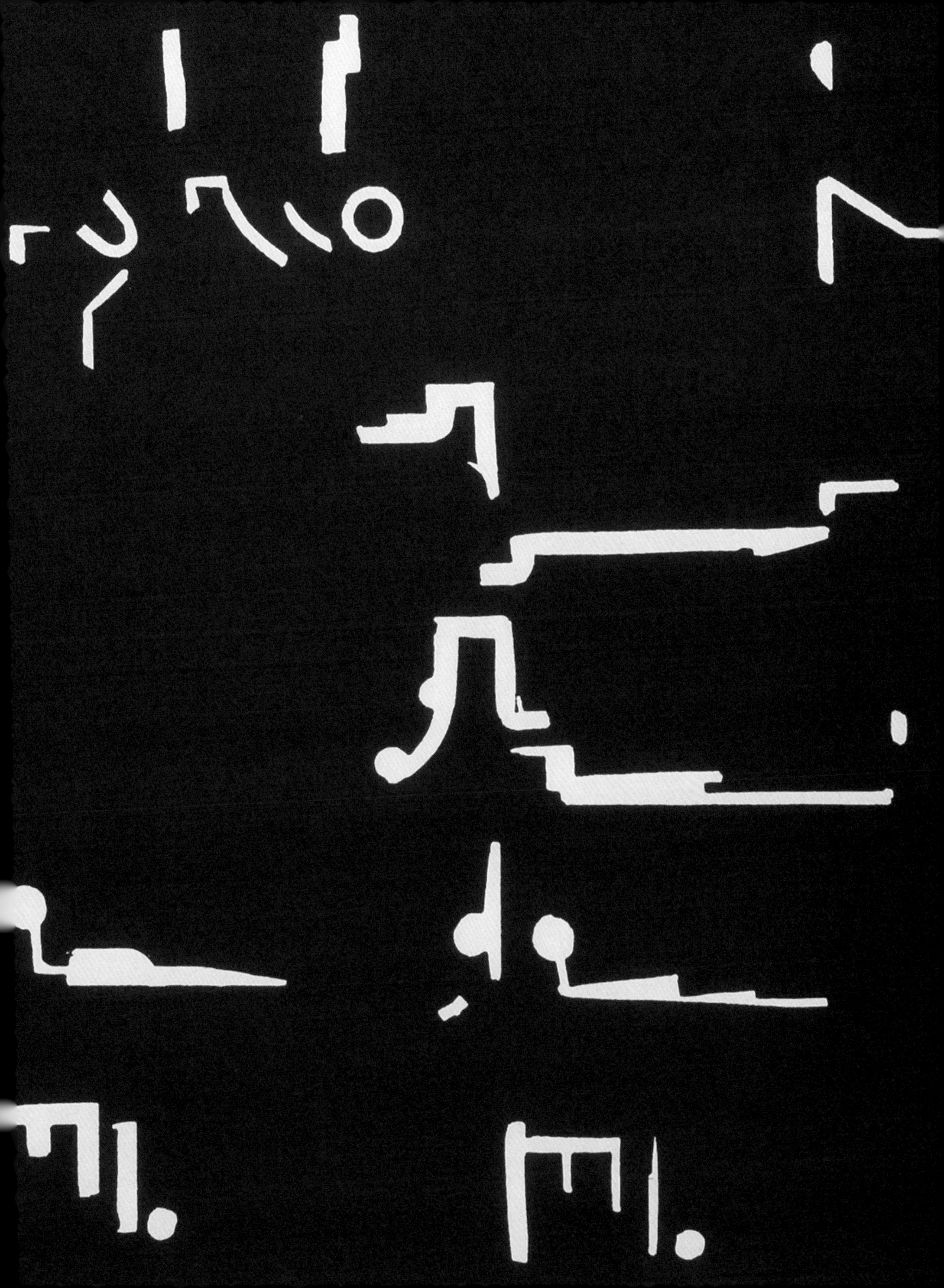

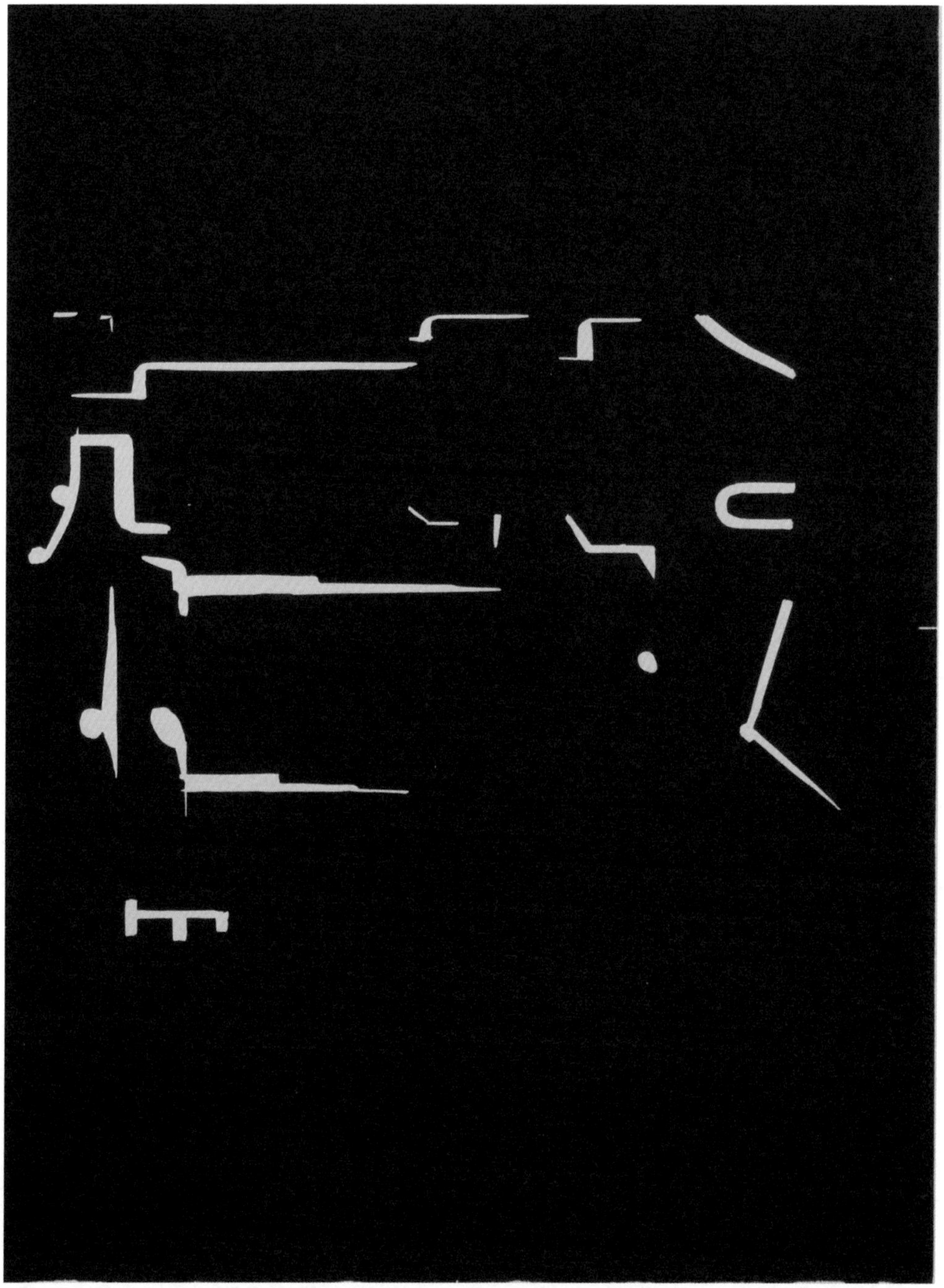

Birdsong 4

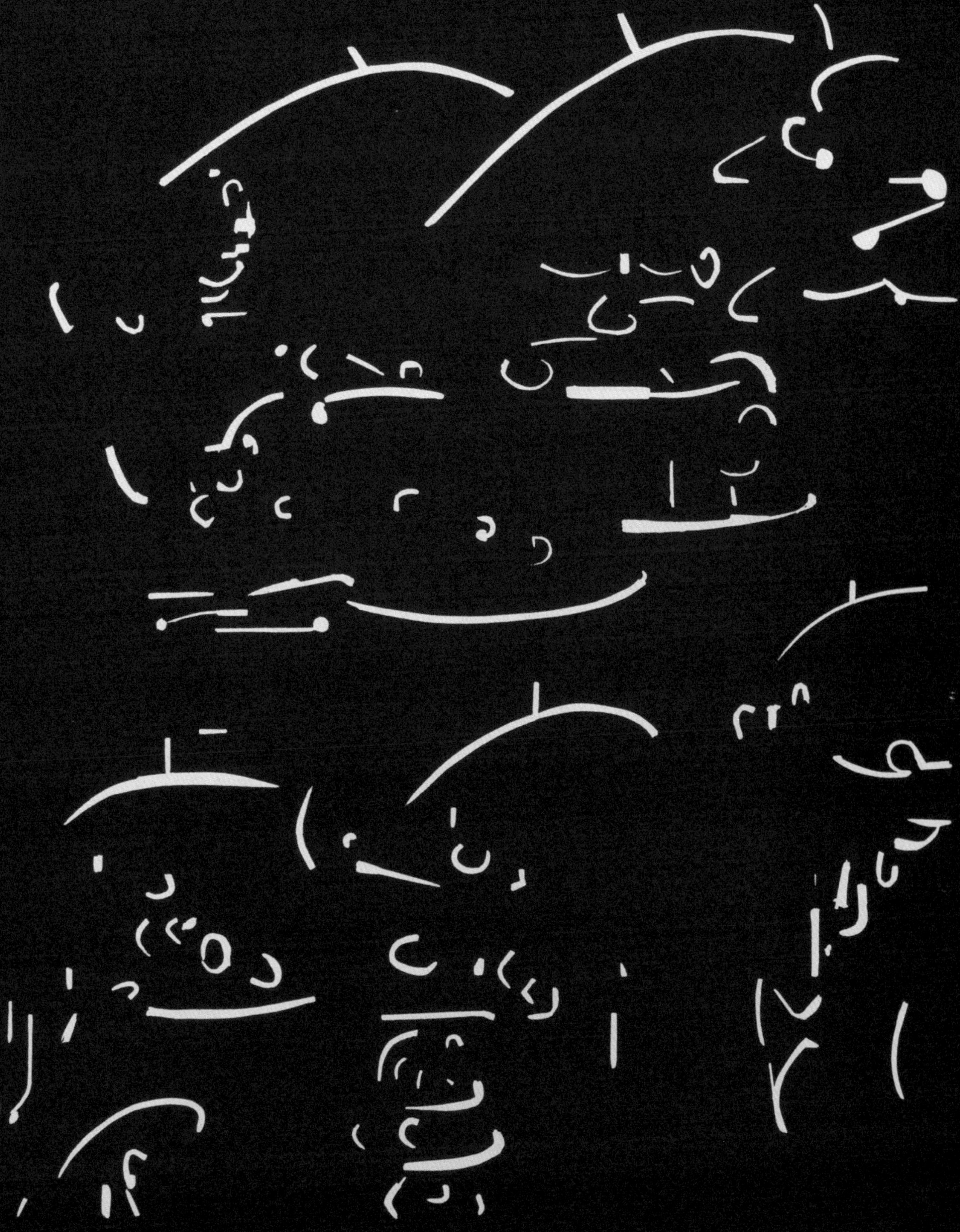

Japan

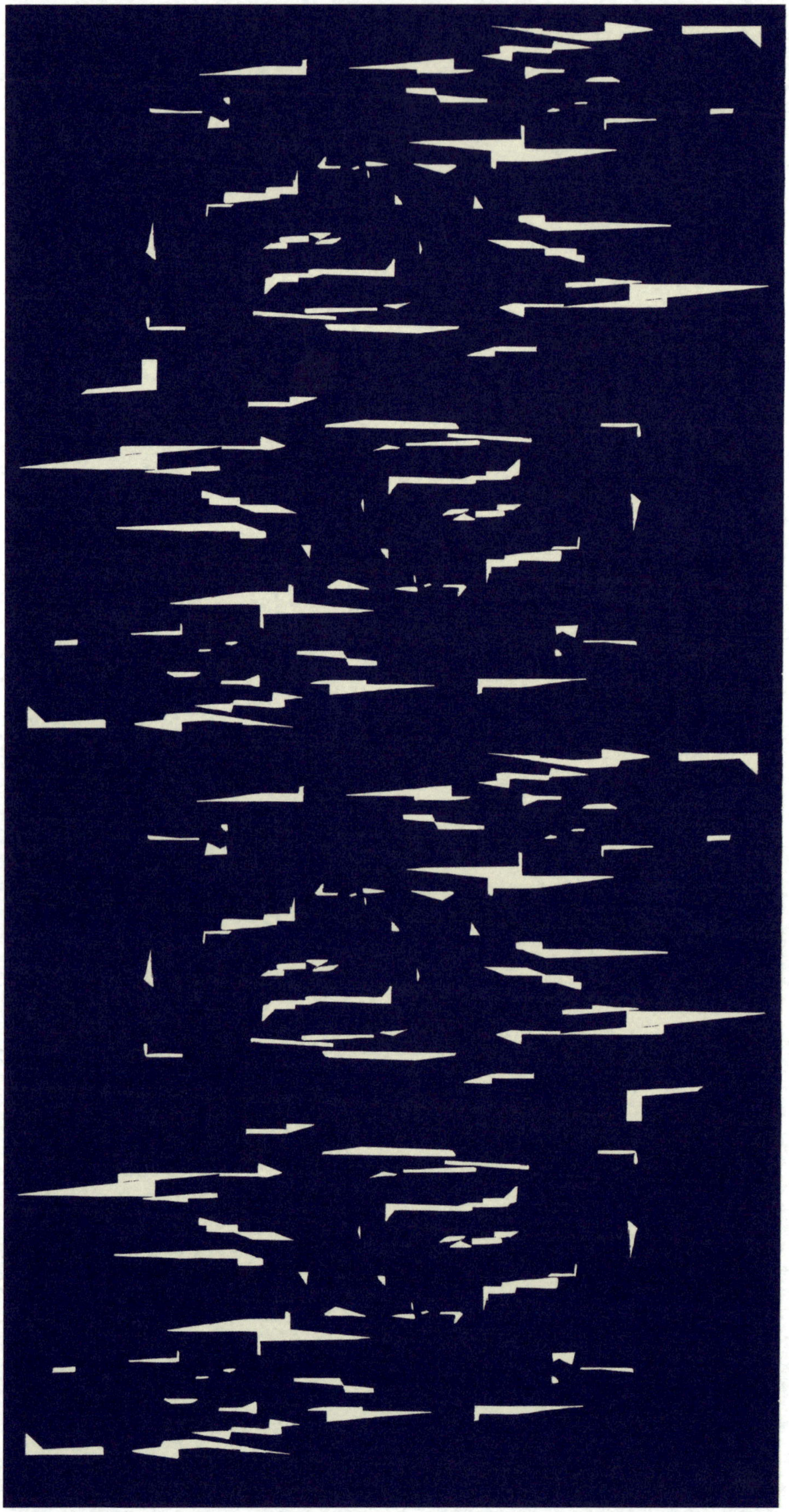

Met transparante diepzeegebaren
het groeien koesteren en de tijdstroom keren,
met flitsen uit het verleden
het zinken van het vlak doorbreken,
met bedwongen hoogtevrees
zweven tussen deze leegte
en de oeverloze tijd.

Zo springt het moment keer op keer
uit het zog van de vergetelheid,
ankert zich in het verleden
en steekt de draak met de eeuwigheid.

Zo plichtsgetrouw de ongeschreven wetten
beheren, van teken tot teken
geschiedenis schrijven.
Maar als de tijd verstek laat gaan
verkrampen de diepzeegebaren.

Marcel van Maele, 'Ontmantelen', portfolio 'Koppelteken', Antwerp, January 1985

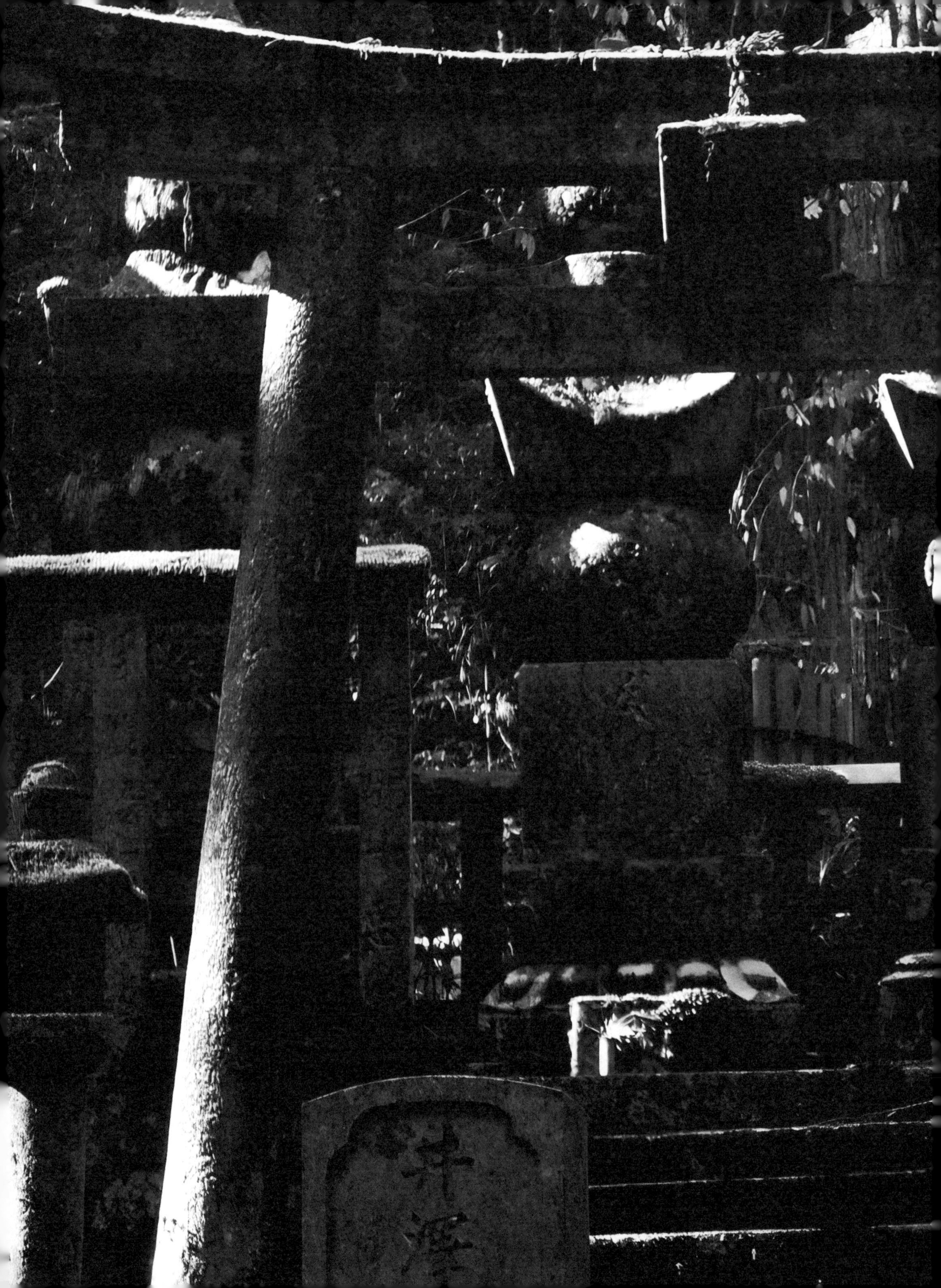

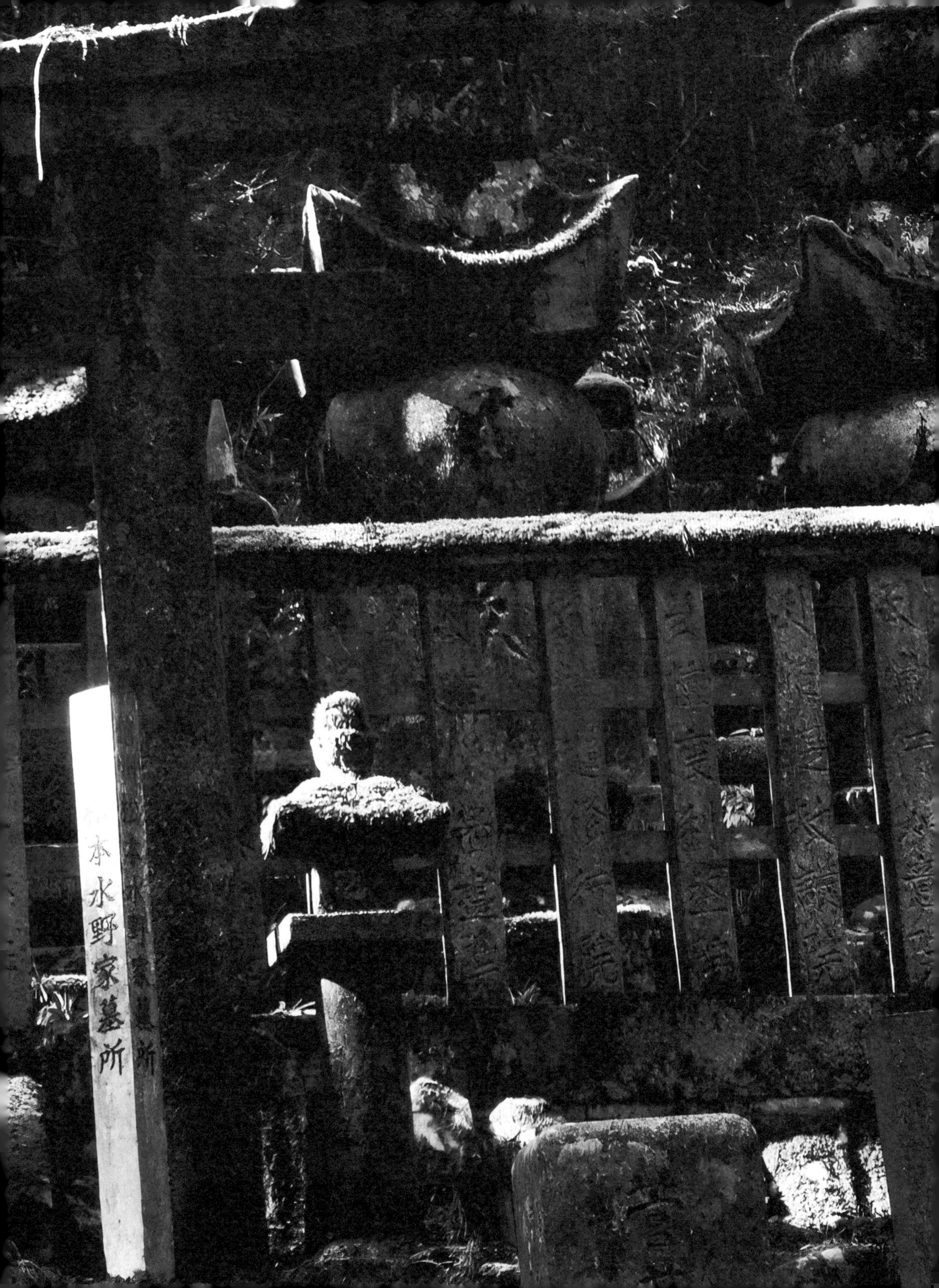
水野家墓所

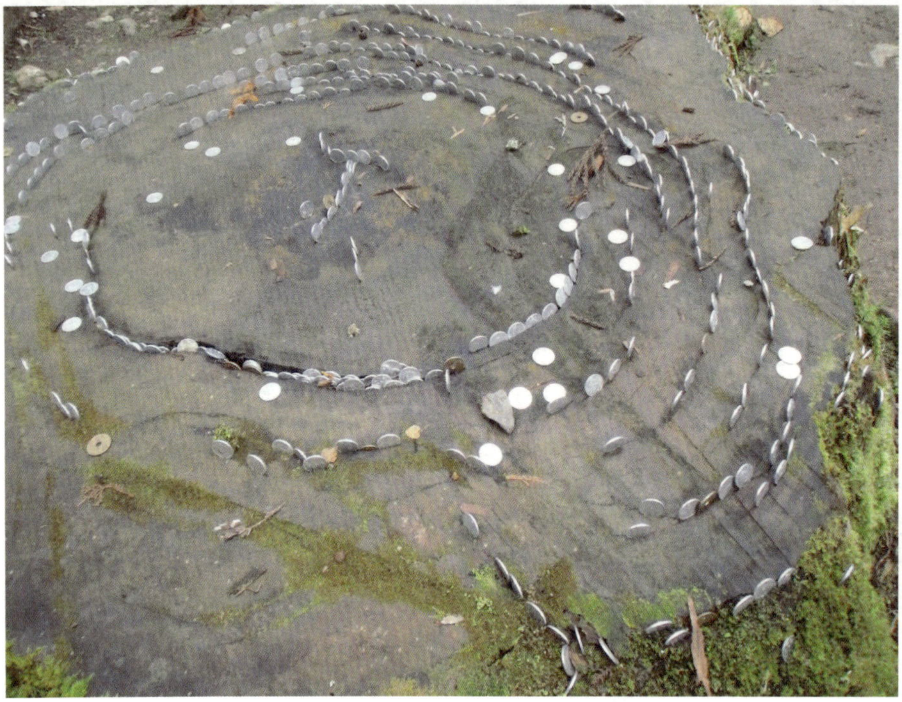

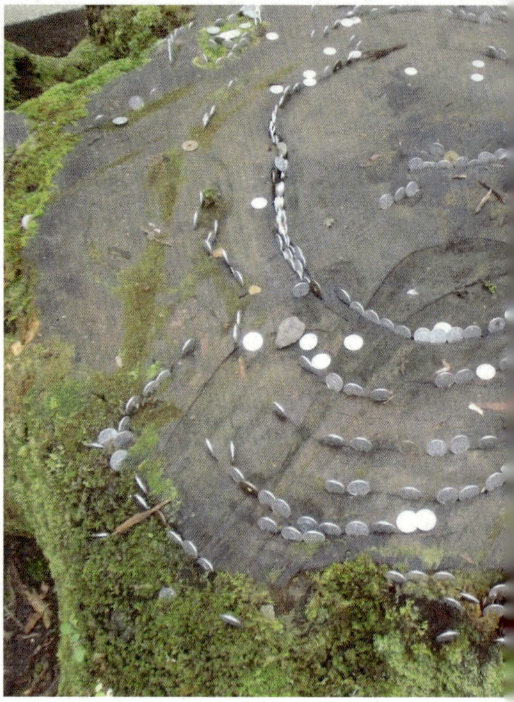

Vinck's work refers strongly to the structure of modern musical pieces (i.e. Giacinto Scelsi or Wolfgang Rihm). The use of repetitions, of clusters with single or limited notes, ensuring in the musical score breaks and cuts, amplifications or sequences, testifies of a composition process close to the one artistically applied in her linocuts.

 João Vário, from 'Linda Vinck: A special case of enumeration in painting', Antwerp, July 1994

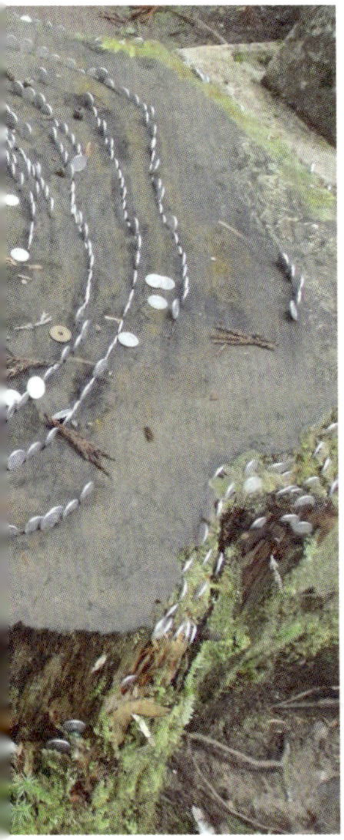

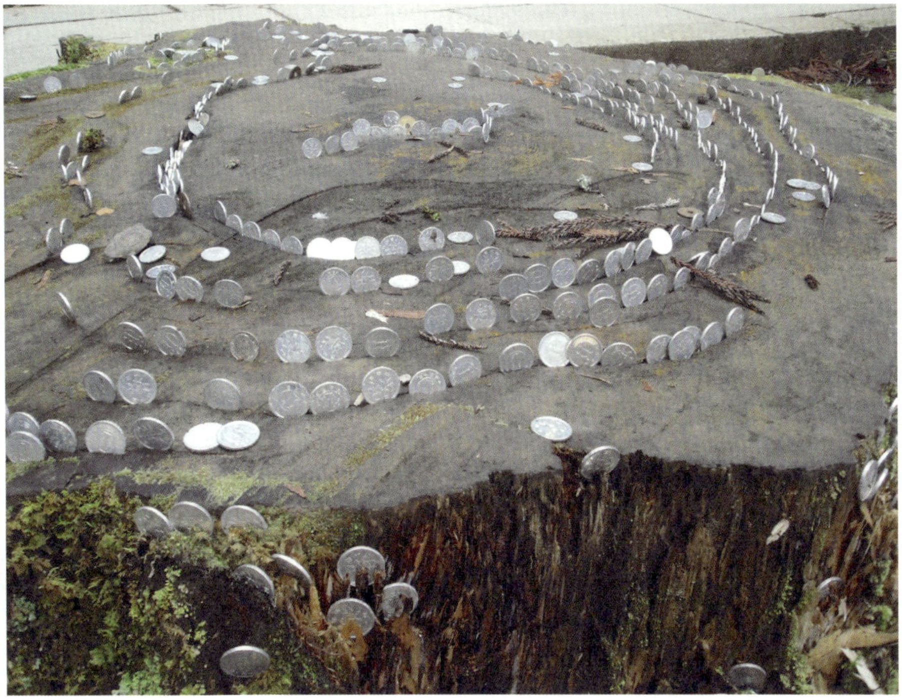

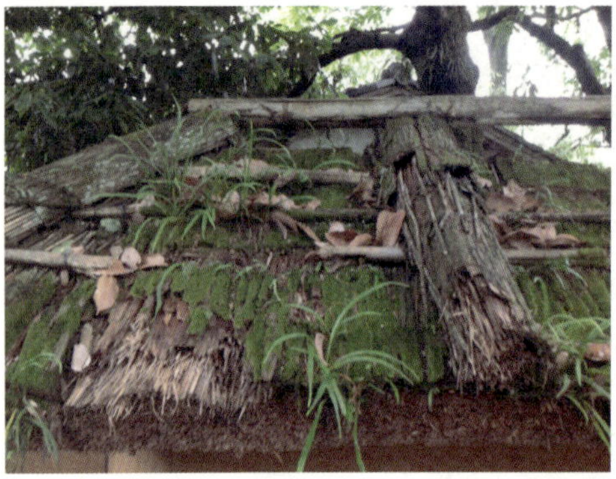
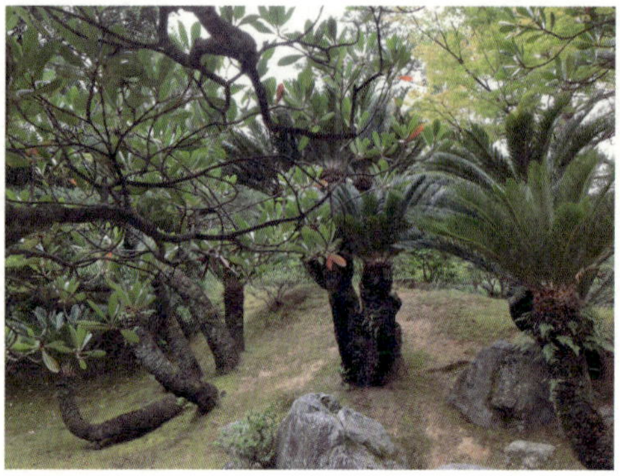
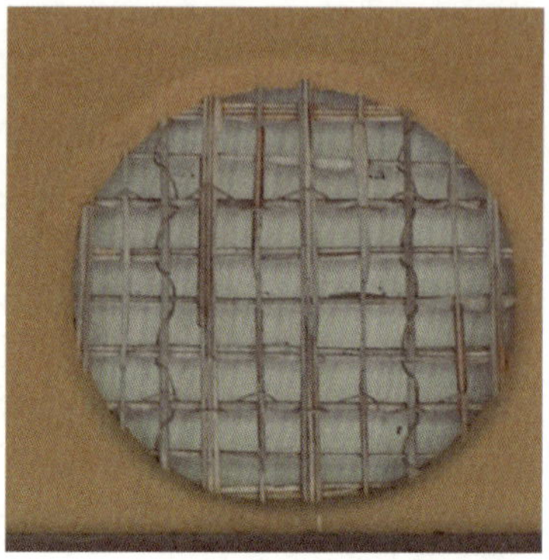
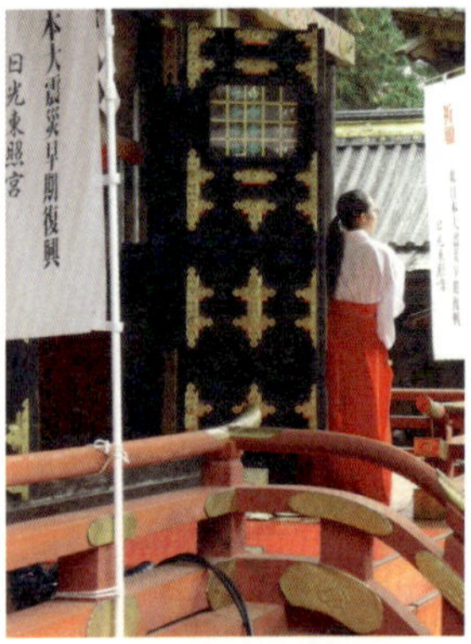
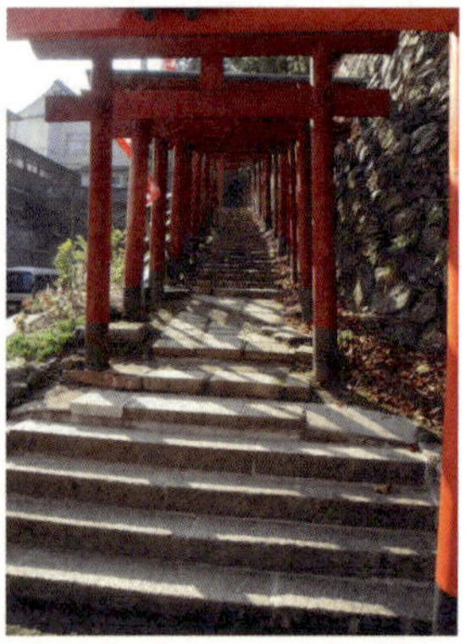
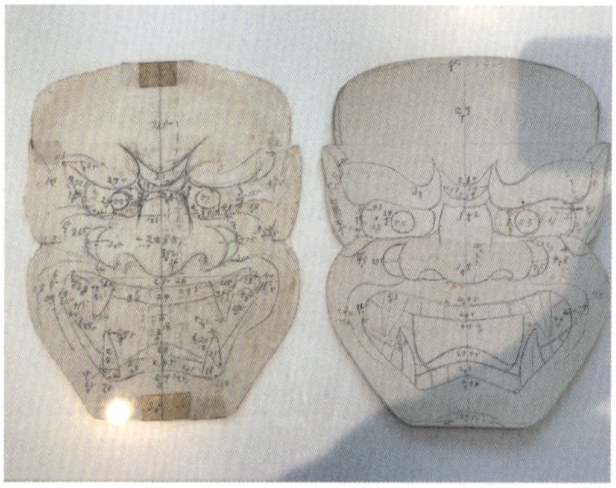
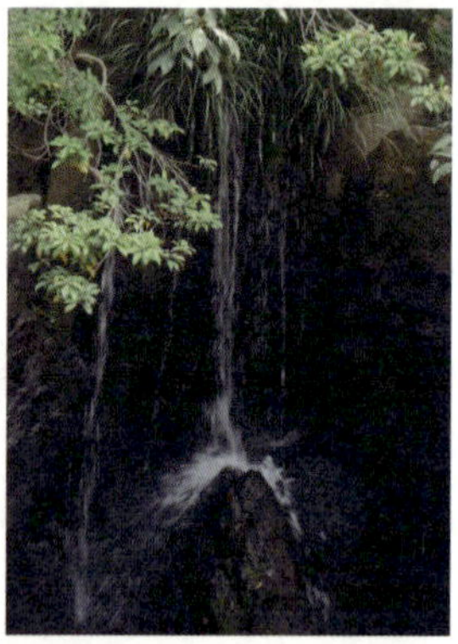

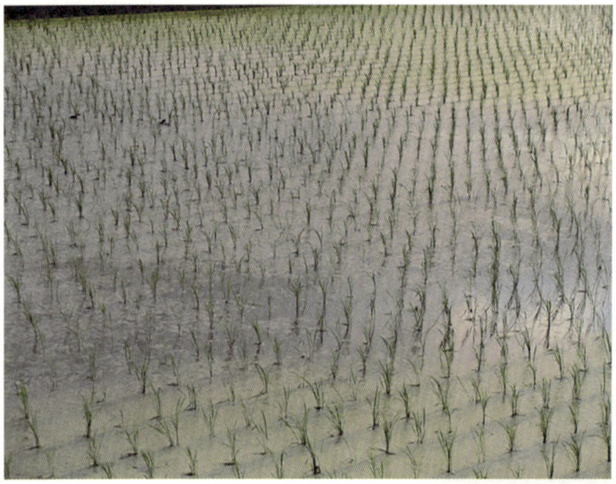
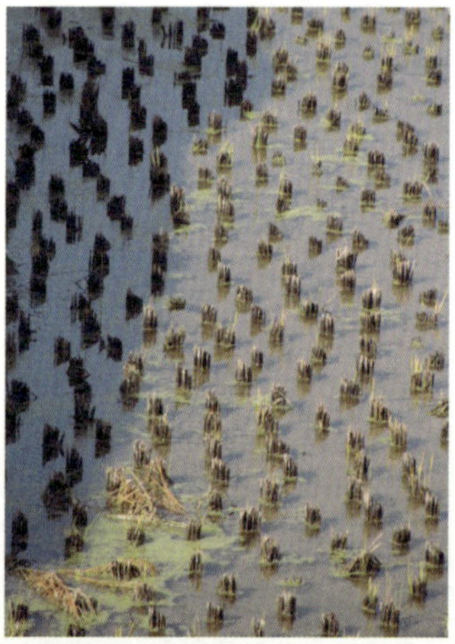
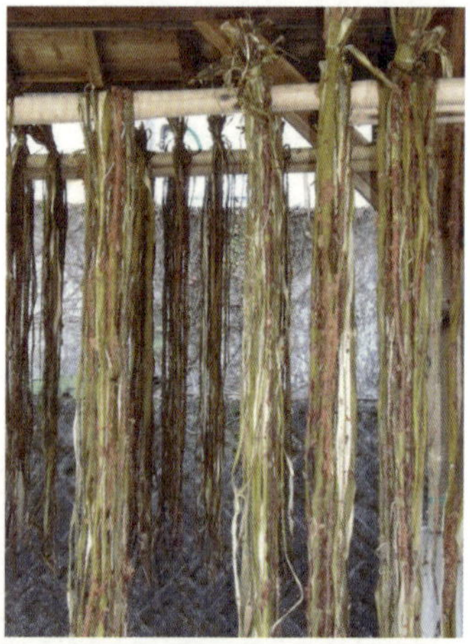
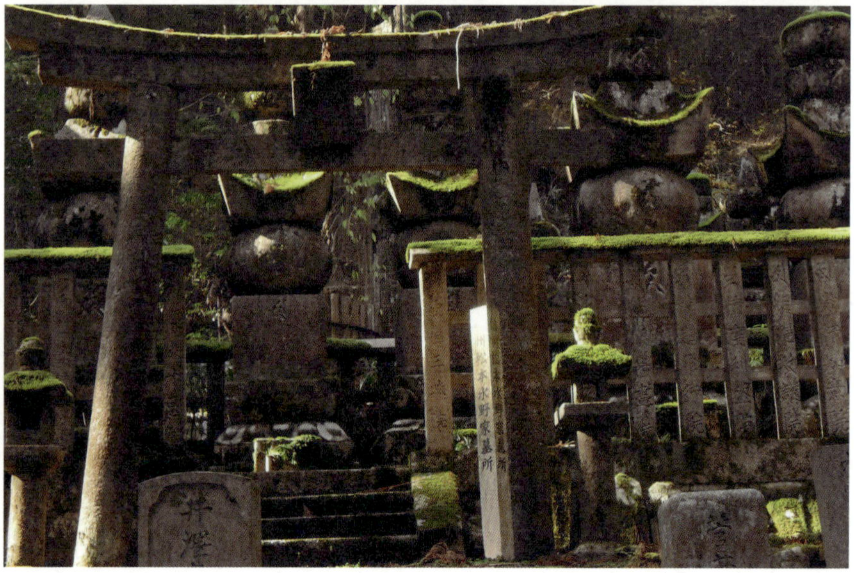
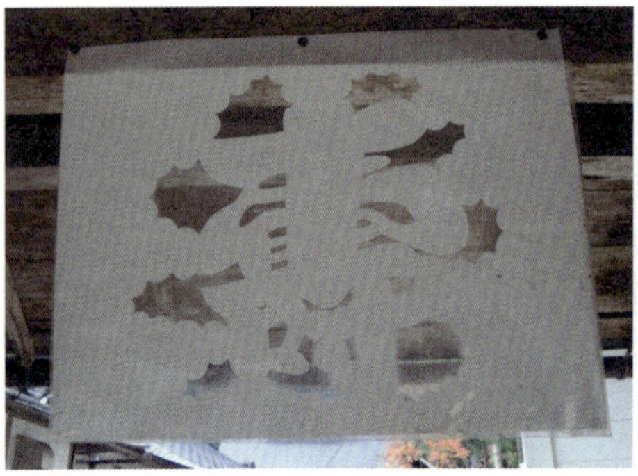

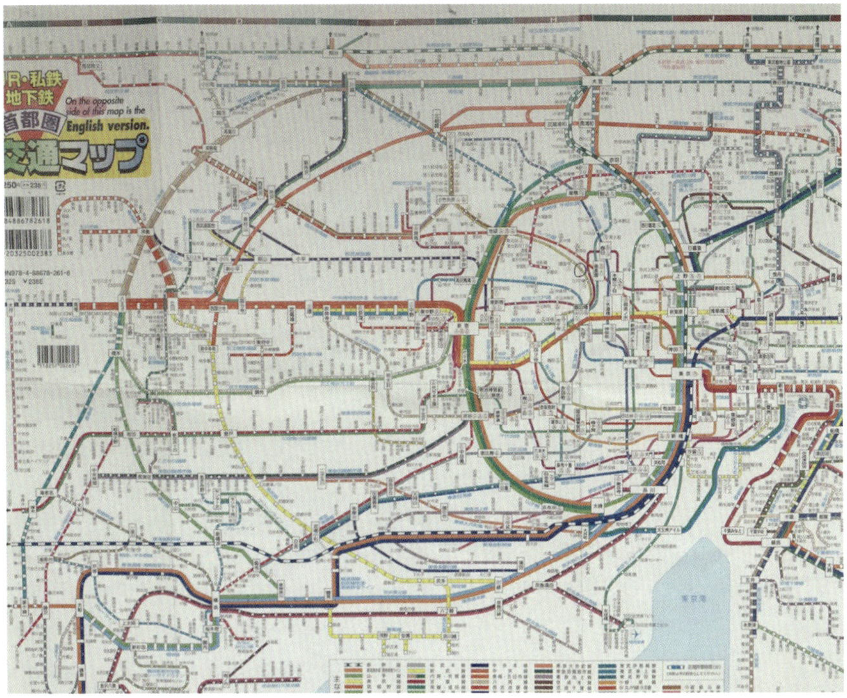
R・私鉄
地下鉄
首都圏
交通マップ
On the opposite side of this map is the English version.

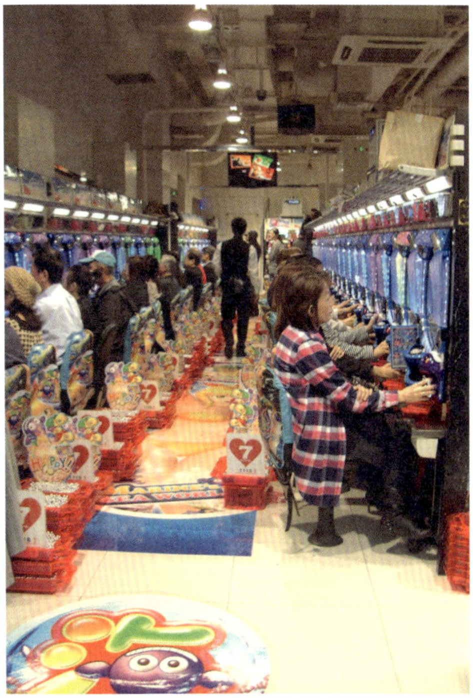

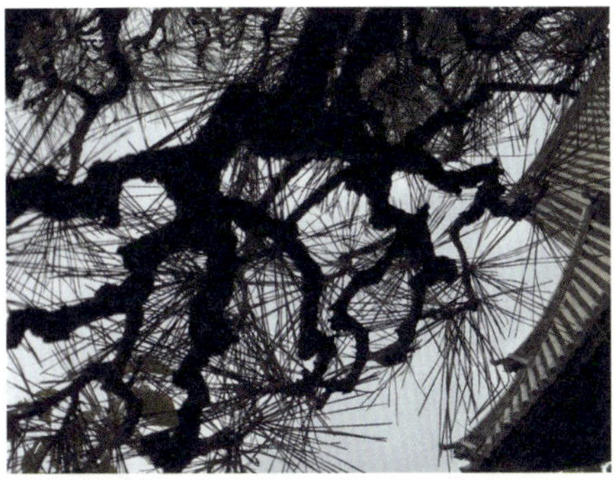

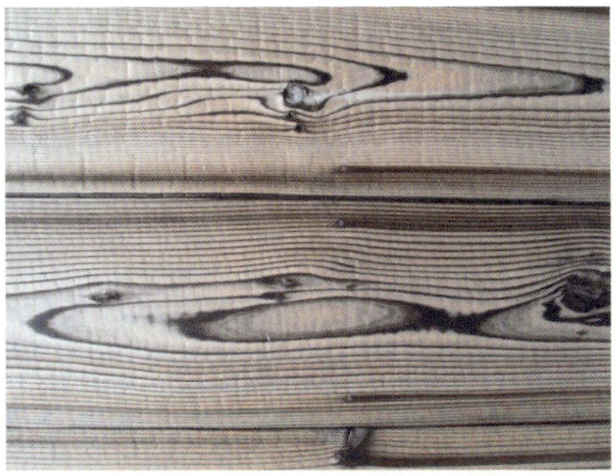

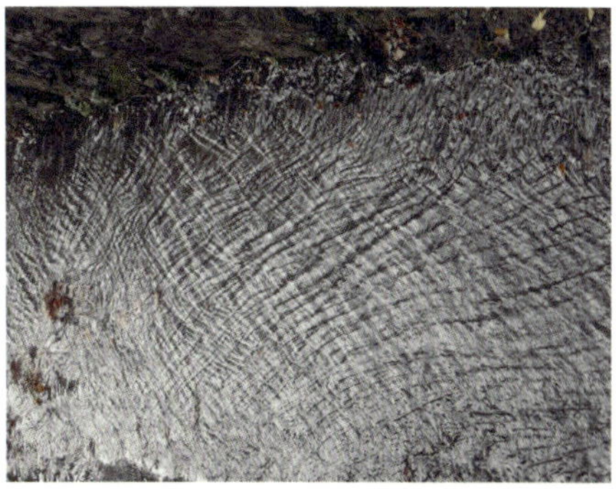

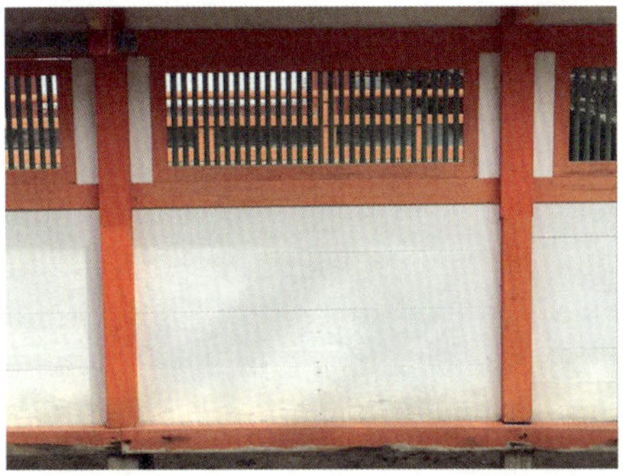

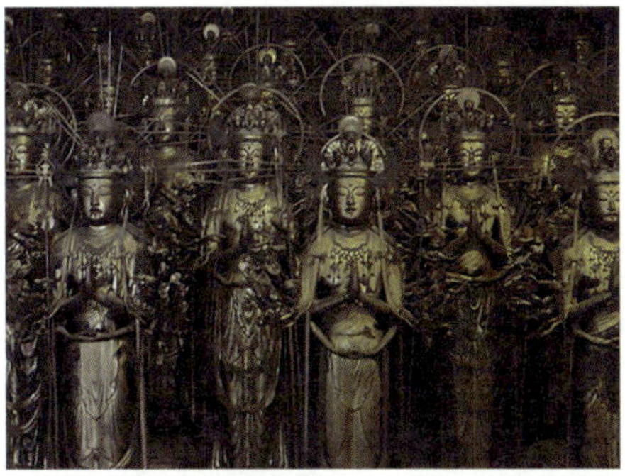

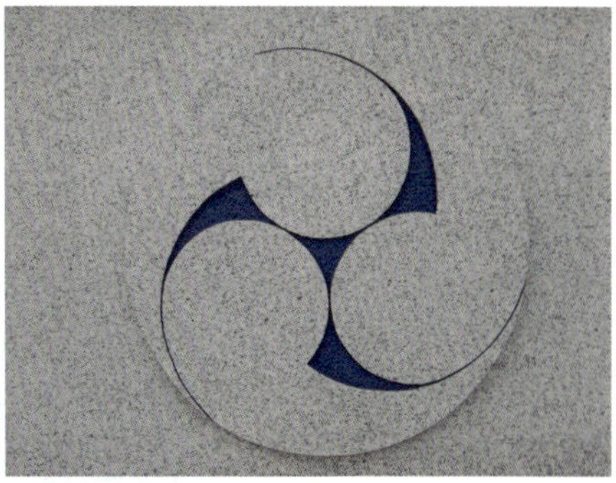

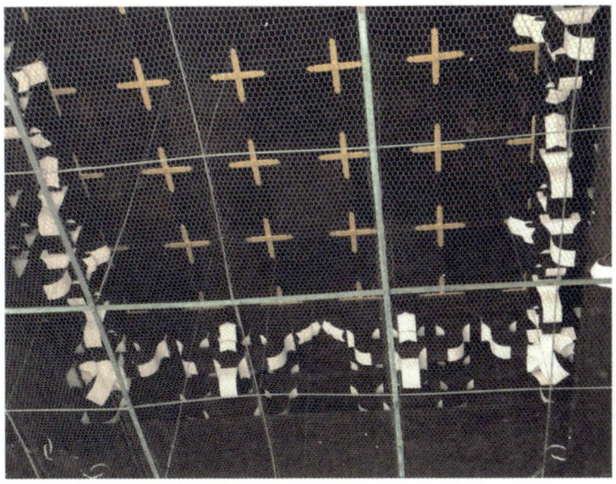

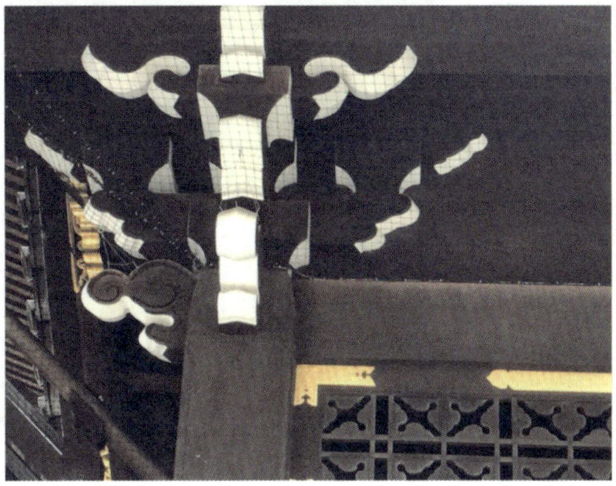

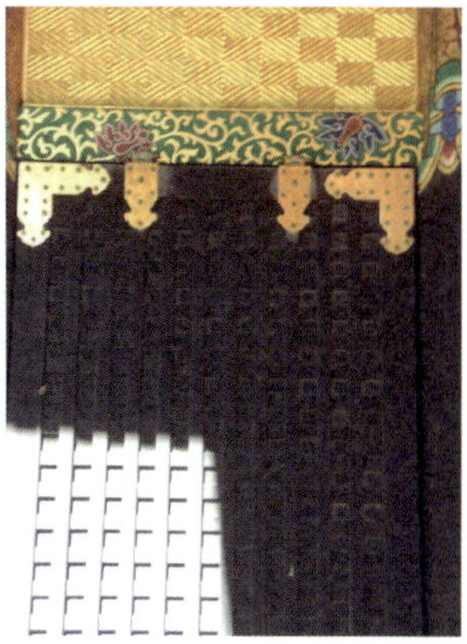

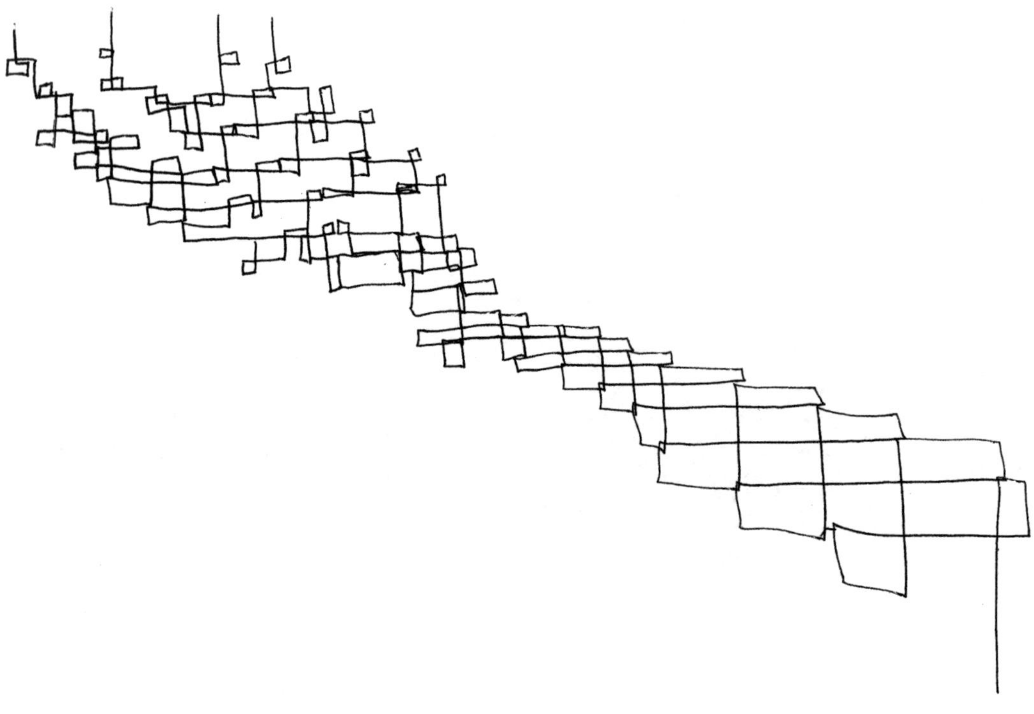

V. A tone is a colour
is a feeling
is a thought
is a star*

Een toon is een kleur
is een gevoel
is een gedachte
is een ster*

When colour takes place

* From book 'De kleuren van de geest, Dans en Trance in Afro-Europese tradities', p. 49, by Paul Vandenbroeck, Snoeck-Ducaju, Ghent, 1997

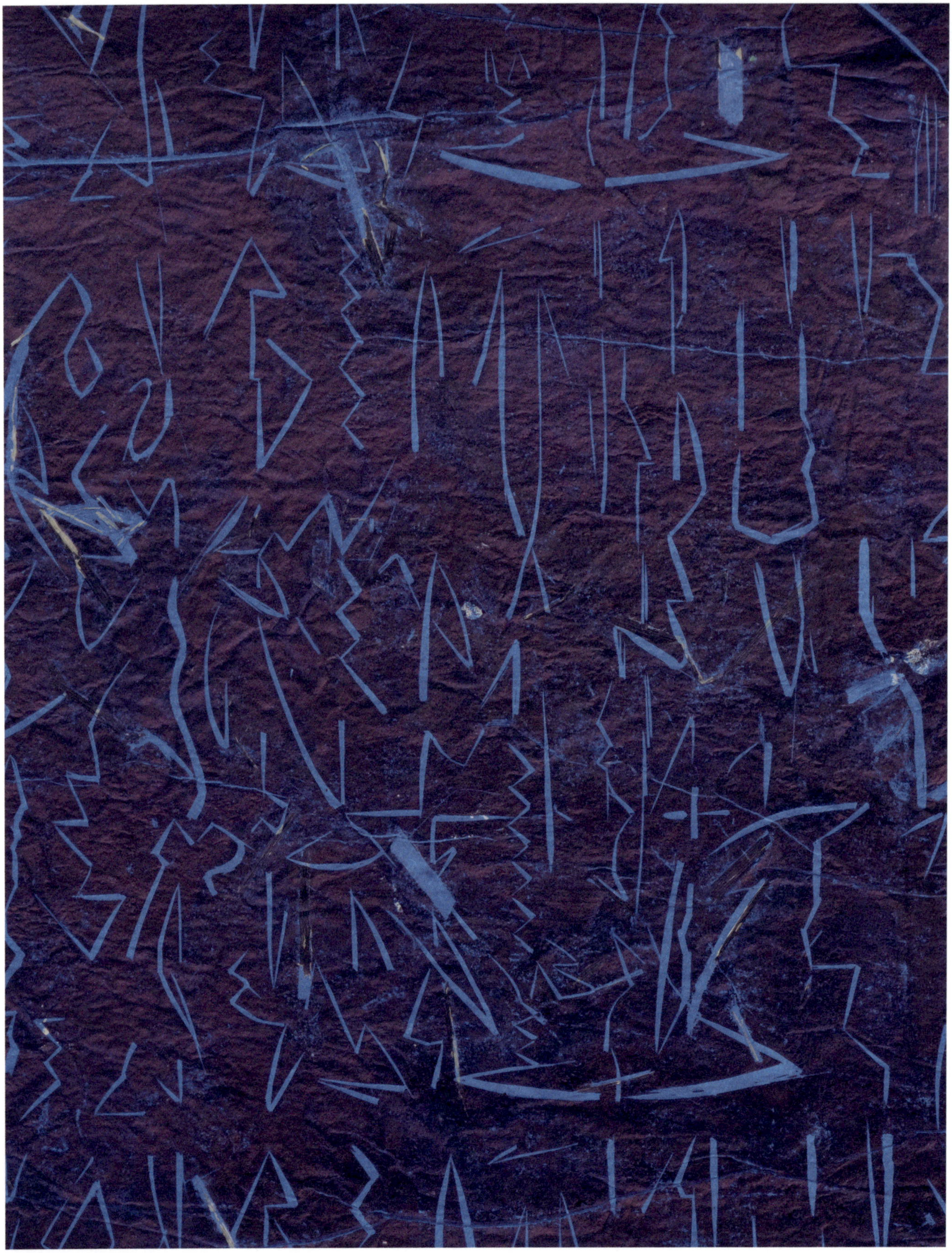

fig. 1

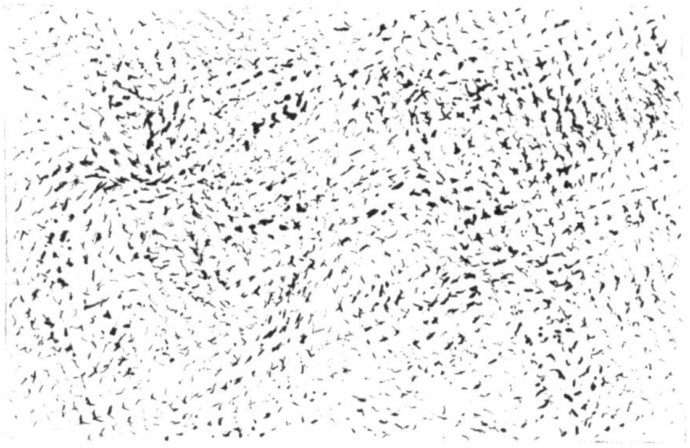

fig. 2

Linda Vinck: Complex and Moving Imagery

Dirk Verhaegen

left page: fig. 1
Patterns of Paradise (detail)

fig. 2
Stretch & Flow, 490 × 720 mm, dry-needle on Arches paper, 1983

A flock of gulls mark themselves out on the clear winter sky. Scripts without language. And yet, they can be read as unity in diversity, as loose cohesion, as chaos adrift. A lively mishmash. Alternating between shadow and light. Relief, movement, transformation.

Perhaps I am leading the audience astray by using such poetic imagery. Indeed, it might suggest that Linda Vinck might also depart from such figurative motifs. But that is not the case. Forget the gulls for now. “I don’t feel any urge to reproduce what I see with my eyes”. Linda Vinck clearly situates herself within an abstract context, seeking out the essential. Her work is clearly fuelled by a perceptible reality. Abstract artists are not blind. But such nurturing only occurs indirectly, through lifelong interaction with perceptible reality. To observe is to acquire knowledge about the world. Evolutionarily speaking, perception predates language itself. Making art is also a way of interweaving knowledge. The globalising, abstracting capabilities of perception and exploratory behaviour form the biological basis of that uniquely human activity: making art. Beyond the visual, Linda’s work also explores our physical impulses, as is the case with both music and especially dance.

Symbols: combinations of linear elements on a background. In turn, they form larger wholes, cohesions, movements, energetic fields. Do they mean anything? Is visual art a form of language? Does it belong within the realm of visual communication? With their text-like appearance, Linda Vinck’s

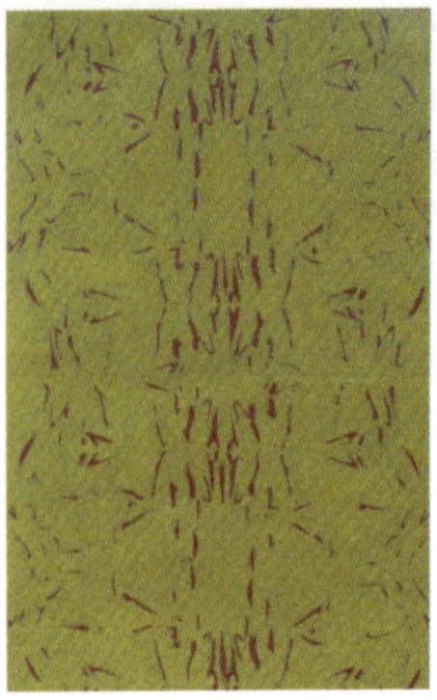

fig. 3

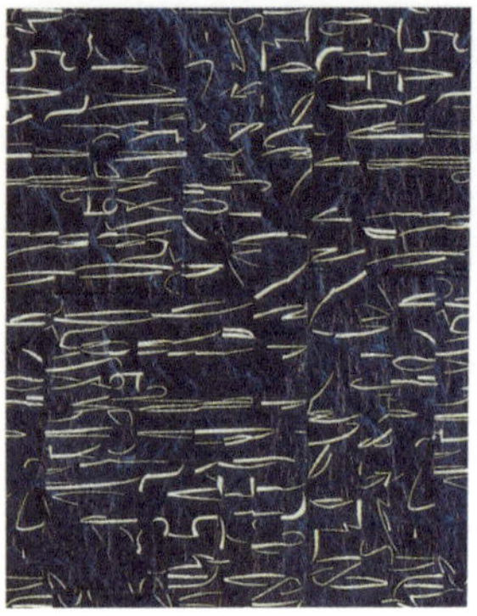

fig. 4

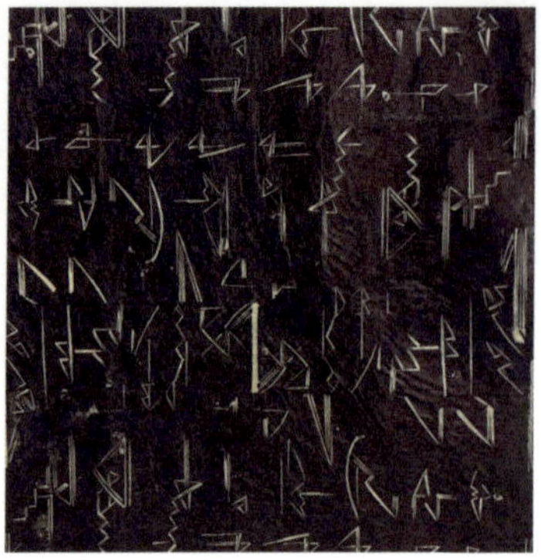

fig. 5

works serve to back up this understanding. They resemble secret writings or scripts taken from foreign civilizations. However, those expecting simple codes will be left wanting. Linda Vinck's symbols have nothing to do with functional language, but rather poetic language. Poetic language does not so much serve to retell something, rather it is to be experienced and lived itself. Here, syntax is more important than semantics. It is ranking, it is ordering. There is also some relationship with ritualism and magical language. Poetic language sets our imagination in motion. With Linda Vinck, we can also talk about 'fluid codes'.

fig. 3
Correntes 4, 400 × 700 mm, linocut on canvas, 2005

fig. 4
Reflex Blue – Patterns of Paradise (detail)

fig. 5
Meditation on Peace: Approaching (detail)

Taking an adventurous quest across continents and ages will put us in the right frame of mind here. After all, Linda Vinck loves physical and mental movement. Within modernism, e.g. Paul Klee, Willi Baumeister, Max Ernst, Mark Tobey, Henri Michaux, Christian Dotremont and others have used cryptic symbols. As literate illiterates, we can also look at prehistoric symbols, at markings by medieval stonemasons, at primitive mathematical symbols, at Eastern calligraphy, at stelae and seals, at the celestial alphabet of the Kabbalists, or at the linguistic symbols of the Berbers and Siberian nomads. We can also read the secret language with the romantic poet Novalis on wings, eggshells, in clouds, in snow, in crystals, the strange conjunctures of chance, his *Sensible Chaos*. Alternatively, we can catalogue the characters as level-headed bookkeepers: open or closed, symmetrical or asymmetrical, crossed or not, linear or crooked. Or, we can consider the principles of gestalt perception, observing how the individual characters connect with each other and merge into a whole, much like individual notes within a broader melody.

Creativity and perception have to do with mental processes. Although a work of art is therefore not to be reduced to its purely material manifestation, that material manifestation should not, above all, be disregarded either. On the contrary, imaginative thinking occurs in close relation to material actions, the employing of tangible techniques and processes. Vinck's symbols have arisen from actions, from material work and from tangible

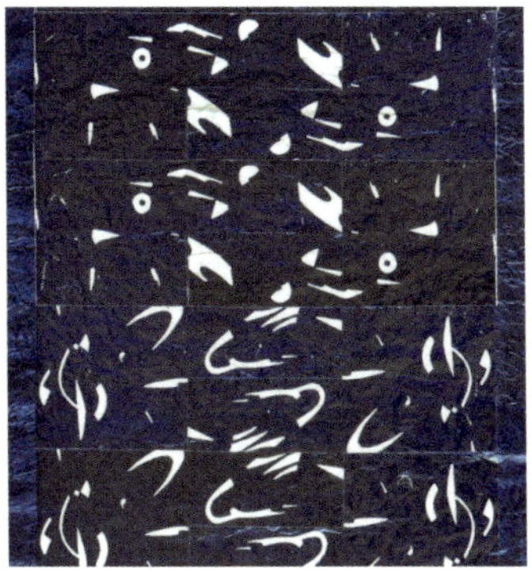

fig. 6

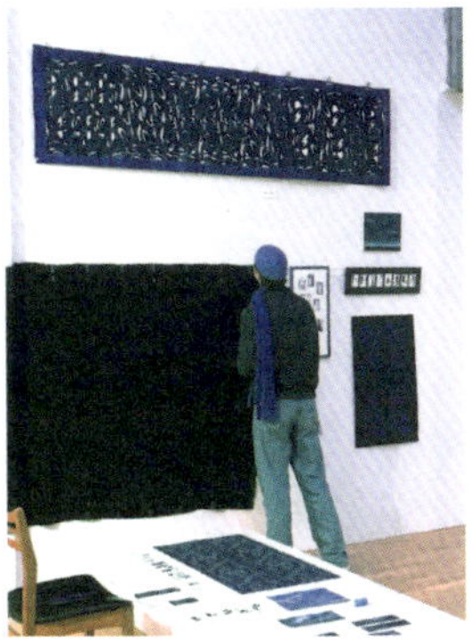

fig. 7

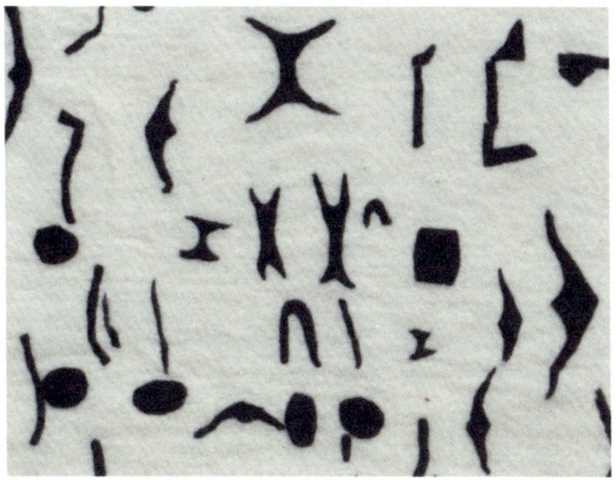

fig. 8

fig. 6
Oceanography 3 (detail)

fig. 7
exhibition *Blauw — Teken van de Nacht* (Blue — Sign of the Night), Kortrijk, 2023

fig. 8
Harpa Doris — Felt (detail)

processes: free hand, the use of grids as a gentle guide, the movements of gouges or scissors, the shifting and arranging of individual elements, mechanical repetition, the twisting and turning of groupings. The material and processes form part of the creation process, helping to determine the specific characteristics of the form. With Linda Vinck, neither the materials nor the techniques are of value in themselves. They are, in fact, usually used in a rather unorthodox manner. They are also in a constant state of change. The pen becomes the paintbrush, then the gouge, then the scissors. The cork becomes splintered wood, which then gives way to felt. For her, the medium is given special attention, often forming an integral part of the work and the process. Sometimes layered, sometimes collage and structured like patchwork. The image boundary therefore bears the irregular traces of the process, becoming a lecture in the margin, i.e. an external manifestation of an internal process. The printing techniques are not used to create editions, rather to manipulate modules, cells, repetitions, rotational symmetries, movements, to realise a rhythmic reading, creating complex, dynamic 'musical' structures.

Linda Vinck's work demonstrates a rich and continuous inventiveness, exploring the limits of her medium in fascinating ways. While her work is repetitive in nature, it never repeats itself. Her creativity does not stem from the spectacular. For her, authenticity may prove more important. Through her use of imagery, she is able to 'symbolize' the complex and dynamic rhythm of the world around us, becoming one with that rhythm and inviting us to share in its vital and joyful energy. Thus, we can once again let go of all scholarly approach, free to simply experience everything without overthinking. And there they are once more, the gulls, squawking with glee!

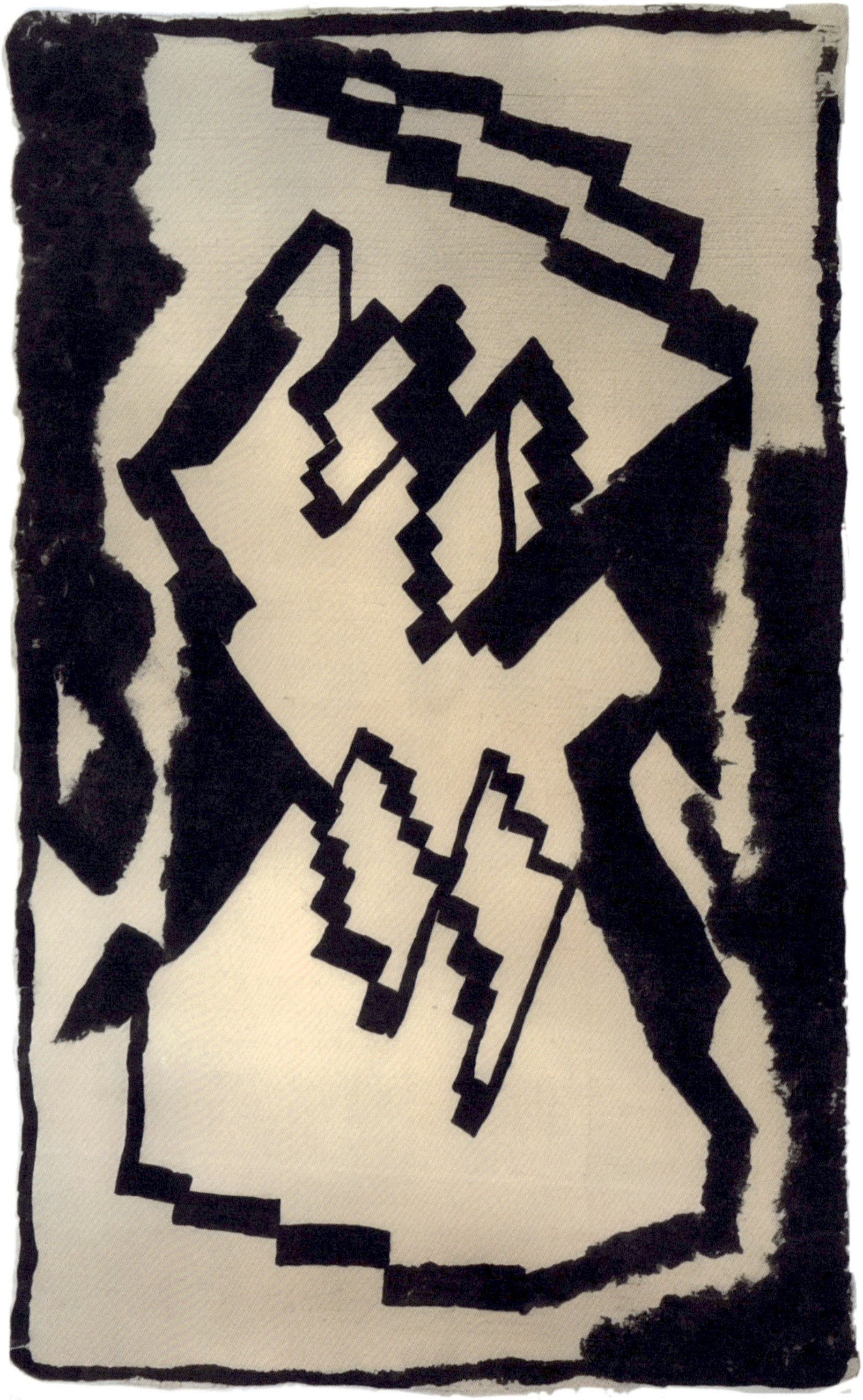

fig. 9

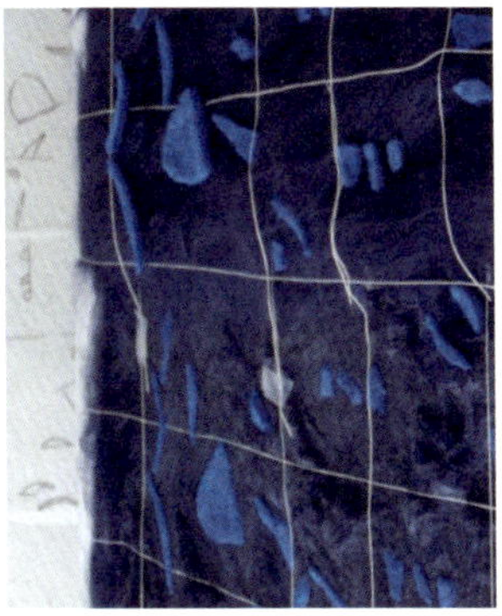

fig. 10

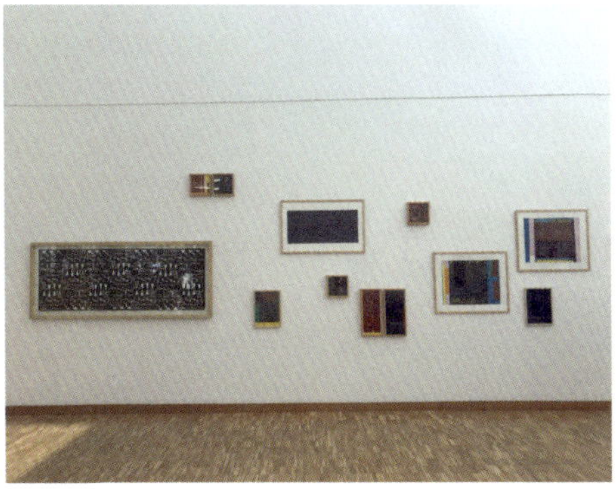

fig. 11

Linda Vinck: Complexe en Bewogen Betekening

Dirk Verhaegen

left page: fig. 9
Parallel Worlds
– Felt
fig. 10
Felt (method)

fig. 11
Rituals of Homecoming, K.I.H. Leuven, 2019

Een zwerm meeuwen tekent zich af op de heldere winterlucht. Schrifttekens zonder taal. En toch kunnen zij gelezen worden: als eenheid in verscheidenheid, als losse samenhang, als chaos op drift. Wirwar die levendigheid heet. Wisselingen van schaduw en licht. Reliëf, beweging, transformatie.

Misschien breng ik het publiek op een dwaalspoor met zulke poëtische beelden. Zij zouden immers kunnen suggereren dat Linda Vinck van zulke figuratieve motieven vertrekt. En dat is dus niet het geval. Vergeet voorlopig die meeuwen. “Ik voel geen enkele aandrang om wat ik met mijn ogen zie weer te geven.” Linda Vinck situeert zich duidelijk binnen een abstracte context. Ze zoekt het essentiële. Haar werk is uiteraard gevoed door de zichtbare werkelijkheid. Abstracte kunstenaressen zijn niet blind. Maar dat gevoed worden gebeurt slechts op indirecte wijze, door de levenslange omgang met de visuele werkelijkheid. Waarnemen is kennis verwerven over de wereld. Waarnemen is – evolutionair gesproken – ouder dan de taal. Ook kunst maken is een manier om kennis te verwerven. De globaliserende, abstraherende vermogens van de waarneming en het explorerende gedrag vormen de biologische basis van die unieke menselijke activiteit: kunst maken. Buiten het visuele heeft Linda’s werk ook wat met lichamelijke impulsen te maken, zoals dat bij muziek en vooral ook bij dans het geval is.

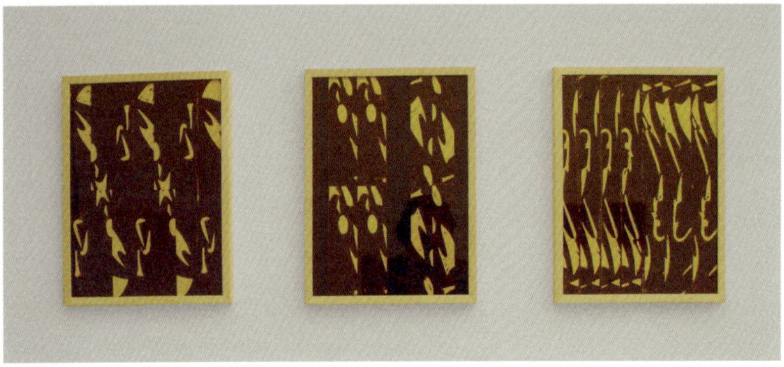

fig. 12

Tekens: combinaties van lineaire elementen op een achtergrond. Op hun beurt vormen zij grotere gehelen, samenhang, beweging, energetische velden. Betekenen zij iets? Is beeldende kunst taal? Behoort zij tot het domein van de visuele communicatie? Met hun tekstachtig uitzicht zouden de werken van Linda Vinck dat extra kunnen suggereren. Zij lijken op geheimschrift of op schriftbeelden uit vreemde culturen. Wie echter op simpele codes rekent zal van een kale reis thuiskomen. De tekens van Linda Vinck hebben niets met functionele taal te maken, wel met poëtische taal. Poëtische taal dient niet zozeer om iets anders te vertellen maar om zelf beleefd en ervaren te worden. Syntaxis is hier belangrijker dan semantiek. Het is rangschikking, het is ordening. Er is ook wel verwantschap met ritueel handelen en magisch taalgebruik. De poëtische taal zet onze verbeelding in beweging. Met Linda Vinck kunnen we ook over 'vloeiende codes' spreken.

fig. 12
Kebra Kanela, FUNANÁ o.a.
Galerie Wollondilly, Antwerp, 2004

right page:
fig. 13
Concentric Circles, (wood printing blocks)

Een avontuurlijke zoektocht over continenten en tijdperken zal ons in een geschikte stemming brengen. Linda Vinck houdt immers van fysieke en mentale verplaatsing. Binnen het modernisme hebben b.v. Paul Klee, Willi Baumeister, Max Ernst, Mark Tobey, Henri Michaux, Christian Dotremont en anderen zich van cryptische tekens bediend. Als geletterde analfabeten kunnen we ook naar prehistorische tekens kijken, naar merktekens van middeleeuwse steenhouwers, naar primitieve wiskundige tekens, naar oosterse kalligrafie, naar stèles en zegels, naar het hemelse alfabet van de kabbalisten, of naar de taaltekens van Berbers en Siberische nomaden. We kunnen ook met de romantische dichter Novalis de geheimtaal lezen op vleugels, eierschalen, in wolken, in sneeuw, in kristallen, de vreemde conjuncturen van het toeval, zijn Sensibele Chaos. Of we kunnen de tekens als nuchtere boekhouders catalogeren: open of gesloten, symmetrisch of asymmetrisch, gekruist of niet, rechtlijnig of krom. Of we kunnen de principes van de gestaltwaarneming in ogenschouw nemen. Zien hoe de individuele tekens verbanden aangaan met elkaar en opgaan in het geheel zoals noten in een melodie.

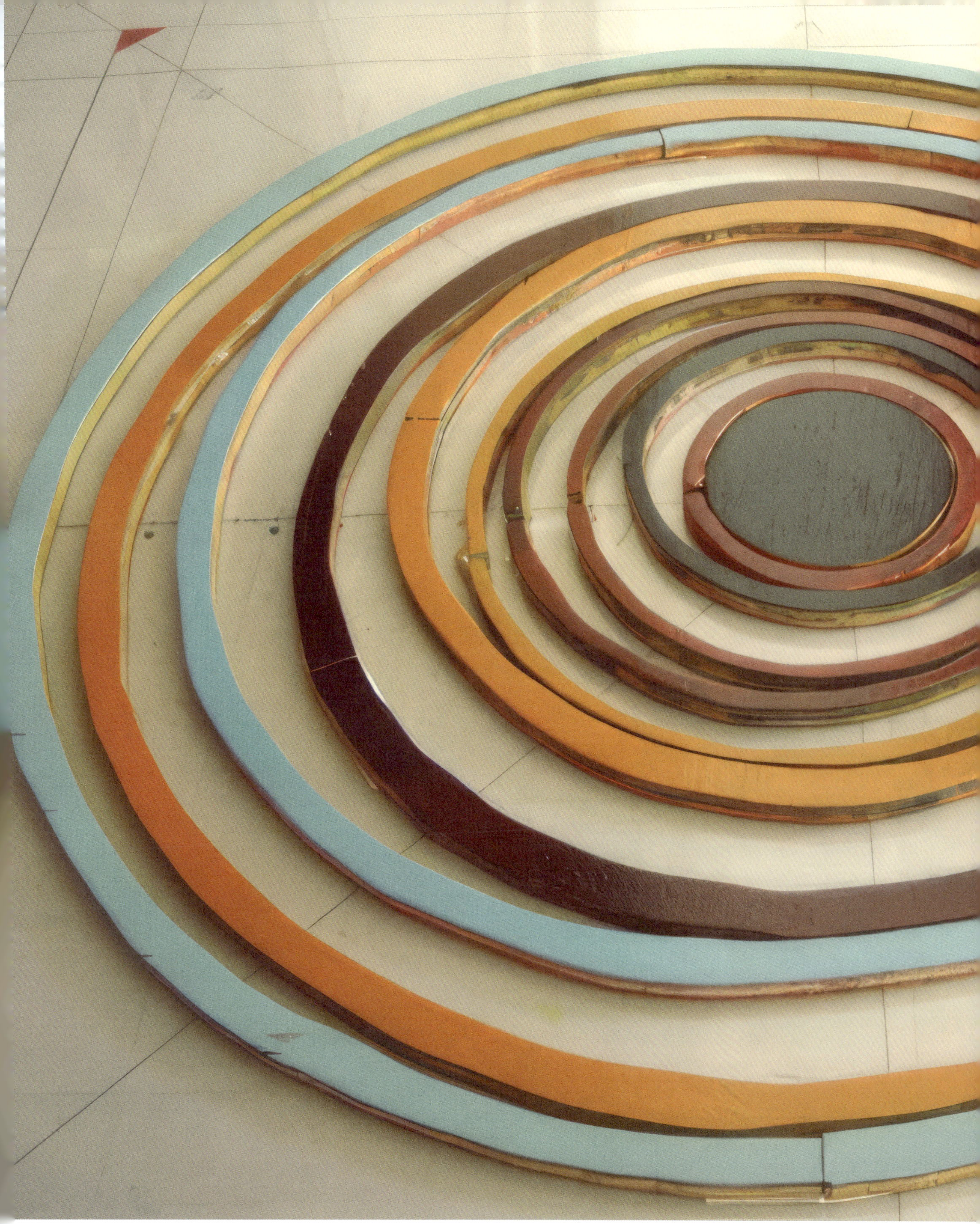

ig. 13

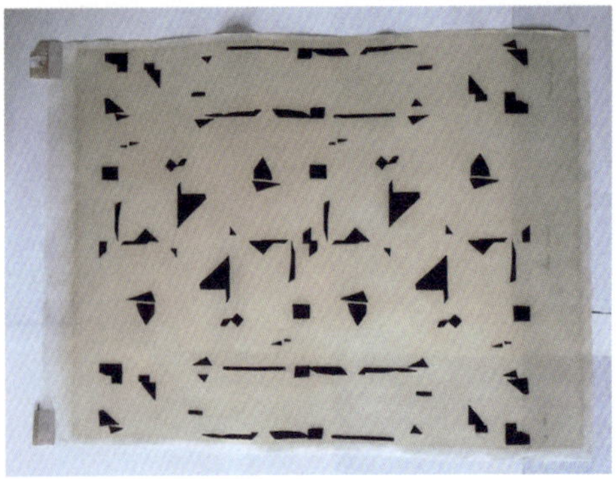

fig. 14

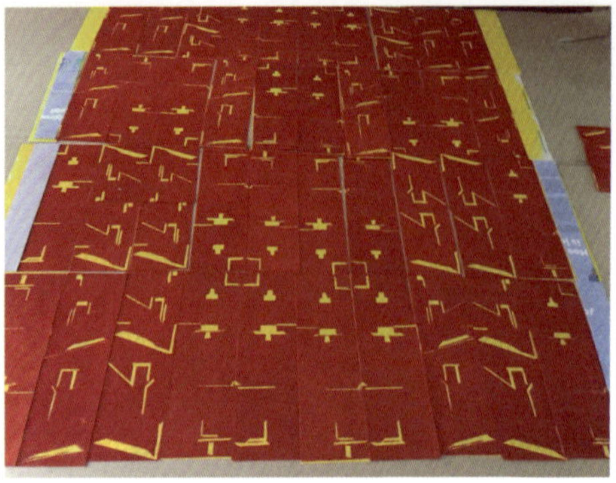

fig. 15

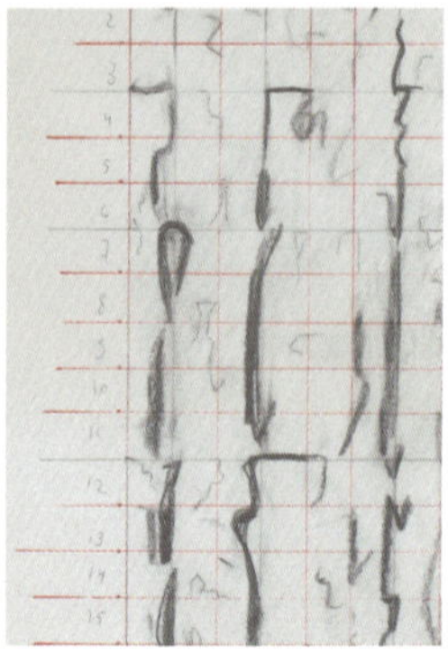

fig. 16

fig. 14
Genetic Process (in the making)

fig. 15
Bugaku (assemblage)

fig. 16
Pencil drawing (detail)

right page:
fig. 17
Alphabet I

Creativiteit en waarneming hebben met mentale processen te maken. Alhoewel een kunstwerk dus niet te herleiden is tot zijn louter materiële verschijningsvorm, valt die materiële verschijningsvorm vooral ook niet te veronachtzamen. Integendeel, beeldend denken gebeurt in nauwe relatie met handelingen in de materie, hanteren van concrete technieken en procédés. De tekens zijn uit handelingen, uit materiaalbewerking en uit concrete procédés ontstaan: het vrije handschrift, het gebruik van rasters als milde leidraad, de bewegingen van guts of schaar, het schuiven en schikken van losse elementen, het mechanische herhalen, het draaienen keren van groepen. Het materiaal en de procédés nemen deel aan het scheppingsproces, bepalen mee de specifieke karakteristieken van de vorm. Noch de materialen, noch de technieken zijn bij Linda Vinck waarde op zich. Zij worden trouwens meestal vrij onorthodox gebruikt. Zij zijn ook in voortdurende verandering. De pen wordt penseel wordt guts wordt schaar, de kurk wordt gesplinterd hout wordt vilt. De drager krijgt bij haar een bijzondere aandacht, is dikwijls een integrerend deel van het werk en van het werkproces. Soms is hij gelaagd, soms is hij collage en als patchwork gestructureerd. De beeldbegrenzing draagt aldus de onregelmetige sporen van het werkproces, wordt een lectuur in de marge, het is een externe resultante van een interne organisatie. De druktechnieken worden niet gebruikt om oplagen te maken maar om modules te hanteren, cellen, repetities, draaisymmetrieën, verplaatsingen, om een ritmische lectuur te organiseren, om complexe, dynamische 'muzikale' structuren te laten ontstaan.

Linda Vinck haar werk getuigt van een rijke en voortdurende inventiviteit, en zij verkent op boeiende wijze de grenzen van haar medium. Haar werk heeft een repetitief karakter, maar herhalen doet zij zich nooit. Haar creativiteit is niet van het spectaculaire genre. Authenticiteit is voor haar wellicht nog belangrijker. Met haar beelddtaal 'betekent' zij het ritme van de wereld, complex en dynamisch, zij voegt zich in dat ritme en zij nodigt ons uit deelachtig te worden in dat vitale geluk. We kunnen dus alle geleerdheid opnieuw loslaten en alles gewoon gedachtenloos beleven. En daar zijn ze weer, de meeuwen, en ze krijsen welgezind!

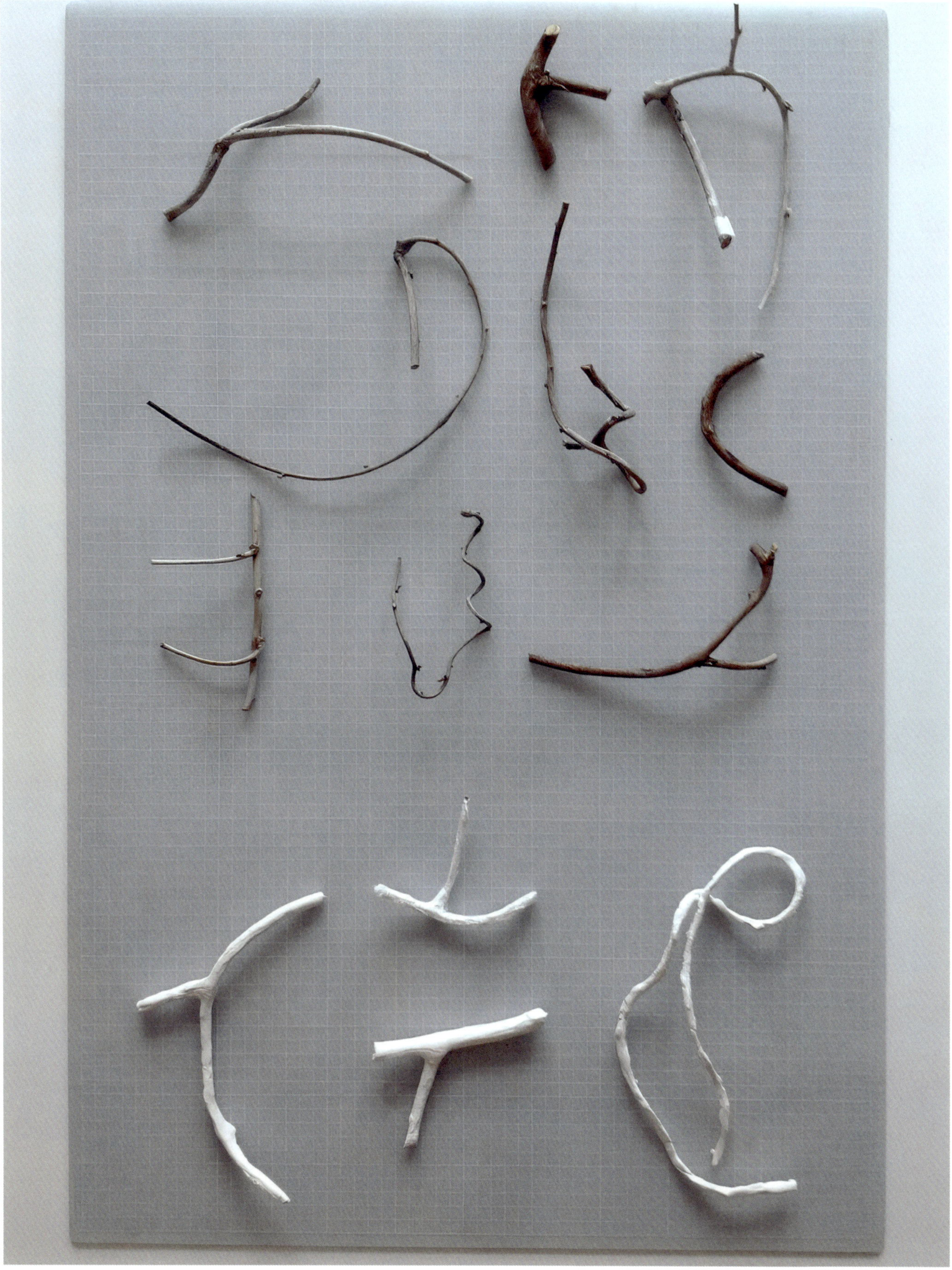

fig. 17

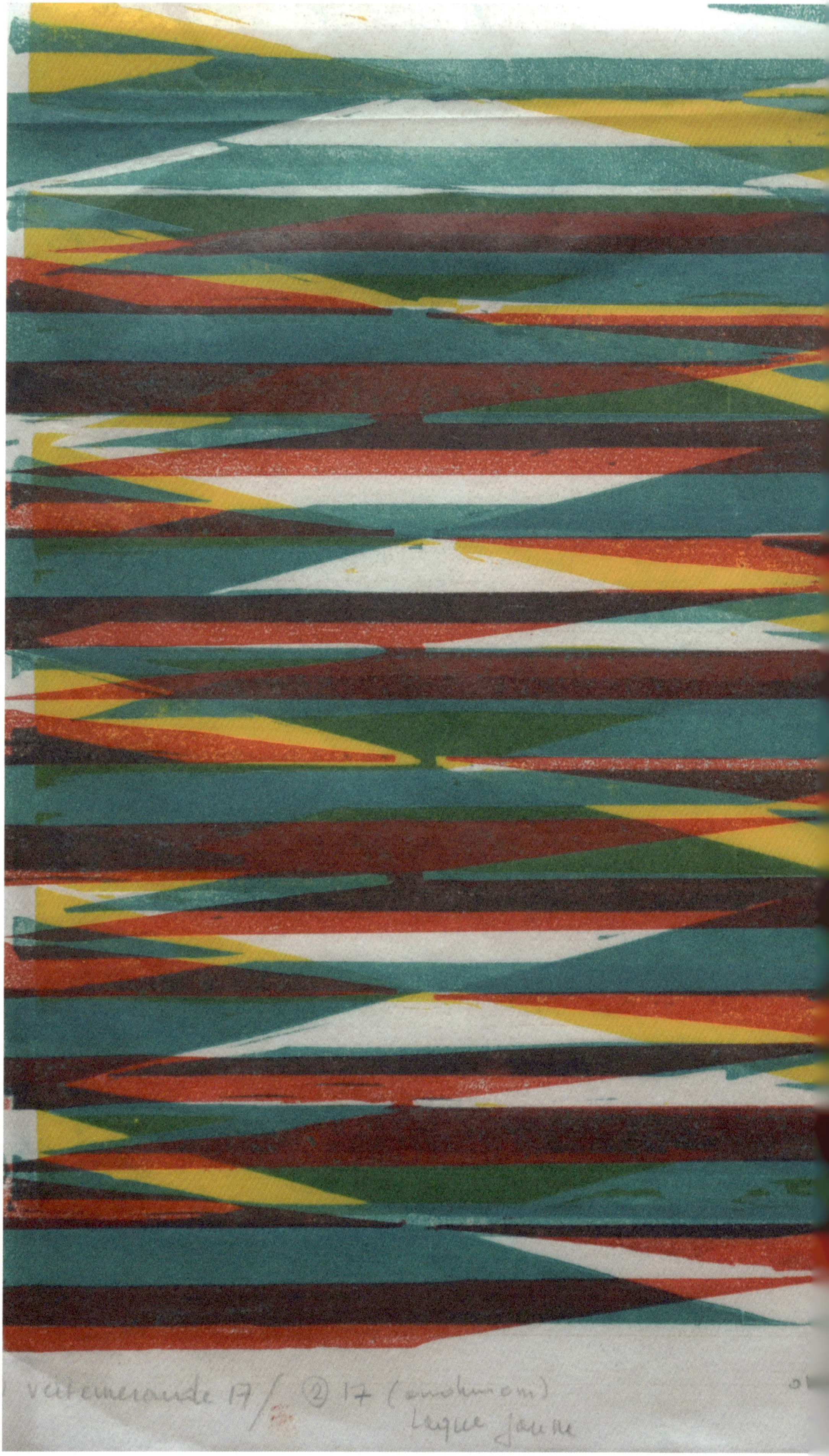
vert emeraude 17/
② 17
laque jaune

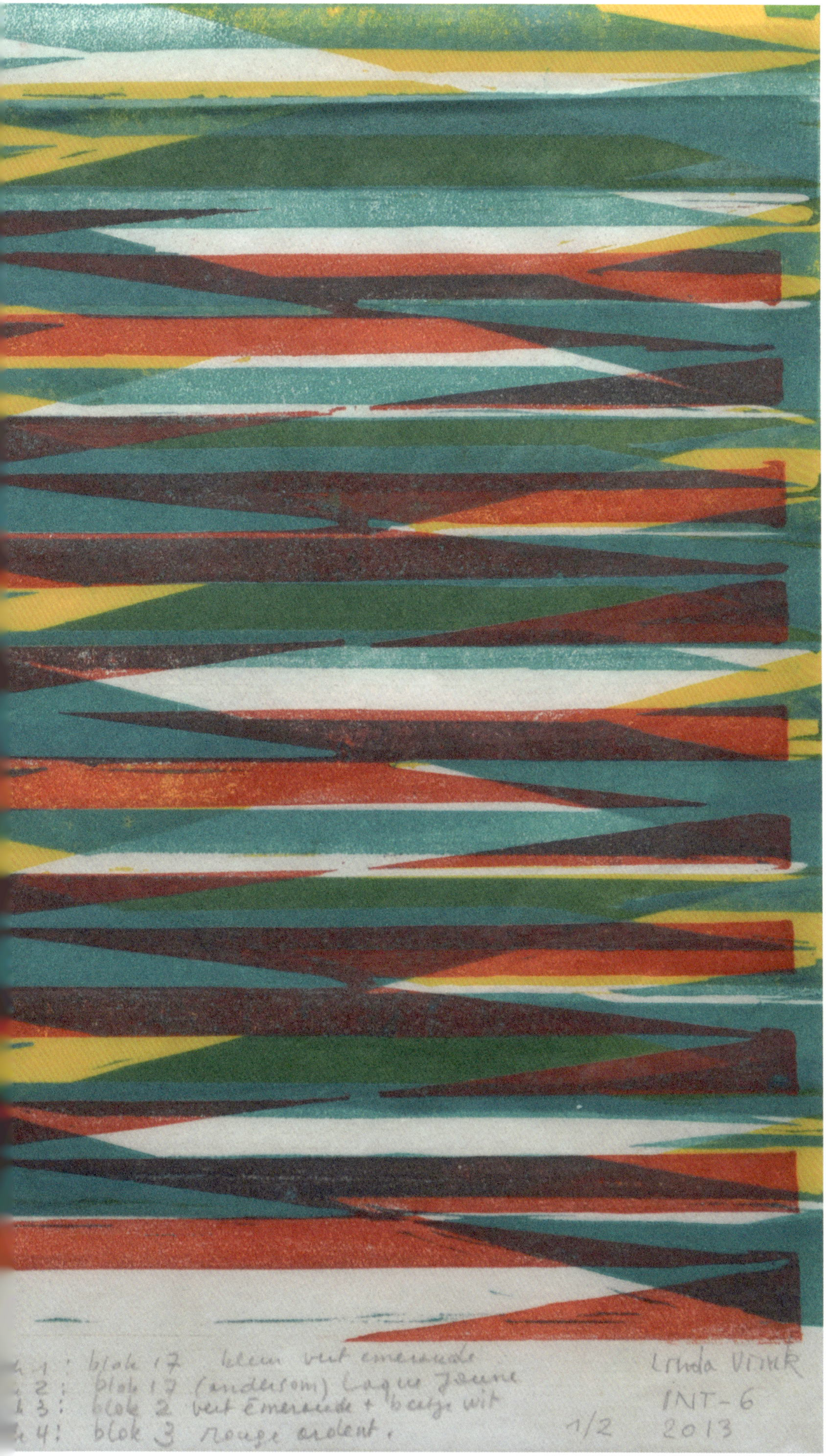
blok 17 bleu vert emeraude
blok 17 (andersom) Laque Jaune
blok 2 vert Emeraude + beige wit
blok 3 rouge ardent.
1/2
INT-6
2013

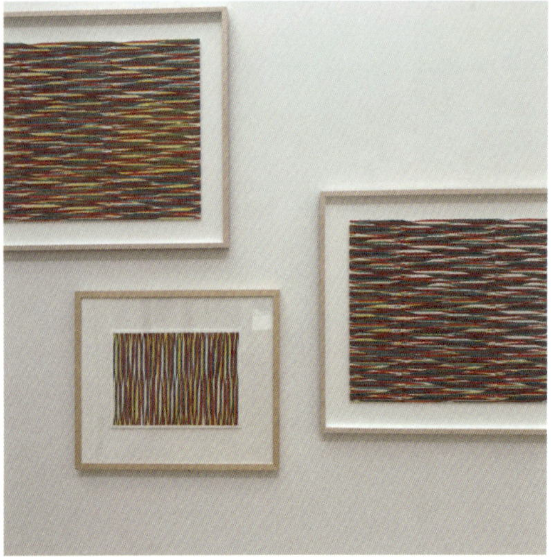

Exhibition Rituals of Homecoming,
K.I.H. Leuven, 2023

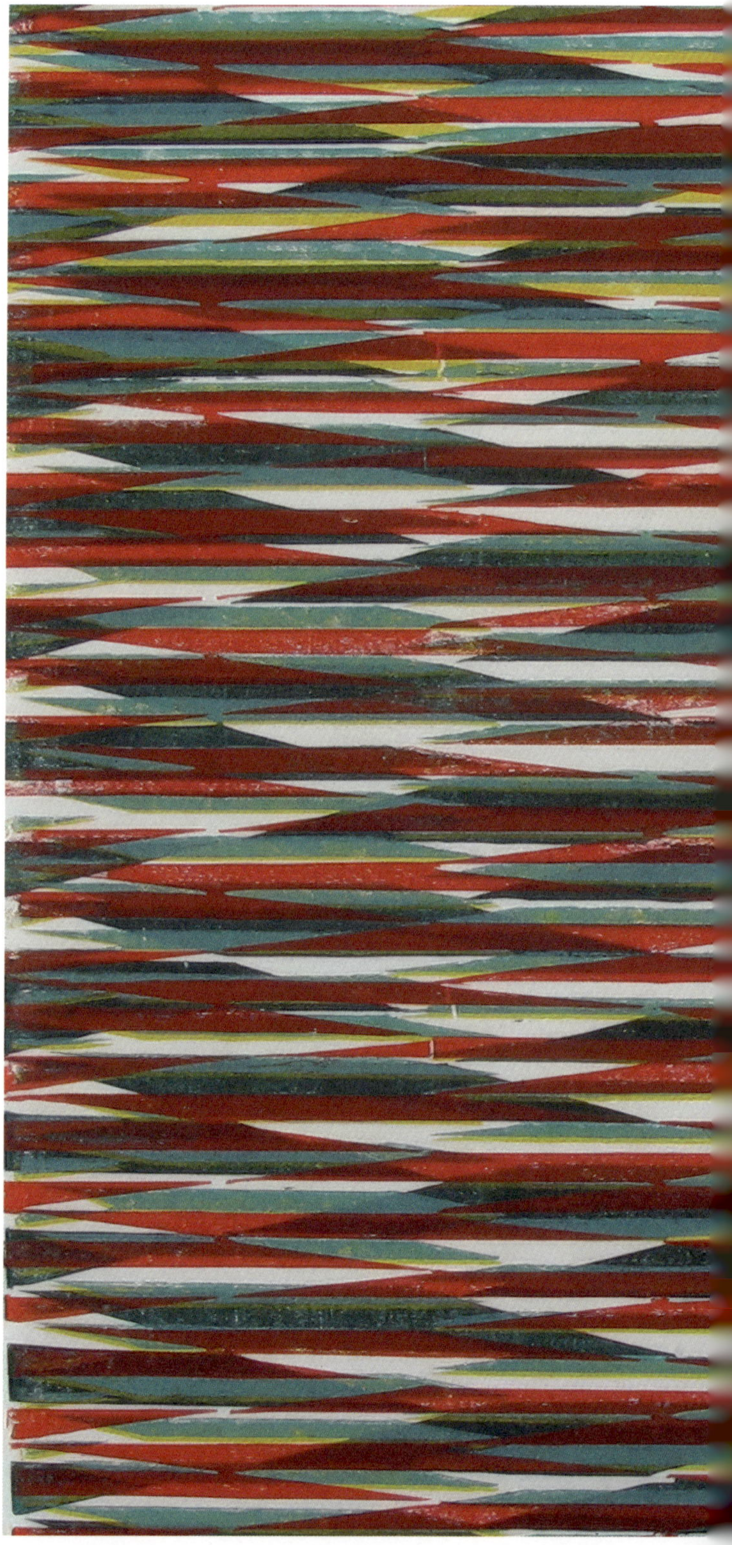

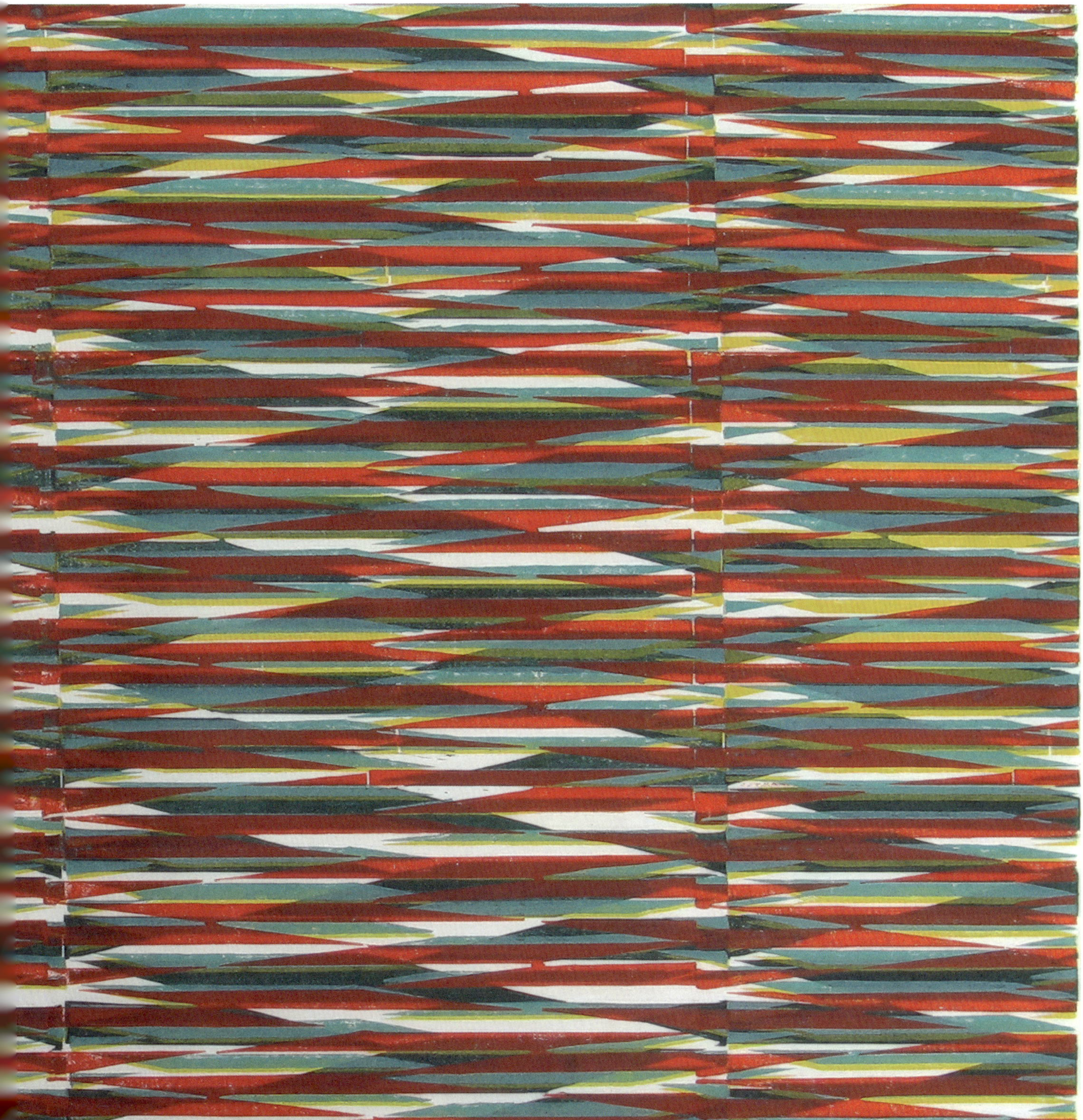

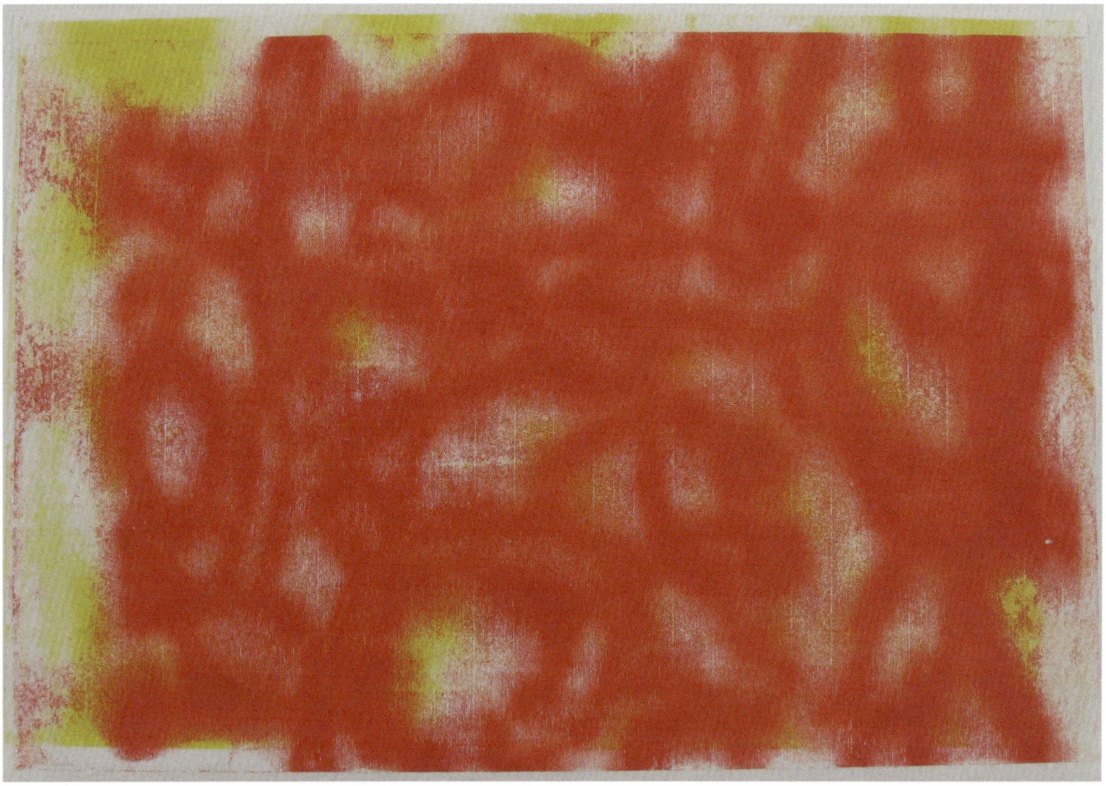

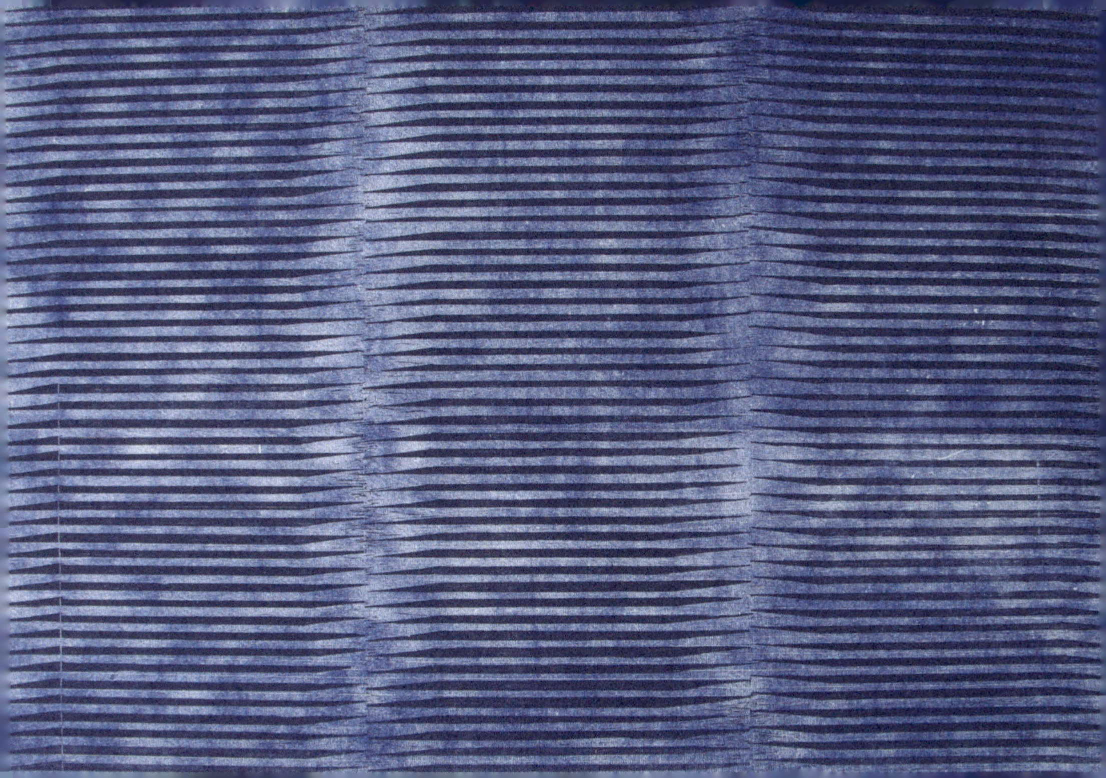

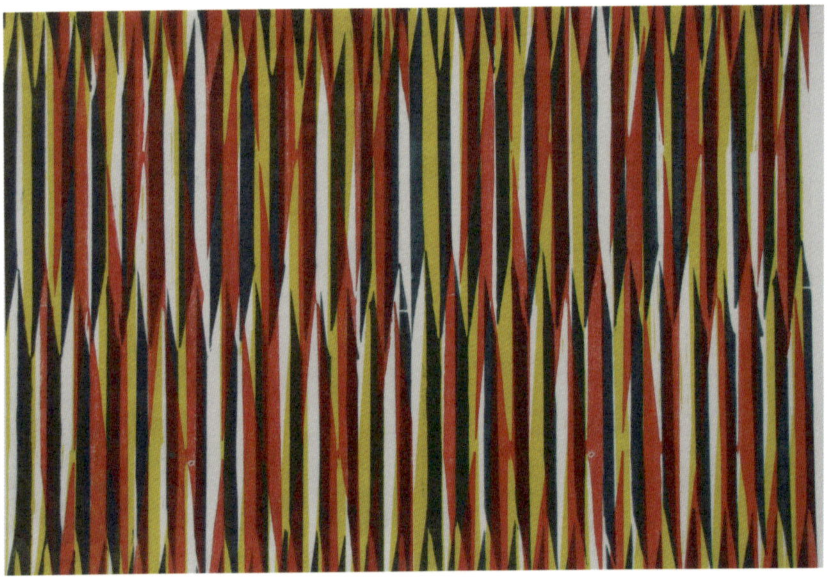

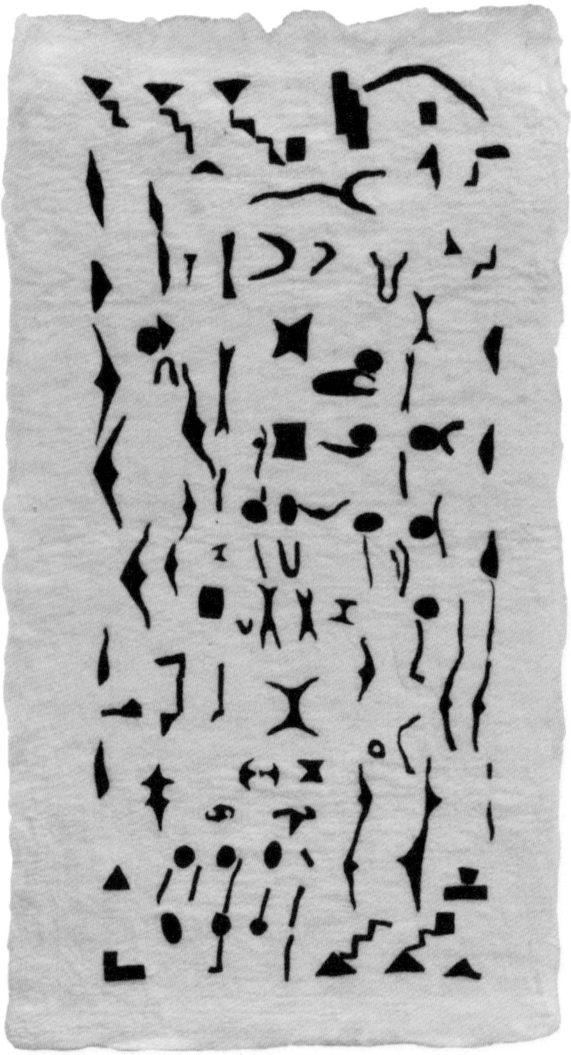

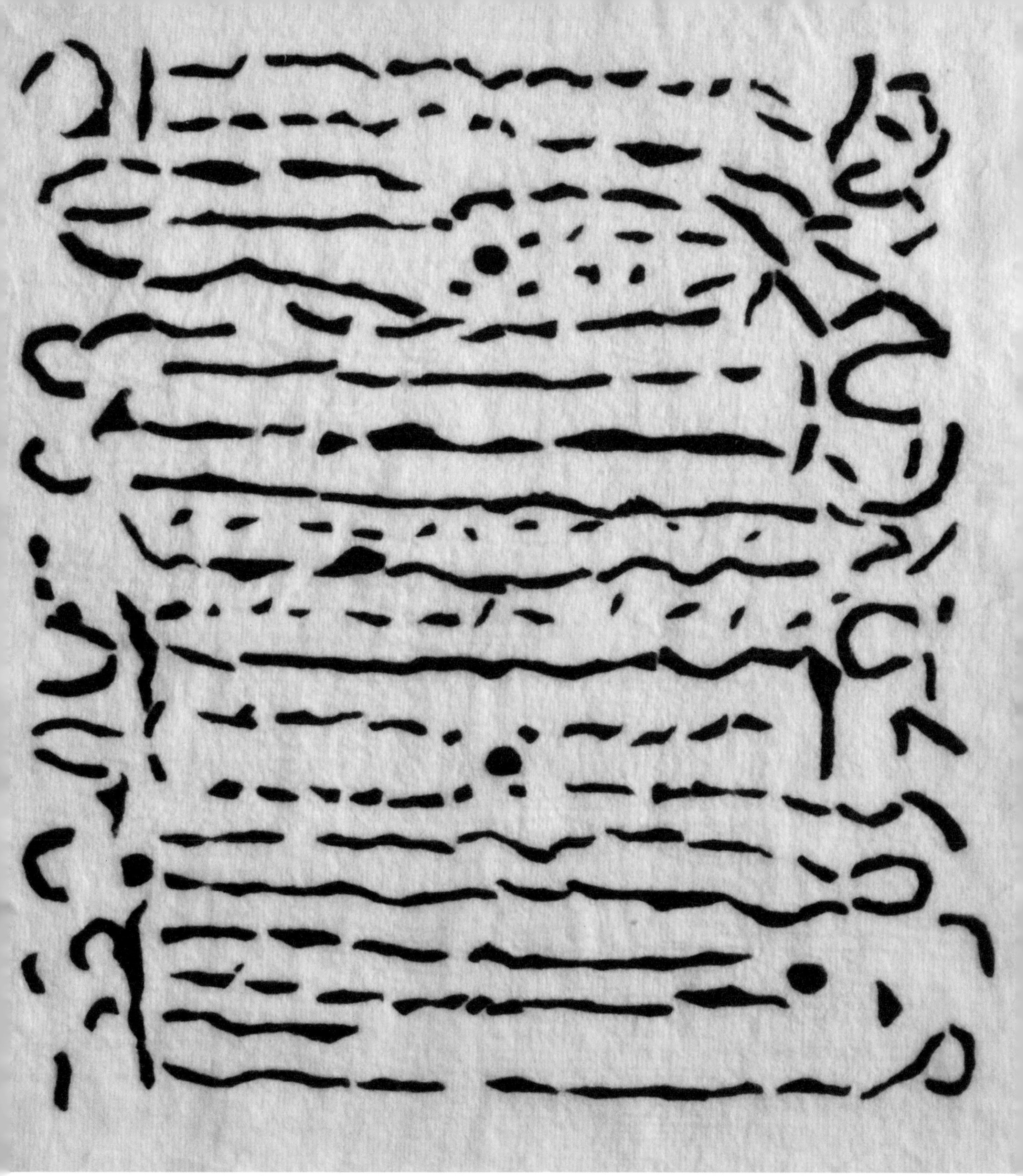

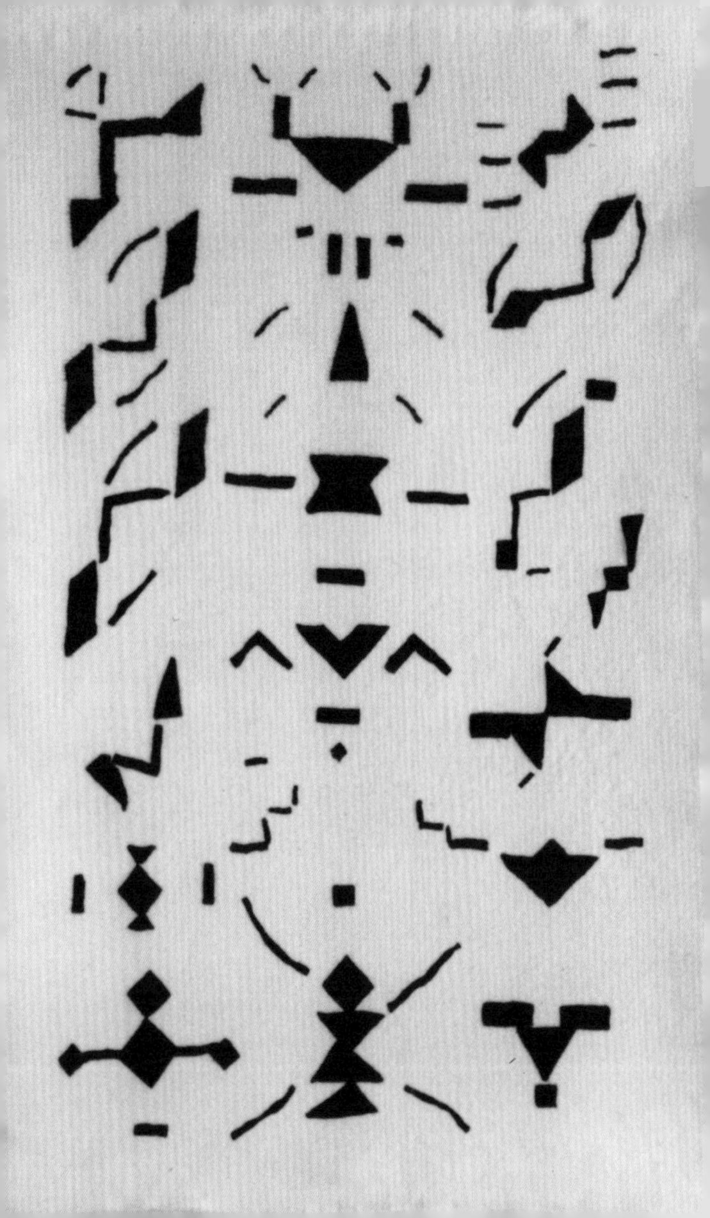

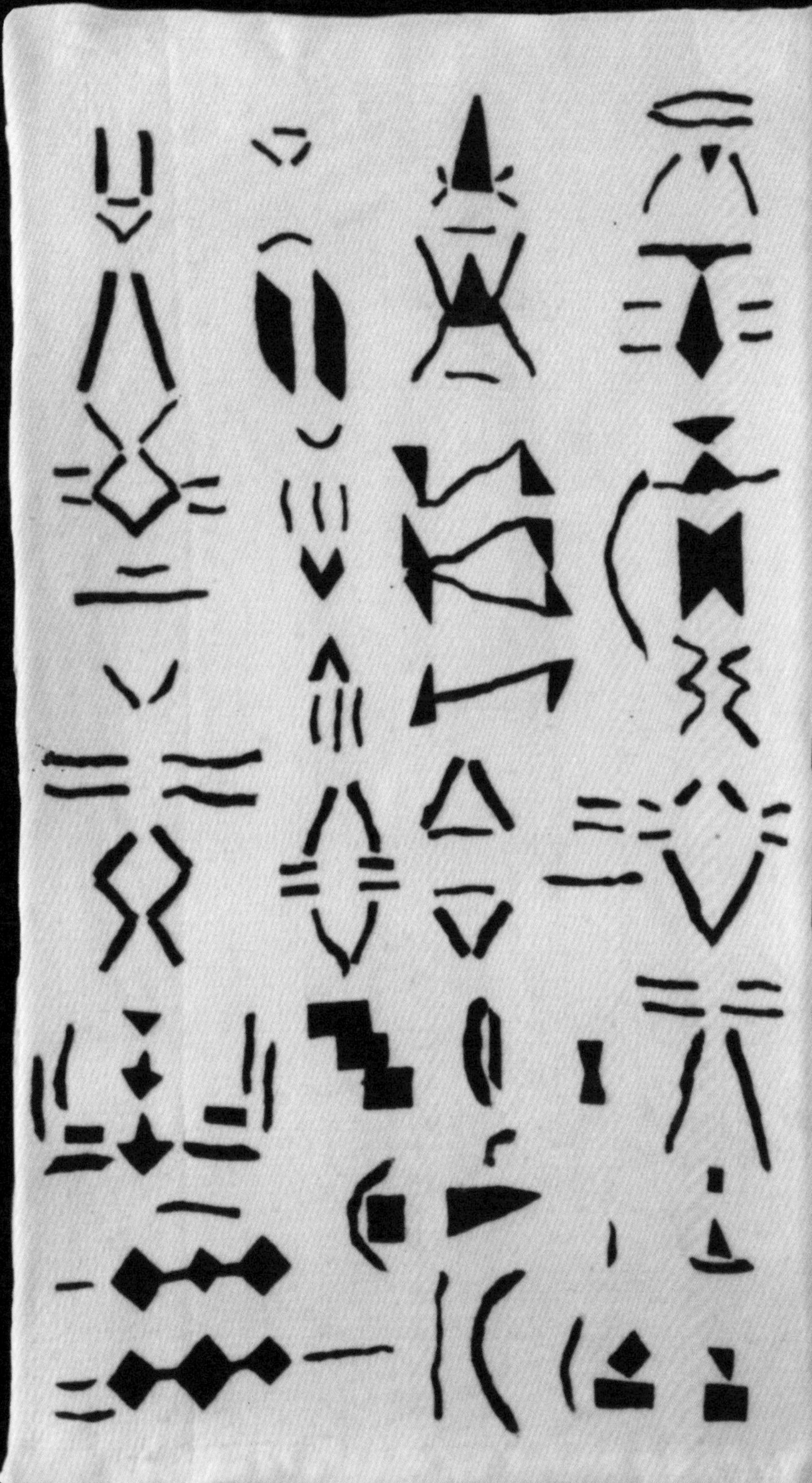

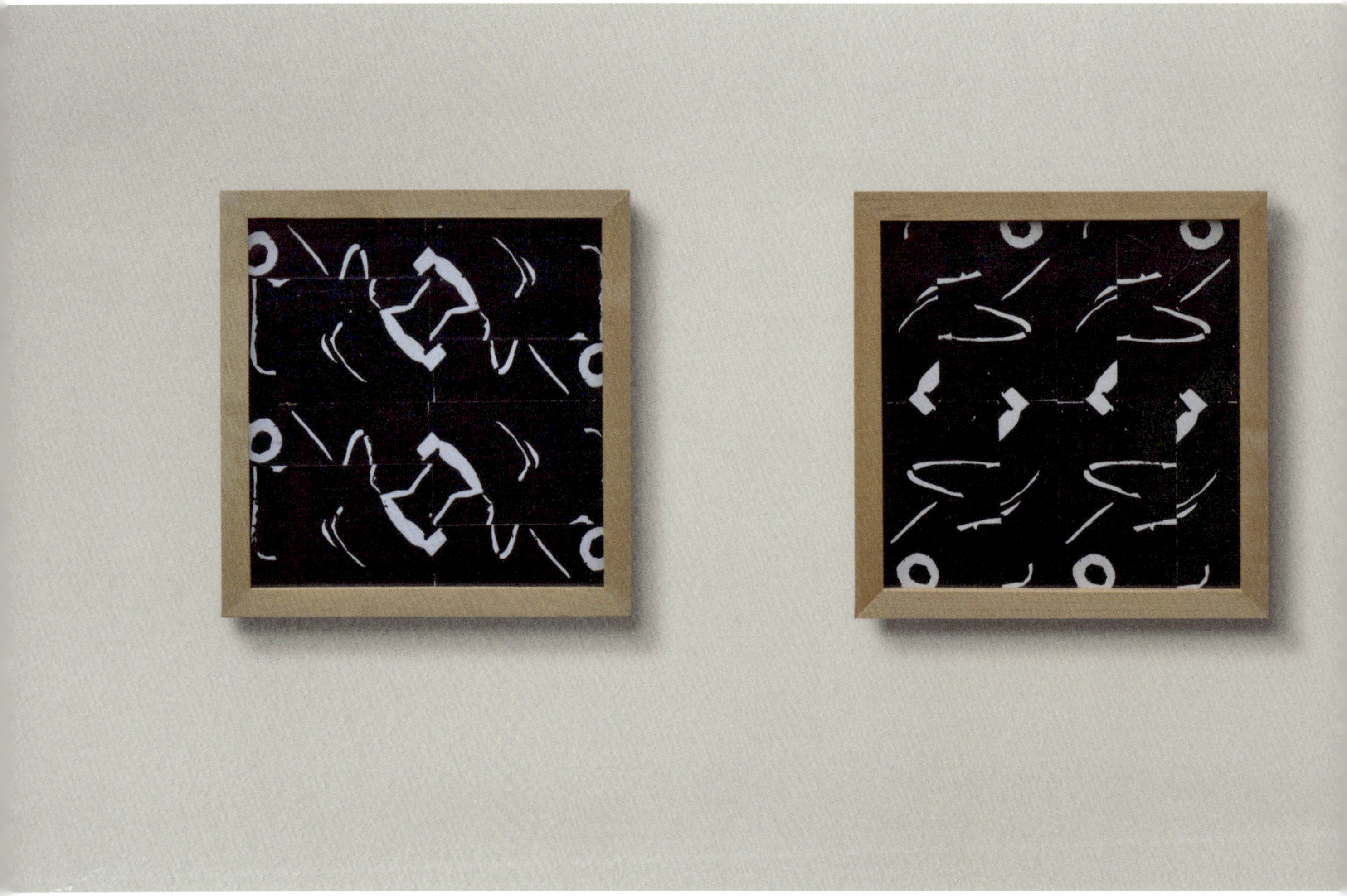

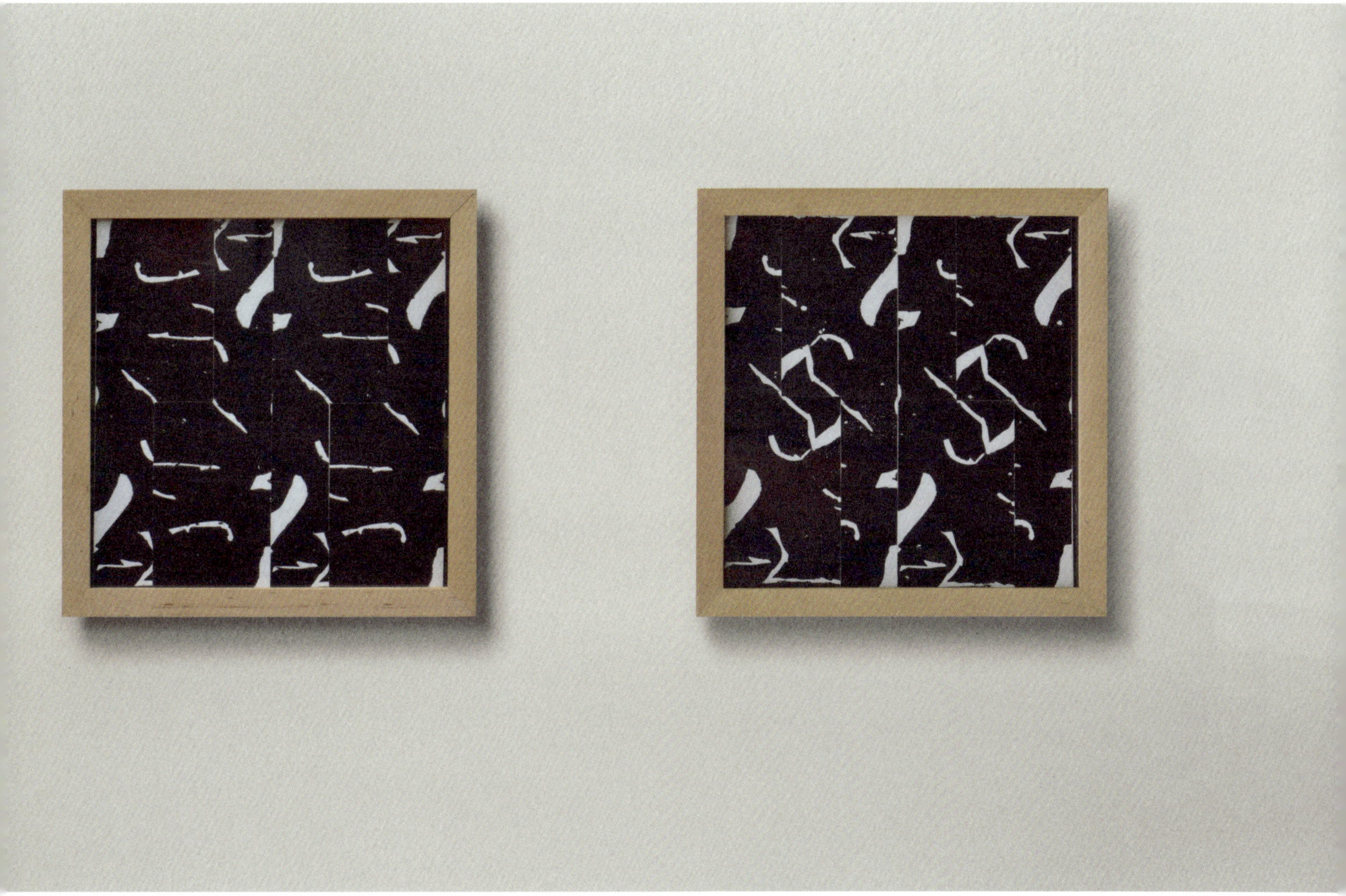

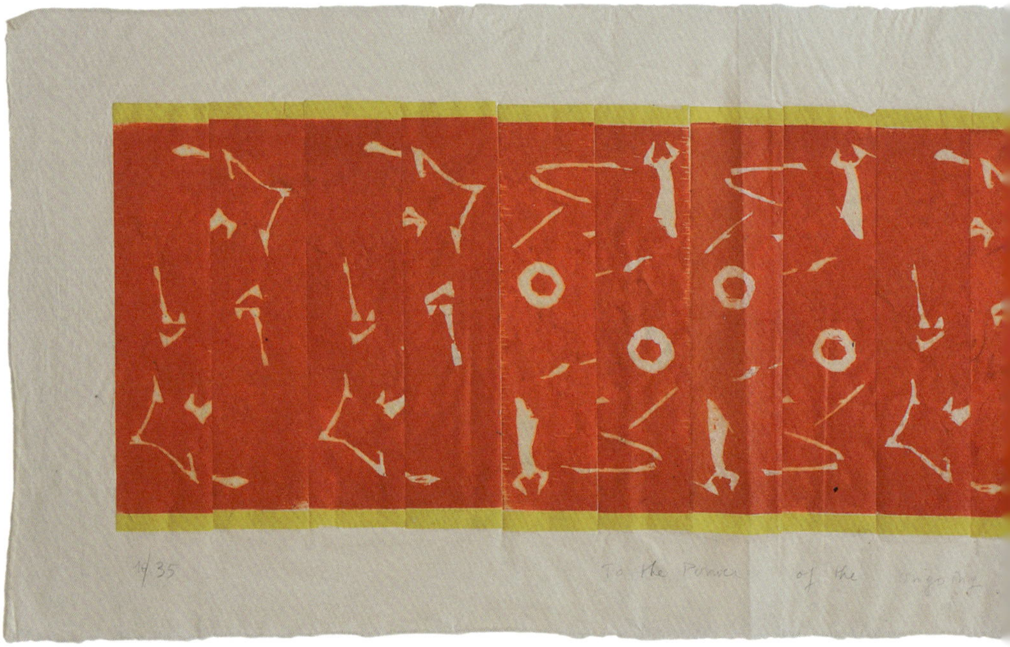

Since there is narrative art, I question, what does this art narrates?

...It unfolds a blazing moment, I presume. It recounts of dazzled and grave emotions of the artist, largely unwittingly, confronted with the miracle that are patterns:

How is it possible that with a limited number of elements, one can make an infinite number of patterns, of structures, in this world? It is a question that artists and scientists have been attempting to answer for centuries and, Linda Vinck continues, in her own way, to offer this magical discontinuity: the inexpressible fascination of the visible.

To this point, if we choose space fragmentation, as a metaphoric display of signs, there is a moment to which this discontinuity creates the intangibility of figuration and becomes an overloaded and trapped questioning about the unpredictability of beauty. That being said, this is how chance recognizes its lack of maturity, when beauty is a necessity of splendor.

 João Vário, from 'Linda Vinck: A special case of enumeration in painting', Antwerp, July 1994

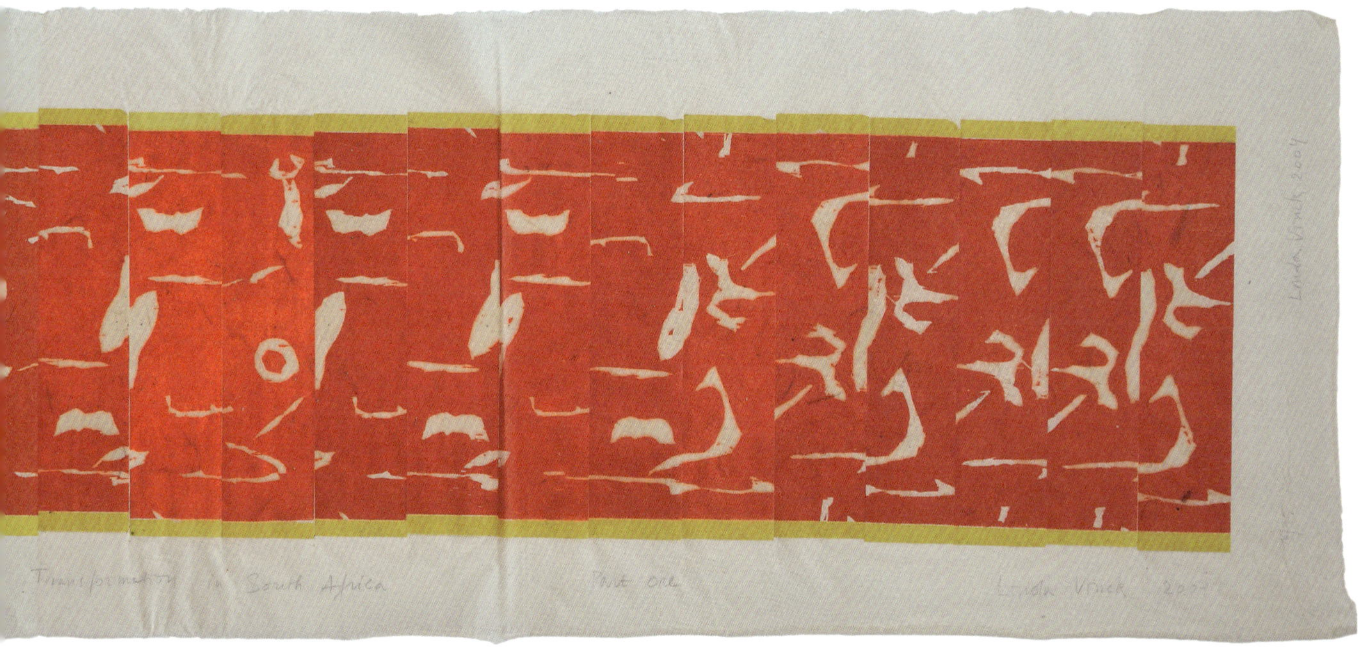

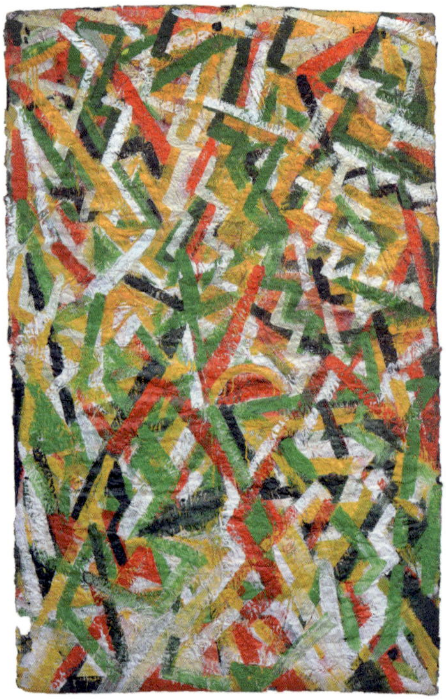

 left: Crossroads 3, right: Dart Away

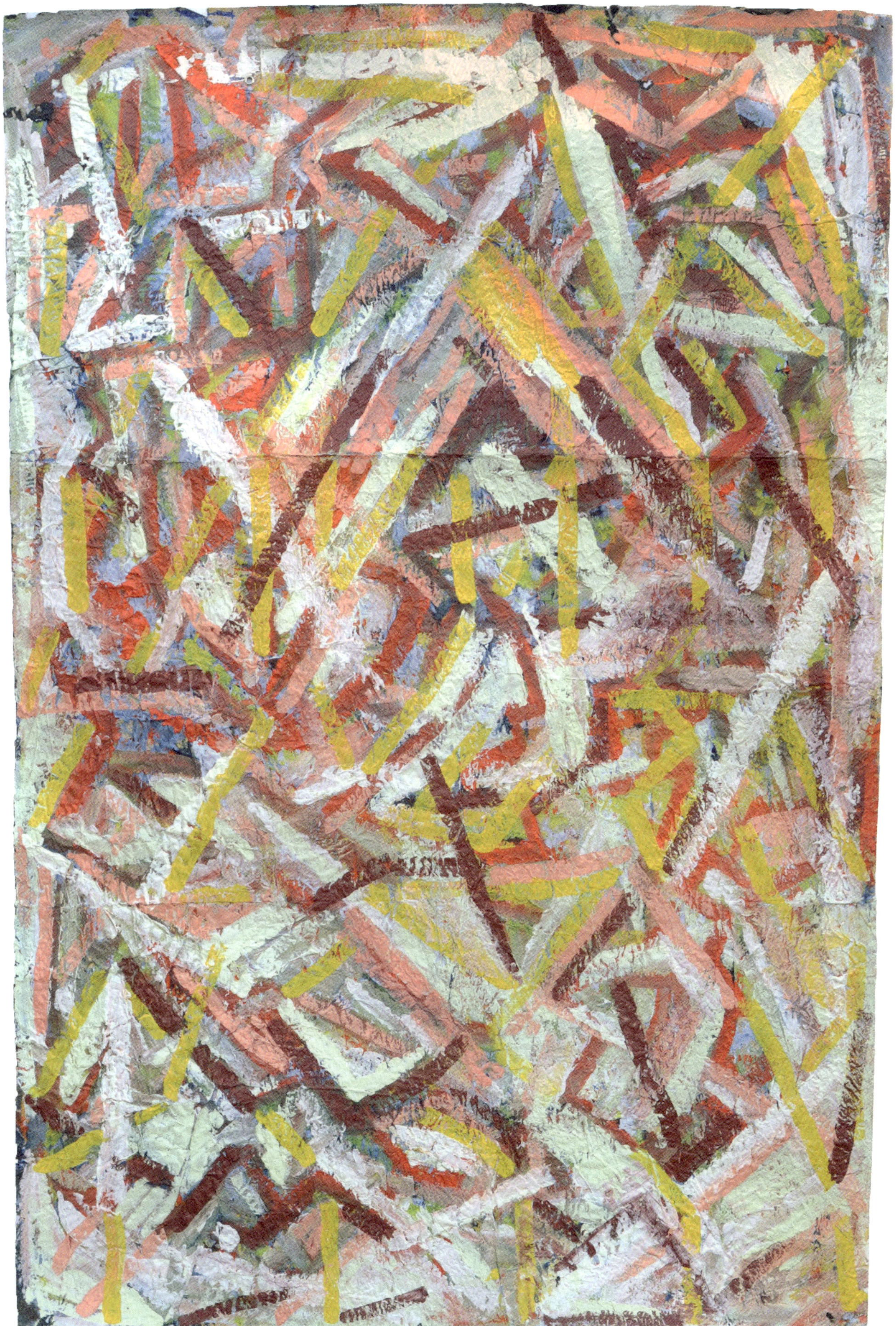

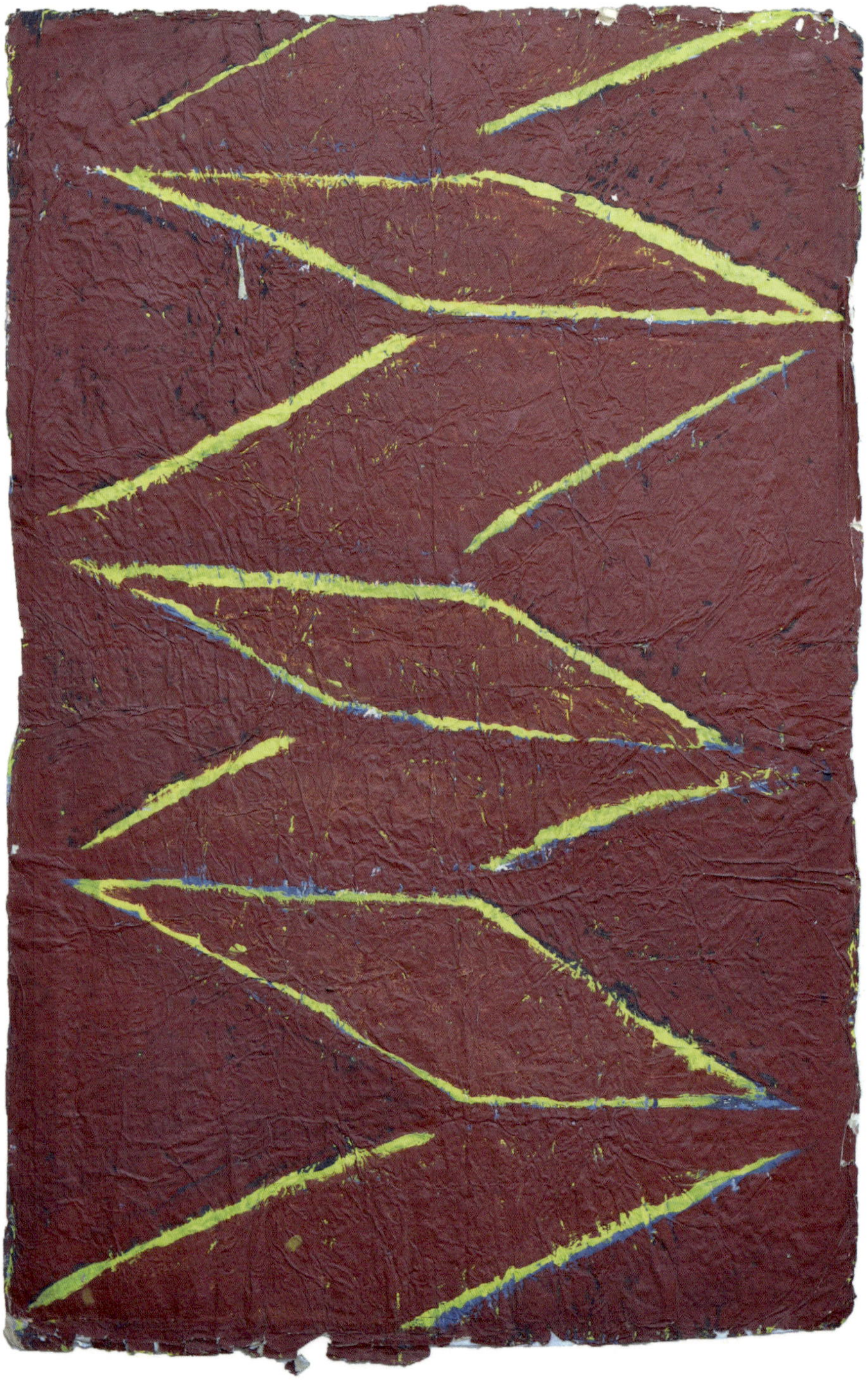

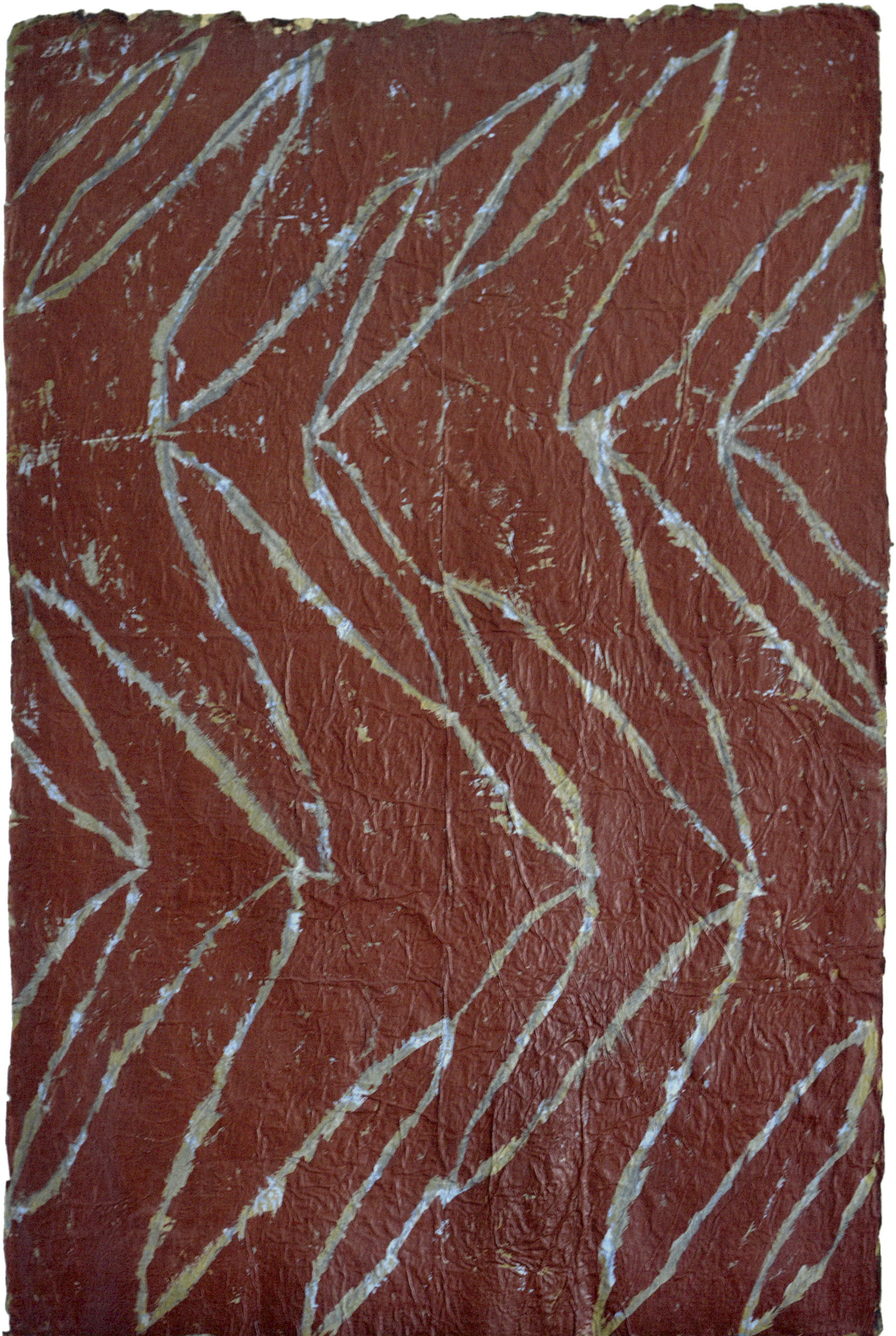

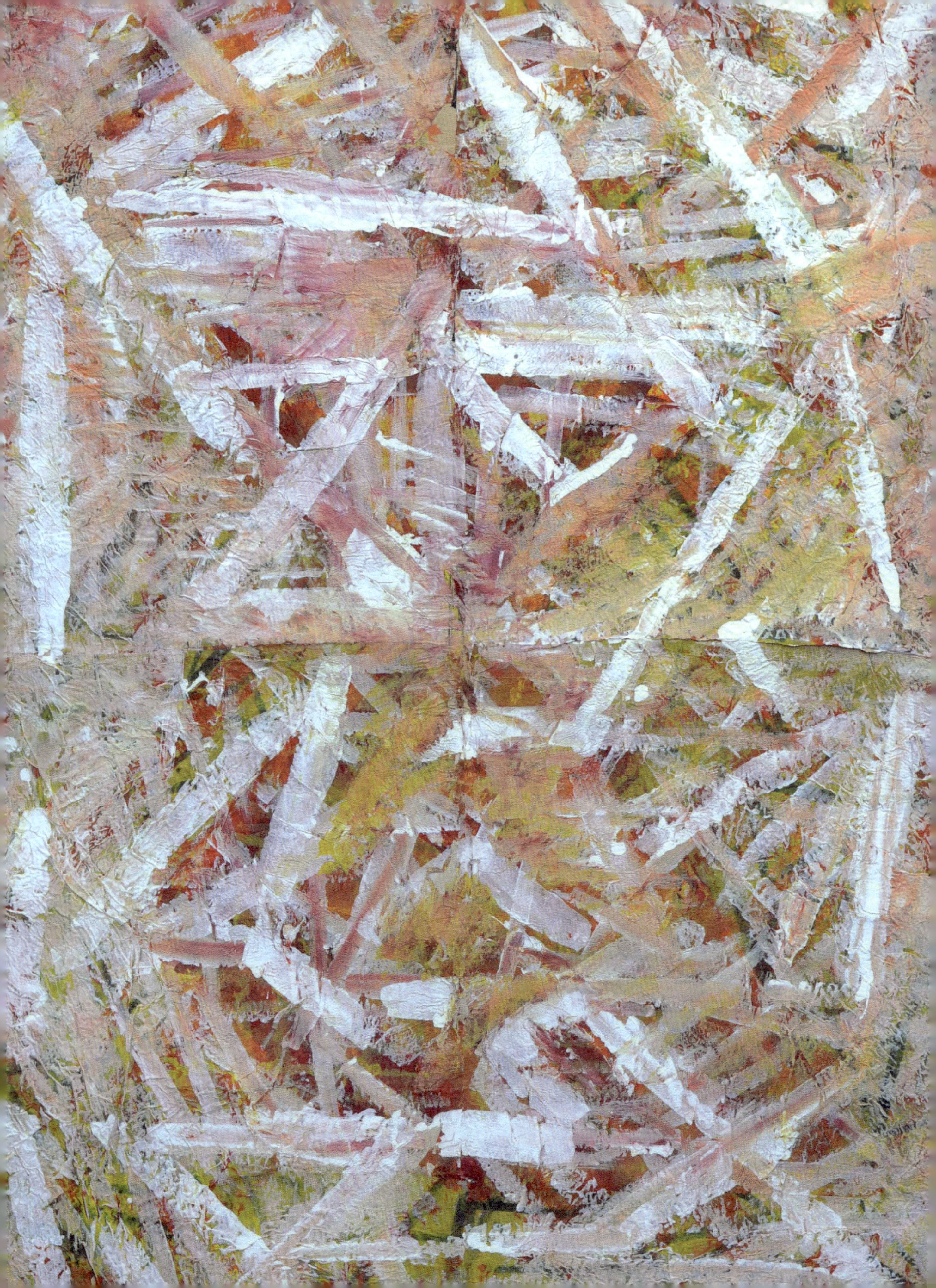

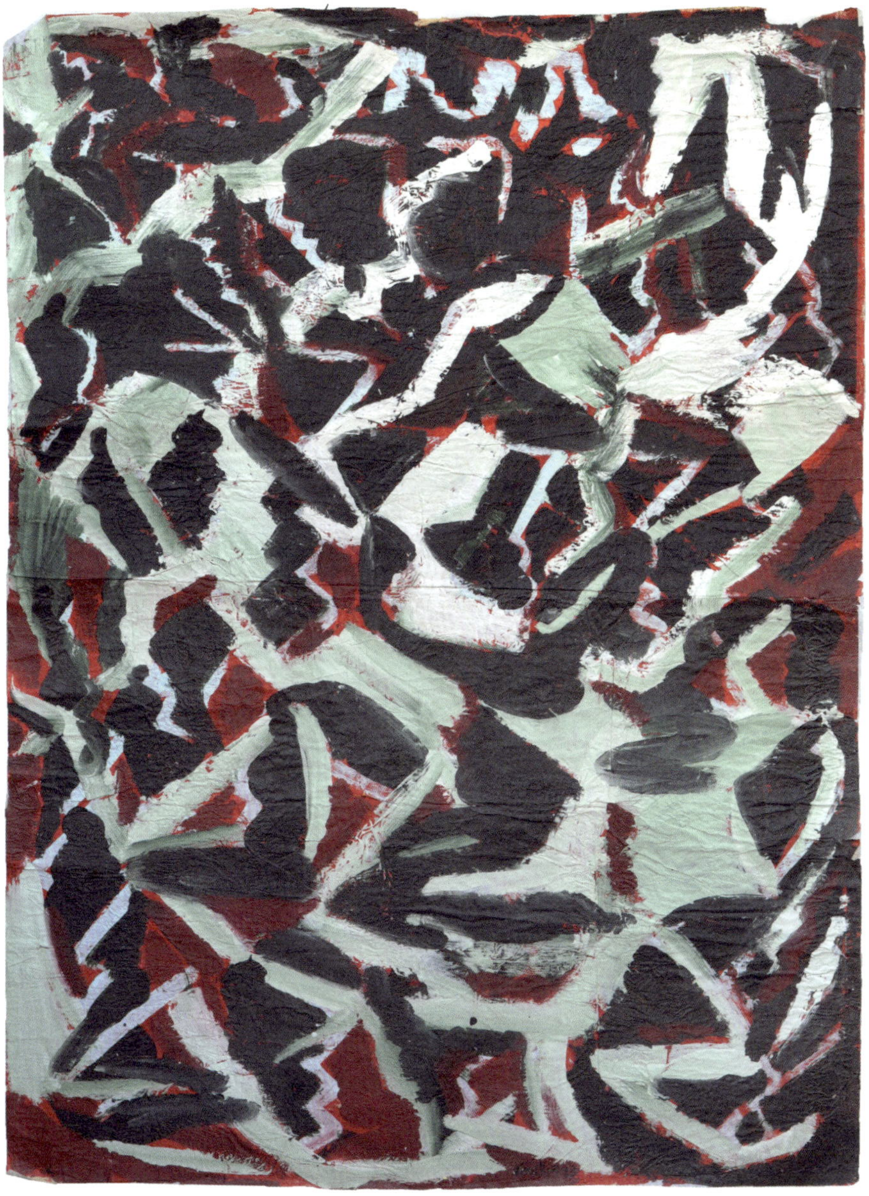

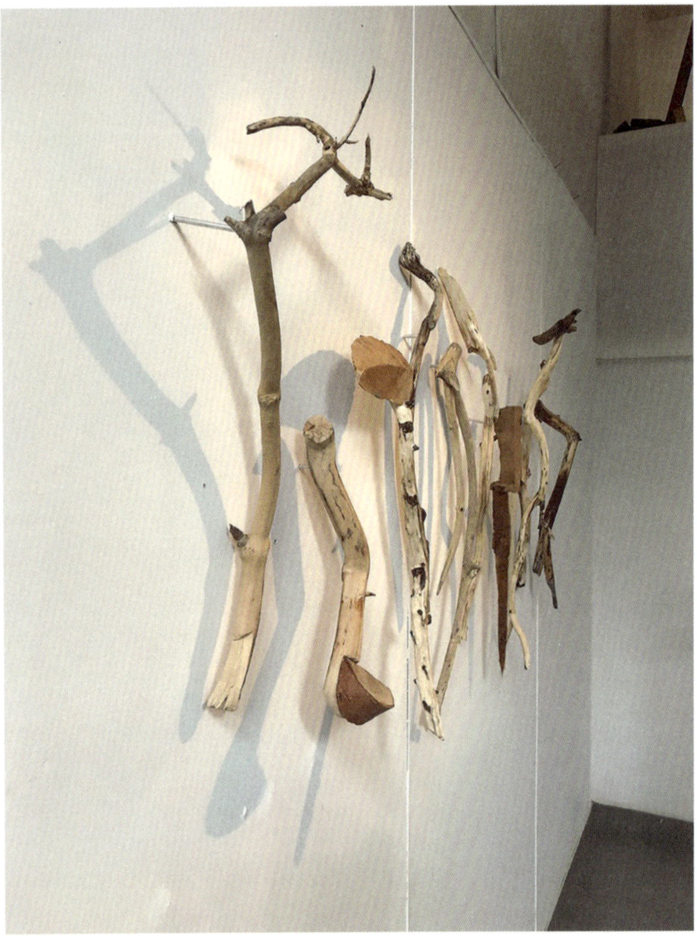

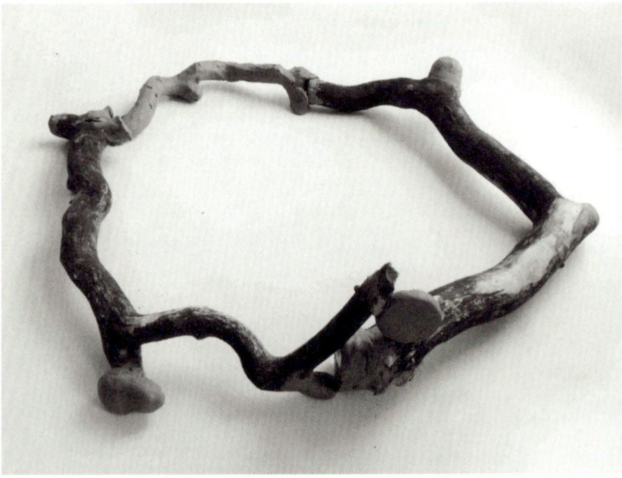

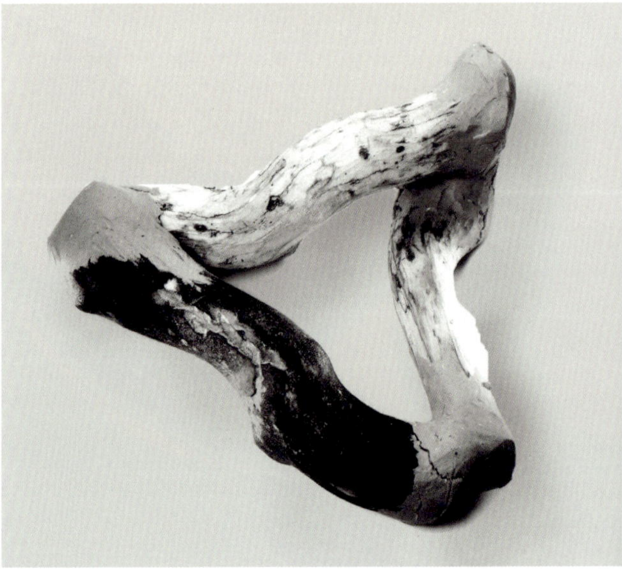

top: Ouroboros 1, bottom: Ouroboros 2

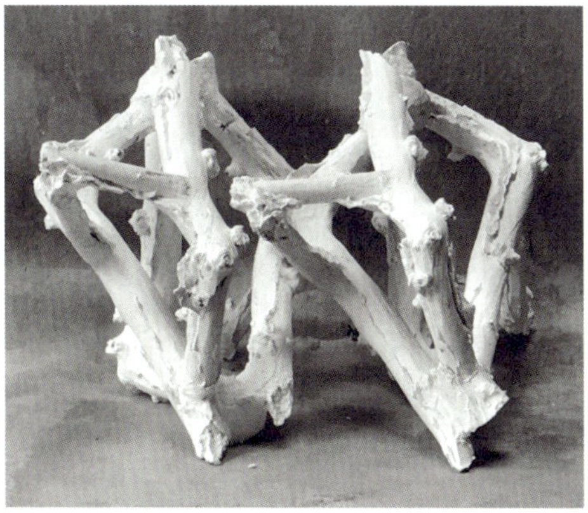
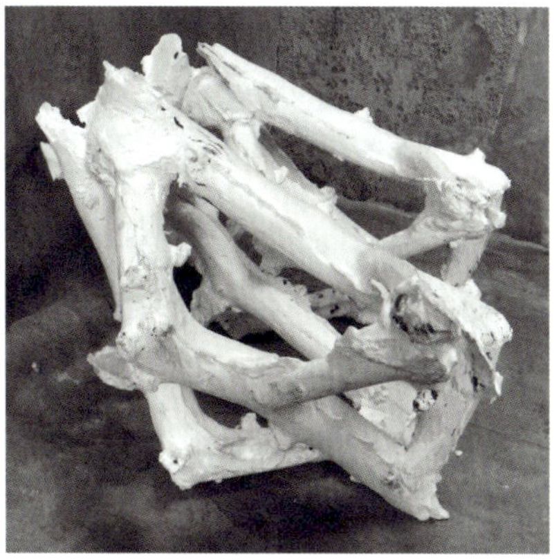
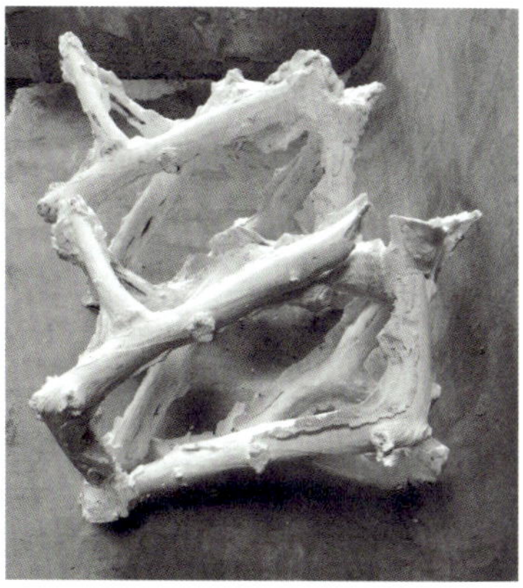
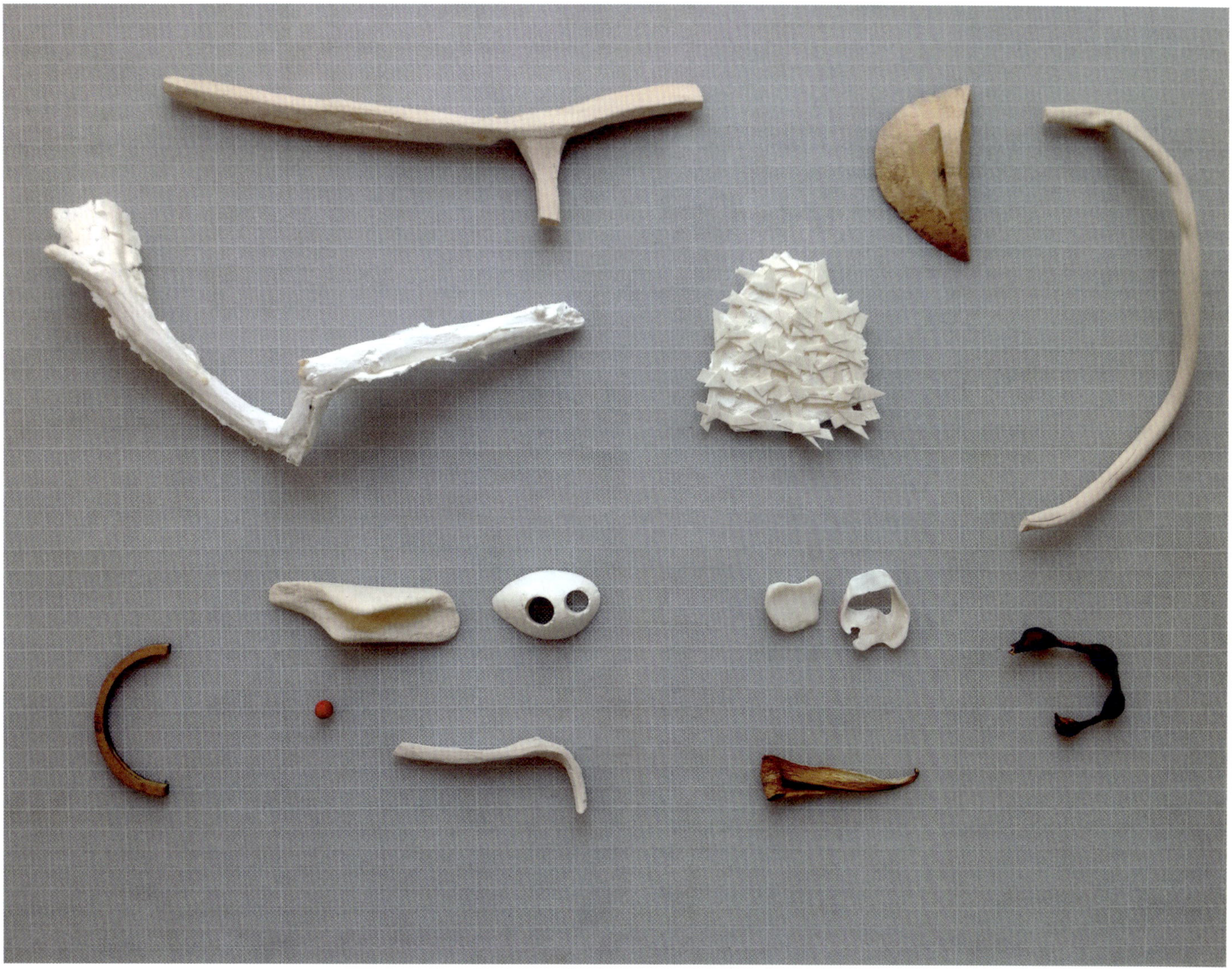

top, from left to right: Pas de deux 1, 2 & 3
bottom: Alphabet 2

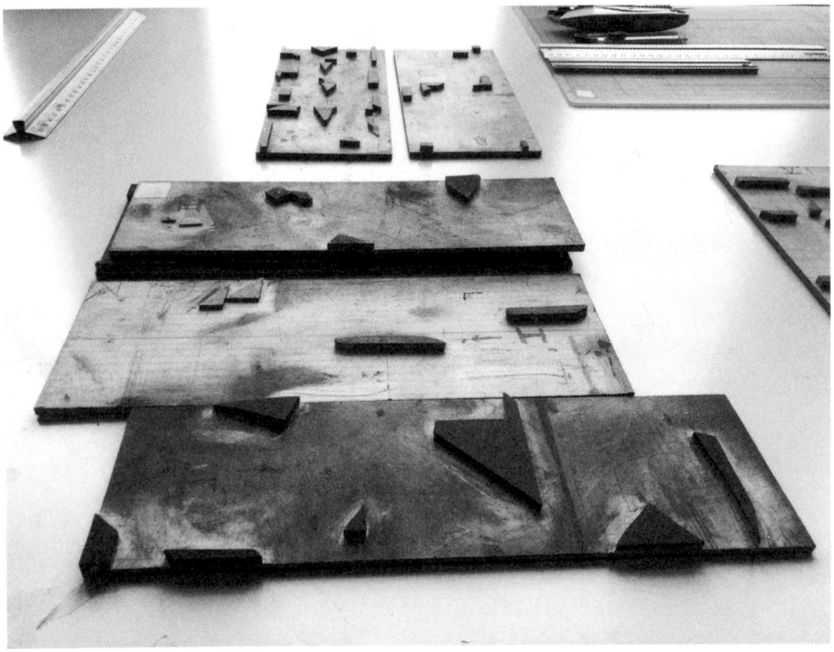

 Wooden blocks for Genetic Process, analogue process

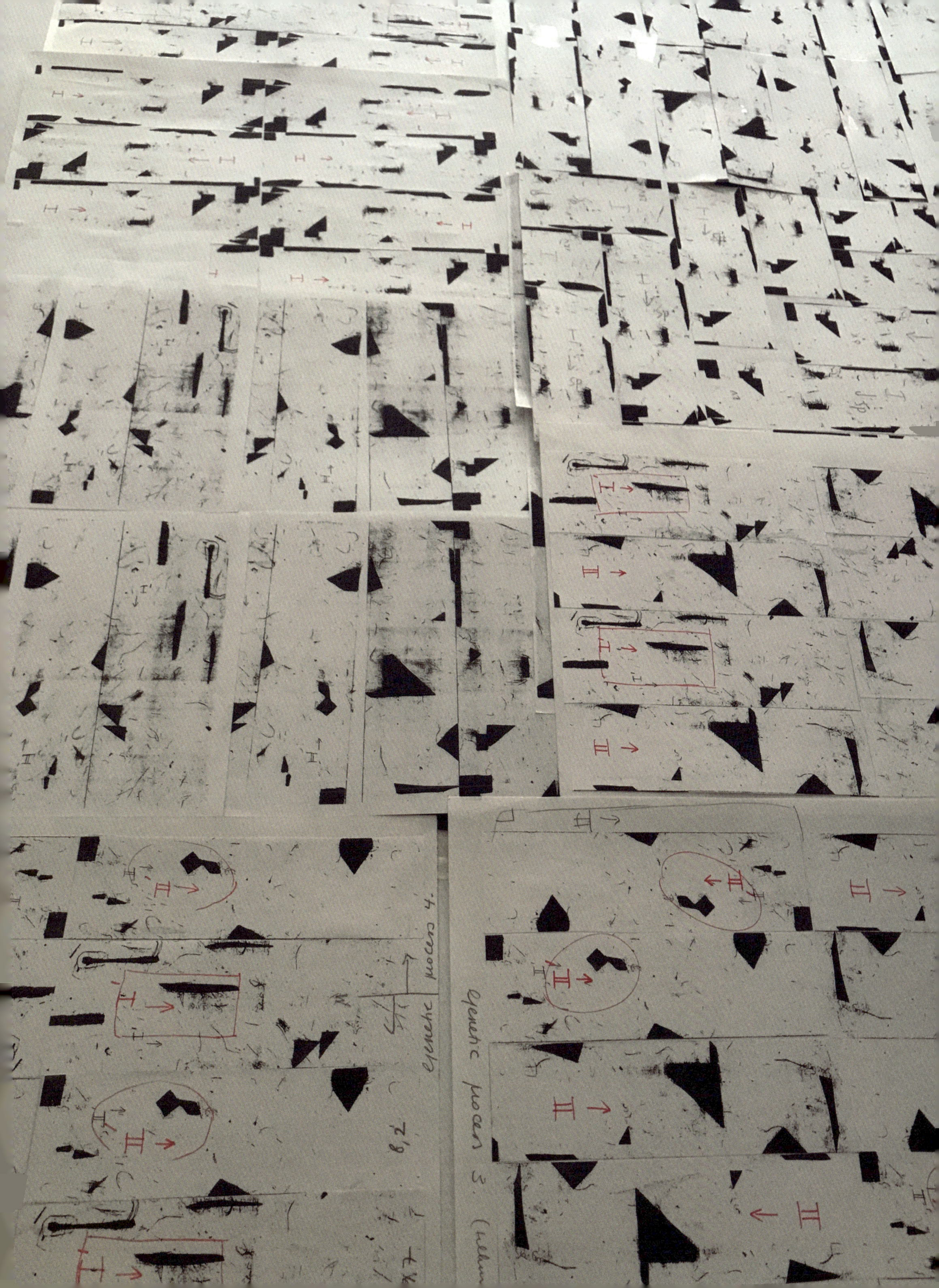

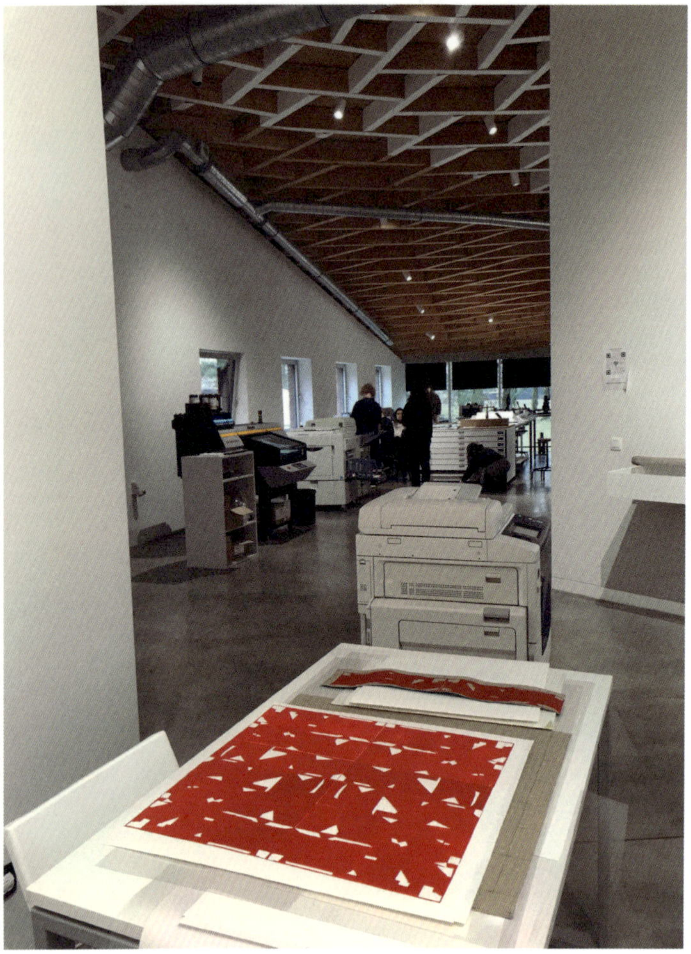

During a residency at the Frans Masereel Centrum (FMC) in February and March 2024
Linda Vinck became acquainted with the very latest graphical techniques. For the first time,
she worked with digital laser cutters that enabled her to cut out her previously analogue designs
in several different sizes, giving her fresh options for her compositions called Genetic Process.

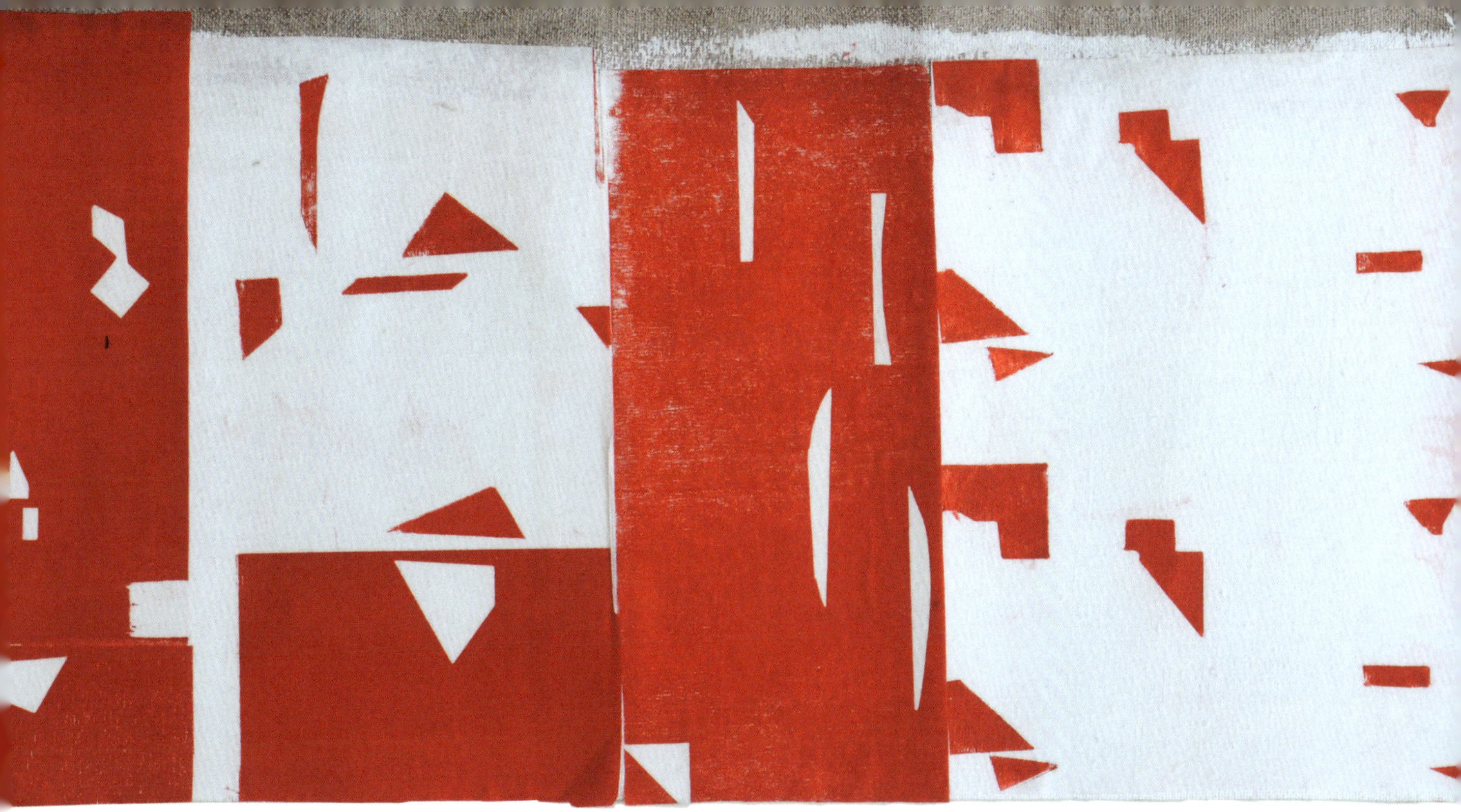

Artist's proof on canvas, mixed media, laser cutting in wood and analogue printing techniques

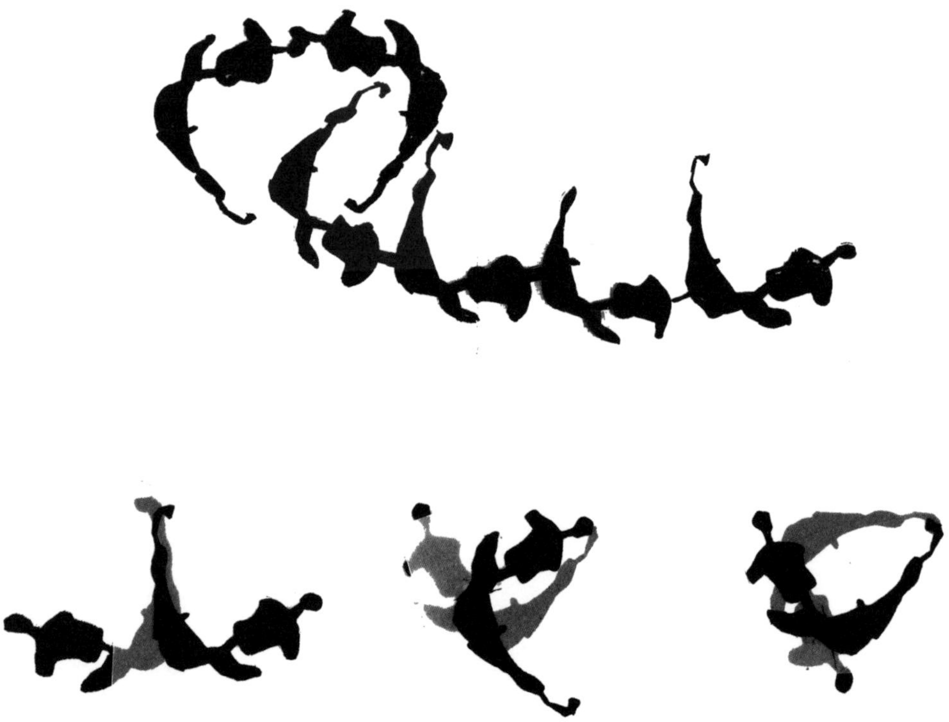

VI. Index

About the artworks, exhibitions and text contributors

I. Vibration, Sequencing, Energy

page 15 to 49

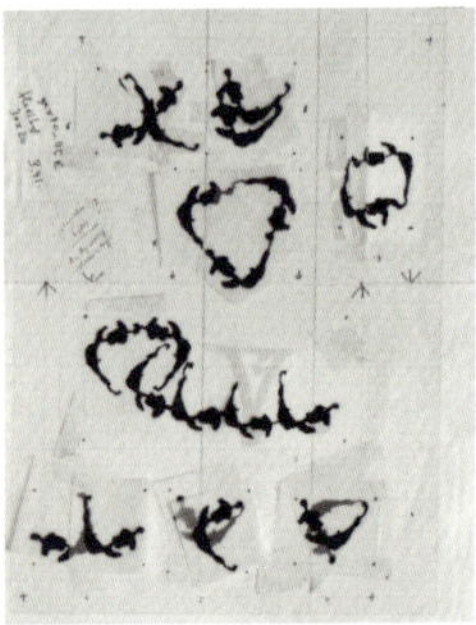
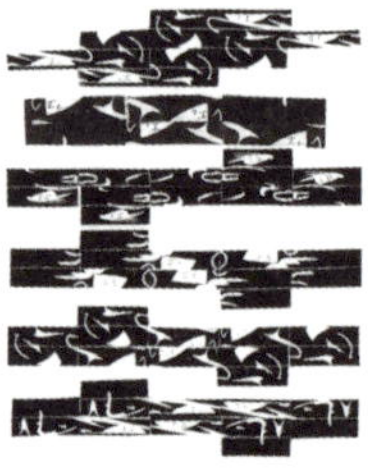
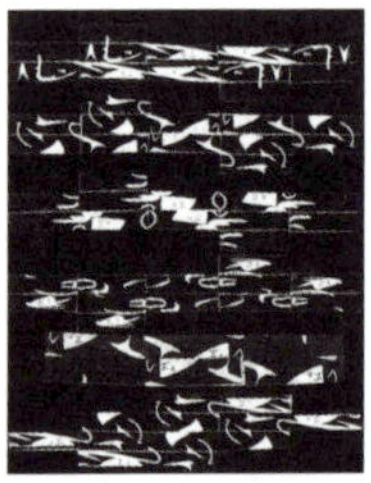
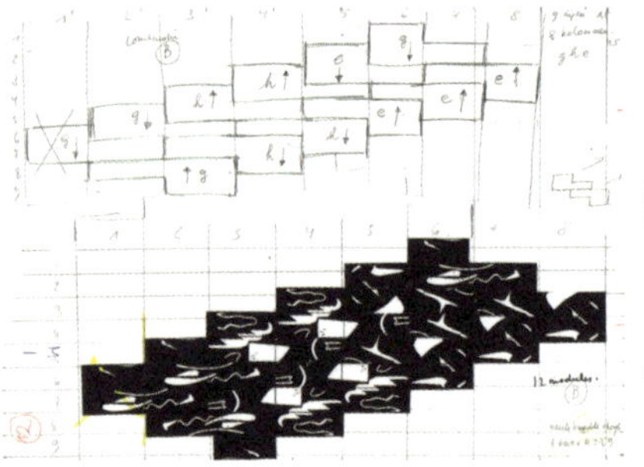
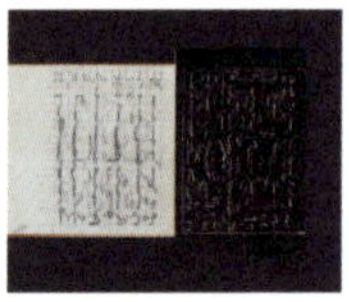
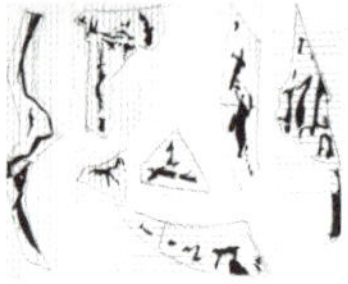
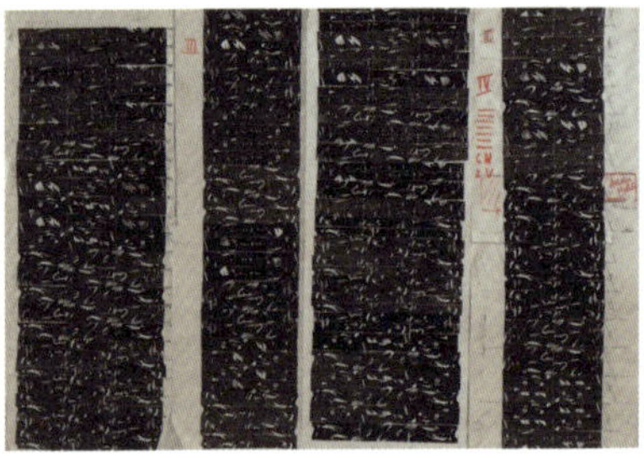
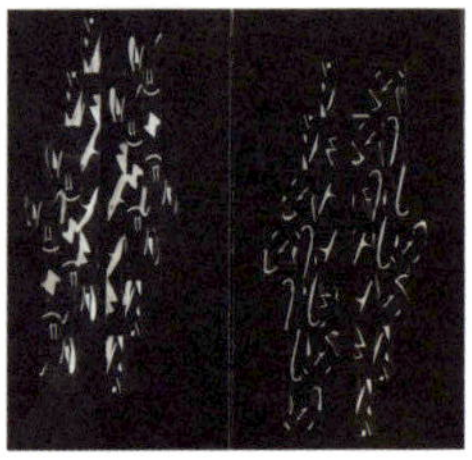
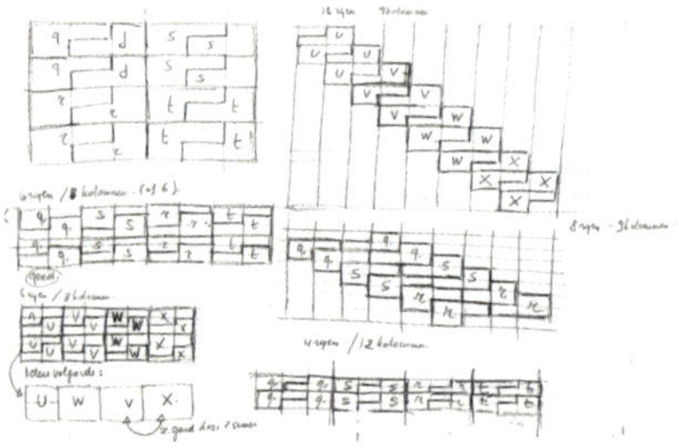
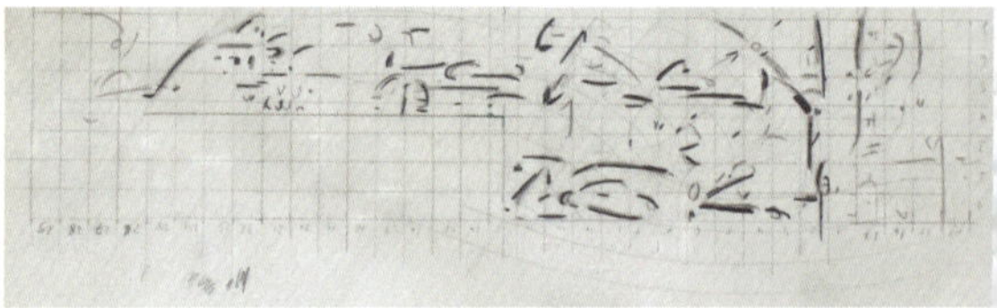
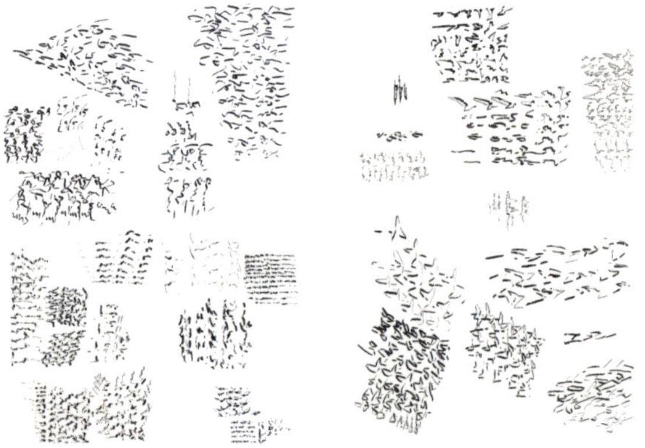
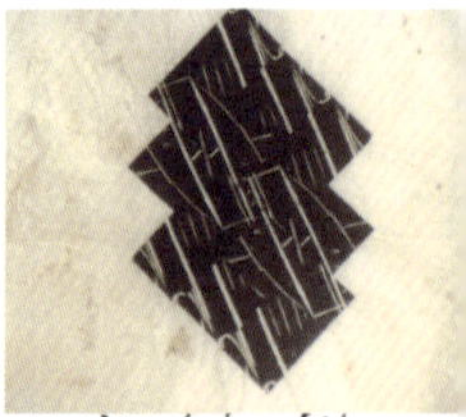
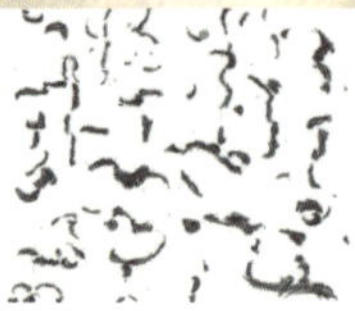
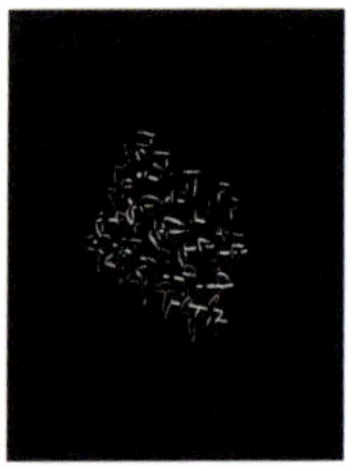
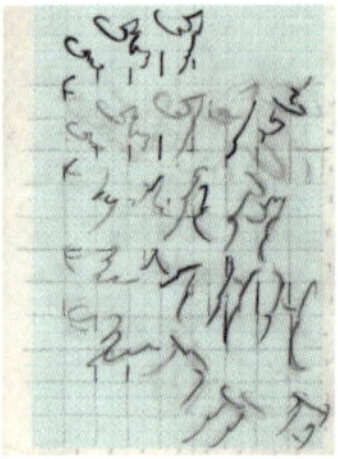
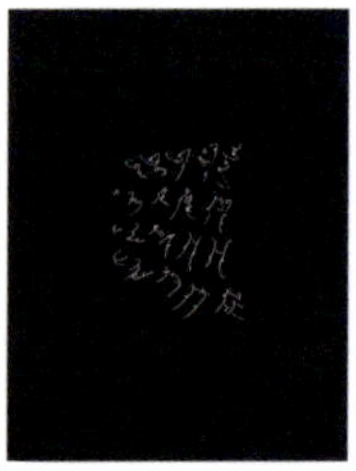
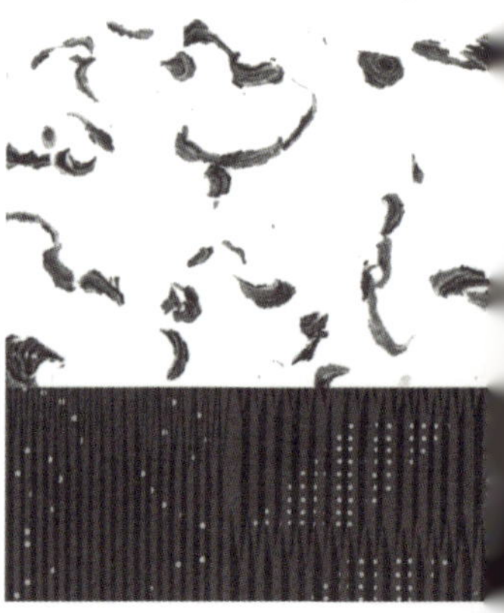

automatic drawing, *seismographic* notations, composing, assemblages
— including Matrix series & Little Nepal series

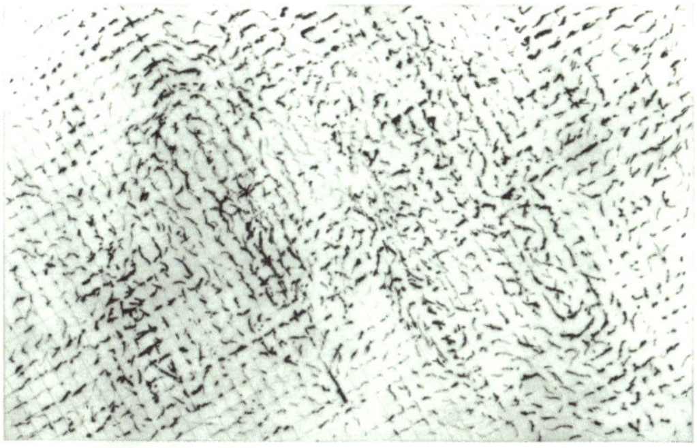

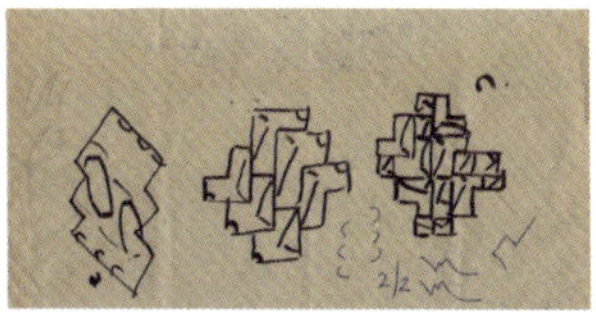

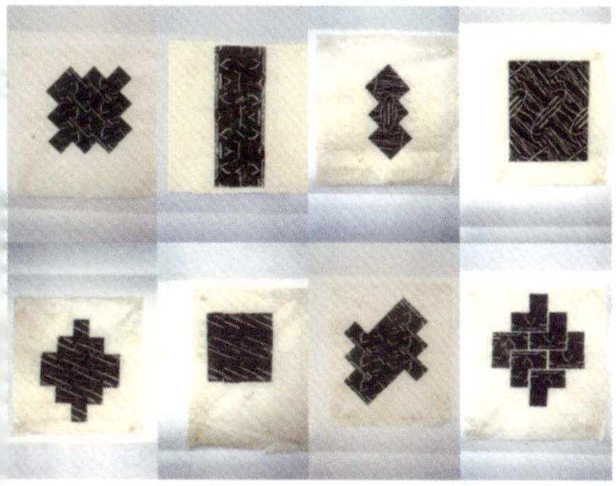

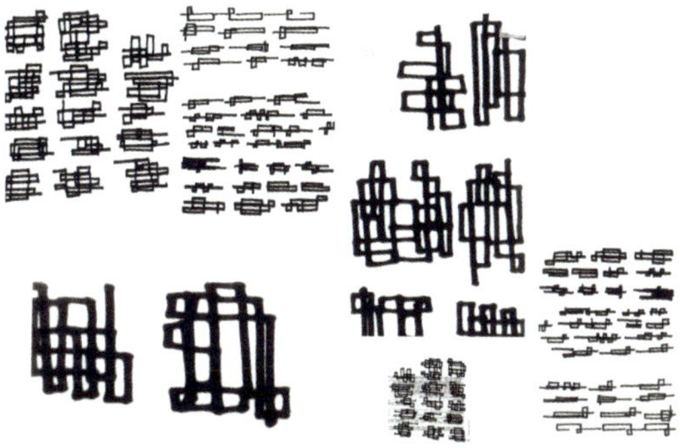

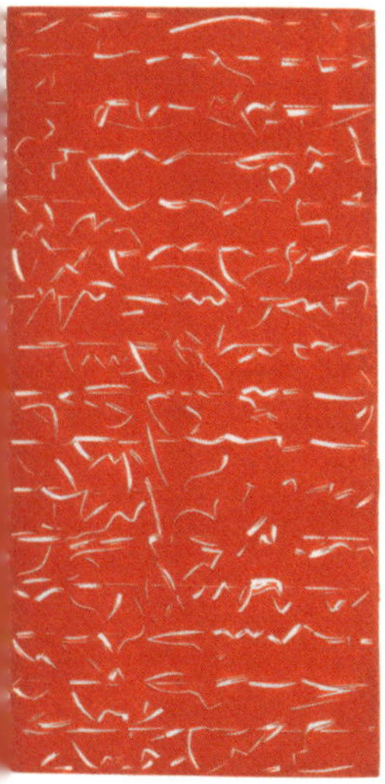

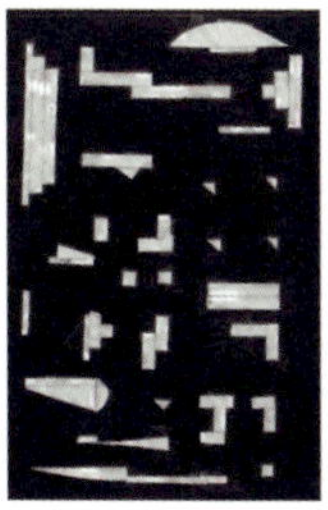

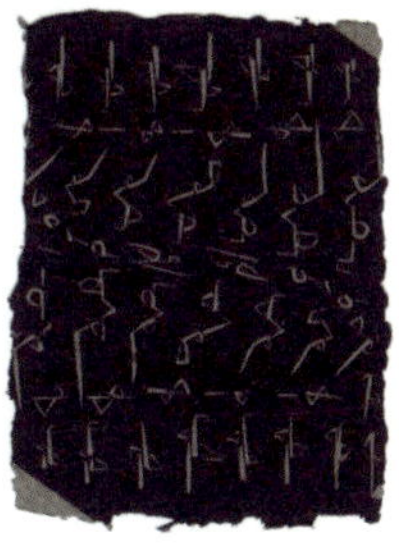

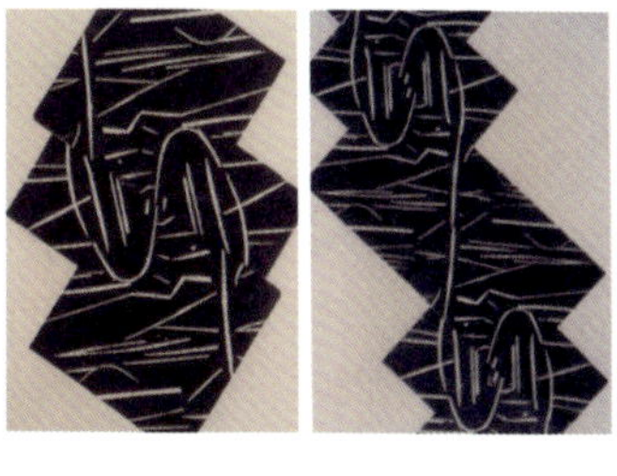

II. Ongoing Stream

page 51 to 80

2.

10.

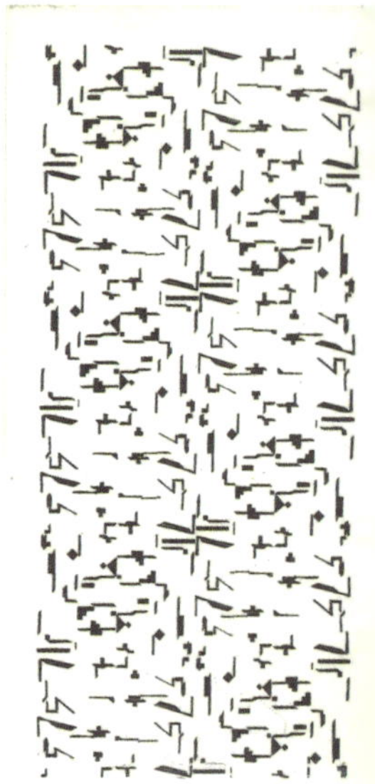

1.

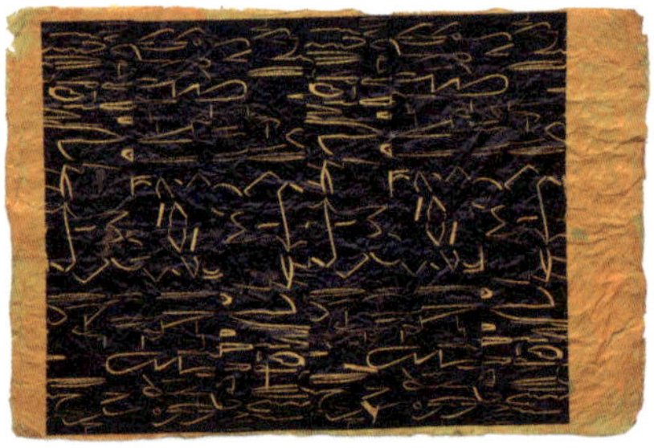

3.

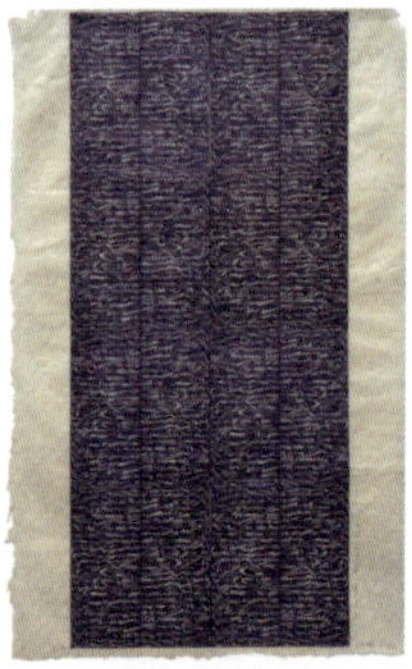

4.

5.

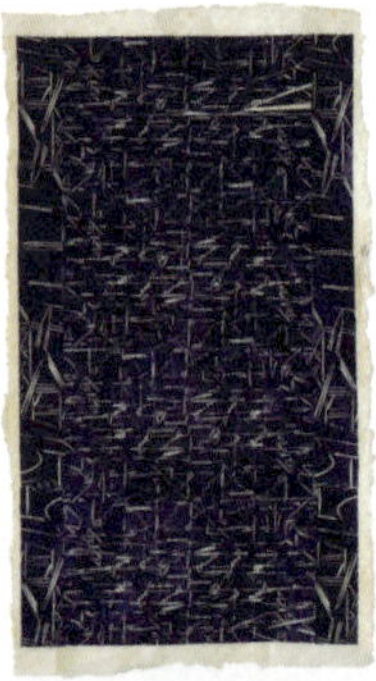

7.

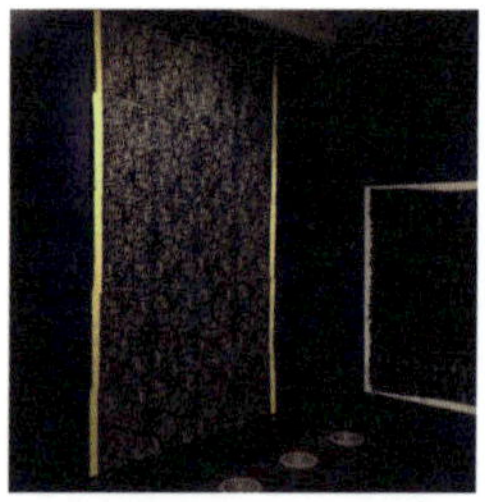

12.

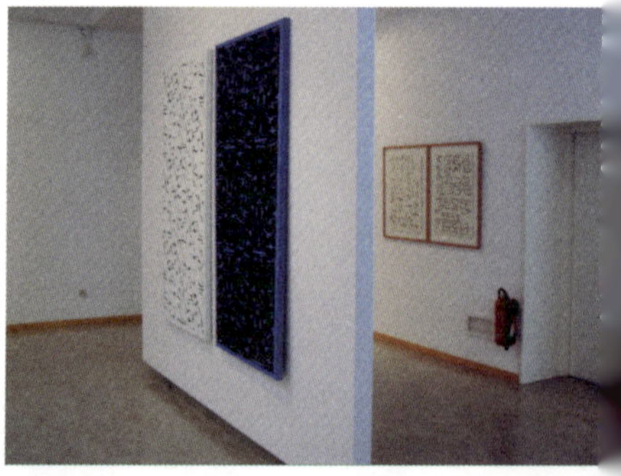

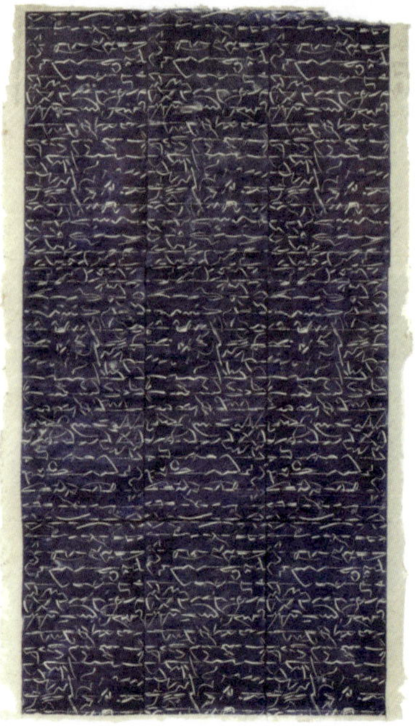

6.

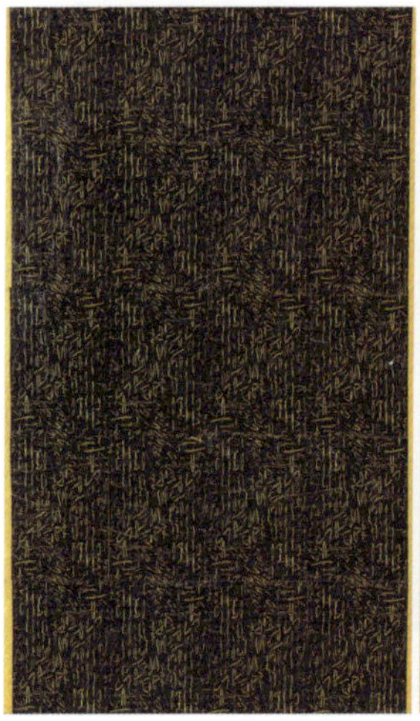

8.

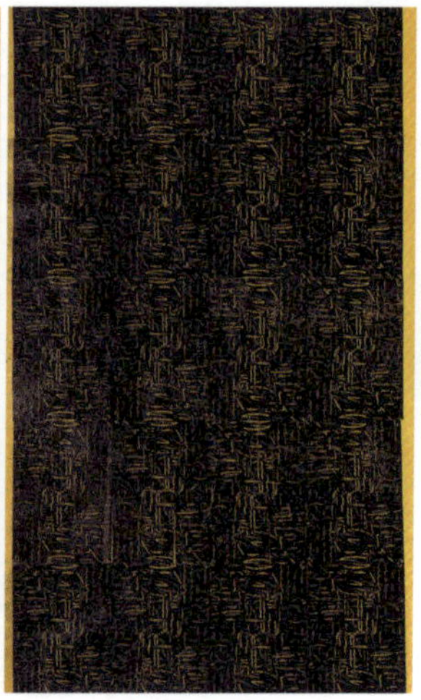

9.

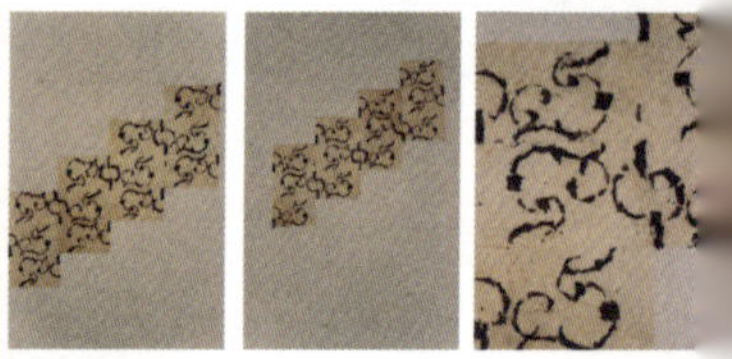

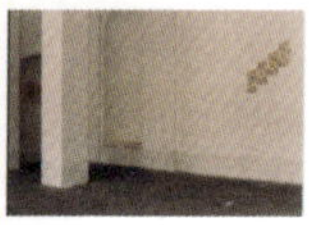

13.

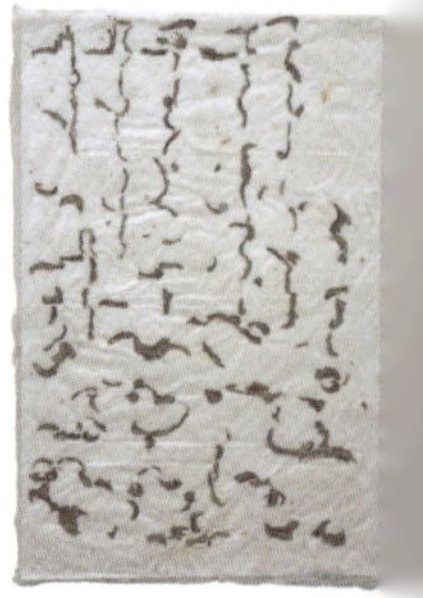

14.

1. **Reflex Blue on Saffron · artist's proof — Patterns of Paradise 6**
   480 × 74 mm, handprinted on handmade Nepalese paper, 1992
2. **Reflex Blue on White — Patterns of Paradise 3**
   2350 × 1300 mm, lino assemblage on layered paper, 1992
3. **Contemplation — Meditation on Peace 2**
   1000 × 610 mm, handprinted on handmade Nepalese paper, 1988
4. **Approaching — Meditation on Peace 3**
   1000 × 600 mm, handprinted on handmade Nepalese paper, 1988
5. **Run — Meditation on Peace 1**
   1300 × 500 mm, handprinted on handmade Nepalese paper, 1988
6. **Humility — Meditation on peace 4**
   980 × 570 mm, handprinted on handmade Nepalese paper, 1988
7. **Pattern of Paradise 2, exhibition 'Bodies of Lace', Museum Texture Kortrijk, 2016**
   2350 × 1300 mm, lino assemblage on layered paper, 1992
   — private collection
8. **Patterns of Paradise 1a**
   2350 × 1400 mm, lino assemblage on layered paper, 1992
   — Collection University of Antwerp
9. **Patterns of Paradise 1b**
   2350 × 1400 mm, lino assemblage on layered paper, 1992
   — Collection University of Antwerp
10. **Kemper meets Chladni 2a**
    860 × 1800 mm, paint-woodcut on canvas, 1997
11. **Kemper meets Chladni 1b**
    860 × 1800 mm, paint-woodcut on canvas, 1997
12. **Kemper meets Chladni, exhibition 'Survey', exhibition view**
    Sint-Jorispoort, Elzenveld, Antwerp, Belgium
13. **Fungus: work in situ**
    450 × 700 mm, wasp material on Japanese paper,
    Klášter Plasy, Czech Republic, 1994
14. **Comment dire 1 & 2**
    450 × 700 mm, wasp material on Japanese paper, 1994
15. **Anthiagrammes series, exhibition 'Papier als Middelpunt'**
    tower in the Castle of the Grand Commandery Alden Biesen, Bilzen, Belgium, 1994
16. **Anthiagrammes 3, 4, 5, 6**
    400 × 300 mm, linocut on Japanese paper, 1994
17. **Anthiagramme 9**
    400 × 300 mm, linocut on Japanese paper, 1994
18. **Anthiapolis 1 & 2**
    1950 × 700 mm, lino assemblage on layered paper, 1998

11.

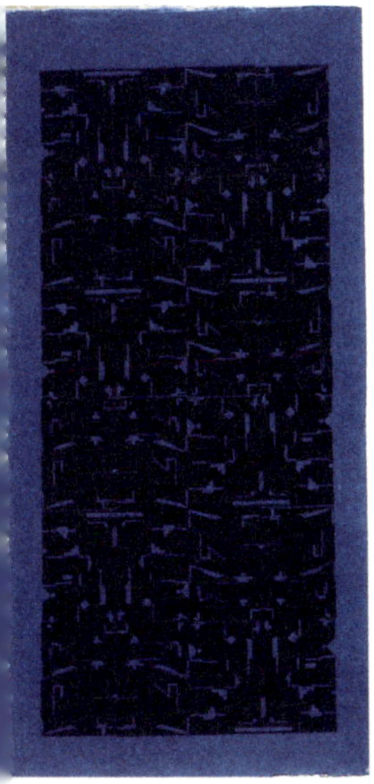

16.

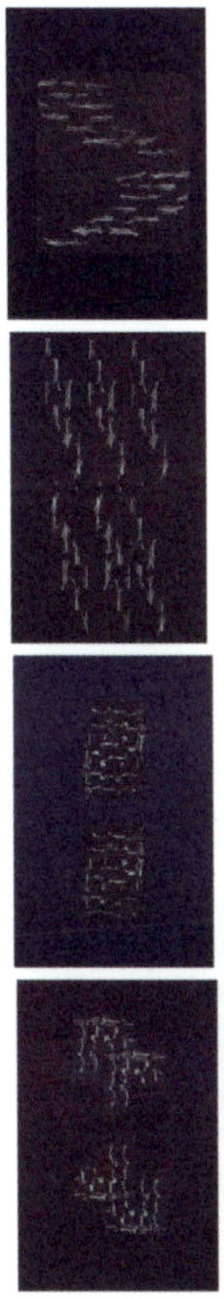

17.

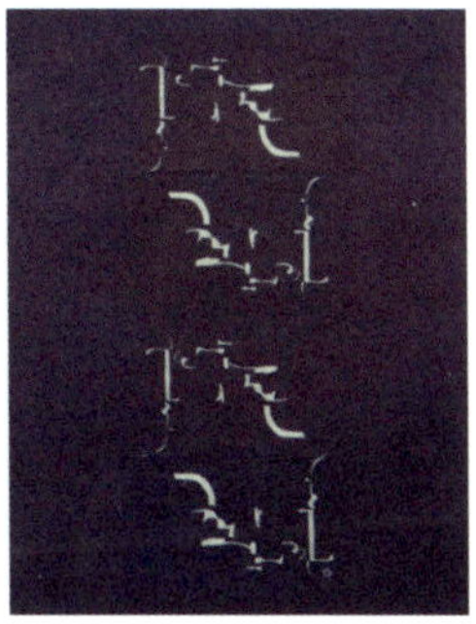

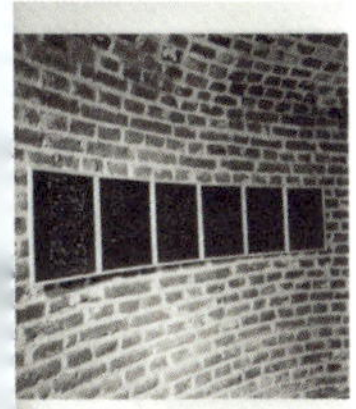

15.

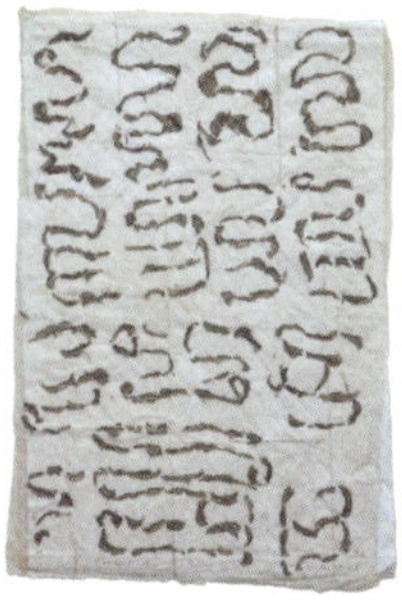

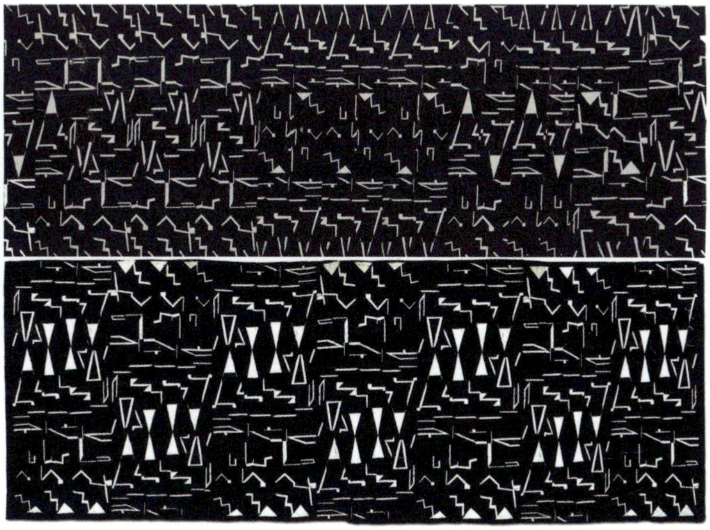

18.

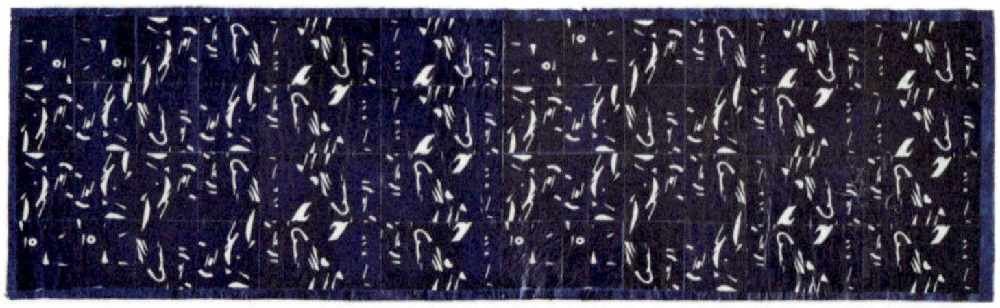

19.

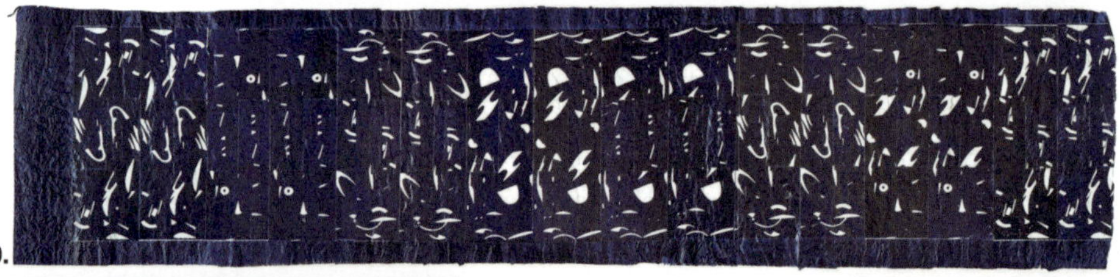

20.

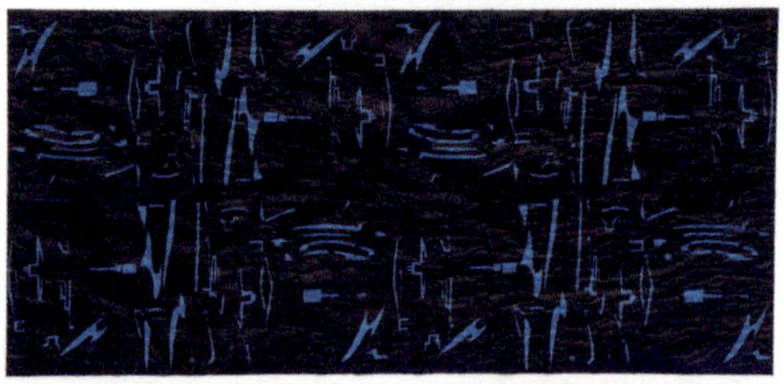

21.

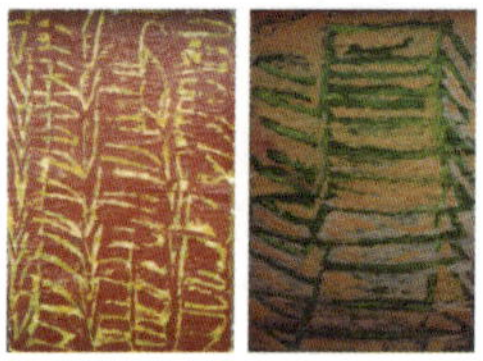

22.

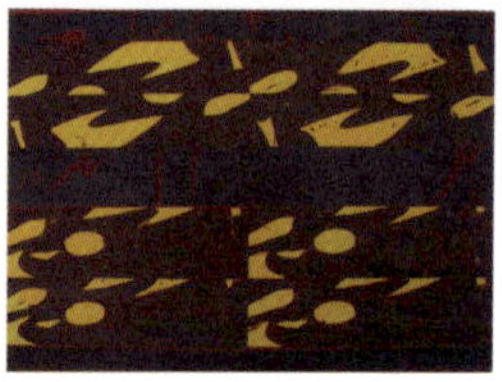

26.

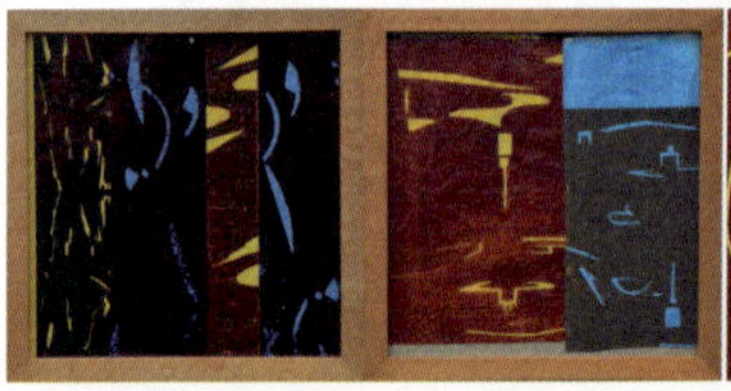

23.

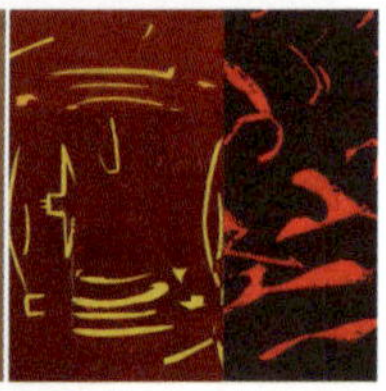

25.

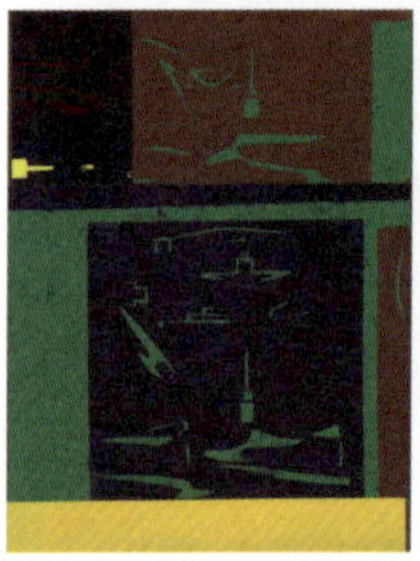

24.

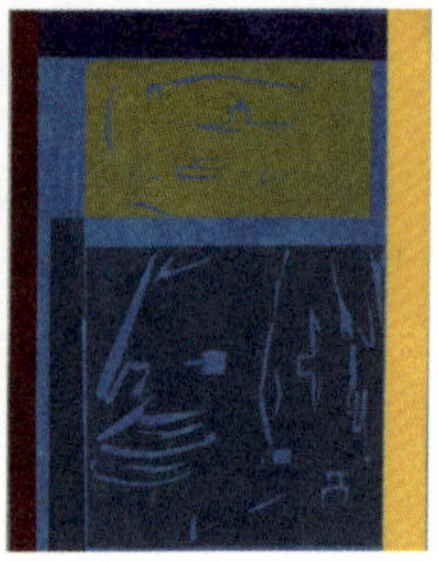

28.

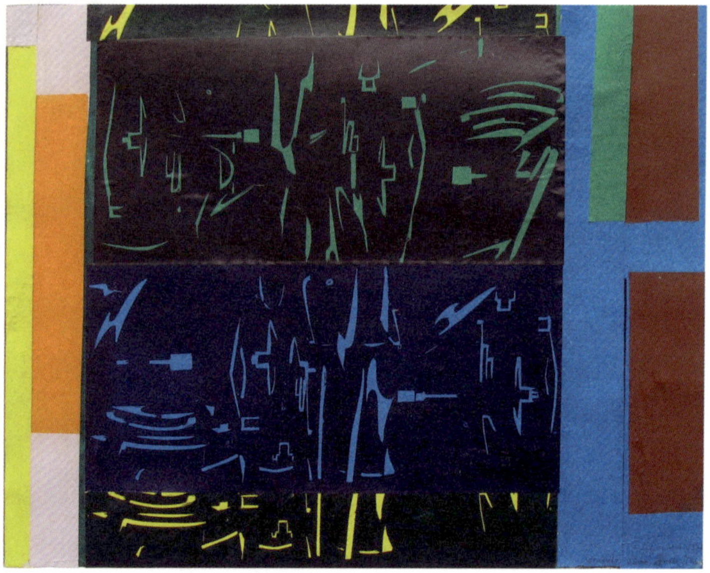

27.

19. **Oceanography 1**
2290 x 600 mm, lino assemblage on layered paper, 2002
20. **Oceanography 3**
2310 x 700 mm, lino assemblage on layered paper, 2002
21. **Arquipélago 3**
385 x 840 mm, lino on layered paper, 2004
22. **Acrylic on layered paper 1 & 2**
1460 x 960 mm, lino on layered paper, 2004
23. **Salamansa 10 & 12**
227 x 227 mm, lino assemblage, 2004
24. **Salamansa 4**
400 x 300 mm, lino assemblage, 2004
25. **Salamansa 11**
227 x 227 mm, lino assemblage, 2004
26. **Kebra Kanela 3**
400 x 300 mm, linocut on Zerkall paper, 2004
27. **Salamansa groot 1a**
505 x 650 mm, lino assemblage, 2004
28. **Salamansa 3**
400 x 300 mm, lino assemblage, 2004
29. **The pulse of new sound (Times Between I)**
350 x 500 mm, screen printing, KwaZulu-Natal, 2004
30. **Hunting Scene**
280 x 400 mm, brush drawing & indian ink, 2004
31. **Underwater Figures**
230 x 230 mm, indian ink paintings, 2004
· artist composition of 5 artworks for the book
32. **Mama Wata**
250 x 180 mm, linocut on Japanese paper, 2004
33. **Sangoma**
165 x 110 x 18 cm, firewood, 2019
34. **S.A.Sister NdB**
300 x 300 mm, gouache painting, 2002
35. **Changing Rhythms (Times Between III)**
350 x 500 mm, screen printing, KwaZulu-Natal, 2004
36. **Bugaku, work in progress, colour and paper tests**
2400 x 1100 mm, mixed media, non-woven cotton, acrylic paint, oil-based ink, 2021

29.

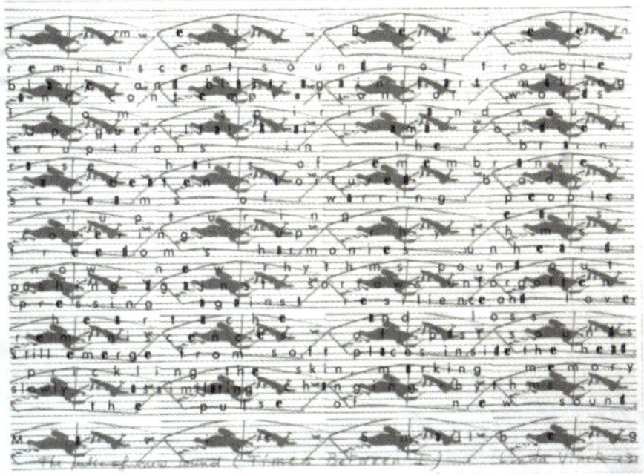

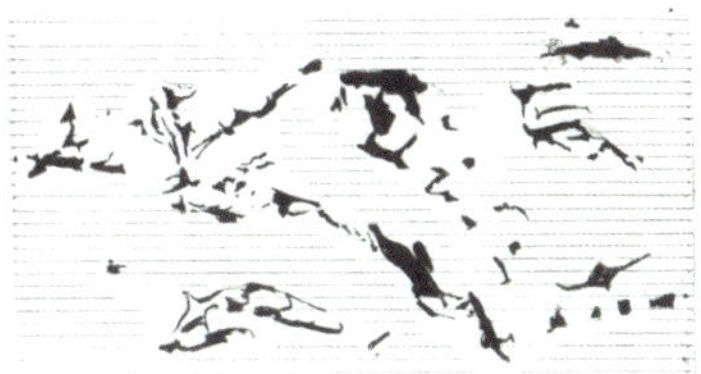

30.

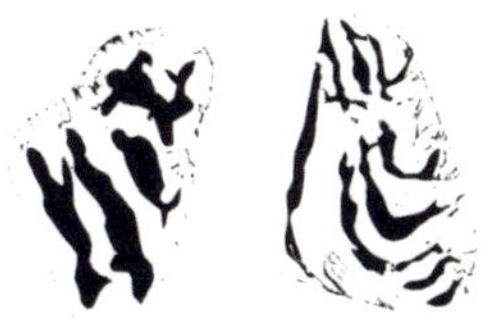

32.

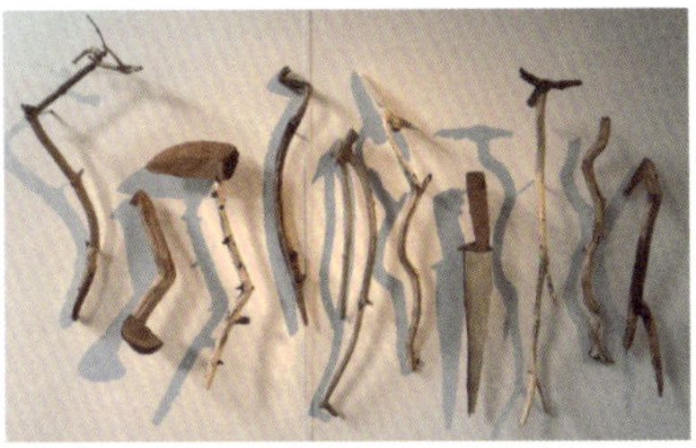

33.

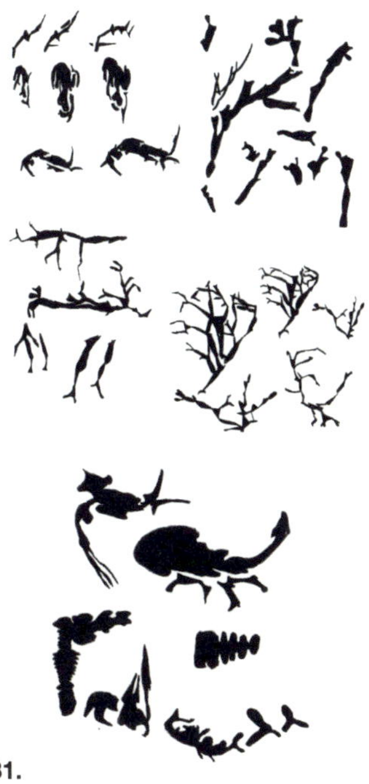

31.

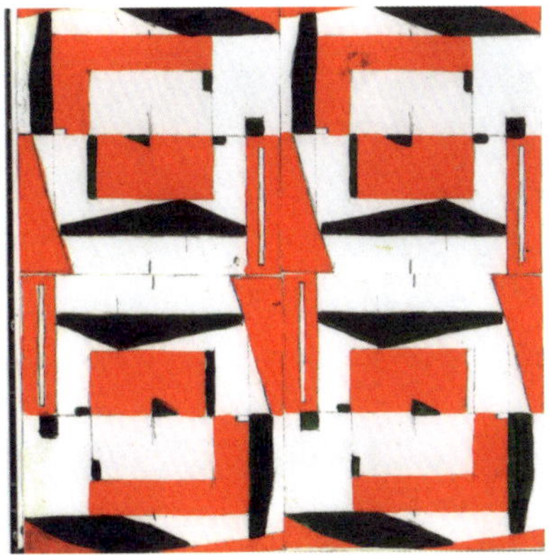

34.

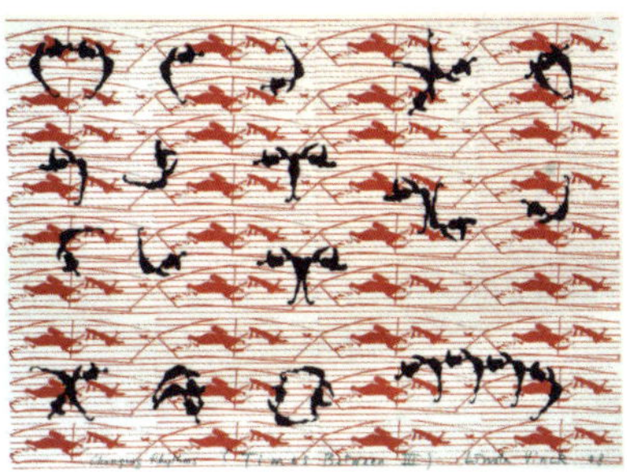

35.

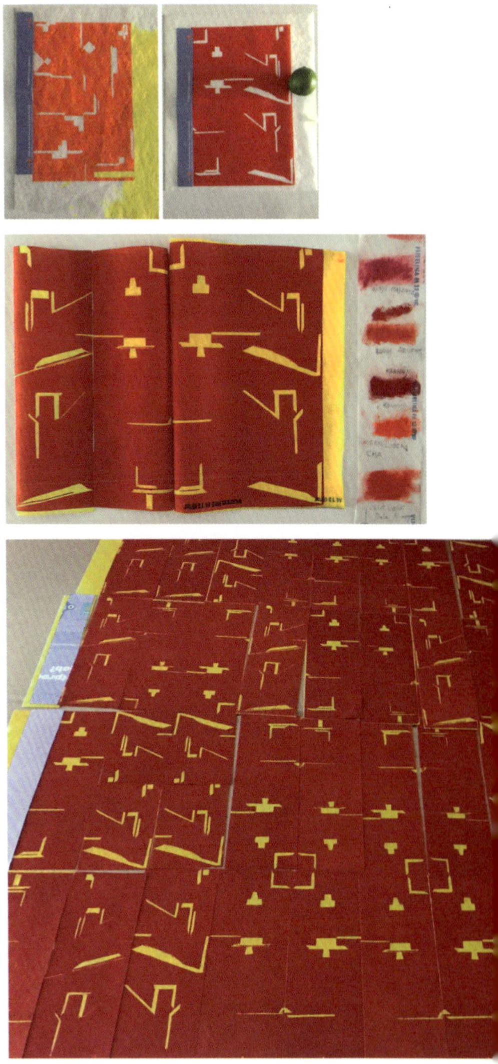

36.

page 127 to 199

38.

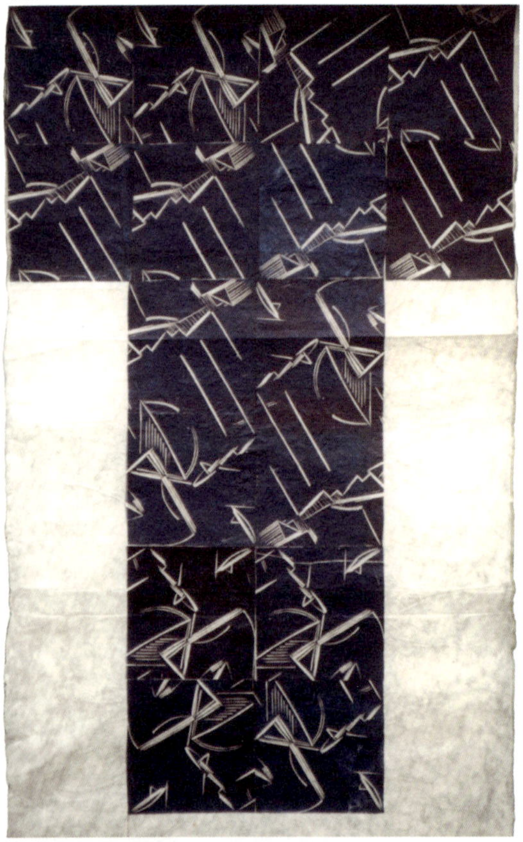

39.

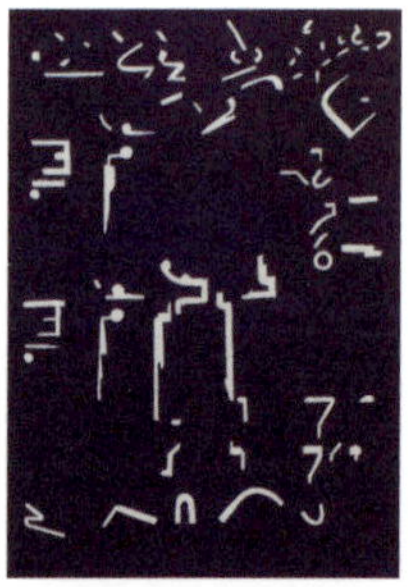

42.

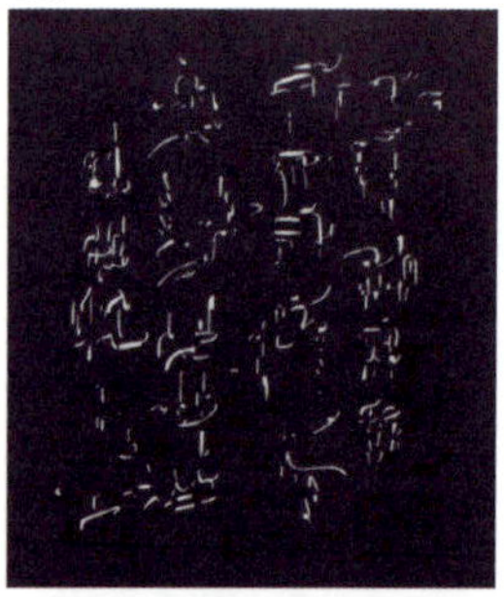

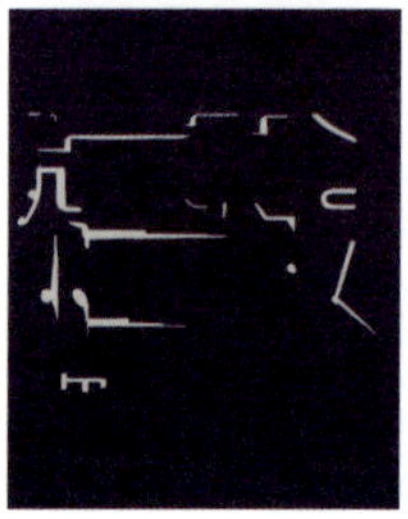

40.

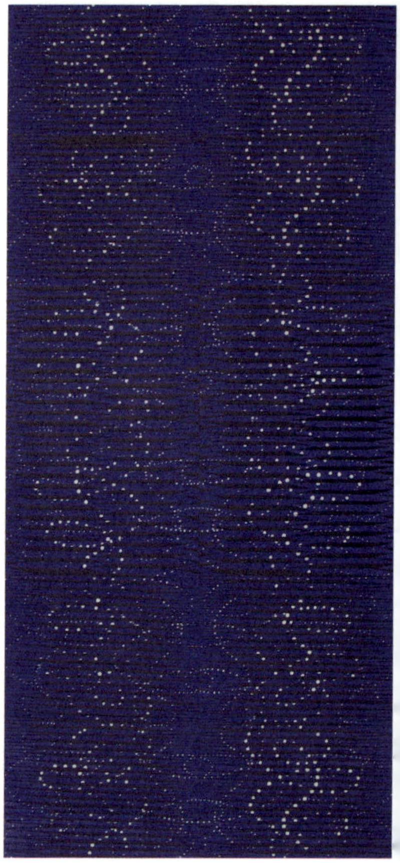

43.

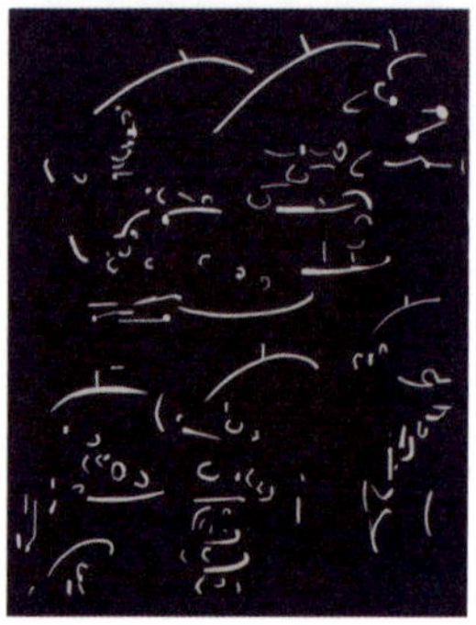

41.

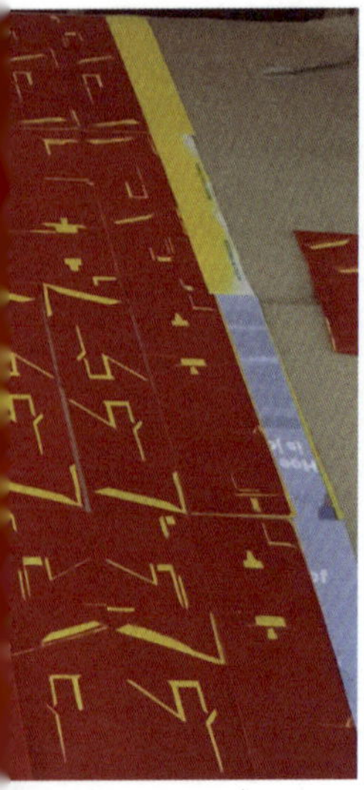

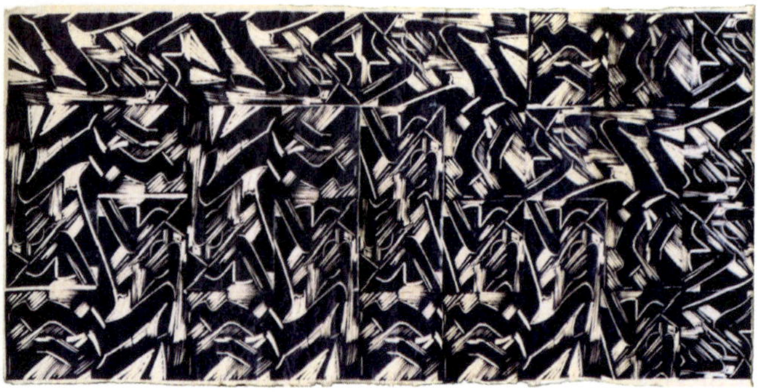

37.

37. Kimono 2
550 × 1270 mm, linocut on Nepali Paper, 1989
38. Kimono 1
540 × 1320 mm, linocut on Nepali Paper, 1989
39. Birdsong 5
295 × 195 mm, linocut on paper, 2019
40. Birdsong 3
308 × 235 mm, linocut on paper, 2019
41. Birdsong 4
281 × 224 mm, linocut on paper, 2019
42. Birdsong 6
308 × 235 mm, linocut on paper, 2019
43. Twisting Around — Blue Patterns
1360 × 600 mm, xylography, Japanese paper, 2011
44. Particles of Light — Blue Patterns
1360 × 600 mm, xylography, Japanese paper, 2011
45. Kodo
600 × 1680 mm, linocut on Zerkall paper, 2016

44.

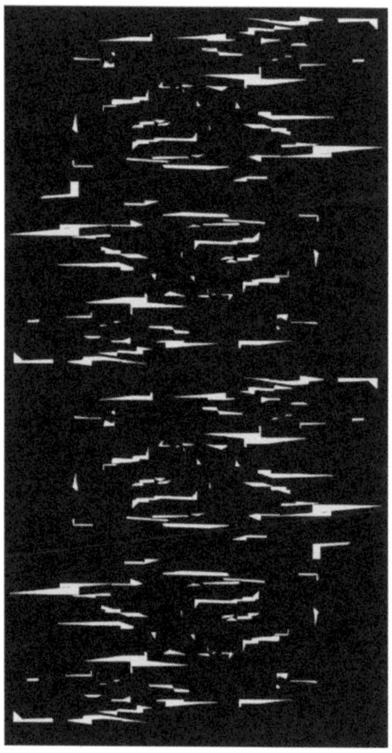

45.

V. A tone is a colour, is a feeling, is a thought, is a star

page 201 to 239

47.

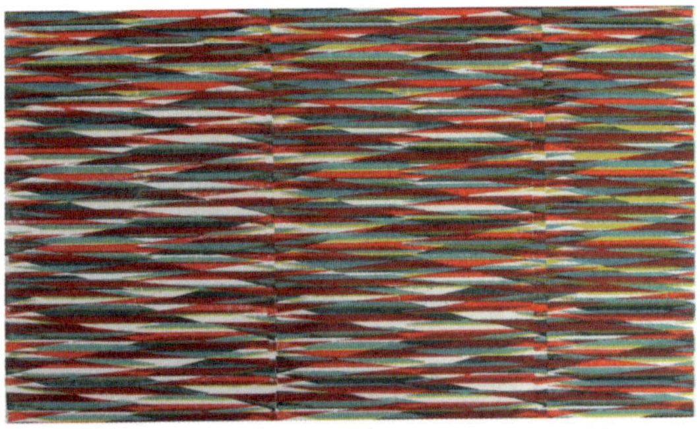

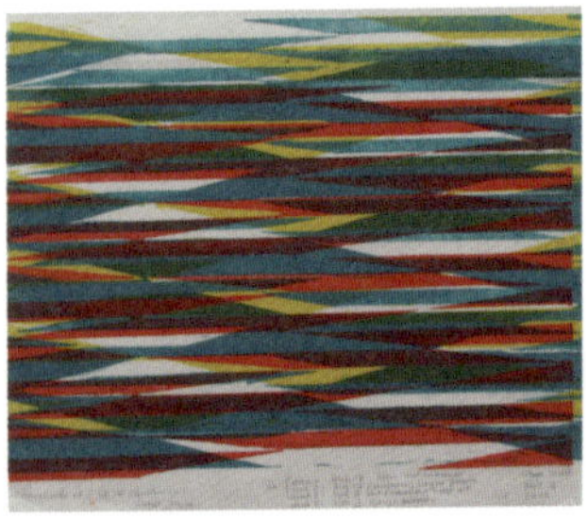

46.

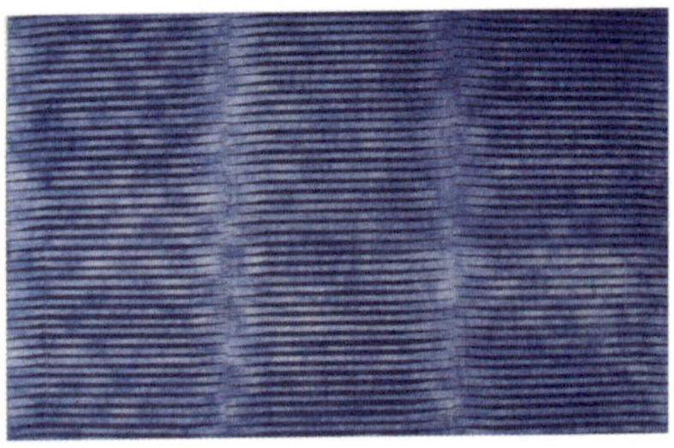

48.

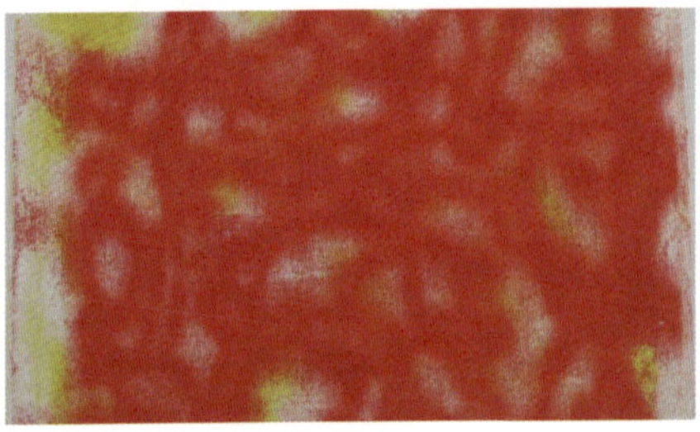

49.

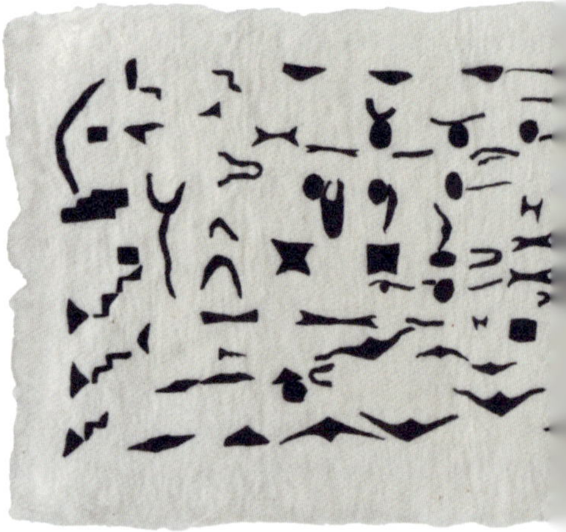

50.

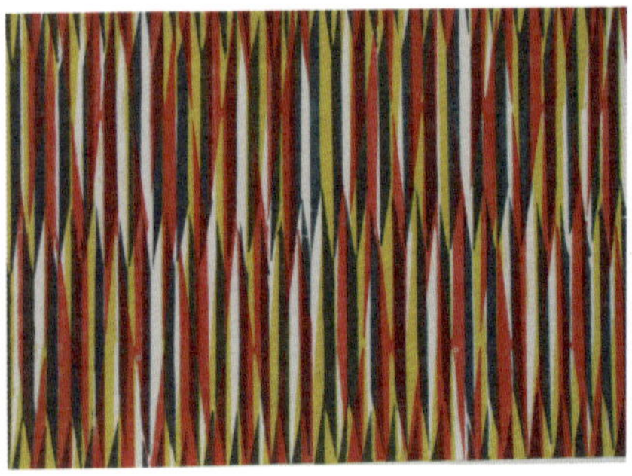

51.

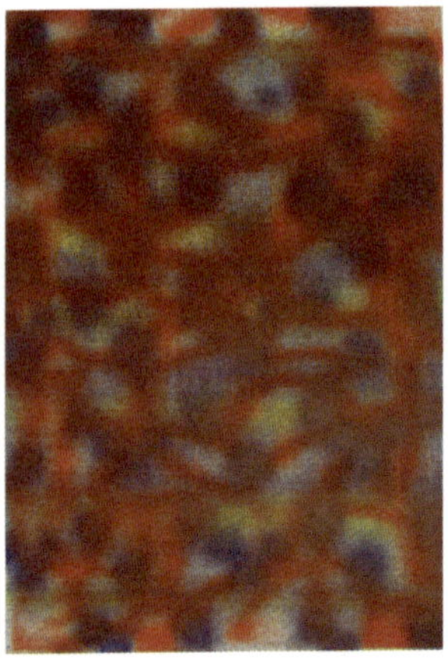

52.

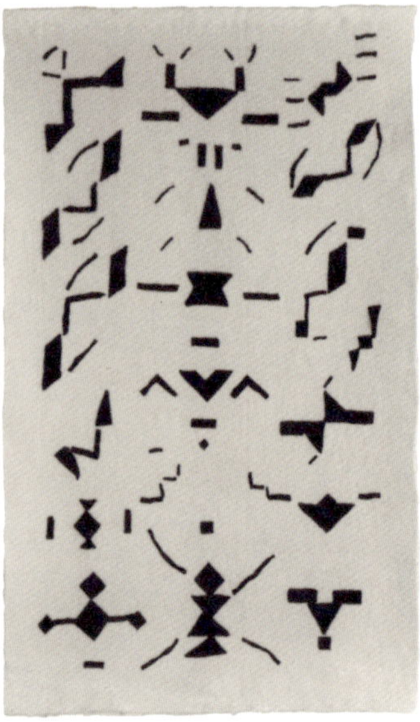

53.

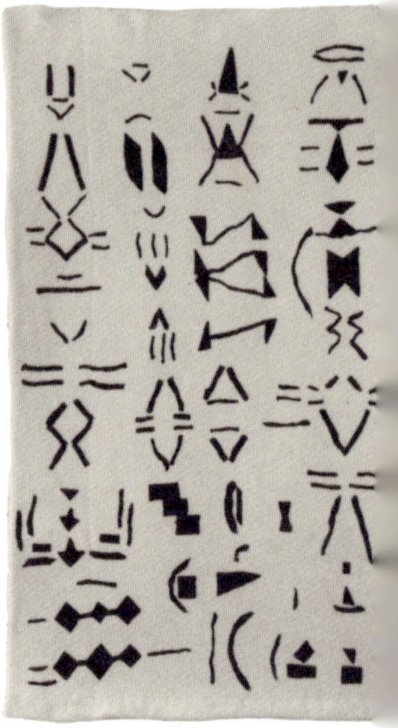

54.

46. Weaver Bird 4
230 × 280 mm, handprinted linocut on Zerkall paper, 2015

47. Weaver Bird 1
540 × 750 mm, handprinted linocut on Zerkall paper, 2015

48. Interaction of Colour 4 [blue-grey]
500 × 750 mm, woodcut, 2012

49. Interaction of Colour 6 [white-red-yellow]
500 × 750 mm, woodcut, 2012

50. Harpa Doris — Felt
1400 × 780 mm, felt assemblage, 2006

51. Weaver Bird 3
300 × 400 mm, handprinted linocut on Zerkall paper, 2015

52. Interaction of Colour 2 [rust-brown]
500 × 750 mm, woodcut, 2012

53. Birch Tree 2 — Felt
1800 × 1100 mm, felt assemblage, 1992

54. Birch Tree 1 — Felt
1850 × 1080 mm, felt assemblage, 1992

55. Chladni's Choice 2 — Felt
830 × 690 mm, felt assemblage, 2006

56. Transformation
1340 × 350 mm, woodcut on Gampi paper Yellow/Vermillion red, 2008

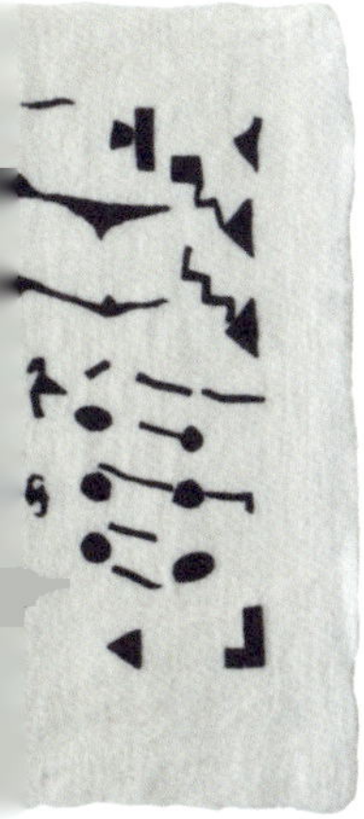

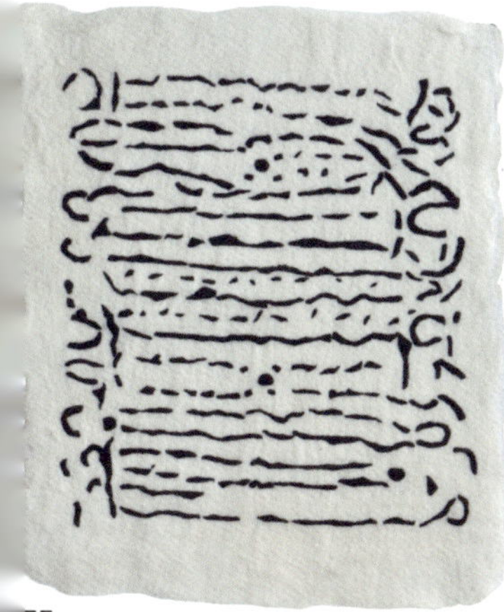

55.

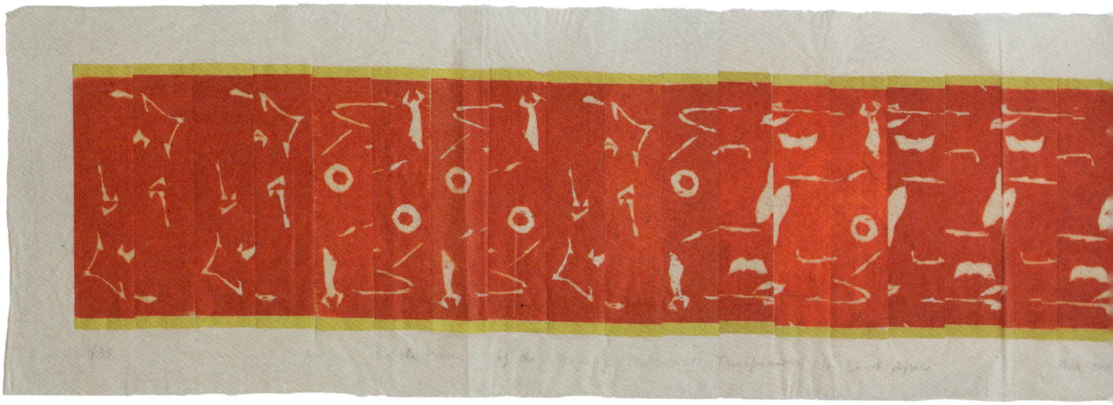

56.

V. A tone is a colour, is a feeling, is a thought, is a star

page 201 to 239

57.

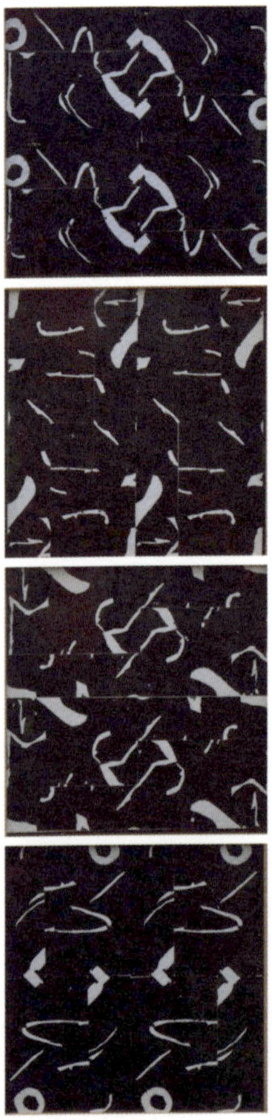

58.

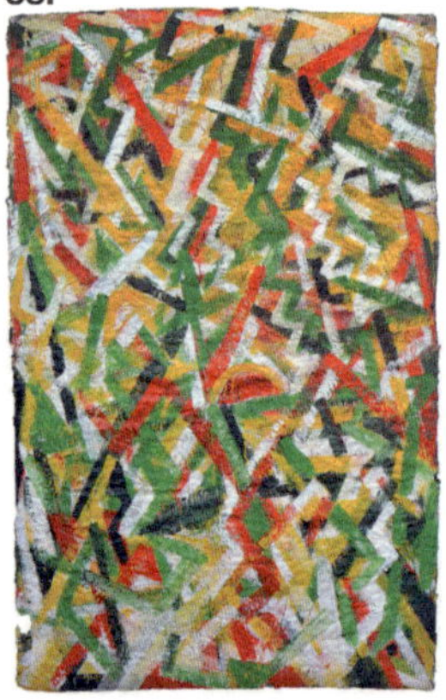

59.

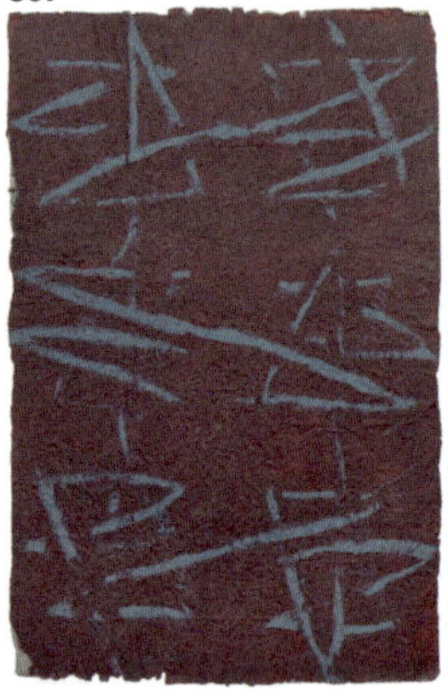

60.

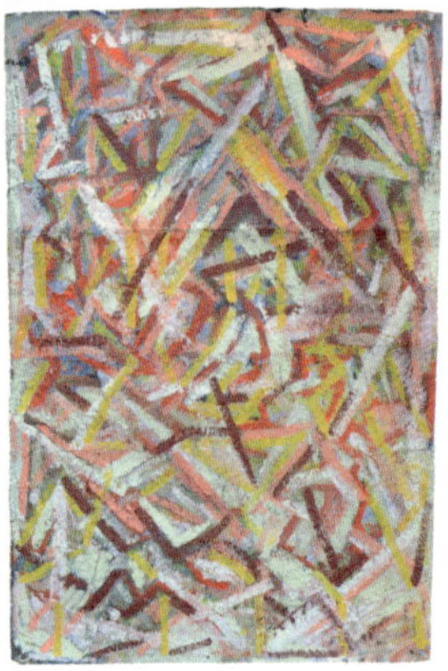

64.

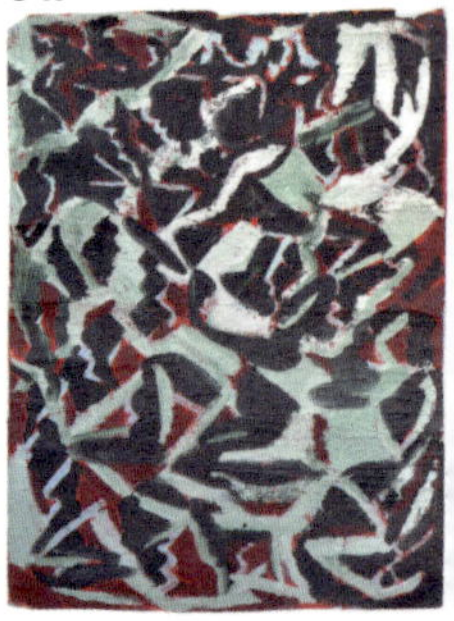

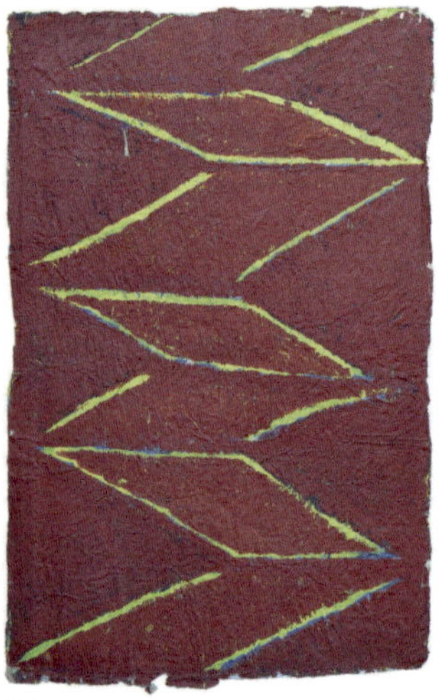

61.

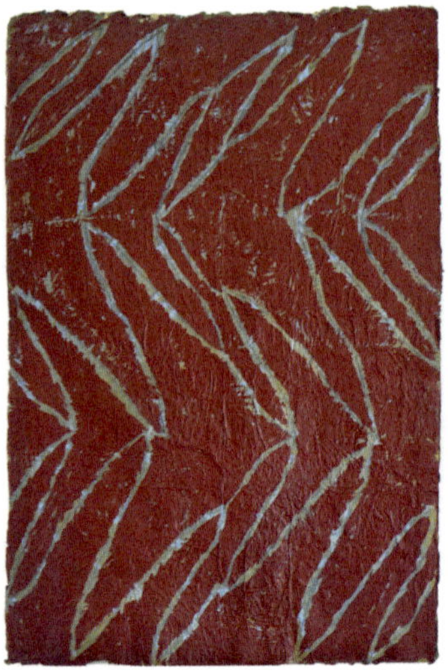

62.

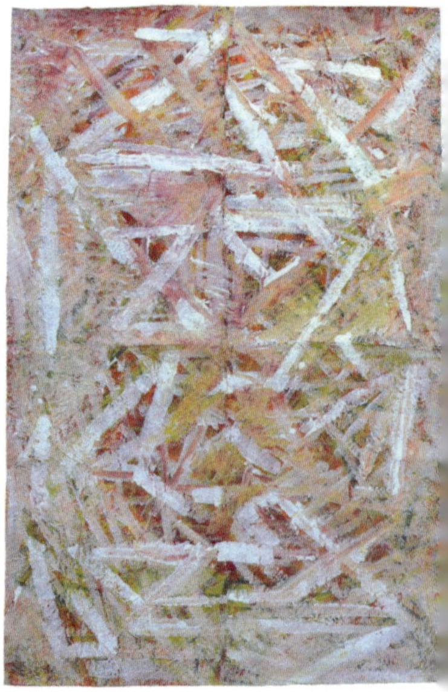

63.

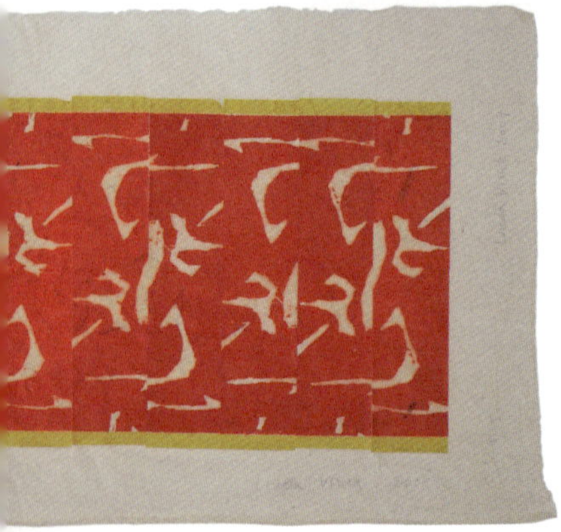

57. **Monkey Monkey 1, 2, 3, 4**
227 × 227 mm, linocut on paper, 2004

58. **Crossroads 3**
1420 × 940 mm, acrylic painting on layered paper, 1987

59. **Dart Away**
400 × 900 mm, acrylic painting on layered paper, 1991

60. **Crossroads 1**
1470 × 960 mm, acrylic painting on layered paper, 1989

61. **Parallelogram**
1400 × 940 mm, acrylic painting on layered paper, 1991

62. **Growth**
1400 × 940 mm, acrylic painting on layered paper, 1991

63. **Crossroads 2**
1470 × 960 mm, acrylic painting on layered paper, 1985

64. **African Market**
1460 × 1040 mm, acrylic painting on layered paper, 1993

65. **Pas de deux**
84 × 17,5 × 15 cm, acrylic resin, 2019

66. **Sangoma**
1650 × 1100 × 180 mm, firewood, 2019

67. & 68. **Ouroboros 1 & 2**
35 × 40 × 15 cm (Ouroboros 1),
22 × 20 × 12 cm (Ouroboros 2),
firewood, plasteline, 2019

69. **Alphabet 2**
60 × 90 × 8 cm, wood, bone, terracotta, organic material,
acrylic resin, 2019

70. **Genetic Process · artist's proof on canvas**
250 × 620 mm, mixed media, laser cutting in wood
and analogue printing techniques, 2024

65.

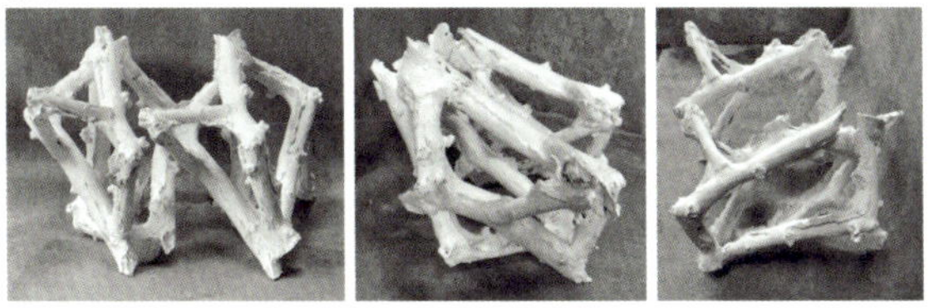

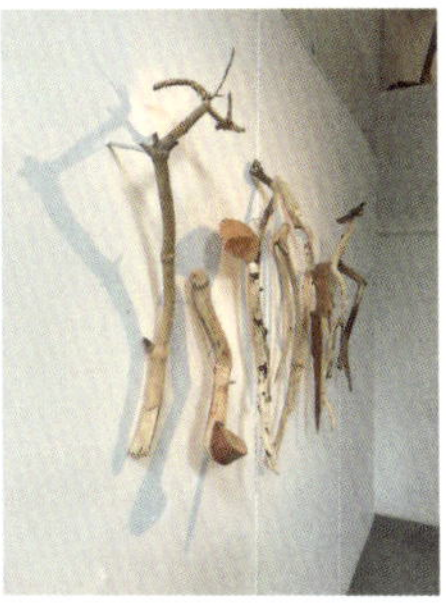

66.

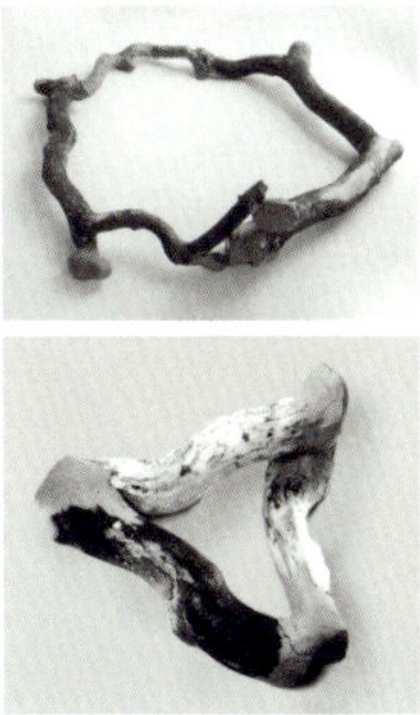

67. & 68.

69.

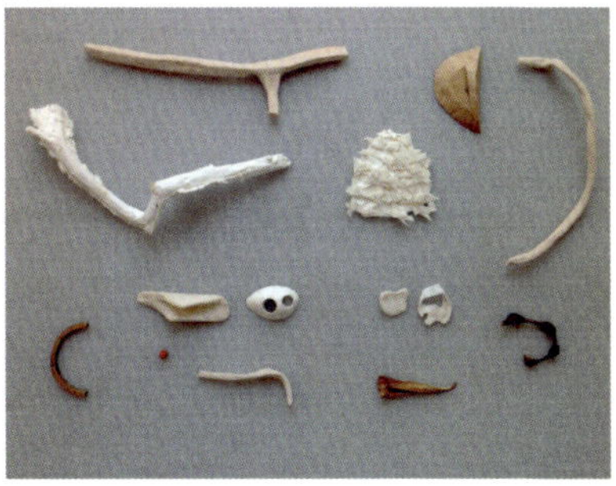

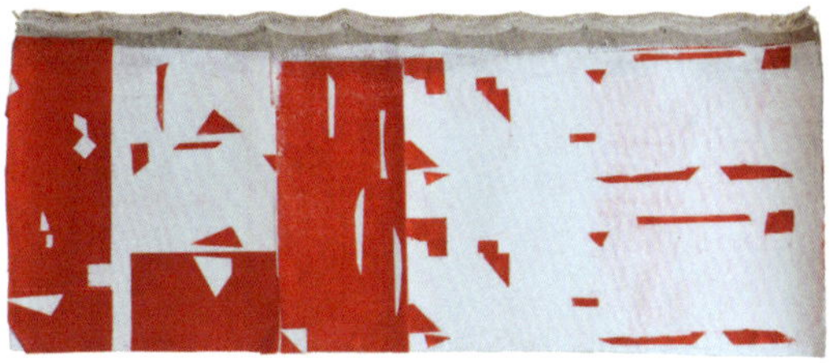

70.

A selection of solo exhibitions, group shows & residencies

2024
Genetic Process
— Artist in Residence
Frans Masereel Centrum
Kasterlee, Belgium

Basic Rhythms of Being
a life in patterns
— book launch
M HKA
Antwerp, Belgium

Linda Vinck
— solo show
Gallery Epreuve d'Artiste
Antwerp, Belgium

2023
Blauw — Teken van de Nacht
— group show
Salon Radical
Kortrijk, Belgium

2022
Bolero
— group show
Golden Gate area
Kyiv, Ukraine

Herinneringen en sequenties
— group show
CC De Bijl
Zoersel, Belgium

2021
Global Print Biennale
Douro Museum
Douro, Portugal

Splitgraphic Biennial
Split, Croatia

Red Oxygen 2
— group show
Salon Radical
Kortrijk, Belgium

2020
Human(ART)istic Festival for Arts.
Science. Philosophy
Rouge Respirant / Red Oxygen
— group show
huisvandeMens
Brussels, Belgium

— group show
Bebop Pop-Up Store
Utrecht, Netherlands

Salon Blanc International
Exhibition of Contemporary Art
National Art Centre
— group show
Tokyo, Japan

10th Bienal do Douro
Alijó, Portugal

2019
Anabasis, Rituals of Homecoming
— solo show
Kunst In Huis
Leuven, Belgium

Belgium – Japan Exchange
Exhibition
U-Forum Museum
Tokyo, Japan

— group show
Gallery OTOKOGURA
Gunma prefecture, Japan

Global Print Douro
Douro Museum
Alijó, Portugal

2018
Peace of Art
— group show
Brussels, Belgium

9th Bienal do Douro
Alijó, Portugal

— group show
Bebop Pop-Up Store
Utrecht, The Netherlands

2017
Splitgraphic Biennial
Split, Croatia

Encounters: body / intuition / art
— group show
MAS & KMSKA
Antwerp, Belgium

Bolero: an international art project
on the move
Eos Gallery
Athens, Greece

2016
Bodies of Lace
— group show
Texture Museum
Kortrijk, Belgium

8th Bienal do Douro
Alijó, Portugal

Yurinkan in Kiryu City Art Biennale
Kiryu, Japan

2015
Belgium – Japan exchange
exhibition
U-Forum Museum
Tokyo, Japan

— group show
Museum of Nature
Watarase Shizenkan, Japan

Ik ben de draad, ik ben de rots
(Ana el khyt / Ana el hyt)
— group show
Kortrijk, Belgium

Global Print Douro
Douro Museum
Alijó, Portugal

Artist in Residence
M_EIA
Mindelo, Cabo Verde

2014
HANGA – Japanese and Belgian
Printmaking Today
SteM
Sint-Niklaas, Belgium

Mayyi Zttan ounfousinou?
Wat weeft in mij?
CC De Brouwerij
Ronse, Belgium

7th Bienal do Douro
Alijó, Portugal

2013
The International Print Biennale
'IOSIF ISER'
Ploiesti, Romania

Art at Wharepuke
International Print Show
Kerikeri, New Zealand

Global Print Douro
Douro Museum
Alijó, Portugal

2012
— Artist in Residence
Guanlan Print Base
Guanlan, China

Prints Tokyo 2012:
International Print Exhibition
Tokyo, Japan

2011
Belgium & Japan Modern Print
Exchange Exhibition
National University Gallery
Kyoto, Japan

Hoogland-Laagland
— group show
The Wittockiana
Brussels, Belgium

2010
Man and Landscape
Schloss Haldenstein
Graubünden, Switzerland

Hot Plate Project
— group show
Phoenix Gallery
Brighton, UK

2009
6th International Novosibirsk
Print Biennale
Novosibirsk State Art Museum
Novosibirsk, Russia

2008
E-POS, Personal Vocabulary
— Traveling group exhibition
Stellenbosch, Pretoria and
Johannesburg, South Africa

2006
Survey
— solo show
Sint-Jorispoort, Elzenveld
Antwerp, Belgium

Ponta seca
— solo show
Galeria Alternativa Mindelo
Mindelo, Cabo Verde

2005
12th Biennial of Contemporary Art
in Flanders
Aalter, Belgium

Aspects of Contemporary Print
in Flanders
Museum of Aalst, Belgium

Towards the Ocean
— solo show
CCM
Mindelo, Cabo Verde

2004
E-POS, Personal Vocabulary
— Cooperative project between Flanders and South Africa
Antwerp/Hasselt, Belgium
Amsterdam, The Netherlands

Funaná e.a.
— solo show
Galerie Wollondilly
Antwerp, Belgium

2003
Printmakers
— group show
Edinburgh, Scotland, UK

2002
Hedendaagse Internationale Grafische Kunst
Antwerp, Belgium

Under the Vulcano
— solo show
Palácio da Cultura
Praia, Cabo Verde

2000
Créolité, the right of being different
— group show
CCM Mindelo
Mindelo, Cabo Verde

Autour de Frans Masereel
Musée des Beaux-Arts Le Locle
Le Locle, Switzerland

LINDA VINCK
— solo show
Galerie Francis van Hoof
Puurs, Belgium

— group show
Galerie Francis van Hoof,
Puurs, Belgium

1999
La Estampa Contemporánea en Flandes
— group show
Gijón, Spain

Grafiek op de grens (1+2)
Cultureel Centrum Scharpoord
Knokke-Heist, Belgium

1998
4 African artists and 1 Belgian
Mindelo, Cabo Verde

Grafiek op de Grens
De Brakke Grond
Amsterdam, The Netherlands

1997
Parcours gravé
— group show
Galerie Epreuve d'Artiste
Antwerp, Belgium

Contemporary Flemish Printmaking
SASOL Art Museum
Stellenbosch, South Africa

Grafiek op de Grens 2
Provinciaal Centrum voor Beeldende Kunsten
Hasselt, Belgium

Grafiek op de Grens 2
Nieuwe Brabantse Kunst Stichting
Breda, The Netherlands

1996
Prentenmaaksters
Stedelijk Museum Zwijgershoek
Sint-Niklaas, Belgium

Houtsneden
Gallery Kunstforum
Schelderode, Belgium

Anthiapolis
— group show
Sint-Lucaspassage
Antwerp, Belgium

-VIER X IN DE KIJKER-
Galerie Kunsthuis Loosveldt
Ostend, Belgium

1995
— group show
Galerie De Queeste
Loker-Heuvelland, Belgium

Parcours gravé en Belgique
Centre de la Gravure et de l'Image Imprimée & De Markten
La Louvière, Belgium

Limited Edition
Monumentale grafische kunst
Cultureel Centrum
Berchem, Belgium

1994
4 Flemish Artists
Gordes, France

Fungus: work in situ
— international group show
Klášter Plasy, Czech Republic

Contemporary Drawings
— group show
Yamaha Gallery Hamamatsu
Osaka, Japan

Belgium-Japan Print Exhibition
Yamaha Gallery Hamamatsu
Osaka, Japan

Hedendaagse Tekeningen
— group show
Belgium-Flanders Exchange Center
Osaka, Japan

— group show
Meguro-Ku Gallery
Tokyo, Japan

3X3
Boot-galerij
Tielrode, Belgium

graveurs van heden
Huis Hellemans
Edegem, Belgium

Papier als Middelpunt
— group show
Castle of Alden Biesen,
Bilzen, Belgium

De Houtsnede
— group show
CHZ Cultuurcentrum
Heusden-Zolder, Belgium

Multiples
— group show
Galerie Antartica
Antwerp, Belgium

Onleesbaar-onlesbaar
Kilims from Central Asia
Graphic work Linda Vinck
— group show
BBL Brabo-hall
Antwerp, Belgium

Linda Vinck
— group show
Galerie 't Zand
Lille, Belgium

1993
— group show
Klammer Gallery
Tokyo, Japan

— group show
Le Musée du Petit Format
Turnhout, Belgium

3X3: 3 generaties 3 technieken
Galerie Witteveen
Amsterdam, The Netherlands

Tjok Dessauvage en Linda Vinck
Kunsthuis Loosveldt
Oostende, Belgium

1992
Linda Vinck
— solo show
Galerie Novanta Nova
Amsterdam, The Netherlands

Linda Vinck
— solo show
Fein Arts Gallery
Brussels, Belgium

Linda Vinck
— group show
Galerie Atrium
Stockholm, Sweden

Linda Vinck
— group show
Galerie Francis van Hoof
Antwerp, Belgium

3x3 — Frans Masereel Centrum 20-jarig bestaan
Frans Masereel Centrum
Kasterlee, Belgium

Linda Vinck, Renée Rohr, Philippe Jacques
Das Belgische Haus
Köln, Germany

undeviginti
— group show
't Elzenveld,
Antwerp, Belgium

1991
Intergrafik
Katowice, Poland

Contemporary Graphic Art
Sofia, Bulgaria

LINDA VINCK
Peintures et Linos
— solo show
Business Faculty
Font Saint Landry
Brussels, Belgium

1990
Lineart art fair Ghent
Galerie Francis van Hoof
Antwerp, Belgium

Contemporary Graphic Art
Sofia, Bulgaria

Internationale grafiek
De Brakke Grond
Amsterdam, The Netherlands

Internationale grafiek
ICC
Antwerp, Belgium

Voelbare Grafische Kunst
'Feeling'
— Prix Mediatine
Woluwe-Saint-Lambert, Belgium

1989
Mini-Print
Taller Galería Fort
Barcelona, Spain

Artists Against War
XYLON European Traveling
Exhibition for Peace
Warschau–Berlin
Museum Schwetzingen
Poland, France & Germany

BLAU-BLAUW-BLEU-BLUE
Belgisches Haus
Cologne, Germany

A(rt)ssenede
Assenede, Belgium

Linda Vinck
— solo show
Galerie Francis van Hoof
Antwerp, Belgium

1988
Mini-Print
Taller Galería Fort
Barcelona, Spain

Het verbeelde woord
Xe Europees Poesie Festival
Leuven, Belgium

Happening '88'
Ghent, Belgium

A(rt)ssenede
Assenede, Belgium

1987
Mini-Print
Taller Galería Fort
Barcelona, Spain

Voorstelling Portfolio 'Pijl'
Nic van Bruggen,
tentoonstelling Linda Vinck
— solo show
Galerij De Grootte Witte Arend
Antwerp, Belgium

1986
–group show
San José Art League
California, USA

A(rt)ssenede
Assenede, Belgium

LINDA VINCK
–solo show
Frans Masereel Centrum
Kasterlee, Belgium

1985
FOURFOLD
Gallery Buchmann
Belgium

11th International Exhibition
of Prints
Kanagawa, Japan

Koppelteken
Voorstelling portfolio
De Brakke Grond
Amsterdam, The Netherlands

FOURFOLD
–group show
Antwerp / Amsterdam
Belgium / The Netherlands

1984
Kunst 80
Museum voor Hedendaagse Kunst
Hasselt, Belgium

1983
9th International Exhibition of Prints
Kanagawa, Japan

— solo show
Tarnów–Przemyśl
–Reszów –Krosno
Poland

1982
— group show
7th British International Print
Biennial
Bradford, UK

1981
Gallery 't Lammeken
Antwerp, Belgium

1979
Gallery 't Lammeken
Antwerp, Belgium

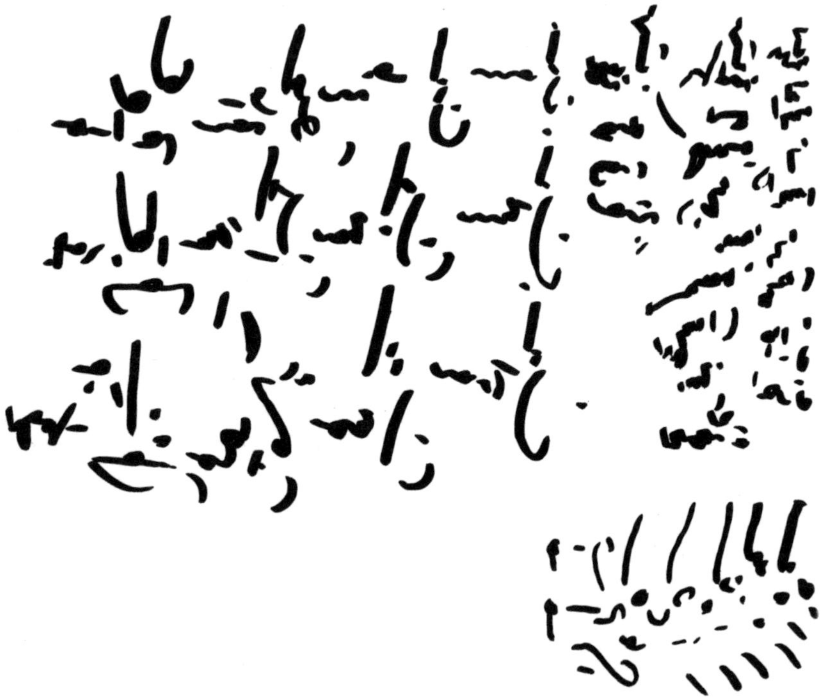

Text contributors

Paul Vandenbroeck, Belgium

Paul Vandenbroeck has held a part-time professorship with the Social Sciences Faculty of KU Leuven since 2003. He is an art graduate from that same university (PhD 1986, on Hieronymus Bosch).

His main research topics are situated on the interface between art and anthropology. His current research focuses on developing a comprehensive theory of the psychocorporeal and transcultural foundations of 'style' and of creative/artistic form; a second research topic is the 'iconography' of North African domestic textile arts.

Paul Vandenbroeck is also the scientific editor of the Annual of the Antwerp Royal Museum, where he has worked with the Collection Research Department since 1980.

Ernest Van Buynder, Belgium

Ernest Van Buynder was chairman of the Willemsfonds. In this capacity he was also chairman of the Consultation Center of Flemish Associations for a while. He was also chairman of the Museum of Contemporary Art Antwerp (M HKA) and of the Flemish Commission for Visual Arts. Until 1999 he was vice-chairman of the University of Antwerp. He remained there until his retirement in 2010. Since 2014 he has worked as an external advisor in the office of Flemish Minister of Culture Sven Gatz. He is currently chairman of the Friends of the M HKA and honorary chairman of M HKA.

Dirk Verhaegen, Belgium

Dirk Verhaegen makes artistic work with logical, mathematical systems. He exhibited frequently with like-minded artists in an international context. He was teaching at LUCA School of arts until 2015.

João Vário, Cabo Verde

(b. 1937 – d. 2007, Mindelo, São Vicente Island, Cabo Verde)

João Vário – main pseudonym of João Manuel Varela, also known as Timóteo Tio Tiofe or G.T. Didial –, was a Cape Verdean writer, poet, essayist and neurobiologist. He was a scientific researcher at the University of Antwerp.

Norimasa Mizutani, Japan

Graduated from the Print Art Course of Sokei Academy of Fine Arts, Norimasa is a member artist of The Printsaurus International Print Exchange Association of Japan. Master in Japanese printmaking techniques, he participated at several exhibitions around the world including Russia, Belgium, Canada, France, etc.

Nic van Bruggen, Belgium

(b. 1938, Merksem – d. 1991, Antwerp)

Flemish poet, co-founder of the Pink Poets, publicist, art critic, sports journalist, advertising copywriter and visual artist. As a graphic artist he used the name Nikolaas.

Frans Boenders, Belgium

Belgian writer. He graduated in Germanic philology and philosophy at the Katholieke Universiteit Leuven. He worked for the Belgian radio as a producer and wrote for various cultural magazines. He also was editor-in-chief of the magazine *Kunst en Cultuur.* He devoted several books to philosophy and eastern religions and cultures.

María del Mar Díaz González, Spain

PhD at the University of Oviedo, where she teaches. She has obtained the Extraordinary Bachelor's Prize (2000) and the Extraordinary Doctorate Prize (2005).

Industrial heritage and contemporary art determine her main lines of research, within the analysis of the printed image in artistic, graphic or reproductive terms.

Author of various books and articles related to the lithographic industry, her dual research orientation has been reflected in her participation in several national and transnational European research projects.

Octavio Paz, Mexico

(b. 1914 – d. 1998, Ciudad de Mexico)

He was a Mexican poet and diplomat. For his body of work, he was awarded the 1977 Jerusalem Prize, the 1981 Miguel de Cervantes Prize, the 1982 Neustadt International Prize for Literature, and the 1990 Nobel Prize in Literature.

Marcel van Maele, Belgium

(b. 1931, Bruges – d. 2009, Antwerp)

Marcel van Maele was a writer, performer and visual artist. As a nonconformist, he was critical and rebellious. His oeuvre expresses a penchant for total individual freedom.

Mavis Smallberg, South Africa

She has been published in at least eight publications during and before 1994, including Qabane Labantu: Poetry in the Emergency: Poesie in die Noodtoestand (1989), Siren Songs: An Anthology of Poetry Written by Women (1989), Breaking the Silence: A Century of South African Women's Poetry (1990), and many others.

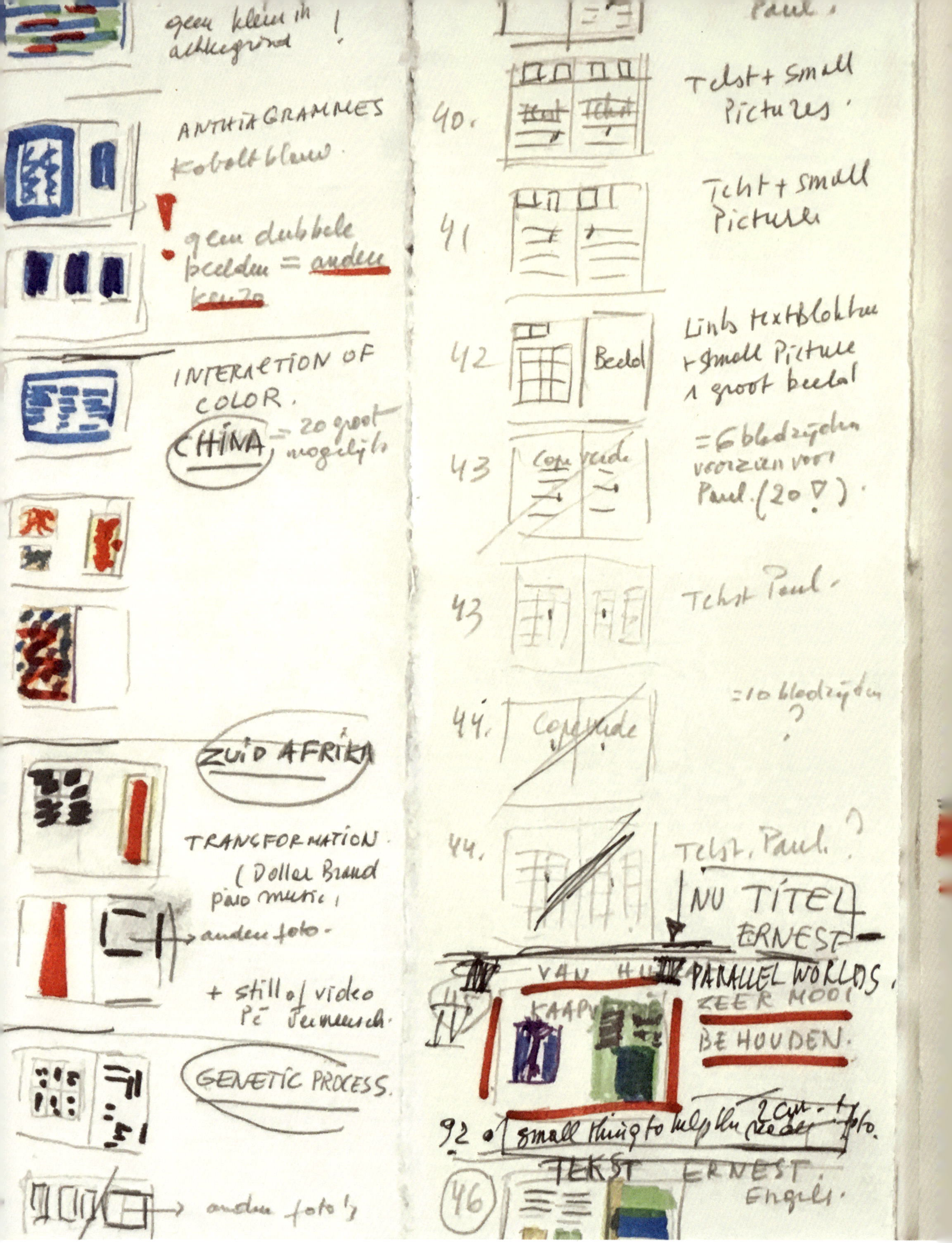

 Linda Vinck sketching for book concept & graphic design of *Basic Rhythms of Being, a life in patterns*, 2024

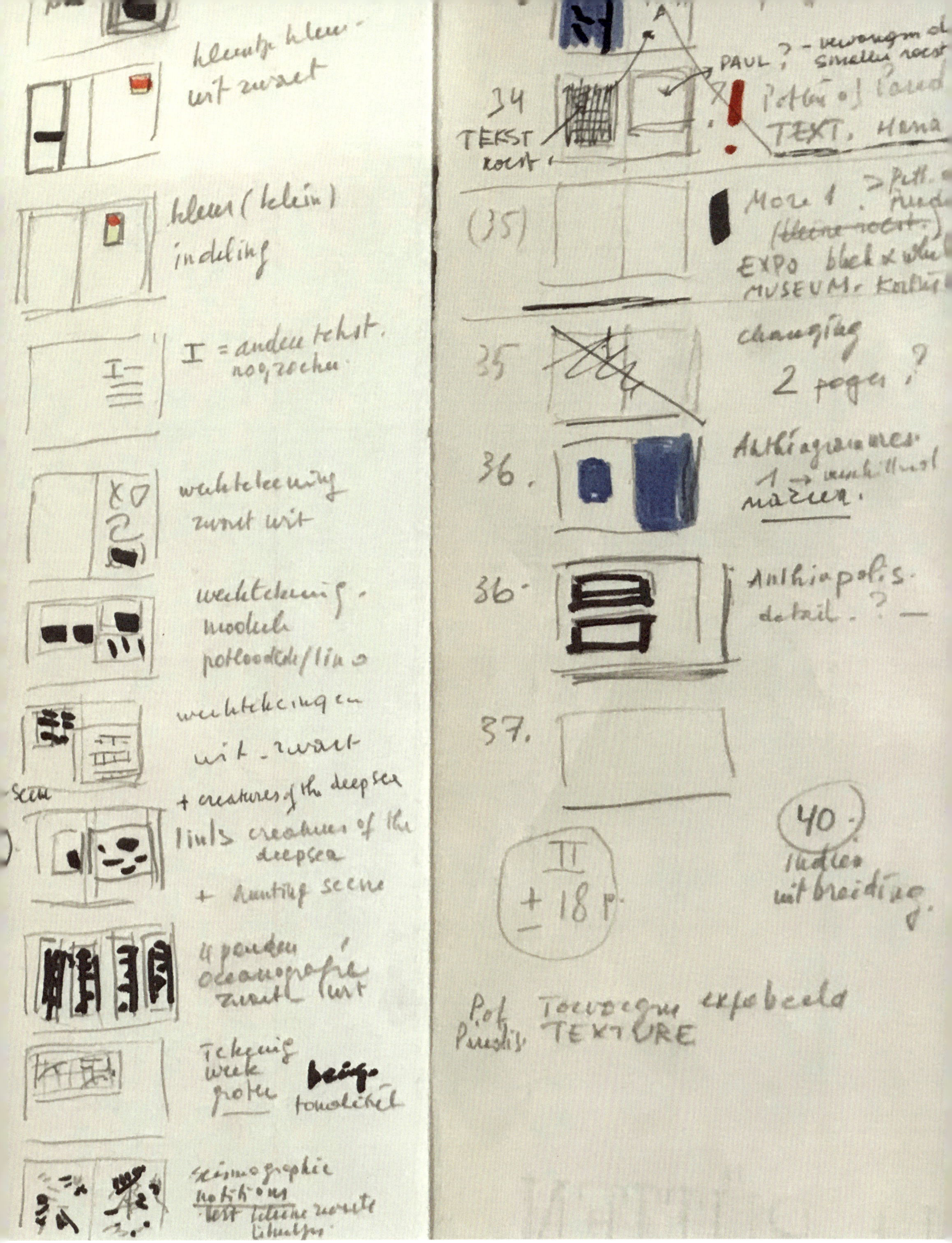

PAUL ?
34
TEKST
TEXT
(35)
EXPO
MUSEUM
35
changing
2 pages ?
36.
36.
37.
40.
II
± 18 p.
TEXTURE

Colophon

Book curator
Bruno Devos
Publisher
HOPPER&FUCHS
Publishing year
2024
Creative and editorial concept
Linda Vinck in conversation with Elena Bollette
Graphic concept & design
Linda Vinck
Graphic and executive design
Elena Bollette
Texts
Paul Vandenbroeck, Ernest Van Buynder,
Dirk Verhaegen
Contributors of quotes, poems & fragments
João Vário, Octavio Paz, Nikola Tesla,
Nic van Bruggen, María del Mar Díaz González,
Frans Boenders, Mavis Smallberg, Marcel van Maele,
Norimasa Mizutani
Additional texts
Jeroen Lejeune
Photography
Mark Bosselaers, Sarah Stone, Linda Vinck
Text & book editing
Jeroen Lejeune, Bruno Devos, Linda Vinck
Translation
ElaN Languages
Production
Zwartopwit (BE)
Typefaces
Helvetica Neue
Papers
Printed in the EC on Munken Lynx Rough 120 & 300 gsm,
Munken Pure 100 gsm by Arctic Paper

Acknowledgements

Linda Vinck would like to thank her family and friends.
Paul Vandenbroeck, Ernest Van Buynder, Jeroen Lejeune,
Mark Bosselaers, and everybody who made the making
of this book possible.

Note to the Reader

HOPPER
&FUCHS

ISBN 9789464002485